WATERWAYS GUIDE 6

Nottingham, York & the North East

CONTENTS

Map showing the waterways of Britain	4
Key to map pages	6
General information for waterways users	8
Aire & Calder Navigation	15
Chesterfield Canal	30
River Derwent and the Pocklington Canal	51
Fossdyke & Witham Navigations	65
River Ouse, River Ure and Ripon Canal	88
Selby Canal	112
South Yorkshire Navigations	119
River Trent	136
Index	174

Also available:

⟪ Collins NICHOLSON
Waterways guides and map

1 Grand Union, Oxford & the South East
2 Severn, Avon & Birmingham
3 Birmingham & the Heart of England
4 Four Counties & the Welsh Canals
5 North West & the Pennines
7 River Thames & the Southern Waterways
Inland Waterways Map of Great Britain

Published by Nicholson
An imprint of HarperCollins*Publishers*
Westerhill Road, Bishopbriggs,
Glasgow G64 2QT

www.harpercollins.co.uk
www.bartholomewmaps.com

River Thames Guide first published by Nicholson 1969
Waterways guides 1 South, 2 Midlands and 3 North first published by Nicholson 1971
This edition first published by Nicholson and Ordnance Survey 1997
New edition published by Nicholson 2000, 2003, 2006, 2009
Reprinted 2006, 2007, 2009, 2011
New edition 2012

Copyright © HarperCollins*Publishers* Ltd 2012

Wildlife text from *Collins Complete Guide to British Wildlife* and *Collins Wild Guide*.

This product uses map data licensed from Ordnance Survey® with the permission of the Controller of Her Majesty's Stationery Office.
© Crown copyright 1999. All rights reserved. Licence number 399302.

Ordnance Survey is a registered trade mark of Ordnance Survey, the national mapping agency of Great Britain.

The representation in this publication of a road, track or path is no evidence of the existence of a right of way.

Researched and written by Jonathan Mosse, Cicely Frew and Ann Malcolm.

The publishers gratefully acknowledge the assistance given by British Waterways and their staff in the preparation of this guide.

Grateful thanks is also due to the Environment Agency and members of the Inland Waterways Association.

All photographs reproduced by kind permission of Derek Pratt Photography, apart from:
Jonathan Mosse p71, 118; Shutterstock p48 Beth Whitcomb (Canada goose), p48 Gertjan Hooijer (Lapwing), p48 Borislav Borisov (Green woodpecker), p48 David Dohnal (Redshank), p49 Rick Thornton (Goldfinch), p49 Marcin Perkowski (Great tit), p49 Karel Gallas (Kingfisher), p51–7 Tom Curtis, p58 Artur Bogacki, p65–87, 71 Mark William Richardson, p143 Norma Cornes (Otter); Paul Huggins (www.paulhugginsphotography.com) p48 (Mallard duck), p49 (Moorhen, Grey heron & Swan), p85.

Every care has been taken in the preparation of this guide. However, the Publisher accepts no responsibility whatsoever for any loss, damage, injury or inconvenience sustained or caused as a result of using this guide.

The Publisher makes no representations or warranties of any kind as to the operation of the websites and disclaims all responsibility for the content of the websites and for any expense or loss incurred by use of the websites.

All rights reserved. No part of this publication may be reproduced, stored in a retrieval system or transmitted in any form, or by any means, electronic, mechanical, photocopying, recording or otherwise without the prior written consent of the publishers and copyright owners.

Printed in China.

ISBN 978-000745261-3

Wending their quiet way through town and country, the inland navigations of Britain offer boaters, walkers and cyclists a unique insight into a fascinating, but once almost lost, world. When built this was the province of the boatmen and their families, who lived a mainly itinerant lifestyle: often colourful, to our eyes picturesque but, for them, remarkably harsh. Transporting the nation's goods during the late 1700s and early 1800s, negotiating locks, traversing aqueducts and passing through long narrow tunnels, canals were the arteries of trade during the initial part of the industrial revolution.

Then the railways came: the waterways were eclipsed in a remarkably short time by a faster and more flexible transport system, and a steady decline began. In a desperate fight for survival canal tolls were cut, crews toiled for longer hours and worked the boats with their whole family living aboard. Canal companies merged, totally uneconomic waterways were abandoned, some were modernised but it was all to no avail. Large scale commercial carrying on inland waterways had reached the finale of its short life.

At the end of World War II a few enthusiasts roamed this hidden world and harboured a vision of what it could become: a living transport museum which stretched the length and breadth of the country; a place where people could spend their leisure time and, on just a few of the wider waterways, a still modestly viable transport system.

The restoration struggle began and, from modest beginnings, Britain's inland waterways are now seen as an irreplaceable part of the fabric of the nation. Long-abandoned waterways, once seen as an eyesore and a danger, are recognised for the valuable contribution they make to our quality of life, and restoration schemes are integrating them back into the network. Let us hope that the country's network of inland waterways continues to be cherished and well-used, maintained and developed as we move through the 21st century.

If you would like to comment on any aspect of the guides, please write to Nicholson Waterways Guides, Collins Geo, Westerhill Road, Bishopbriggs, Glasgow G64 2QT or email nicholson@harpercollins.co.uk.

Since 1948, British Waterways has been the branch of government responsible for caring for Britain's canals and rivers. At the time this book went to press, however, the organisation was scheduled to go through a major upheaval, as the part of DEFRA which looked after the 2000 mile network of canals and rivers in England and Wales leaves public ownership and becomes a charitable body, the Canal & River Trust. The Welsh name for the new charity is Glandwr Cymru which translates literally as 'Waterside Wales'. Scotland's canals will remain under the direct authority of the Scottish government. This change is scheduled to take place in April 2012, but is dependent on the approval of an Act of the UK Parliament. If the scheduled change occurs please be aware that all references to British Waterways within this publication, can then be replaced with the Canal & River Trust; postal addresses should change accordingly and all email addresses ending in @britishwaterways.co.uk will become @canalrivertrust.org.uk, so for example enquiries@britishwaterways.co.uk becomes enquiries@canalrivertrust.org.uk.

The Waterways of Britain

KEY

- Waterways featured in this guide
- Unnavigable section

Waterways featured in:
- Guide 1
- Guide 2
- Guide 3
- Guide 4
- Guide 5
- Guide 7

The Inland Waterways Map of Great Britain covers the canal and river navigations of England, Scotland and Wales.

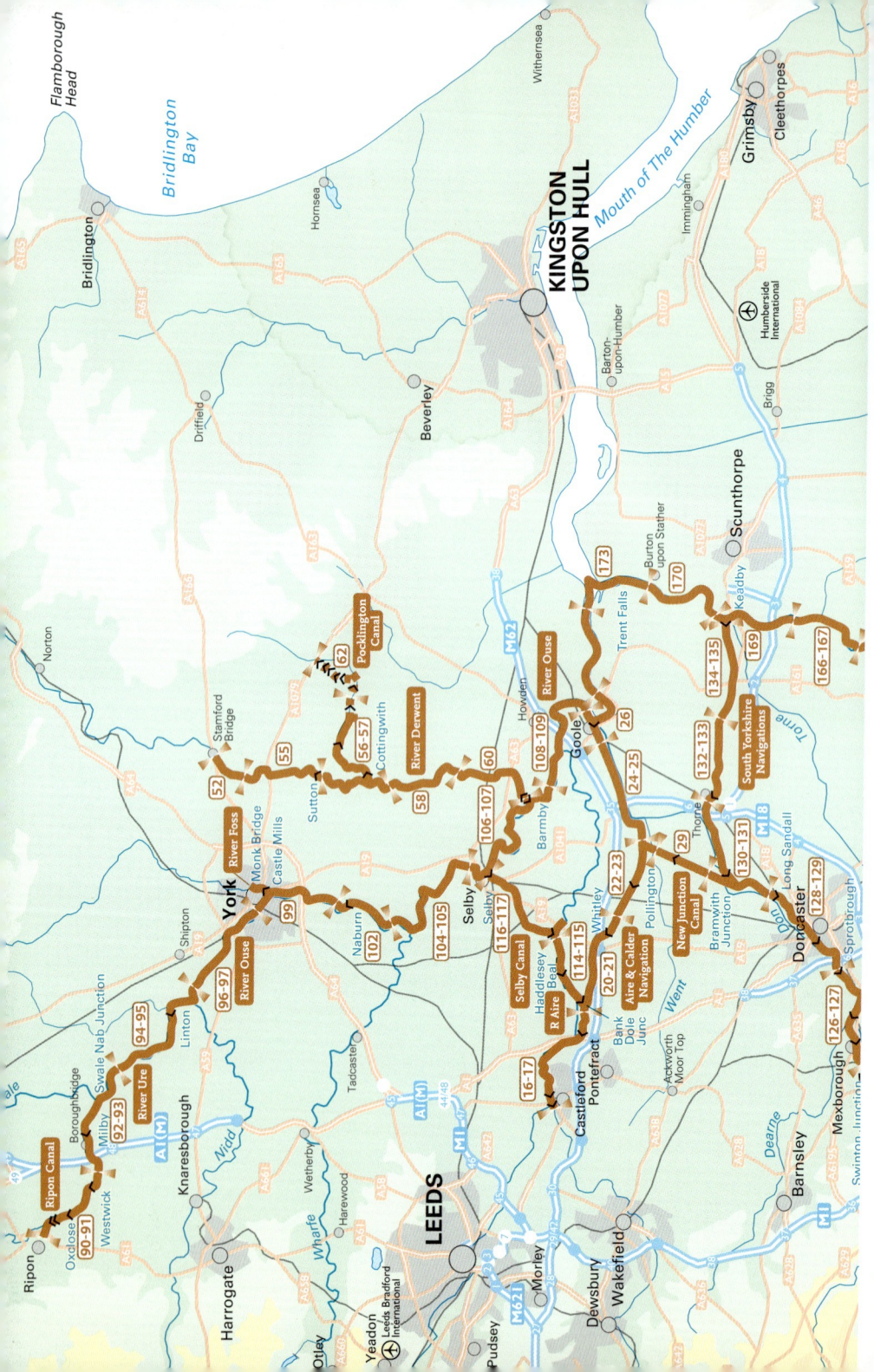

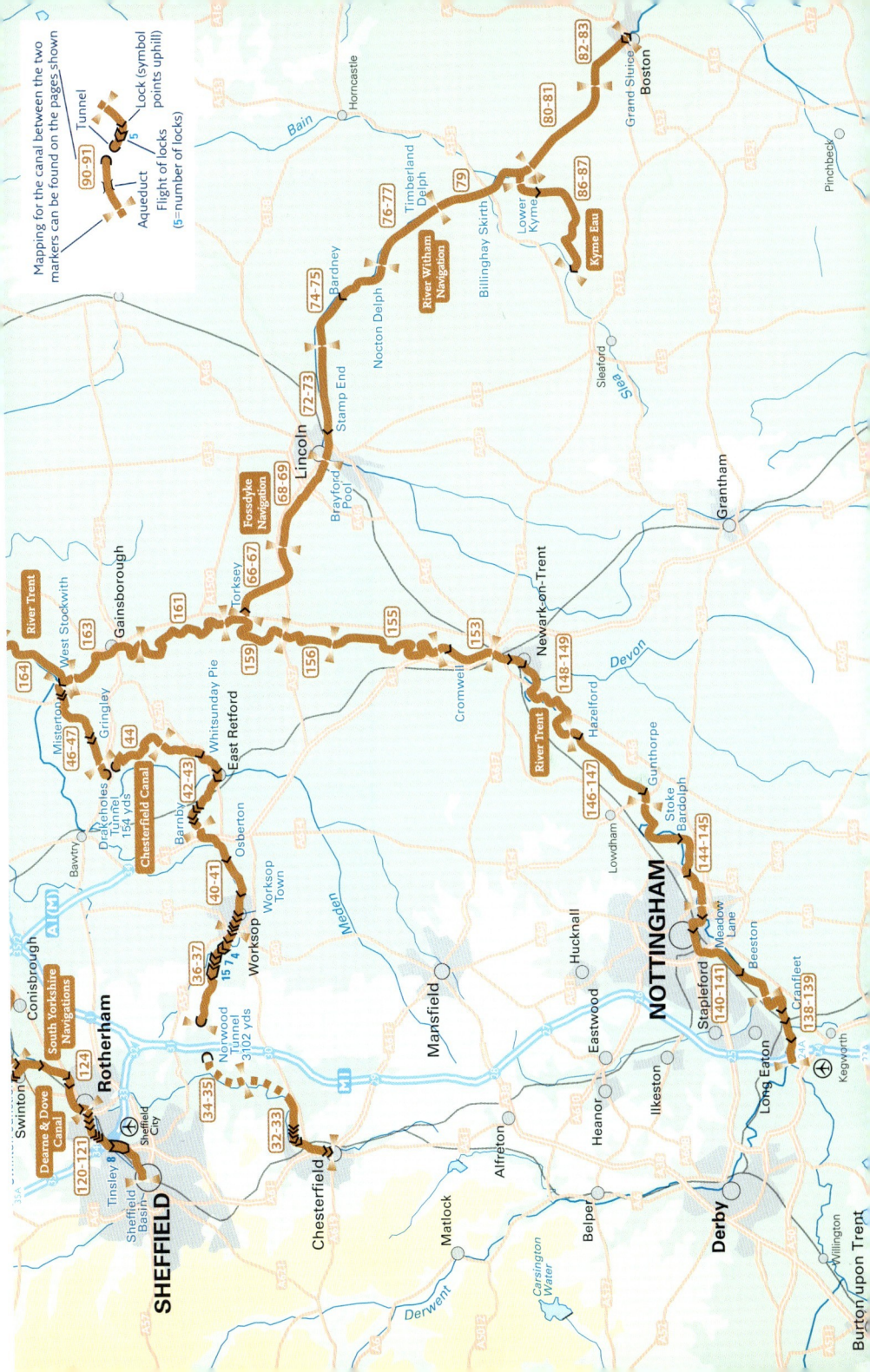

GENERAL INFORMATION FOR WATERWAYS USERS

INTRODUCTION

Boaters, walkers, fishermen, cyclists and gongoozlers (on-lookers) all share in the enjoyment of our quite amazing waterway heritage. British Waterways and the Environment Agency, along with other navigation authorities, are empowered to develop, maintain and control this resource. It is to this end that a series of guides, codes, and regulations have come into existence over the years, evolving to match a burgeoning – and occasionally conflicting – demand. Set out in this section are key points as they relate to everyone wishing to enjoy the waterways.

The *Boater's Handbook* is available from all navigation authorities. It contains a complete range of safety information, boat-handling know-how, warning symbols and illustrations.

THE WATERWAYS CODE

The Waterways Code gives advice and guidance to visitors on how to enjoy the inland waterways safely. It, and the *Boater's Handbook*, are available from the Customer Service Centre or from www.waterscape.com/downloads. BW Customer Service Centre is staffed Mon–Fri, 08.00–18.00. The helpful staff will answer general enquiries and provide information about boat licensing, boating holidays and activities on the waterways. They can be contacted on 01923 201 1120; enquiries.hq@britishwaterways.co.uk; British Waterways Customer Service Centre, 64 Clarendon Road, Watford WD17 1DA. Visit www.waterscape.com for up-to-date information on almost every aspect of the inland waterways, from news and events to moorings.

Emergency Helpline Available from BW outside normal office hours on weekdays and throughout weekends. For emergency help, or to report something dangerous, such as serious damage to structures or water escaping, call 0800 47 999 47.

ENVIRONMENT AGENCY

The Environment Agency (EA) manages around 600 miles of the country's rivers, including the Thames and the River Medway. For general enquiries or to obtain a copy of the *Boater's Handbook*, contact EA Customer Services on 03708 506 506; enquiries@environment-agency.gov.uk. To find out about their work nationally (or to download a copy of the *Handbook*) and for lots of other useful information, visit www.environment-agency.gov.uk. The website www.visitthames.co.uk provides lots on information on boating, walking, fishing and events on the river.

Incident Hotline The EA maintain an Incident Hotline. To report damage or danger to the natural environment, damage to structures or water escaping, telephone 0800 80 70 60.

LICENSING – BOATS

The majority of the navigations covered in this book are controlled by BW and the EA and are managed on a day-to-day basis by local Waterway Offices (you will find details of these in the introductions to each waterway). All craft using the inland waterways must be licenced and charges are based on the dimensions of the craft. In a few cases, these include reciprocal agreements with other waterway authorities (as indicated in the text). BW and the EA offer an optional Gold Licence which covers unlimited navigation on the waterways of both authorities. Permits for permanent mooring on BW waterways are issued by BW.

Contact the BW Boat Licensing Team on 01923 201120; www.britishwaterways.co.uk/licenseit; British Waterways Boat Licensing, PO Box 162, Leeds LS9 1AX.

For the Thames and River Medway contact the EA. River Thames: 0118 953 5650; www.environment-agency.gov.uk; Environment Agency, PO Box 214, Reading RG1 8HQ. River Medway: 01732 223222 or visit the website.

BOAT SAFETY SCHEME

BW and the EA operate the Boat Safety Scheme – boat construction standards and regular tests required by all licence holders on BW and EA waterways. A Boat Safety Certificate (for new boats, a Declaration of Conformity), is necessary to obtain a craft licence. BW also requires proof of insurance for Third Party Liability for a minimum of £1,000,000 for powered boats. The scheme is gradually being adopted by other waterway authorities. Contact details are: 01923 201278; www.boatsafetyscheme.com; Boat Safety Scheme, 64 Clarendon Road, Watford, Herts WD17 1DA. The website offers useful advice on preventing fires and avoiding carbon monoxide poisoning.

TRAINING

The Royal Yachting Association (RYA) runs one and two day courses leading to the Inland Waters Helmsman's Certificate, specifically designed for novices and experienced boaters wishing to cruise the inland waterways. For details of RYA schools, telephone 023 8060 4100 or visit www.rya.org.uk. The practical course notes are available to buy. Contact your local boat clubs, too. The National Community Boats Association (NCBA) run courses on boat-handling and safety on the water. Telephone 0845 0510649 or visit www.national-cba.co.uk.

LICENSING – CYCLISTS

Not all towpaths are open to cyclists. Maps on www.waterscape.com show the stretches of towpath open to cyclists, and local offices can supply more information. A cycle permit is usually required. Cycling along the Thames towpath is generally accepted, although landowners have the right to request that you do not cycle. Some sections of the riverside path, however, are designated and clearly marked as official cycle ways. No permits are required but cyclists must follow London's Towpath Code on Conduct at all times. For further information, to obtain a permit or a copy of the Towpath Code, contact BW Customer Services or visit www.waterscape.com.

TOWPATHS

Few, if any, artificial cuts or canals in this country are without an intact towpath accessible to the walker at least and the Thames is the only river in the country with a designated National Trail along its path from source to sea (for more information visit www.nationaltrail.co.uk). However, on some other river navigations, towpaths have on occasion fallen into disuse or, sometimes, been lost to erosion. The indication of a towpath in this guide does not necessarily imply a public right of way or mean that a right to cycle along it exists. Horse riding and motorcycling are forbidden on all towpaths.

INDIVIDUAL WATERWAY GUIDES

No national guide can cover the minutiae of detail concerning every waterway, and some BW Waterway Managers produce guides to specific navigations under their charge. Copies of individual guides (where available) can be obtained from the relevant BW Waterway Office or downloaded from www.waterscape.com/boatersguides. Please note that times – such as operating times of bridges and locks – do change year by year and from winter to summer. For a free copy of A User's Guide to the River Thames – visit www.visitthames.co.uk/form/75/publications.html.

STOPPAGES

BW and the EA both publish winter stoppage programmes which are sent out to all licence holders, boatyards and hire companies. Inevitably, emergencies occur necessitating the unexpected closure of a waterway, perhaps during the peak season. You can check for stoppages on individual waterways between specific dates on www.waterscape.com/stoppages, lockside noticeboards or by telephoning 01923 201401; for stoppages and river conditions on the Thames, visit www.visitthames.co.uk or telephone 0845 988 1188.

NAVIGATION AUTHORITIES AND WATERWAYS SOCIETIES

Most inland navigations are managed by BW or the EA, but there are several other navigation authorities. For details of these, contact the Association of Inland Navigation Authorities on 0113 243 3125 or visit www.aina.org.uk. The boater, conditioned perhaps by the uniformity of our national road network, should be sensitive to the need to observe different codes and operating practices.

BW is a National Waterways charity, responsible to the Department for Environment, Food and Rural Affairs in England and Wales, and is linked with an ombudsman. BW has a comprehensive complaints procedure and a free explanatory leaflet is available from Customer Services. Problems and complaints should be addressed to the local Waterway Manager in the first instance. For more information, visit their website.

The EA is the national body, sponsored by the Department for Environment, Food and Rural Affairs, to manage the quality of air, land and water in England and Wales. For more information, visit its website.

The Inland Waterways Association (IWA) campaigns for the use, maintenance and restoration of Britain's inland waterways, through branches all over the country. For more information, contact them on 01494 783453; iwa@waterways.org.uk; www.waterways.org.uk; The Inland Waterways Association, Island House, Moor Road, Chesham HP5 1WA. Their website has a huge amount of information of interest to boaters, including comprehensive details of the many and varied waterways societies.

STARTING OUT

Extensive information and advice on booking a boating holiday is available from the Inland Waterways Association, www.visitthames.co.uk and www.waterscape.com. Please book a waterway holiday from a licensed operator – only in this way can you be sure that you have proper insurance cover, service and support during your holiday. It is illegal for private boat owners to hire out their craft. If you are hiring a holiday craft for the first time, the boatyard will brief you thoroughly. Take notes, follow their instructions and don't be afraid to ask if there is anything you do not understand. BW have produced a short DVD giving basic information on using a boat safely. Copies are available from BW Customer Services (charge).

PLACES TO VISIT ALONG THE WAY

This guide contains a wealth of information, not just about the canals and rivers and navigating on them, but also on the visitor attractions and places to eat and drink close to the waterways. Opening and closing times, and other details often change; establishments close and new ones open. If you are making special plans to eat in a particular pub, or visit a certain museum it is always advisable to check in advance.

MORE INFORMATION

An internet search will reveal many websites on the inland waterways. Those listed below are just a small sample:
National Community Boats Association is a national charity and training provider, supporting community boat projects and encouraging more people to access the inland waterways. Telephone 0845 0510649; www.national-cba.co.uk.

National Association of Boat Owners is dedicated to promoting the interests of private boaters on Britain's canals and rivers. Visit www.nabo.org.uk.
www.canalplan.org.uk is an online journey-planner and gazetteer for the inland waterways.
www.canals.com is a valuable source of information on anything related to cruising the canals, with loads of links to canal and waterways related websites.
www.saveourwaterways.org is the website of Save Our Waterways, a campaign which embraces all waterways users and is dedicated to securing the long-term future of the inland waterways.
www.ukcanals.net lists services and useful information for all waterways users.

GENERAL CRUISING NOTES

Most canals and rivers are saucer shaped, being deepest at the middle. Few canals have more than 3-4ft of water and many have much less. Keep to the centre of the channel except on bends, where the deepest water is on the outside of the bend. When you meet another boat, keep to the right, slow down and aim to miss the approaching craft by a couple of yards. If you meet a loaded commercial boat keep right out of the way and be prepared to follow his instructions. Do not assume that you should pass on the right. If you meet a boat being towed from the bank, pass it on the outside. When overtaking, keep the other boat on your right side.

Some BW and EA facilities are operated by pre-paid cards, obtainable from BW and EA regional and local waterways offices, lock keepers and boatyards. Weekend visitors should purchase cards in advance. A handcuff/anti-vandal key is commonly used on locks where vandalism is a problem. A watermate/sanitary key opens sanitary stations, waterpoints and some bridges and locks. Both keys and pre-paid cards can be obtained via BW Customer Service Centre.

Safety

Boating is a safe pastime. However, it makes sense to take simple safety precautions, particularly if you have children aboard.
- Never drink and drive a boat – it may travel slowly, but it weighs many tons.
- Be careful with naked flames and never leave the boat with the hob or oven lit. Familiarise

yourself and your crew with the location and operation of the fire extinguishers.
- Never block ventilation grills. Boats are enclosed spaces and levels of carbon monoxide can build up from faulty appliances or just from using the cooker.
- Be careful along the bank and around locks. Slipping from the bank might only give you a cold-water soaking, but falling from the side of, or into a lock is more dangerous. Beware of slippery or rough ground.
- Remember that fingers and toes are precious! If a major collision is imminent, never try to fend off with your hands or feet; and always keep hands and arms inside the boat.
- Weil's disease is a particularly dangerous infection present in water which can attack the central nervous system and major organs. It is caused by bacteria entering the bloodstream through cuts and broken skin, and the eyes, nose and mouth. The flu-like symptoms occur two-four weeks after exposure. Always wash your hands thoroughly after contact with the water. Visit www.leptospirosis.org for details.

Speed

There is a general speed limit of 4 mph on most BW canals and 5 mph on the Thames. There is no need to go any faster – the faster you go, the bigger a wave the boat creates: if your wash is breaking against the bank, causing large waves or throwing moored boats around, slow down. Slow down also when passing engineering works and anglers; when there is a lot of floating rubbish on the water (try to drift over obvious obstructions in neutral); when approaching blind corners, narrow bridges and junctions.

Mooring

Generally you may moor where you wish on BW property, as long as you are *not causing an obstruction*. Do not moor in a winding hole or junction, the approaches to a lock or tunnel, or at a water point or sanitary station. On the Thames, generally you have a right to anchor for 24 hours in one place provided no obstruction is caused, however you will need explicit permission from the land owner to moor. There are official mooring sites along the length of the river; those provided by the EA are free, the others you will need to pay for. Your boat should carry metal mooring stakes, and these should be driven firmly into the ground with a mallet if there are no mooring rings. Do not stretch mooring lines across the towpath and take account of anyone who may walk past. Always consider the security of your boat when there is no one aboard. On tideways and commercial waterways it is advisable to moor only at recognised sites, and allow for any rise or fall of the tide.

Bridges

On narrow canals slow down well in advance and aim to miss one side (usually the towpath side) by about 9 inches. *Keep everyone inboard when passing under bridges and ensure there is nothing on the roof of the boat that will hit the bridge.* If a boat is coming the other way, the craft nearest to the bridge has priority. Take special care with moveable structures – the crew member operating the bridge should be strong and heavy enough to hold it steady as the boat passes through.

Going aground

You can sometimes go aground if the water level on a canal has dropped or you are on a particularly shallow stretch. If it does happen, try reversing *gently*, or pushing off with the boat hook. Another method is to get your crew to rock the boat from side to side using the boat hook, or move all crew to the end opposite to that which is aground. Or, have all crew leave the boat, except the helmsman, and it will often float off quite easily.

Tunnels

Again, ensure that everyone is inboard. Make sure the tunnel is clear before you enter, and use your headlight. Follow any instructions given on notice boards by the entrance.

Fuel

Hire craft usually carry fuel sufficient for the rental period.

Water

It is advisable to top up daily.

Lavatories

Hire craft usually have pump out toilets. Have these emptied *before* things become critical. Keep the receipt and your boatyard will usually reimburse you. The Green Blue, an organisation providing environmental advice for boating and watersports, has produced a series of maps locating pump out facilities within the UK. Visit www.thegreenblue.org.uk/youandyourboat for these and other advice.

Boatyards

Hire fleets are usually turned around at a weekend, making this a bad time to call in for services.

VHF Radio

The IWA recommends that all pleasure craft navigating the larger waterways used by freight carrying vessels, or any tidal navigation, should carry marine-band VHF radio and have a qualified radio operator on board. In some cases the navigation authority requires craft to carry radio and maintain a listening watch. Two examples of this are for boats on the tidal River Ouse wishing to enter Goole Docks and the Aire & Calder Navigation, and for boats on the tidal Thames, over 45ft, navigating between Teddington Lock and Limehouse Basin. VHF radio users must have a current operator's certificate. The training is not expensive and will present no problem to the average inland waterways boater. Contact the RYA (see Training) for details.

PLANNING A CRUISE

Don't try to go too far too fast. Go slowly, don't be too ambitious, and enjoy the experience. Mileages indicated on the maps are for guidance only. A *rough* calculation of time taken to cover the ground is the lock-miles system:

Add the number of *miles* to the number of *locks* on your proposed journey, and divide the resulting figure by three. This will give you an approximate guide to the number of *hours* your travel will take.

TIDAL WATERWAYS

The typical steel narrow boat found on the inland waterways is totally unsuitable for cruising on tidal estuaries. However, the adventurous will inevitably wish to add additional 'ring cruises' to the more predictable circuits of inland Britain. Passage is possible in most estuaries if careful consideration is given to the key factors of weather conditions, tides, crew experience, the condition of the boat and its equipment and, perhaps of overriding importance, the need to take expert advice. In many cases it will be prudent to employ the skilled services of a local pilot. Within the text, where inland navigations connect with a tidal waterway, details are given of sources of advice and pilotage. It is also essential to inform your insurance company of your intention to navigate on tidal waterways as they may very well have special requirements or wish to levy an additional premium. This guide is to the inland waterways of Britain and therefore recognizes that tideways – and especially estuaries – require a different approach and many additional skills. We do not hesitate to draw the boater's attention to the appropriate source material.

LOCKS AND THEIR USE

A lock is a simple and ingenious device for transporting your craft from one water level to another. When both sets of gates are closed it may be filled or emptied using gates, or ground paddles, at the top or bottom of the lock. These are operated with a windlass. On the Thames, the locks are manned all year round, with longer hours from April to October. You may operate the locks yourself at any time.

If a lock is empty, or 'set' for you, the crew open the gates and you drive the boat in. If the lock is full of water, the crew should check first to see if any boat is waiting or coming in the other direction. If a boat is in sight, you must let them through first: do not empty or 'turn' the lock against them. This is not only discourteous, and against the rules, but wastes precious water.

In the diagrams the *plan* shows how the gates point uphill, the water pressure forcing them together. Water is flooding into the lock through the underground culverts that are operated by the ground paddles: when the lock is 'full', the top gates (on the left of the drawing) can be opened. One may imagine a boat entering, the crew closing the gates and paddles after it.

In the *elevation*, the bottom paddles have been raised (opened) so that the lock empties. A boat will, of course, float down with the water. When the lock is 'empty' the bottom gates can be opened and the descending boat can leave.

Remember that when going *up* a lock, a boat should be tied up to prevent it being thrown about by the the rush of incoming water; but when going *down* a lock, a boat should never be tied up or it will be left high and dry.

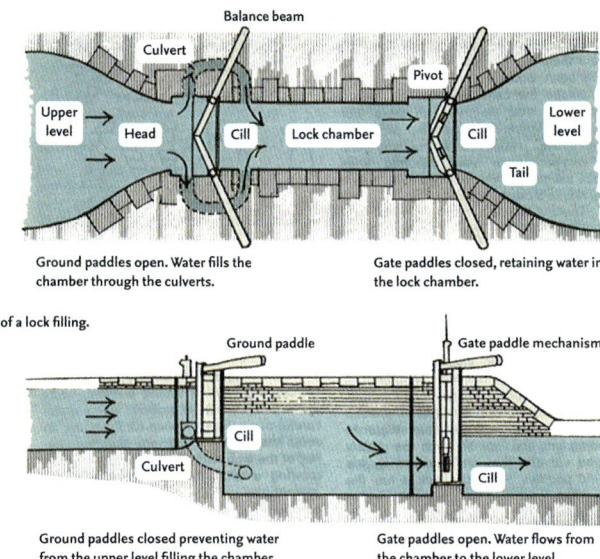

A plan of a lock filling.

An elevation of a lock emptying.

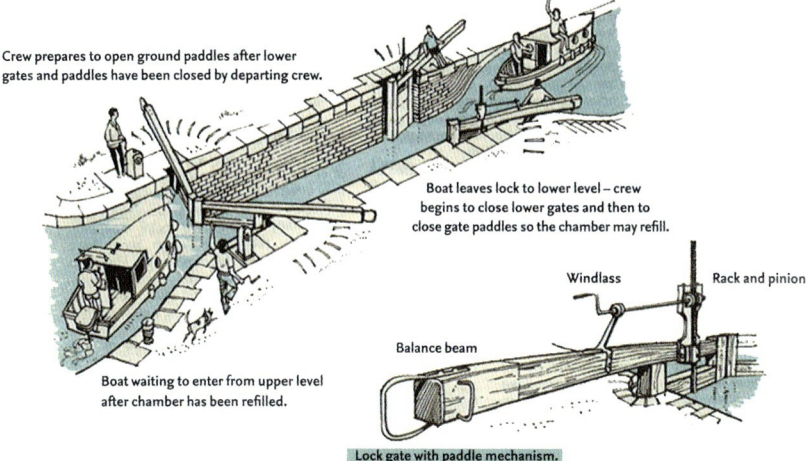

Lock gate with paddle mechanism.

- Make safety your prime concern. *Keep a close eye on young children.*
- Always take your time, and do not leap about.
- Never open the paddles at one end without ensuring those at the other end are closed.
- Keep to the landward side of the balance beam when opening and closing gates.
- Never leave your windlass slotted onto the paddle spindle – it will be dangerous should anything slip.

- Keep your boat away from the top and bottom gates to prevent it getting caught on the gate or the lock cill.
- Never drop the paddles – always wind them down.
- Be wary of fierce *top gate* paddles, especially in wide locks. Operate them slowly, and close them if there is *any* adverse effect.
- Always follow the navigation authority's instructions, where given on notices or by their staff.

Boroughbridge (see page 92)

AIRE & CALDER NAVIGATION

MAXIMUM DIMENSIONS
Castleford to Goole
Length: 200'
Beam: 20'
Headroom: 11' 9" *(see note 5 on page 27)*
Draught: 8' 2"

MANAGER
0113 281 6800; enquiries.northeast@britishwaterways.co.uk

MILEAGE
CASTLEFORD to:
Bank Dole: 7 miles, 3 locks including Castleford
New Junction Canal: 16½ miles, 5 locks
Goole: 24 miles, 5 locks

SAFETY NOTES
BW produce excellent Cruising Notes for the pleasure boater using this waterway, obtainable from the manager's office or downloadable from www.waterscape.com. This is both a commercial waterway and one developed from a river navigation: both pose their own disciplines highlighted in the notes.

The National Association of Boat Owners (NABO) produce a Skipper's guide for the Aire & Calder, available from their website (www.nabo.org.uk). Each lock on the waterway has a set of traffic lights both upstream and downstream of the lock chamber. The purpose of these lights is to convey instructions and advice to approaching craft.

Red light
Stop and moor up on the lock approach. The lock is currently in use.

Amber light *(between the red and green lights)*
The lock keeper is not on duty. You will need to self-operate.

Green light
Proceed into lock.

Red & green lights together
The lock is available for use. The lock keeper will prepare and operate the lock for you.

Flashing red light
Flood conditions – unsafe for navigation.

Most lock approach moorings are immediately upstream and downstream of the lock chamber; however, **please note**:

Ferrybridge Lock upstream approach mooring is located on the river side of the lock island.

Locks at Castleford, Bulholme, Ferrybridge and Bank Dole allow access to river sections of the navigation. River level gauge boards indicate conditions as follows:

GREEN BAND – Normal river levels safe for navigation.

AMBER BAND – River levels are above normal. If you wish to navigate the river section you are advised to proceed on to and through the next lock.

RED BAND – Flood conditions unsafe for navigation. Lock closed.

All locks between Castleford and Goole (except Bank Dole) are equipped with VHF Marine Band Radio. They monitor and operate on channel 74.

See page 21 for details of self-operation of these locks.

In an emergency non-VHF users should contact the manager's office.

The River Aire was first made navigable to Leeds in 1700 and rapidly became a great commercial success, taking coal out of the Yorkshire coalfield and bringing back raw wool, corn and agricultural produce. Improvements were then made to the difficult lower reaches, with first Selby and later Goole becoming Yorkshire's principal inland port. The opening of the New Junction Canal in 1905 further secured its suitability for commercial traffic, which until recently amounted to some 2 million tons, mainly coal, sand and petroleum. However, the current cessation of coal carrying to Ferrybridge Power Stations has, at a stroke, transferred 1½ million tons from the navigation onto road and rail annually, together with its associated environmental cost.

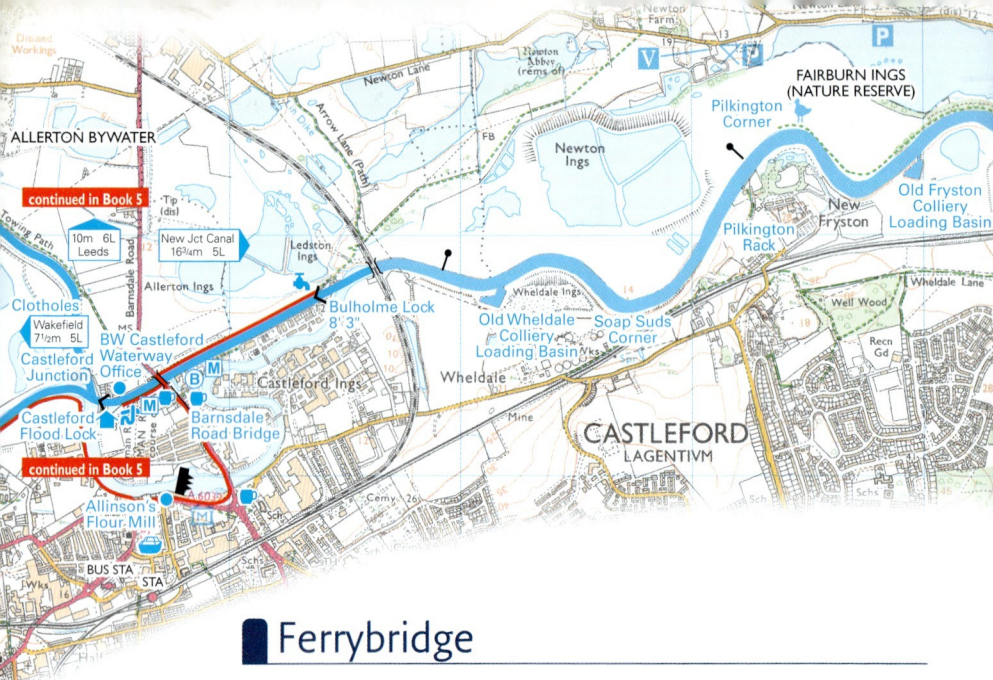

Ferrybridge

At Bulholme Lock is a sign directing walkers to Newton. This walk should not be attempted in wet weather as the footpath becomes waterlogged. The lock keeper's bungalow, built on stilts, replaces a traditional canalside cottage. At this point the canal enters the river which is surrounded by large areas of derelict land. Landscaping of the now-abandoned Fryston and Wheldale collieries is still being undertaken but will, no doubt, lead to the establishment of plants and trees in the area. The lower land to the north of the navigation forms the Ings, a word dating back to Viking times which denotes areas of riverside water meadows which are subject to seasonal flooding. Mining subsidence in the area, particularly over the last 50 years, has meant that much of this land has now become permanently waterlogged, resulting in the loss of a considerable area of agricultural land. These wetlands have, however, provided a habitat for all forms of wildlife, the area between the river and the village of Fairburn being recognised as a nature reserve since 1957. Owned by the Coal Authority, formerly the National Coal Board, and leased to the RSPB, the 618-acre site was designated a statutory bird sanctuary in 1968 – 251 species of birds have been recorded, of which about 170 are regular visitors. Originally the land was acquired in order to provide space for tipping spoil from the collieries. The Coal Authority still retains tipping rights in the area but, in the interest of wildlife, has restricted its activities. Continued work on the spoil heaps prevents the natural establishment of vegetation, although tree planting on the mature spoil heaps between Castleford and Ferrybridge has proved most effective. The river eventually traces a surprisingly pretty course as it meanders through banks now well established with silver birch, larch and alder. Just before the skew railway bridge are some sluice gates, installed in order to regulate the water levels within the washland areas of the reserve. These levels can vary considerably, often having a disastrous effect on nesting birds. Boaters should note that the only recognised access to the reserve is from the Fairburn to Allerton Bywater road to the north of Castleford. On no account should visitors try to gain access from the river, as the land here is the property of the Coal Authority and is prone to subsidence. The village of Fairburn is a good walk from Castleford but would provide a useful refreshment point for anyone visiting the bird sanctuary. On arrival at the Ferrybridge Power Stations the river suddenly resumes its industrial character as the massive cooling towers overpower the landscape. Coal has been transported to Ferrybridge from over 30 collieries throughout the north east and until fairly recently approximately 25 per cent of this was carried by water. Hargreaves alone carried well over 1,000,000 tons of coal to

Aire & Calder Navigation

Ferrybridge

NAVIGATIONAL NOTES
See page 19.

	Castleford	New Jct Canal
	6½m 3L	10¼m 2L

Ferrybridge
C each year.
Leaving
behind the
gaunt buildings
of the power stations,
the graceful 18th-C bridge
which once carried the Great
North Road comes into sight.
This has now been superseded by
the concrete viaduct which carries the A1
dual carriageway. Here the River Aire leaves the
navigation, flowing off to the left, as the canal traces a
more southerly course through Knottingley. All craft should bear right
and await the traffic lights controlling the entrance to the Ferrybridge Flood Lock. Moorings
immediately beneath the viaduct are for the use of boats waiting to enter the lock only. Long-
stay moorings are to be found on the river to the left of the lock. Care should be exercised on
this section as the river terminates in a weir. Pubs and shops in Ferrybridge can be reached
from the lock. The navigation now enters an artificial cut which continues all the way to
Goole. The canal skirts an industrial complex on the right and passes the tall gaunt buildings
of King's Flour Mills on the left, before entering a pleasantly green, wooded cutting. Here is
evidence of limestone quarrying over and above the need to make passage for the waterway
and indeed the approaches to both Gaggs and Jacksons bridges remain as solid rock.

17

Passing Thorpe Marsh Power Station, Barnby Dun (see page 130)

- **Fairburn**
  W. Yorks. PO, tel, stores. Limestone and alabaster were once quarried here. There is also a record of a tunnel, 350yds long, which extended under the village connecting it to the river. Perched on the hillside above the Ings, the village has several pubs and shops.

- **Ferrybridge**
  W. Yorks. PO, tel, stores, garage. The town takes its name from the bridge over the River Aire which was built at the point where, for many centuries, travellers were ferried across the water. Possession of the site has been contested in the past by the Romans and much later by the armies of York and Lancaster. The area is now dominated by the three power stations, Ferrybridge A, B and C. Ferrybridge A is now given over to workshops devoted to the repair and testing of machinery, Ferrybridge B has closed, whilst C station still produces electricity for the national grid.

NAVIGATIONAL NOTES

1. All the locks on the Aire & Calder operate mechanically and, although largely under the control of mobile lock keepers, can be boater-operated out of hours. Obey the traffic light signals.
2. Remember that this is a river navigation. Many of the locks are accompanied by large weirs, so keep a sharp lookout for the signs which direct you safely into the locks.
3. When the river level rises after prolonged heavy rain, the flood locks will be closed. Pleasure craft should stay put until they are advised by a lock keeper that it is safe to proceed.
4. This is a commercial waterway, used by 600-tonne tanker and sand barges. Keep a lookout for them, and give them a clear passage, especially on the many bends that the river describes on this stretch. Moor carefully on the canal sections of the navigation, using bollards or fixed rings rather than mooring stakes, since the wash from these craft can be substantial.
5. Ferrybridge Power Stations are not far away and navigators should be prepared for any activity in that area. There is nowhere suitable to moor on this part of the river.

Boatyards

ⓑ **CPL Hargreaves** Navigation Road Dockyard, Lock Lane, Castleford WF10 2LG (01977 553685). Boat repairs, dry dock, wet dock, DIY facilities, crane.

Pubs and Restaurants

The Golden Lion The Square, Knottingley WF11 8ND (01977 279339). Riverside at Ferrybridge Lock. A friendly pub overlooking the River Aire. Real ale. Meals available *L and E*, *Sun carvery 12.00–16.00*.. Children welcome. Outside seating. B & B.

WALKING & CYCLING

At the present time there is no recognisable towpath beyond Bulholme Lock. It is possible to follow a series of footpaths on the north bank of the river, to reach the canal towpath at Ferrybridge.

Whitley Bridge

Immediately through Shepherds Bridge the navigation forks: straight ahead leads to Bank Dole Lock into the River Aire and thence to the Selby Canal, while the main line bends right. Care should be exercised here on account of both moored commercial craft and laden barges approaching under Skew Bridge. They require first call on the available water to line up for Shepherds Bridge. For much of this journey the canal is steel-piled to

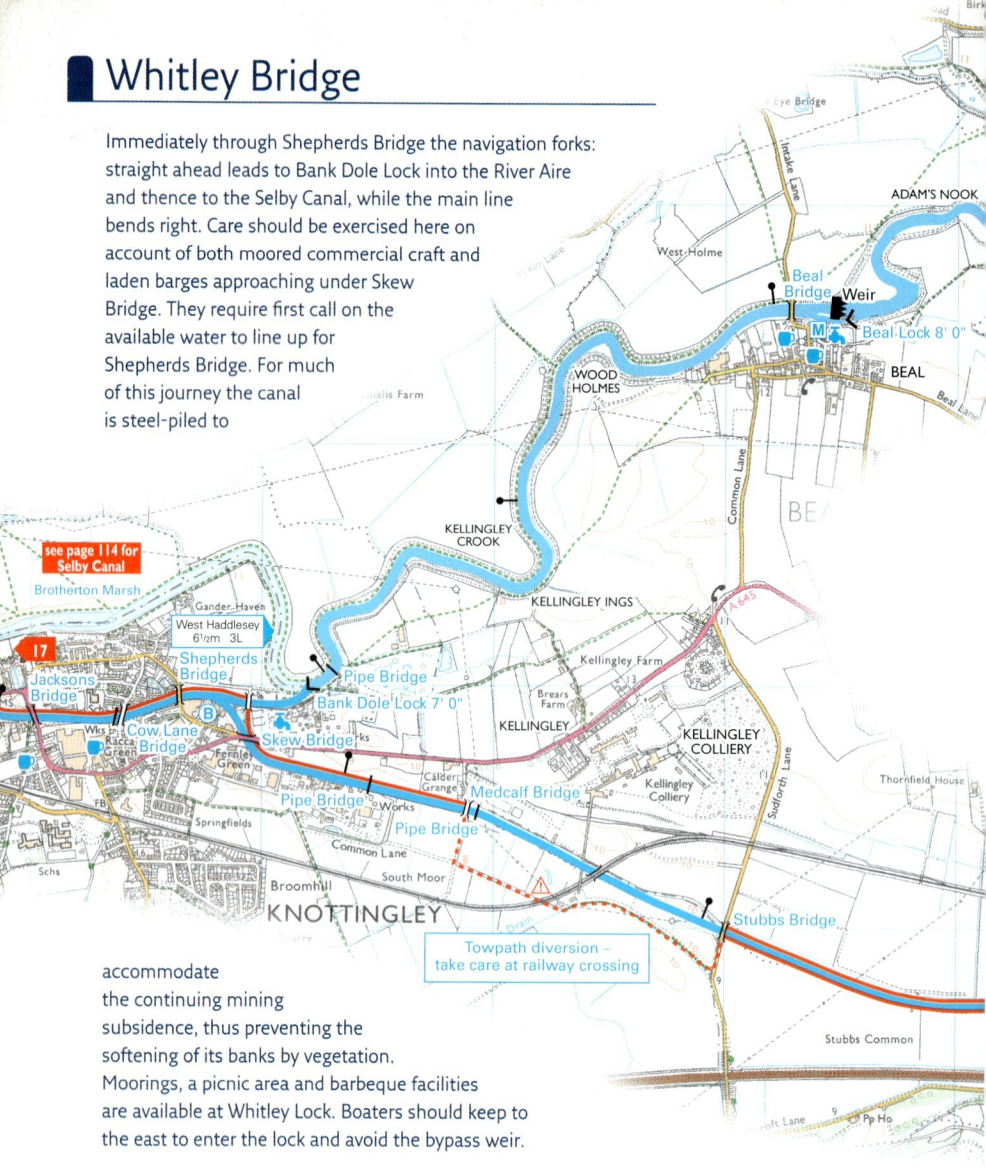

accommodate the continuing mining subsidence, thus preventing the softening of its banks by vegetation. Moorings, a picnic area and barbeque facilities are available at Whitley Lock. Boaters should keep to the east to enter the lock and avoid the bypass weir.

● **Knottingley**
W. Yorks. All services. Once famous for the making of clay tobacco pipes and for its pottery, Knottingley now depends on the manufacture of synthetic chemicals, hydrocarbons, cosmetics and glassware. The local glassworks, its production now limited to scent bottles, once manufactured the majority of the glass containers found in our homes and supermarkets. The pretty church of St Botolph can be seen at the north end of Jacksons Bridge. The church has some impressive carvings around the doorway and an interesting campanile tower.

The area next to the church was once the site of Knottingley Old Hall, an Elizabethan residence demolished in 1830 'for the sake of the limestone beneath it'.

● **Eggborough**
N. Yorks. Tel, PO, stores, garage, station (limited service). The original settlement of Whitley Bridge has now been lost amidst a sprawling development of new housing in Low Eggborough. There are two feed mills in the area. Eggborough Power Station, one of the largest in Yorkshire, is situated halfway between the canal and the old course of the River Aire.

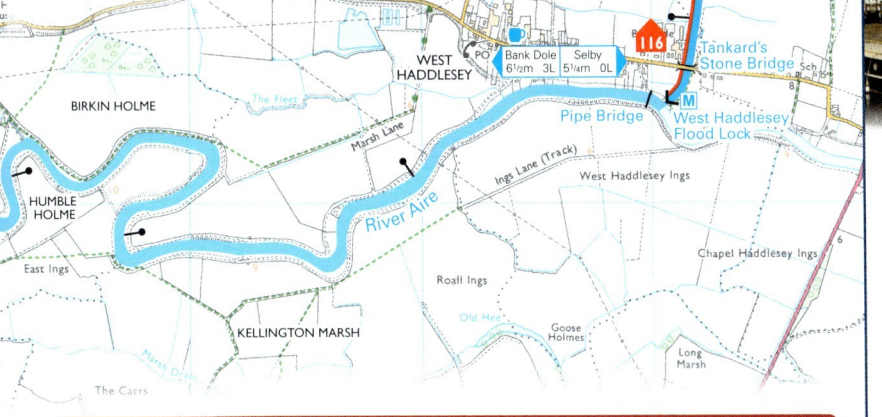

NAVIGATIONAL NOTES

1. **Lock operation** Lock gate and sluice operating pedestals are located adjacent to the upstream and downstream gates. You will need to insert a BW Watermate key into the pedestal to activate the system and allow use. Follow the step by step instructions on the operating panel in order to open the gates/sluices safely. Each pedestal can only be used to operate the adjacent gate/sluice.

2. **Emergency breakdown telephone** In the event of a breakdown in the operating system a red fault light will illuminate. Should this occur an emergency telephone is located in the front of the lockside control building. The cabinet door will automatically unlock or use your Watermate key. Dial 0800 4799947 and advise of your location and fault details. Remain by the telephone in case the duty engineer calls back for further information.

Aire & Calder Navigation

Whitley Bridge

Pollington

Soon Heck Bridge appears, giving access to local pubs. There used to be a quaint village shop, where only the sign outside gave the visitor any indication of its function. Once inside it soon became apparent that the shop was no more than a room set aside in someone's house. Sadly this is yet another whimsical feature of English village life that has passed away. Just beyond Heck Bridge is the home of the South Yorkshire Boat Club, making use of the basin once excavated to provide transhipment of stone to Goole from the local quarry. Immediately beyond the village the east coast main railway from London to Edinburgh crosses the navigation. Now electrified, this line carries the Class 91 Electra locomotives capable of hauling passenger trains at speeds of up to 140mph yet still restricted to 125mph pending a viable signalling system and an ever-receding line upgrade. To the north stand the twin chimneys of the disused quarry, now the site of a concrete pipe works. The navigation now adopts a fairly bleak and monotonous course through a flat but fertile landscape. Trees are scarce, and hedges and livestock are nowhere to be seen. There are numerous drainage ditches. The straggling village of Pollington lies to the north of Pollington Bridge; there is a *post office*, *pub* and *restaurant*. The school and a brick-built chapel with a bell tower are on the south side of the bridge. To the west of the village, facing the canal, stands Pollington Hall, an attractive 18th-C house with pleasingly proportioned narrow windows and a door pediment. Beyond the lock is Manor Farm where there is evidence of a moat. These buildings, along with Pollington Grange to the south of the navigation, indicate a former prosperity. At Pollington Lock the lock keeper's pretty cottage is one of the best examples of its type, with attractively rounded brick arches above the windows and a particularly deep overhang to the roof at the gable ends. Beyond Crow Croft Bridge the demolished abutments of an old railway bridge can be seen, unusual in that it once pivoted upwards at one end.

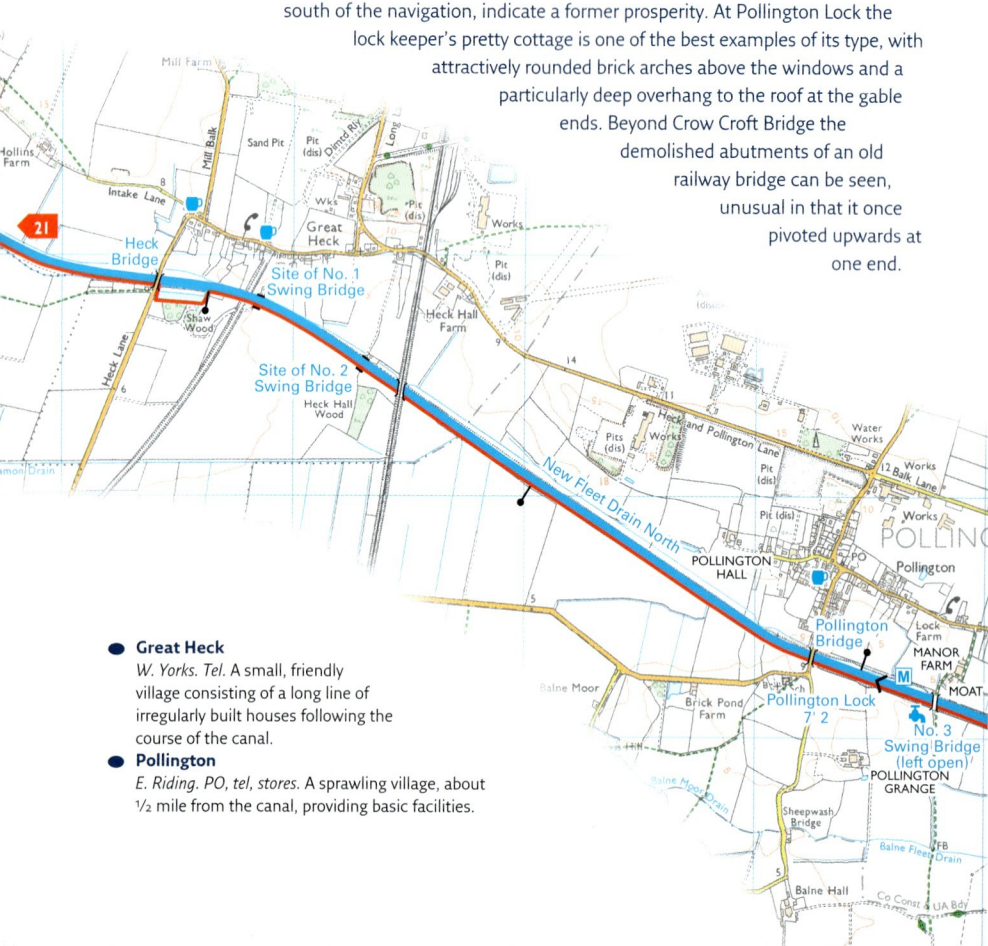

- **Great Heck**
  W. Yorks. Tel. A small, friendly village consisting of a long line of irregularly built houses following the course of the canal.
- **Pollington**
  E. Riding. PO, tel, stores. A sprawling village, about 1/2 mile from the canal, providing basic facilities.

At this point the River Went draws close and follows the line of the navigation towards Goole. The dinghies of the Beaver Sailing Club at Southfield Reservoir add an unexpected and welcome splash of colour to the landscape. The 110-acre reservoir, built at the turn of the century, marks the beginning of the New Junction Canal leading south to Sheffield. Its construction provided a water supply to meet the needs of the much larger locks installed on the navigation, and it effectively maintains the water levels of the docks at Goole.

NAVIGATIONAL NOTES

See page 21 for details of self-operation of locks.

Pubs and Restaurants

Simply Indian Restaurant Main Street, Pollington, South Yorkshire, DN14 0DN (01405 869618). *Open daily 17.00–24.00*. Takeaway also available.

The Bay Horse Main Street, Great Heck DN14 0BQ (01977 661121; www.oldmillbrewery.co.uk). 300yds north of Heck Bridge. A cosy pub, popular with boaters, serving real ale and good meals *Tue–Fri L and E, Sat–Sun all day*. Children welcome, outside seating. Occasional entertainment.

The King's Head Main Street, Pollington, Goole DN14 0DN (01405 861507). At the east end of the village. Friendly pub serving real ale. Children welcome, dogs only on a lead outside. Garden and children's play area.

Also try the **New Inn** Main Street, Great Heck DN14 0BQ.

Aire & Calder Navigation

Pollington

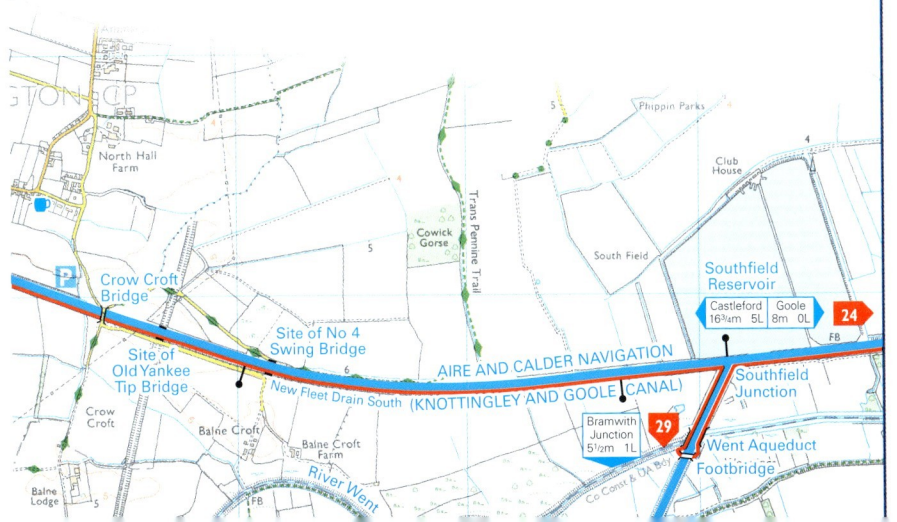

Rawcliffe Bridge

Beyond the turning to Keadby and Sheffield, up the unerringly straight New Junction Canal, the Aire & Calder performs an exaggerated dogleg and then sets off on an equally straight course for its terminus in Goole Docks. This manoeuvre is brought about by the appearance of the River Don from the south, joined near Beever Bridge by the diminutive River Went. In times of high rainfall the Went becomes more aggressive, flooding the surrounding farmland and leaving large deposits of silt in its wake. The turf-growing enterprise in this area bears witness to the inherent fertility of this regular fluvial performance and to man's ability to capitalise on one of nature's excesses. Having swung hard left, the boater is now in alignment with the Dutch River, the artificial channel cut by Cornelius Vermuyden to contain the River Don's previous exuberance. Before his intervention the Don had two mouths: one across the Isle of Axholme into the Trent near Trent Falls and a second into the River Aire, little more than a mile north of here. Were the boater not to swing right, under New Bridge, but to carry on straight ahead (with the addition of the odd wiggle or two) he would, in fact, be following the Don's old course. As the tidal Dutch River, Vermuyden's Don now accompanies the canal all the way to Goole.

● **Rawcliffe Bridge**
E. Riding. Tel, PO, stores, garage, station (limited service). A small, straggling settlement, running down to the canal and Dutch River to the south, and up to the main village of Rawcliffe 1½ miles to the north.

Both navigations - the Dutch River is used by experienced skippers - duck under the M18 (a sheltered 'berth' much fancied by local barge owners for painting their boats) and passes the site of both an old tar works and of a disused brickworks. Both works used to rely heavily on the canal for raw materials and the export of their finished products. To the east of Rawcliffe Bridge BW have established a safe haven mooring available for craft on either a short- or long-term basis. Contact 0113 281 6800; enquiries.northeast@britishwaterways.co.uk for further details.

Aire & Calder Navigation

Rawcliffe Bridge

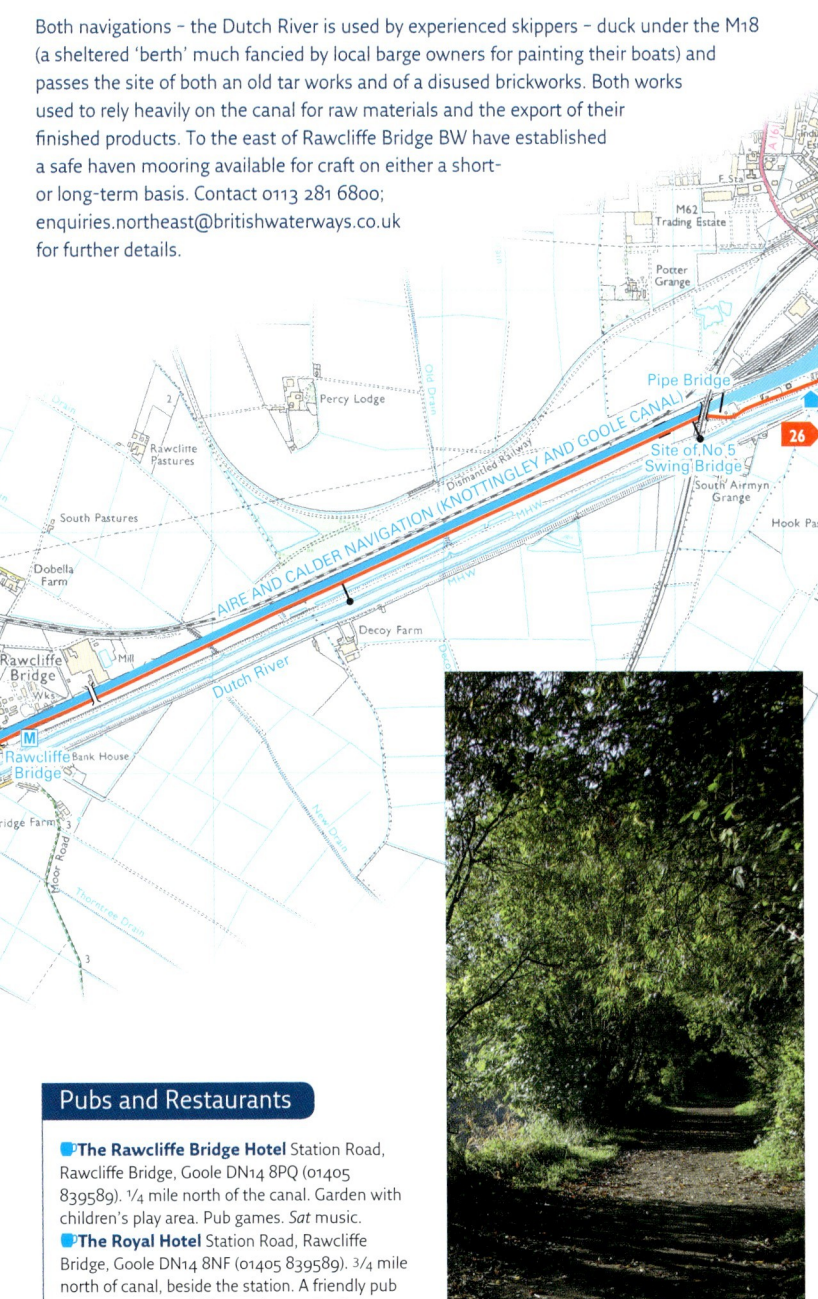

Beside the River Don

Pubs and Restaurants

● **The Rawcliffe Bridge Hotel** Station Road, Rawcliffe Bridge, Goole DN14 8PQ (01405 839589). ¼ mile north of the canal. Garden with children's play area. Pub games. *Sat* music.
● **The Royal Hotel** Station Road, Rawcliffe Bridge, Goole DN14 8NF (01405 839589). ¾ mile north of canal, beside the station. A friendly pub serving real ales. Children welcome. Pool, darts and dominoes. Live music *Sat*.

25

BOAT TRIPS
Yorkshire Waterways Museum Dutch Riverside, Goole DN14 5TB (01405 768730; www.waterwaysmuseum.org.uk). Hourly tours around the docks *weekends, Easter–Sep. Other times by appointment.*

Goole

Immediately before the railway bridge, marking the effective start of Goole Docks, is the site of the old No 5 swing bridge, replaced by a device replicating the stop planks found on narrow canals. A 'curtain' resting in the bottom of the waterway was winched across from one bank to the other. It was originally installed at the outbreak of World War II in anticipation of the docks being bombed. Once through the bridge, it can be plainly seen that there is far more boat capacity than there is waterborne traffic to fill it. To the north is a small basin, the remains of what was a proposed connection to the West Dock. It was here that Humber keels removed their lee-boards, masts and cog boats before heading inland. Fuel barges berth beside a boatyard in the first basin on the left (known as the 'dog and duck'), followed by John Branford's sand barges (cargoes from the Trent to Whitewood, near Castleford) at the aggregate wharf, and the occasional Waddington's boat. On the right is a concrete plant which receives materials by water, the Waterways Museum, commercial wharves and finally William Bartholomew's No 5 Boat Hoist, now restored. Bartholomew devised the system of trains of floating tubs – known as Tom Puddings – towed in a long snaking line (as many as 19 at a time) behind a tug, to be up-ended into a coaster, via the Boat Hoist, on their arrival in the docks.

Boatyards

Ⓑ**Goole Boathouse** The Timber Pond, Dutch Riverside, Goole DN14 5TB (01405 763985). 🛥 D E Gas, overnight mooring and long-term mooring (6' max draught), winter storage, slipway, crane, dry dock, boat repairs, chandlery, books, maps, toilets, showers, limited groceries, solid fuel, laundrette.

Ⓑ**Viking Marine** Albert Street, Goole DN14 5SY (01405 765737; www.vikingmarine.co.uk). D mooring, gas, 20 ton hoist, winter storage, maintenance and repair service, chandlery. Approved Honda main dealer (outboards and generators). Closed *Sun*.

NAVIGATIONAL NOTES

1. There are British Waterways visitor moorings at the sanitary station, by Goole Boathouse.
2. At the west end of South Dock the navigation ceases to be the responsibility of BW and comes under the jurisdiction of Associated British Ports (ABP). They may be contacted on VHF radio channel 14 – call *Goole Docks* – or by telephoning 01482 327171. **Boats using the tideway and Ocean Lock must carry VHF radio and have at least two persons on board.**
3. Beyond this point ocean-going shipping is manoeuvring and contact must be made with Ocean Lock Control before continuing.
4. Overnight mooring in this area will incur a substantial charge and temporary mooring, whilst awaiting a lock or bridge swing is only permitted if the crew are in attendance. Mooring on any pier whilst on the tideway (unless awaiting a lock) will also incur a charge.
5. Headroom under the swing bridge is approximately 11' 6" (the level of the dock can vary) and contact should be made with the lock keeper to arrange for it to be opened.
6. Lock operating times are 2$^{1}/_{2}$ *hours before high tide and 1 hour after* for which no charge is made. Outside these times special pens are always available on payment of a fee, which is in turn dependent on the time of day or night.
7. The lock keeper will willingly offer advice and information on navigating the tideway. For his part the boater must inform ABP that he is on the river and make his position known. ABP maintain a continuous watch on Channel 14. **At high tide the River Ouse is a busy navigation, carrying ocean-going shipping.**

Aire & Calder Navigation

Goole

● **Goole**
E. Riding. All services. When the Aire & Calder Navigation applied for an Act to build a canal from Knottingley to Goole in 1819, Goole was no more than a few cottages scattered around the marshes on the banks of the Ouse. Work commenced on cutting the canal in 1822 and by the following year a new town was developing rapidly as dwellings were built for the employees of the company. By 1828 foreign trade had begun with Hamburg and the local people entertained themselves by going down to the docks in the evening to await the arrival of foreign vessels on the spring tides. It is said of Goole that it was 'born under Victoria and died with her'. The docks are still very much the focal point of Goole, handling cargoes from Europe and Scandinavia. Lock Hill, near the Leisure Centre, is a good vantage point for watching vessels manoeuvring.
Goole Leisure Centre North Street, Goole DN14 5QX (01405 769005). Excellent facilities for the whole family.
Goole Museum and Art Gallery Carlisle Street, Goole DN14 5DS (01405 768963; www.eastriding.gov.uk). The museum houses an interesting exhibition depicting the development of Goole and the surrounding area, with an emphasis on the docks and shipping. *Open Tue, Thu, Fri 10.00–17.00, Wed 10.00–19.00, Sat 09.00–16.00.* Free.
Yorkshire Waterways Museum Dutch Riverside, Goole DN14 5TB (01405 768730; www.waterwaysmuseum.org.uk). Museum displays, boat tours of Goole Docks. Regular special events. Café. *Open all year Mon–Fri 09.00–16.00; weekends 11.00–16.00.* Free.

Pubs and Restaurants

●**The Macintosh Arms** 13 Aire Street, Goole DN14 5QW (01405 763850). Close to the main docks, this former courthouse offers a friendly welcome together with a selection of real ales. Dogs welcome. Outside seating and pub games. Regular entertainment. *Open all day.*
●**The Victoria Hotel** Hook Road, Goole DN14 5JB (01405 763839). Typical homely northern pub with dark wooden panelling and cream paintwork, built in 1794, where the landlord prides himself on his well-kept real ale. Food available *L and E.* Children welcome *until 21.00.* Beer garden, pool, darts and dominoes.

Other pubs in Goole, close to the docks and frequented by boaters, include the Vermuyden, the First and Last and the Middle House.

New Junction Canal

The New Junction Canal provides a link between the Aire & Calder and the South Yorkshire Navigations and was one of the last canals to be constructed in this country. The waterway is 5½ miles long and completely straight all the way, the monotony being broken only by a series of bridges and a lock. There are aqueducts at each end of the long corridor formed by the navigation, the first carrying the canal over the River Went; the more southerly over the River Don. Two smaller aqueducts are to be found at Chequer Lane and Westfields. Although the countryside here is flat, it is not without character. Moorings are available beside Sykehouse Lift Bridge and from here the village of Sykehouse and its pub may be reached, approximately 3/4 mile to the west of the canal. Further moorings are available close to Sykehouse Lock. Beyond Top Lane Lift Bridge is Low Lane Swing Bridge, carrying the road leading into Kirk Bramwith, with its interesting Norman church. Then the Don aqueduct appears. It presents a rather forbidding feature as it is contained by large guillotine gates at either end. Passing boats, although protected by a barrier on one side, have no more than railings on the other side, to prevent their descent into the river below. Once over the aqueduct, the canal is joined by the Stainforth & Keadby section of the navigation meeting at a very fine angle from the left. Its junction is masked by trees growing on the narrow spit of land formed between the two canals.

NAVIGATIONAL NOTES

1. All locks and moveable bridges can be boater-operated using a BW Watermate key.
2. Sykehouse Lock: when locking upstream keep away from the top gates to avoid excessive turbulence. Similarly, boats below the lock should keep well clear of the bottom gates when it is emptying. The swing bridge is interlocked with the operation of the lock so follow the instructions on the pedestal.

Sykehouse

S. Yorks. Tel, garage. A linear settlement which sprawls extensively to either side of the canal. A pub and a shop can be found to the west where there is attractive housing, much of which has been thoughtfully constructed of old brick. Holy Trinity Church has an attractive brick tower which was added to the original stone structure in 1724. The stone was subsequently replaced by a Victorian brick edifice. The village virtually closes down during the winter months.

Pubs and Restaurants

●**The Old George Inn** Broad Lane, Sykehouse DN14 9AU (01405 785635). It is a brave man who would interfere with a Yorkshireman's cricket! Once the home of the local cricket team, the adjoining field now contains an adventure playground which has made this a popular pub with families from the surrounding towns and villages. The building dates back some 500 years, the pub having been formed from what was once a terrace of cottages consisting over the years of a shop, a dame school, a farrier, a butcher and a slaughter house. The original wheel for hoisting the animals aloft for slaughter still hangs in the dining area. Real ale is served here and food *L and E, daily*. Large patio seating area and children's play area.

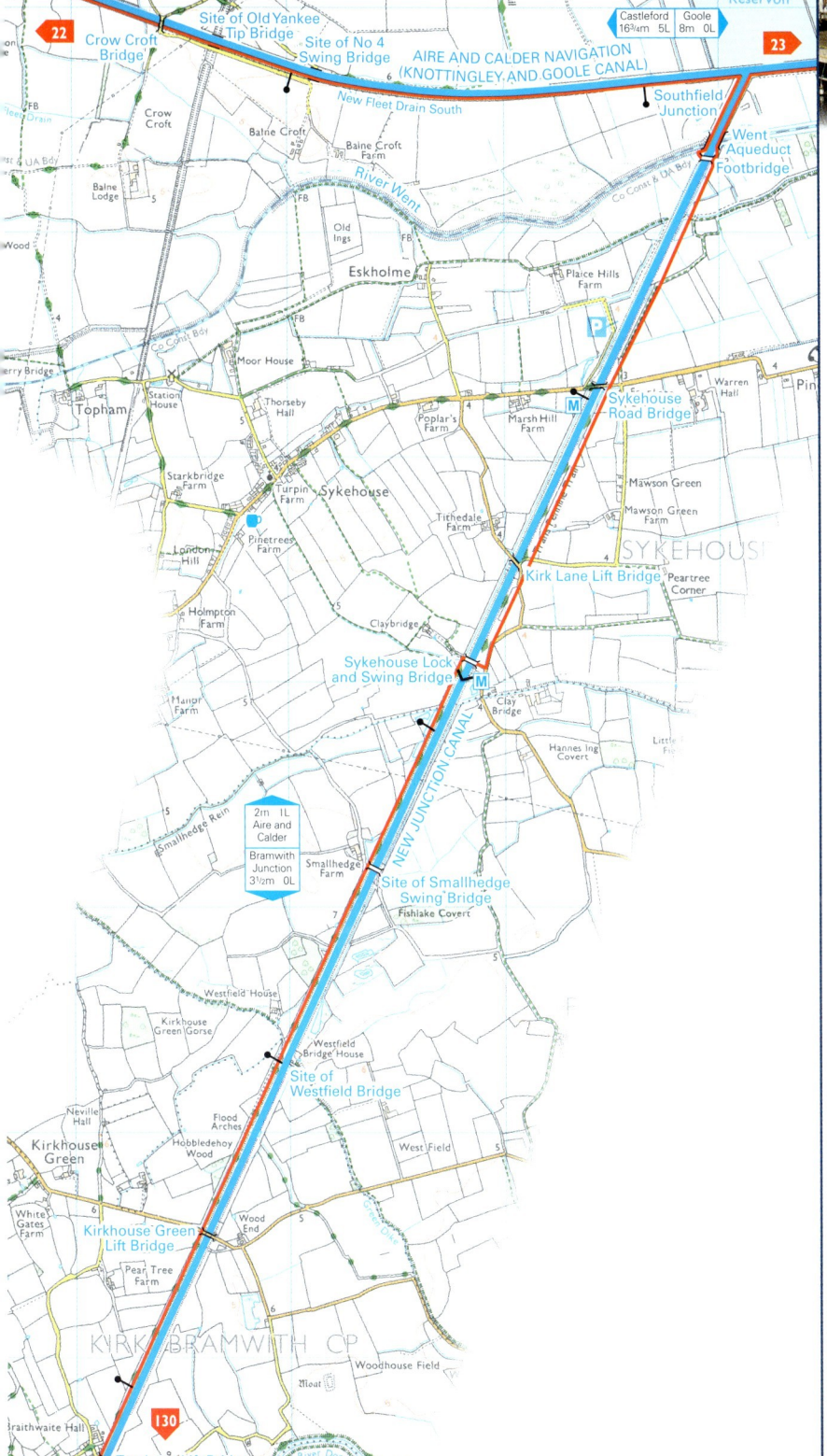

CHESTERFIELD CANAL

MAXIMUM DIMENSIONS
Length: 72'
Beam: 6' 10"
Headroom: 7' 1"
Draught: 2' 6"
(Craft of 7' 6" beam, on leaving the River Trent, *may* be able to proceed as far as Clayworth, depending on the height of the superstructure – Bridge 78 is the most restrictive overall structure.)

MANAGER
01636 704481;
enquiries.eastmidlands@britishwaterways.co.uk

MILEAGE
CHESTERFIELD to:
Staveley: 5 miles
Killamarsh: 10 miles
Norwood Tunnel West End: 12 miles
Norwood Tunnel East End: 14 miles
Ryton Aqueduct: 17½ miles
Worksop Town Lock: 20 miles
Osberton Lock: 23½ miles
Retford Town Lock: 30½ miles
Clayworth Bridge: 36 miles
Drakeholes Tunnel: 39 miles
WEST STOCKWITH, junction with River Trent: 45½ miles

Locks: 65 (Nos 6–19 derelict)

The Chesterfield Canal was initially surveyed in 1768 by John Varley to follow a line between Chesterfield and Bawtry on the River Idle, as an improvement on the trade route already in use. However, both Worksop and Retford were anxious to benefit from the proposed waterway, so Varley undertook a second survey a year later along a route to West Stockwith that bypassed the Idle altogether.

In 1769 James Brindley who had, due to pressure of other work, delegated the initial survey to Varley, called a public meeting at the Red Lion in Worksop. Here he proposed a draft line, terminating near Gainsborough and costing £105,000. This was later re-amended, on the grounds of cost and speed of construction, to meet the Trent at West Stockwith.

Work started in October 1771 with John Varley as resident engineer, Brindley being still too busy with other schemes to be permanently on site. Most of the work, including digging the 2893yds long Norwood Tunnel, constructing the summit level reservoir and building the lock flights, was let as separate contracts and carried out by individual contractors. Brindley's method was to make each section of the canal navigable as soon as it was completed to enable the company to benefit from the carriage of the heavy construction materials.

Brindley's death in September 1772 was a sad blow to the project and led to Varley being placed in overall charge of this, his first large project. Ultimately Hugh Henshall, Brindley's brother-in-law, was made inspector of works, later to become chief engineer with a salary of £250 per annum. In the following year he discovered work, carried out by John Varley's father and two brothers, in the construction of Norwood Tunnel, to be unsatisfactory. Soon other examples of dubious contractual arrangements and slack management came to light, all reflecting badly on the Varley family. The extent of John Varley's complicity in these matters remains to this day a matter for debate.

On 4 June 1777 the canal was officially opened from West Stockwith to Chesterfield. Norwood Tunnel caused problems from the outset, as did the shortage of water to the summit pound. Boats travelling less than 12 miles empty, or lightly laden, were penalised when using a lock. Over the next 25 years a more satisfactory solution was provided by the building of three large reservoirs at Killamarsh, Woodhall and Harthill.

As had always been envisaged by the canal's promoters, coal was the principal cargo carried, followed by stone, corn, lime, lead, timber and iron. Pottery and ale were also regular cargoes. Traffic peaked at over 200,000 tons in 1848, when records show the average load as 22 tons.

Early in 1841 a cargo of Anston stone, bound for the construction of the new Houses of Parliament, was carried for transhipment at West Stockwith, the first of approximately 250,000 tons despatched over a period of four years. As always, amalgamation with a railway company, in this case the Manchester & Lincoln Union Railway, led to a steady decline in the canal's fortunes and a reduction in maintenance. By 1904 it was reported that the minimum headroom in Norwood Tunnel was reduced to 4' 10", owing to subsidence, while a roof collapse on 18th October 1907 led to its final closure. Between the wars, now under London & North Eastern Railway (LNER) ownership, the canal was reasonably maintained, while the tidal lock into the Trent was enlarged and repaired in 1923-5. Attempts were also made to reduce the weed which had appeared in 1852 and remains, to some extent, a problem today. The navigation was temporarily resuscitated by the transport of munitions during World War II, but traffic virtually came to an end in 1955 when the small trade from Walkeringham brickworks (near Gringley) to the Trent finished. One cargo that did linger on into the early 1960s was that of warp: a fine natural silt dredged from the Trent at Idle Mouth and used as a metal polishing material in the Sheffield cutlery trade. To the end all boats - known as 'Cuckoos' - remained horse-drawn.

WALKING & CYCLING

To find the start of the navigation in Chesterfield, take the B6543 Brimington Road north east from its junction with Malkin Street, close to the Railway Station's main forecourt. Where this road crosses the river, walkers can access the towpath to the north west via Holbeck Close. Cyclists should, however, continue along Brimington Road to a point just south of the sharp bend under the railway. Here a waymarked path leads down to the junction of river and canal. From here the towpath is in excellent condition for both walkers and cyclists to a point just north of Staveley, as it is both the Cuckoo Way and a spur leading down from the Trans Pennine Trail - National Cycle Network Route 67. The waymarked Bluebank Loop, commencing at bridge 3, offers a very worthwhile diversion, or a separate walk in its own right. This is depicted on a most attractive, incised interpretation board. To the east of Eckington Road Bridge, the trail divides, with a second spur heading south whilst the main route turns almost due north. The Cuckoo Way follows the line of the canal in a north easterly direction and this section is only suitable for walkers. Cyclists should use the trail at least as far as Renishaw. For further details on the coast to coast Trans Pennine Trail telephone (01226) 772574 or visit www.transpenninetrail.org.uk.

North of Barlborough Road Bridge the Trans Pennine Trail still remains the easiest way of following the line of the canal - part in water, part infilled - certainly as far as cyclists are concerned. At Forge Bridge the line can be followed east into Killamarsh, as far as Bridge Street, without too much difficulty. At this point the faint-hearted are best advised to head north to Sheffield Road (the B6058) and then turn right and rejoin the somewhat overgrown towpath towards the top of the hill at Nether Green, where a Cuckoo Way finger post points due north. The purist may wish to stick, as far as possible, to the old line of the canal, avoiding the housing development alongside Kirkcroft Avenue and, via a section of Pringle Drive, meeting the aforementioned finger post at Belk Lane Lock (now very much an ornamental garden feature). At Norwood the path, although on private property, is a public right of way and leads to a stile above the tunnel mouth. From here, skirt along the right hand field boundary to a tunnel under the motorway, beyond which the path runs steadily downhill, finally meeting Hard Lane beyond newly landscaped open-cast workings. It continues east of the road, crossing a meadow to rejoin the fully navigable waterway at the eastern tunnel portal. When in doubt look out for the Cuckoo Way waymarking.

Chesterfield

The canal itself begins at Tapton Mill Bridge, where it leaves the River Rother above a weir. The original intention was to cross over the river at this point and continue the waterway into Chesterfield. However, a shortage of funds dictated that the cheaper option, provided by a short section of river navigation, was chosen, hence the present terminus south of Wharf Lane Changeover Bridge. This in fact superseded the original terminal basin and warehouse (slightly further north) that were severed from the river by the building of the Manchester, Sheffield and Lincolnshire Railway in the late 19th C – which has, in turn, been replaced by the Inner Relief Road. A single floodgate protects the canal at its junction with the Rother and before long the navigation becomes embroiled in a group of road crossings, bracketing the first lock and the excellent Tapton Lock Visitor Centre. Beyond are two further bridges – this time carrying the main line railway junction – as the waterway turns north east and heads for open countryside. There is little to remind the boater of the proximity of town and industry as the canal enters a side cutting overhung with the trees of Bluebank Wood. Dixon's Lock was newly reconstructed in a position some 200yds below the original to avoid the ravages of open-cast mining, and newly planted spoil tips are still very much in evidence as the waterway enters a shallow cutting. Hollingwood and Staveley (once the home of a vast canalside iron foundry) maintain a discrete distance from the navigation, separated by a tract of gently rising pastureland, and it is a matter of wonder how rapidly nature (with a little assistance from the bulldozer) regains control. Just to the east of Eckington Road Bridge, waterway and Trans Pennine Trail diverge: the trail heads north along an abandoned railway line, while the largely infilled course of the canal wanders off across the fields towards Mastin Moor.

Pubs and Restaurants

See page 40.

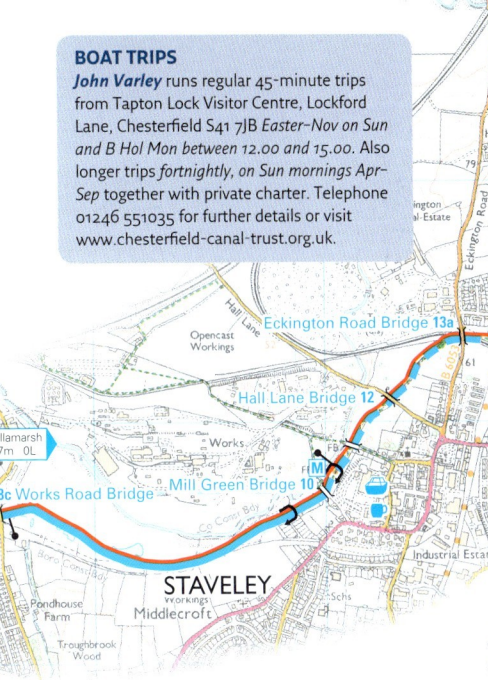

BOAT TRIPS
John Varley runs regular 45-minute trips from Tapton Lock Visitor Centre, Lockford Lane, Chesterfield S41 7JB *Easter-Nov on Sun and B Hol Mon between 12.00 and 15.00.* Also longer trips *fortnightly, on Sun mornings Apr-Sep* together with private charter. Telephone 01246 551035 for further details or visit www.chesterfield-canal-trust.org.uk.

Chesterfield Canal

Chesterfield

● **Chesterfield**
Derbyshire. All services. Probably best known as the town with the crooked spire (*see* St Mary and All Saints Church below), Chesterfield prospered well before the relatively recent wealth introduced by local metalworking industries and coal mining. It was known as Cestrefeld by the Anglo-Saxons, the 'Cestre' prefix indicating that the Romans were active here well before them. In this important market town many street names are of ancient origin and hint at a range of medieval trades that were once dominated by industries linked to the plentiful supply of wool produced on the surrounding hills. George Stevenson lived at Tapton for more than a decade, moving to the area whilst surveying a route for the North Midland Railway between Derby and Leeds. While digging the 'Mile Long' tunnel at Clay Cross, just south of Chesterfield, extensive iron and coal deposits were discovered in 1837, which Stevenson went on to exploit, launching the 'Clay Cross Company'. Today Chesterfield is a prosperous market town, retaining excellent railway connections but with little of its former industry.

The **Chesterfield Canal Trust** (www.chesterfield-canal-trust.org.uk) runs boat trips (*see* above) and promotes the canal and its full restoration. Visit the website for information about their work and events.

Barrow Hill Roundhouse Campbell Drive, Barrow Hill, Chesterfield S43 2PR (01246 472450; www.barrowhill.org). Built in 1870, this is in fact a square building constructed to house, maintain, coal and water and, in many cases, to turn steam locomotives. With the demise of steam haulage, most roundhouses were demolished, but, thanks to its continuing use for diesel traction and the dedication of the Barrow Hill Engine Society, this example survives and now houses one of the largest collections of electric, diesel and steam engines in the country. *Open Sat, Sun 10.00-16.00* and there is a calendar of special events (when there is a free bus service) – telephone for details or visit their website. Café. 1 mile north of Hollingwood Lock or buses 56, 80 or 90 from Chesterfield bus station. Charge.

Chesterfield Museum and Art Gallery St Mary's Gate, Chesterfield S41 7TD (01246 345727; www.visitchesterfield.info). The museum houses the actual builders' wheel used in the construction of the crooked spire, left inside the tower when building was completed. Also insights into Chesterfield life and George Stevenson's preoccupation with growing straight cucumbers. The art gallery contains Impressionist work by local artist Joseph Syddall. *Open Mon-Tue and Thu-Sat 10.00-16.00 (closed Wed and Sun).* Free.

Revolution House High Street, Old Whittington, Chesterfield S41 9JZ (01246 345727; www.visitchesterfield.info). Once an alehouse, known as the Cock & Pynot (magpie), this cottage was the meeting place for three local noblemen intent on overthrowing King James II in favour of William and Mary of Orange. Today the ground floor houses a display of 17th-C furniture; there is a video telling the story of the Revolution and upstairs are changing exhibitions relating to local themes. *Open daily Apr-Sep 11.00-16.00. Also limited Xmas opening.* Free. Bus service from Chesterfield.

St Mary and All Saints Church St Mary's Gate, Chesterfield S41 7TJ (01246 206506; www.chesterfieldparishchurch.org.uk). Whether viewed from near or far, most attention is focused on the spire rather than upon the church itself. Standing 228ft from ground to weathervane, leaning 9½ft out of plumb and grotesquely

33

Killamarsh

When the Great Central Railway built their line from Sheffield to Nottingham in 1890, its straight-as-a-die route between Staveley and Killamarsh conflicted on a very regular basis with the contoured course of the Chesterfield Canal. Rather than incur the substantial cost of building a succession of bridges, the Railway Company straightened the line of the canal, excavating cuttings as required, and it is for this reason that both canal and the now-disused railway run in tandem north and west of Renishaw. Here the navigation makes a second sweep to the east, passing through what was once a vast foundry complex, now demolished and built upon. Moulding sand had, over the years, been tipped into the canal bed and the waterway has only recently been re-excavated. At Forge Bridge and almost doubling back on itself, the navigation finally settles on a more easterly course, picking its way through the houses of Killamarsh. Vociferous protest in the 1970s failed to prevent a part of the canal being built upon and now, in places, the original line is difficult to follow. However, alternative routes are under investigation to link in with future plans at Norwood, where 13 locks await restoration. Here a superb flight of staircase locks – three groups of three and one of four – lift the canal to the bricked-up western portal of Norwood Tunnel. The building at the bottom of the flight was once the Boatman Inn; the large decorative 'lakes' were side pounds: storage for the considerable quantity of water needed to operate the locks, and in turn connected to reservoirs in the hills above. Between the top two staircase lock groups a dwelling has been converted from an old sawmill. This very early example of waterway construction dates, in the main, from 1775 and within 1/3 mile encapsulates some of the very best in canal engineering, all within an idyllic setting.

Pubs and Restaurants

See page 40.

Chesterfield Canal — Killamarsh

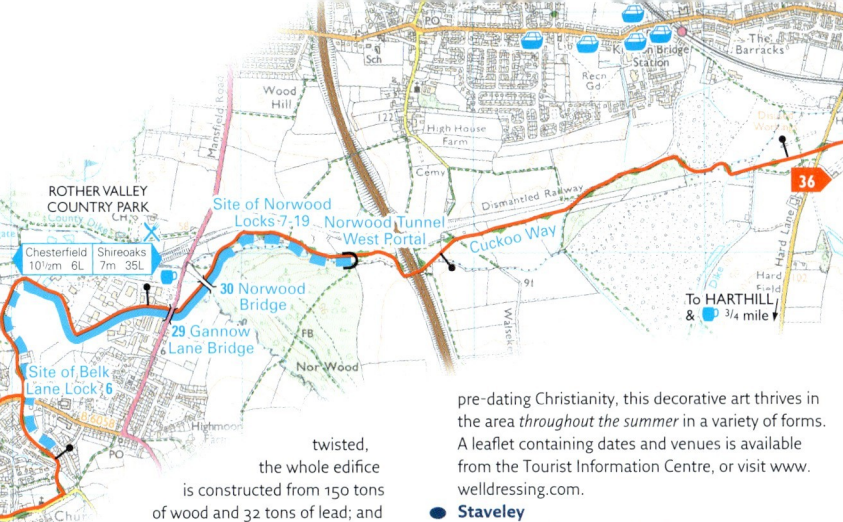

twisted, the whole edifice is constructed from 150 tons of wood and 32 tons of lead; and nothing secures it to the tower save its own mass. Legends abound as to the cause of its twist, involving wizards, devils, blacksmiths and virgins, though not necessarily all at once. More reasonably, the nature of the green oak from which it was constructed over 600 years ago, shrinking as it seasoned *in situ*, is the most likely culprit, aided and abetted by a design that eschews cross-bracing and allowed the bottom timbers to gradually decay over the years. A holy building in one form or another has stood on the site since the middle of the 7th C; the present building was dedicated in 1234 and completed in 1360, when the spire was added. The Norman font was dug up in the vicarage garden in 1848, although the cause of its migration remains a mystery. The spire almost fell prey to a serious fire in December 1961 and was within minutes of total destruction.

Tapton Visitor Centre Lockoford Lane, Chesterfield S41 7JB (01246 551035; www.derbyshire.gov.uk). Focus for much activity along the canal and within the Three Valleys area, the centre is a fund of information and has a well-stocked shop selling a range of useful publications, guides and maps together with free walks leaflets and an exhibition area. Also snacks and hot and cold drinks. *Open daily Apr–Oct 10.00–16.30; weekends Nov–Mar 10.00–16.00*. Free.

Tourist Information Centre Rykneld Square, Chesterfield S40 1SB (01246 345777; www.visitchesterfield.info). *Open Mon–Sat, Easter–Oct 09.00–17.30 and Nov–Easter 09.00–17.00*.

Well Dressing Derbyshire. While its origins remain something of a mystery, but undoubtedly pre-dating Christianity, this decorative art thrives in the area *throughout the summer* in a variety of forms. A leaflet containing dates and venues is available from the Tourist Information Centre, or visit www.welldressing.com.

● **Staveley**
Derbyshire. PO, tel, stores, banks, chemist, butcher, takeaways, fish & chips, garage. Mentioned in the Domesday Book, part of the Frecheville family estates in the 16th C and more recently owned by the Dukes of Devonshire, Staveley has, post Industrial Revolution, been the focus for the iron and coal industries in the area, with large foundries beside the canal at Hollingwood. The shop is *open Mon–Sat 08.00–22.00 & Sun 10.00–16,00*.

● **Renishaw**
Derbyshire. PO, tel, stores, takeaway, off-licence. Another foundry town once producing a vast array of complex castings for a wide range of industries. Shop *open Mon–Fri 06.00–22.00; Sat 07.00–22.00 & Sun 08.00–22.00*.
Renishaw Hall Renishaw, near Sheffield S21 3WB (01246 432310; www.sitwell.co.uk). 3/4 mile north west of Barlborough Road Bridge. The 300-year-old home of the Sitwell family who established themselves as coal magnates and iron founders long before displaying their literary credentials. Gardens, museum, tearoom, craft centre and galleries *open Apr–Oct, Thu–Sun and B Hol Mon 10.30–16.30. Public tours of Hall 2nd Sun in month at 15.00 (Apr–Sep); booking essential*. Charge.

● **Killamarsh**
Derbyshire. PO, stores, tel, chemist, fish & chips, library, butcher, takeaways, garage. Known as Chinewoldemaresc at the time of the Domesday survey, with a manor held by the tenure of providing a horse to the value of five shillings, with a sack and a spur, for the King's army in Wales. More recently and much more prosaically, a coal-mining centre, its deposits now exhausted. Shop *open Mon–Sat 08.00–22.00 & Sun 08.00–16.00*.

WALKING & CYCLING
The Derbyshire Countryside Service (08456 058 058; www.derbyshire.gov.uk) produce excellent walks leaflets (downloadable from the website) covering the Three Valleys area around the western end of the canal. **Creswell Craggs Museum and Education Centre** (01909 720378; www.creswell-crags.org.uk). Visit their website for a fascinating insight into the rich cultural and natural heritage of a former coalfield area. The **Dronfield 2000 Rotary Walk** is 'a countryside walk for all' to the north west of the canal – visit www.thewalk.org.uk for further details. Cycle Hire from Rother Valley Country Park – see page 39.

Shireoaks

Leaving the eastern tunnel portal, the waterway settles into an open cutting before gliding through woodland coppice to emerge beside the Anston stone quarries, the source of the stone used in the construction of the Houses of Parliament. Nothing can prepare the boater for the magic of the next few miles: it is pure waterway witchcraft as beyond, against rolling farmland to the north, the canal heads for the first of the treble locks, followed immediately by three single locks and another treble. So begins a truly awesome length of waterway and an amazing feat of early canal engineering. Two double and two single locks take the navigation down into Turnerwood Basin, ringed by a charming collection of waterside cottages. Thence by seven locks, following in quick succession, the waterway tunnels into a delightful ribbon of woodland on its approach to Ryton Aqueduct and Boundary Lock, newly constructed to accommodate mining subsidence in the area. At Shireoaks the navigation ducks under the rebuilt road bridge sitting beside the local cricket field – a perfect replica of a county ground in miniature. Beyond is the *marina*, dug out on the site of an abandoned colliery and offering *short-term moorings, showers and toilets, a self-operated pump out* and *electrical hook up*, together with all the usual facilities, and a post box.

RECIPROCAL MOVEMENTS

Above John Varley's remarkable flights of locks are woods and stone quarries, areas where natural resources have been exploited in the developments of our age. Anston Quarries not only offered a ready source of stone for the locks and bridges along the canal, they were also the source of almost 250,000 tons of stone used to rebuild the Houses of Parliament when they burnt down in 1834. However the traffic has not been entirely one way. The small community of Shireoaks lost 24 young men in World War I (who are commemorated by a Calvary Cross) and exactly half that number in World War II. In their memory a clock was installed in the turret of St Luke's parish church with a double, three-legged gravity escapement. The significance of this mechanism is that, not only will it resist outside influences – such as wind pressure on the hands – but that it is also a direct copy of Edmund Becket Denison's design for Big Ben.

Chesterfield Canal

Shireoaks

Wales
Derbyshire. PO, tel, stores, chemist, takeaways, library, bank, off-licence, fish & chips, garage, station. A mining community that now sits above the M1. The older area is set around the church. It was here that the body of Sir Thomas Hewitt, the somewhat eccentric owner of Hewitt Hall at Shireoaks, was eventually laid to rest. A confirmed atheist, Sir Thomas had begun to build an elaborate mausoleum at his home but died before it was completed. His servants tried to outwit the family's wishes to bury him at the church in Wales and one night filled the coffin with stones and set off with his body through the local woods at dead of night. Rumour has it that a strong wind blew out their torches and the servants were so frightened that they returned hastily to the hall with the body, which was then buried according to the family's plan. Scratta Wood was eventually felled and burned following reputed hauntings! The village shop is *open Mon-Sat 08.00-22.00 & Sun 10.00-16.00.*

Rother Valley Country Park Mansfield Road, Wales Bar, Sheffield S26 5PQ (0114 247 1452; www.rvcp.co.uk). Entrance just north of Gannow Lane Bridge 29. One thousand acres of parkland catering for a wide variety of leisure pursuits on both land and water. There is an 18th-C working mill, craft centre, and **The Stables Café** - *open daily* for appetising, inexpensive meals and snacks. For enquiries about leisure pursuits including boats, canoes, windsurfers and bicycles, telephone 0114 247 1452. For access by bus, telephone Traveline 0870 608 2 608 or visit www.derbysbus.net. *Open daily dawn to dusk (except Xmas).*

Kiveton Park
Derbyshire. PO box, tel, station. A cluster of houses and industrial units where once there were major stone quarries.

Harthill
Derbyshire. PO, tel, stores, butcher, laundrette. An attractive village whose main street is described in Scott's *Ivanhoe*. Mentioned in the Domesday Book, the first church was established here in 1078 by the son-in-law of William the Conqueror. Its successor houses some fine wooden carvings and an imposing timber roof. It is here that the body of John Varley was buried in 1809. The shop is *open daily 06.00-22.00.*

South Anston
Derbyshire. PO, tel, stores, chemist, butcher, takeaway, garage. A sprawling settlement overlooked by the pretty church of St James with its elegant spire.

Thorpe Salvin
Derbyshire. Tel. A tiny village which has several times been winner of Britain in Bloom and had the onerous task of representing England in the European competition. The small nucleus of attractive stone houses is dominated by the now-ruined Elizabethan Thorpe Hall and the church.

Pubs and Restaurants

See page 41.

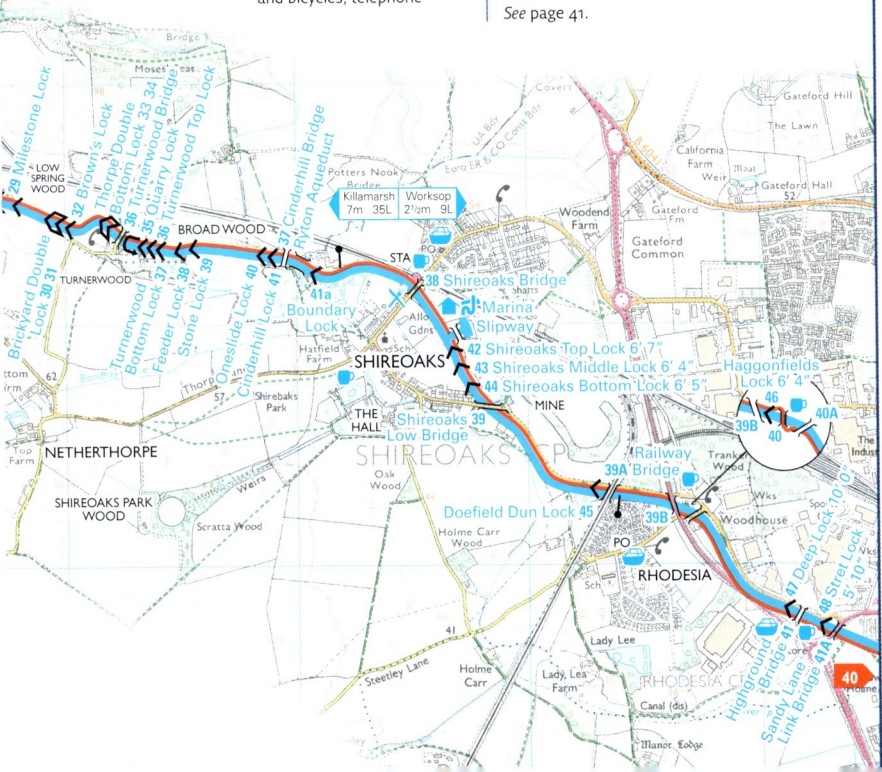

37

A very fine Norman doorway, a chained bible and a font depicting the four seasons are some of the treasures which can be seen within.

● **Shireoaks**
Notts. PO, stores, butcher, off-licence, fish & chips, station. It is worth taking the time to explore this village whose splendid terrace of miners' cottages leads down the hill to the church. The village takes its name from a giant oak tree which cast its shade into Yorkshire, Derbyshire and Nottinghamshire and which was said to have measured 94ft in circumference. The money for both the church and the cottages was given by the 5th Duke of Newcastle following the sinking of the pit. The presence of coal in the area brought work for up to 600 men and it is easy to imagine the impression that the newly-built colliers' cottages of Shireoaks Row must have made on the village. It is still possible to identify some of the original window casements and doors with their elaborate strap hinges, although many of the dwellings have cast history aside for more comfortable 20th-C fitments. The foundation stone of the church was laid in 1861 by Edward VII, then Prince of Wales. The quill pen which he used at the ceremony can still be seen in the church. Dedicated to St Luke, the building houses a beautiful altar, commemorating the Duke of Newcastle, and a painted ceiling. In 1975 the spire of the church had to be removed following subsidence caused by the mining in the area. A miner's lamp hangs above the pulpit as a poignant reminder of the industry which was the lifeblood of the village until the closure of the pit in 1990. The village has twice won the best-kept village award. Just beyond Shireoaks Row stands the impressive half-ruined Jacobean Hall, built in 1612, whose coach-house has been sensitively converted into a pub. The 45 acres of land behind the hall were laid out as a water garden to include a lake, cascade and ornamental canal. The shop is *open daily 06.00-22.00.*

● **Rhodesia**
Notts. PO, tel, stores, takeaway. A small settlement to the south west of the A57 flyover. Gas is available at the village store which is *open Mon-Sat 07.00-20.00 & Sun 10.00-16.00.*

Pubs and Restaurants

● **Market** 95 New Square, Chesterfield S40 1AH (01246 273641). Large town hostelry serving an excellent and ever changing range of real ales together with bar food *L, daily.* Also real cider. Outside seating and children are welcome *when dining. Open all day Mon-Sat and Sun E.*

● ✕ **Rutland** 23 Stephenson Place, Chesterfield S40 1PX (07835 816163; www.therutlandchesterfield.co.uk). Serious real ale establish-ment with regular mini beer festivals. This pub incorporates the former vicarage and is overshadowed by the church-with-the-twisted-spire. Food is available *L and E.* Children welcome if eating. Outside seating. *Open all day.*

✕ **Browsers Coffee Shop** Chesterfield Central Library, New Beetwell Street, Chesterfield S40 1QN (01629 533412). A selection of teas, coffee, snacks and light meals in an unusual setting. Children welcome. *Open Mon-Fri 09.30-16.00 and Sat 09.30-15.30.*

✕ ♥ **Old Post Restaurant** 43 Holywell Street, Chesterfield S41 7SH (01246 279479; www.theoldpostrestaurant.co.uk). A family-friendly restaurant serving traditional English dishes *L and E (closed Sun E and Mon).* Early bird menu available *Tue-Fri 18.00-19.15.*

● **Derby Tup** 387 Sheffield Road, Whittington Moor, Chesterfield S41 8LS (01246 454316). North west of Tapton Lock. Another pub with an ever changing selection of real ales offering a friendly welcome and a warm atmosphere together with food *L Mon, Tue, Thu-Sun L and E, Wed E only.* Also bottled Belgian beers and real cider. Pub games. Quiz *Sun.*

● **Lock Keeper** Tapton, Chesterfield S41 7NJ (01246 560700). East of Tapton Lock. Boater-friendly establishment serving real ales and food *L and E.* Brewers Fayre. Children welcome. Outside seating. B & B.

● **Mill** Brimington, Chesterfield S43 1LT (01246 273807). Real ale pub, overlooking the canal with outside, terraced seating. Inexpensive home-made food and snacks available *Tue-Fri L and E, Sat and Sun 12.00-16.00.* Children welcome. Limited mooring.

Try also **The Beeches Brook**, just the other side of the High Street.

● ✕ **Sitwell Arms** 39 Station Road, Renishaw S21 3WF (01246 435226; www.sitwellarms.com). Hotel offering an extensive à la carte restaurant menu *L and E (not L Mon and Sat).* Bar meals available *L and E, daily.* Real ales. Children welcome; garden. Occasional entertainment. B & B.

● **Angel Inn** 127 Rotherham Road, Killamarsh S21 2DR (0114 248 5607). Immediately north of Gannow Lane Bridge. Friendly pub serving real ale and home-made food *L and E (Sun E until 17.00).* Children welcome in dining room. Garden and children's play area.

SELF-DISCOVERY OR WATERWAYS RECOVERY?

Messing about in the mud has long been the pursuit of little boys (and girls) and is an occupation that some of us have great difficulty in shrugging off, even in later life. Imagine, then, having the opportunity to legitimise this sensory indulgence in the respectable form (in the eyes of some, at least) of canal restoration. There are still many muddy, overgrown ditches festering in their own private world of decay that were once illustrious watery highways. As the more straightforward canal restorations are successfully accomplished, so the more difficult ones become the targets for the doyens of dirty digging, namely the Waterways Recovery Group (www.wrg.org.uk). Formed with the express purpose of resurrecting fallen waterways and familiar to many a boater as the driving force behind the annual National Waterway Festivals, this organisation is able to dig the dirt with the best of them. The Chesterfield Canal is one of many navigations to have benefited from their unstinting ability to mix endeavour with cheerfulness, pleasure with muck and sand with cement.

Chesterfield Canal

Shireoaks

Pubs and Restaurants

The Beehive Union Street, Harthill S26 7YH (01909 770205). Friendly village pub serving real ale and a good choice of reasonably priced food *L and E*. Children welcome if eating, dogs in bar area only. Quiz nights. *Closed Mon*.

The Saxon Station Road, Kiveton Park S26 6QP (01909 770517). North of Kiveton crossroads. Busy modern local. Children welcome.

The Parish Oven Worksop Road, Thorpe Salvin S80 3JU (01909 770685; www.theparishoven.co.uk). Modern pub in the centre of the village, serving real ales and both a bar and restaurant menu *L and E (not Mon)*. Children welcome *until 21.00*. Garden. Quiz night *Thu*, karaoke *Fri*, often live entertainment *Sat*.

The Hewitt Arms Shireoaks Park, Thorpe Lane, Shireoaks S81 8LT (01909 500979). ½ mile south west of the canal. A restrained conversion of the coach house and stables adjoining the hall. A good range of real ales can be enjoyed in comfort overlooking the landscaped park. Meals are served *12.00–15.00 and 19.00–22.00 daily except Sun E*. Children welcome and there is outside seating.

The Lock-Keeper Sandy Lane, Rhodesia S80 1TJ (01909 532565). A family pub between Deep and Stret locks serving real ale together with reasonably priced food available *all day, every day*. Children welcome. Canalside seating and children's play area.

The Woodhouse Inn Woodend, Rhodesia S80 3HD. Real ale, large garden and children's play area. Pool and snooker. Large-screen TV. Regular entertainment. Quiz *Thu*.

Also try the **Duke of Leeds** Church Street, Wales S26 5LQ and the **Leeds Arms** Sheffield Road, South Anston S25 5DT.

Boatyards

Ⓑ **Shireoaks Marina** Worksop S81 8NQ (01636 704481). 🚻🚿⛽ E Pump out, long-term mooring, toilets, showers.

39

Worksop

Once below Worksop Town Lock, you will have descended one of the most splendid flights of locks anywhere on the waterways system: 31 in all over a distance of just four miles. Representing hard work for today's navigator, it also presented an amazing challenge to the canal's original builders and acts as a tantalising preview to the eventual resurrection of the spectacular (and currently derelict) 13 lock flight immediately to the west of Norwood Tunnel. On leaving the town, just south of Bridge 44A, there is a useful *shop* and *several takeaways* before the waterway heads out into open countryside and passes the attractive farm buildings of Osberton Hall. Beyond here it wanders eastward, passing beyond the hubbub of the A1 at Ranby, on its approach to the contrasting peace and isolation of Forest Locks.

Pubs and Restaurants

The Shireoaks Inn Westgate, Worksop S80 1LT (01909 472118). Once a row of cottages, now a welcoming hostelry, dispensing real ale. Excellent value, home-cooked food available *L and E*; fresh fish and roast dinners a speciality. Children welcome. Outside seating and pub games. Quiz *Thu.*

The Greendale Oak Norfolk Street, Worksop S80 1LE (01909 489680). Just off Westgate. Cosy mid-terraced pub dispensing real ales. A selection of freshly prepared sandwiches, home-made food is available *L*. Children and dogs welcome. Garden.

The Mallard Station Approach, Carlton Road, Worksop S81 7AG. An exciting selection of ever-changing real ales from small breweries together with a comprehensive range of continental bottled beers. Outside seating and pub games. Real cider. Filled rolls only. Quiz *Mon*. Disabled access from station platform. *Open L Fri-Sun and E Mon-Sat.*

The Station Hotel Carlton Road, Worksop S80 1PS (01909 474108;

www.thestationhotelworksop.co.uk). Real ales and a comprehensive menu are available *all day, every day (not Sun)*. Children welcome if eating. Quiz *Sun afternoon*. B & B.

The Litten Tree 1 Victoria Square, Worksop S80 1DX (01909 475742). Beside Worksop Town Lock. Traditional locals pub serving bar meals *all day*. Children welcome *until 19.00*.

The Canal Tavern Canal Road, Worksop S80 2EH. Canalside. Real ales and bar meals *L Mon-Sat*. Children welcome, beer garden. Karaoke *Thu*. Moorings for patrons.

The Chequers Inn Ranby, Retford DN22 8HT (01777 703329). Real ales and food are available *L and E (not Sun E)* in this attractive canalside pub. Various meal 'specials' offered. Children welcome. A large outside terrace overlooks the canal. Moorings.

- **Worksop**
  Notts. All services. Old buildings of note in Worksop are the Priory and its gatehouse.
  Mr Straw's House 7 Blythe Grove, Worksop S81 0JG (01909 482380; www.nationaltrust.org.uk). *NT.* When William and Walter Straw's father died in 1932, the brothers kept his house as a shrine and altered nothing. In 1991 William died and left the property, with a legacy of £1.5 million, to the National Trust. They have preserved this time capsule and opened it to visitors. *Open Apr-Oct, Tue-Sat 11.00-17.00.* Entrance by pre-booked time tickets only – telephone or write for tickets.
  The Priory Priorswell Road, Workshop S80 2BU (01909 472 180; www.worksoppriory.co.uk). Near Prior Well Bridge. The church dates from the 12th C. Much rebuilding has taken place since then: in fact from 1970-72 the superstructure was added to, incorporating a new spire. Interesting paintings and monuments are inside the church and a gruesome relic from Sherwood Forest – a skull with the tip of an arrow embedded in it.
  Pilgrim Fathers' Story Worksop Museum, Public Library, Memorial Avenue, Worksop S80 2BP (01909 501148.) *Open Mon, Tue and Fri 09.30-19.00; Wed 09.30-17.30, Thu and Sat 09.30-13.00. Closed B Hols.* Free. Disabled access.
  Tourist Information Centre Worksop Library, Memorial Avenue, Worksop S80 2BP (01909 501148; www.bassetlaw.gov.uk). *Open Mon-Fri 09.30-17.30 and Sat 09.30-15.00. Closed B Hols.*
  Within a few miles of the town there are some interesting places and beautiful countryside to visit, although a car or a bicycle is needed to reach them. All around are the surviving woods of Sherwood Forest, while to the south of the town is the area called the Dukeries, each of the adjacent estates of Thoresby, Clumber and Welbeck having been owned by a duke. Welbeck is now an army college, Thoresby Park is open to the public. Clumber House was demolished in 1938 but the Park, owned by the National Trust, is one of its most visited properties. Three miles west of Worksop is an outstanding building well worth visiting – the tiny Steetley Chapel – described as 'the most perfect and elaborate specimen of Norman architecture to be found anywhere in Europe'. *Open 09.30-16.30.* The quiet villages of north Nottinghamshire were home to the Pilgrim Fathers. The full story is told in Worksop Museum which acts as a starting point for the Mayflower Trail leading out into the villages themselves.

- **Ranby**
  Notts. Tel. A small rambling village with a pub on the canal, the only one for miles in either direction.
  Osberton Hall Built in 1806 by James Wyatt and enlarged and altered in 1853. Private.

- **Scofton**
  Notts. This is the tiny estate village for Osberton Hall. The old stable block is impressive and is surmounted by a clock tower.

Retford

The straight road crossing the canal at Barnby Wharf Bridge was a Roman highway. It was, in fact, the original course of the Great North Road but 200 years ago the citizens of Retford got the road diverted to pass through their town, thereby increasing its importance and prosperity. They must now be equally relieved to have rid themselves of it again. In the open countryside around here are the four Forest Locks, complete with *all facilities* including showers and toilets. At the second lock there are good *moorings* and a *water point* right beside the top gate. Below the locks the outskirts of Retford are clearly visible as the waterway winds its way towards the town, passing through West Retford Lock and over three minute aqueducts, arriving close to the town centre beside a handy *supermarket*. Here is the last of the narrow locks with a large canal warehouse beside it.

> **WALKING & CYCLING**
> Beside bridge 63 there is a nicely presented map setting out all the paths and bridleways within the parish of Hayton. These represent a wealth of walking (and cycling) opportunities throughout the local area.

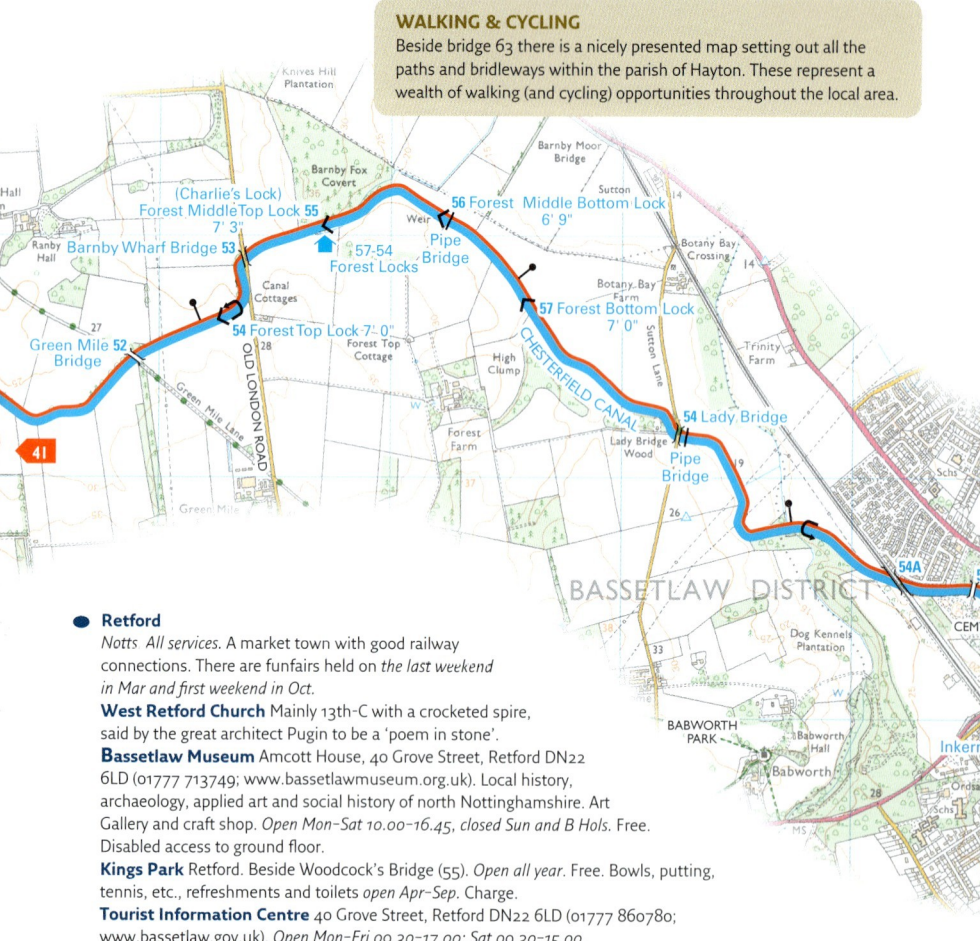

- **Retford**
  Notts *All services*. A market town with good railway connections. There are funfairs held on *the last weekend in Mar and first weekend in Oct*.
  West Retford Church Mainly 13th-C with a crocketed spire, said by the great architect Pugin to be a 'poem in stone'.
  Bassetlaw Museum Amcott House, 40 Grove Street, Retford DN22 6LD (01777 713749; www.bassetlawmuseum.org.uk). Local history, archaeology, applied art and social history of north Nottinghamshire. Art Gallery and craft shop. *Open Mon-Sat 10.00-16.45, closed Sun and B Hols. Free*. Disabled access to ground floor.
  Kings Park Retford. Beside Woodcock's Bridge (55). *Open all year. Free*. Bowls, putting, tennis, etc., refreshments and toilets *open Apr-Sep*. Charge.
  Tourist Information Centre 40 Grove Street, Retford DN22 6LD (01777 860780; www.bassetlaw.gov.uk). *Open Mon-Fri 09.30-17.00; Sat 09.30-15.00*.

- **Clarborough**
  Notts. *PO, tel, stores, off-licence, garage*. The shop is *open Mon-Sat 05.30- 19.00 & Sun 06.00-14.00*.

- **Hayton**
  Notts. *Tel*. In nearby Bolham, where the local inhabitants once lived in caves hewn in the rock, there are the remains of an ancient chapel.

Chesterfield Canal — Retford

Pubs and Restaurants

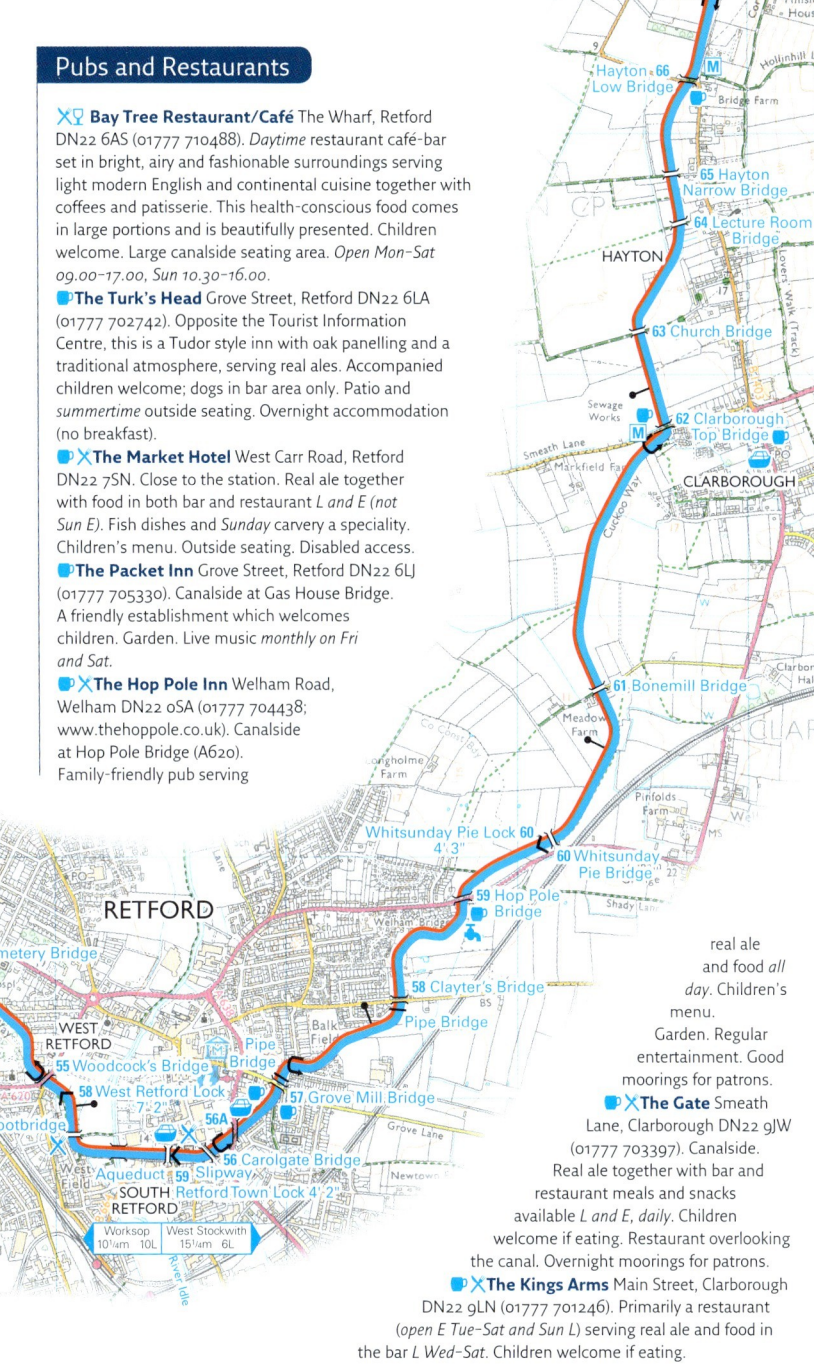

✕♈ Bay Tree Restaurant/Café The Wharf, Retford DN22 6AS (01777 710488). *Daytime* restaurant café-bar set in bright, airy and fashionable surroundings serving light modern English and continental cuisine together with coffees and patisserie. This health-conscious food comes in large portions and is beautifully presented. Children welcome. Large canalside seating area. *Open Mon-Sat 09.00-17.00, Sun 10.30-16.00.*

🍺✕ **The Turk's Head** Grove Street, Retford DN22 6LA (01777 702742). Opposite the Tourist Information Centre, this is a Tudor style inn with oak panelling and a traditional atmosphere, serving real ales. Accompanied children welcome; dogs in bar area only. Patio and *summertime* outside seating. Overnight accommodation (no breakfast).

🍺✕ **The Market Hotel** West Carr Road, Retford DN22 7SN. Close to the station. Real ale together with food in both bar and restaurant *L and E (not Sun E)*. Fish dishes and *Sunday* carvery a speciality. Children's menu. Outside seating. Disabled access.

🍺✕ **The Packet Inn** Grove Street, Retford DN22 6LJ (01777 705370). Canalside at Gas House Bridge. A friendly establishment which welcomes children. Garden. Live music *monthly on Fri and Sat.*

🍺✕ **The Hop Pole Inn** Welham Road, Welham DN22 0SA (01777 704438; www.thehoppole.co.uk). Canalside at Hop Pole Bridge (A620). Family-friendly pub serving real ale and food *all day*. Children's menu. Garden. Regular entertainment. Good moorings for patrons.

🍺✕ **The Gate** Smeath Lane, Clarborough DN22 9JW (01777 703397). Canalside. Real ale together with bar and restaurant meals and snacks available *L and E, daily.* Children welcome if eating. Restaurant overlooking the canal. Overnight moorings for patrons.

🍺✕ **The Kings Arms** Main Street, Clarborough DN22 9LN (01777 701246). Primarily a restaurant (open *E Tue-Sat and Sun L*) serving real ale and food in the bar *L Wed-Sat.* Children welcome if eating.

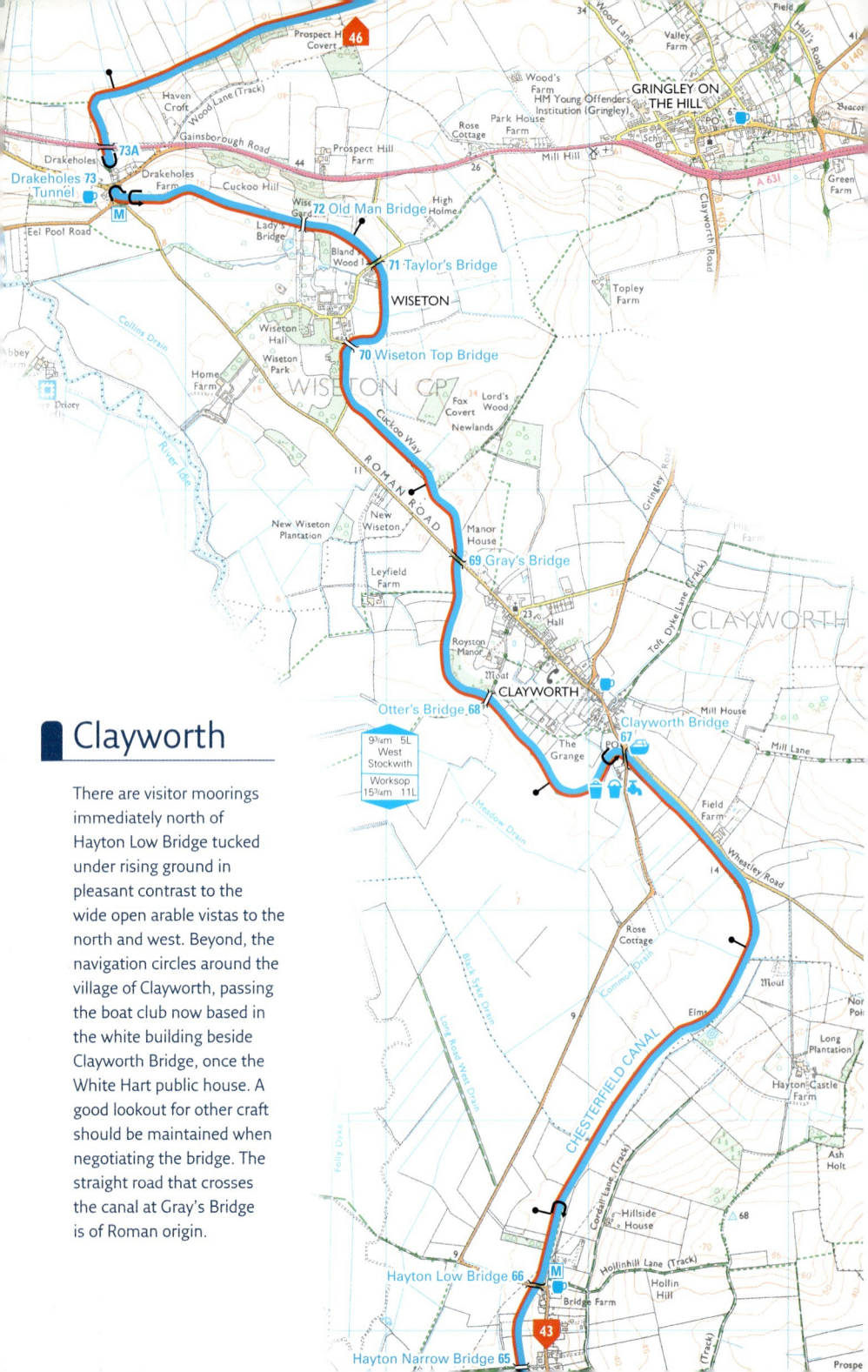

Clayworth

There are visitor moorings immediately north of Hayton Low Bridge tucked under rising ground in pleasant contrast to the wide open arable vistas to the north and west. Beyond, the navigation circles around the village of Clayworth, passing the boat club now based in the white building beside Clayworth Bridge, once the White Hart public house. A good lookout for other craft should be maintained when negotiating the bridge. The straight road that crosses the canal at Gray's Bridge is of Roman origin.

Again the waterway curls around the next habitation, skirting an attractive courtyard housing development built on the site of Wiseton Park's old walled kitchen garden. The brick from the enclosing walls has been put to good use in the construction of many of the houses. Heading towards Drakeholes *(moorings and electrical hook-up)*, the canal passes the stern features of a bearded man on the parapet of Old Man Bridge and, accompanied by woods, reaches the attractive moorings nestling beside the tunnel entrance. Drakeholes Tunnel (154 yds) is cut through rock and is mostly unlined with a slipway and winding hole immediately to the south. The navigation to the north is a thoroughly delightful stretch, heavily overhung with trees from Gringley to Drakeholes, running along the bottom of a ridge of hills. Wildlife near the water's edge includes coots, moorhens, water rats and bats. It is very secluded but the intimate feeling of the thickly wooded cutting beyond the tunnel has been ruined by the construction of a large road bridge.

Clayworth
Notts. PO, tel, stores. A quiet and pleasant village extending along a single main street. The houses are of all periods, the new blending well with the old. The Retford & Worksop Boat Club (01777 817546; www.rwbc.org.uk) is based at the old pub at Clayworth and welcomes visitors to the clubhouse. There are good moorings and all facilities here. In the old days a passenger boat used to run every Saturday from this pub to Retford, so that the villagers of Clayworth, Hayton and Clarborough could take their produce to Retford Market. The goods were loaded into the 'packet' boat on the Friday night, then the people would return early on Saturday morning, leaving at 06.30 to reach Retford by 08.30. The boat used to return in the evening when the market closed. A handsome sundial sits over the porch of the pretty village church, inscribed with the words 'Our days on earth are as a shadow'. Inside there is a series of beautiful wall paintings.

Wiseton
Notts. Tel. A superbly elegant estate village set in a landscaped park, still clearly fulfiling its original manorial function. Trees and grass separate the various buildings, of which the large stable with its handsome clock tower is the most significant. The Hall, a modern red brick building, which replaced the original in 1962, is well hidden behind high walls.

Pubs and Restaurants

The Boat Inn Main Street, Hayton DN22 9LF (01777 700158). Canalside near Hayton Low Bridge. A popular and nicely kept pub offering real ales and a wide range of reasonably priced food available in the bar *L and E, daily*. The carvery restaurant is *open all day Sun Overnight*. Garden and play area. Accommodation (no breakfast).

The Brewers Arms Town Street, Clayworth DN22 9AD (01777 816107; www.brewers-arms.co.uk). Real ale. Traditional bar meals available *L and E Tue-Sun*. Beer garden. Traditional pub games. The pub is combined with a quality country clothing shop supplying outdoor wear (01777 816522).

The White Swan Eel Pool Road, Drakeholes, Wiseton DN10 5DF (01777 817206). Canalside at Drakeholes Tunnel. A smart establishment serving real ale. There is an extensive bar menu, as well as a carvery and restaurant. Food is available *L and E, daily*. Children welcome. Outside seating. B & B.

West Stockwith

The course of the navigation is entirely rural and pleasant, passing well-established but often decaying farm buildings and two disused brickworks, one now the repository for canal dredgings. At Misterton there are two locks close together and between them there once stood the Albion Flour Mill, powered by canal water from a small reservoir beside the top lock. The church spire of East Stockwith stands opposite the point where the Chesterfield Canal enters the Trent. The lock here is keeper-operated. Just above the lock is a basin housing a *boatyard*, a *boat club*, a *hire boat company*, a *slipway* and a *waterpoint* (apply to the lock keeper) and plenty of moored pleasure boats. *Pump out facilities*, *diesel* and *gas* are also available from the lock keeper when on duty. A *pub* and *a farm shop* are nearby.

NAVIGATIONAL NOTES

1. Entering the canal from the Trent can be tricky due to the tidal flow across the entrance to the lock. A leaflet is available from BW 01636 704481 (and from most Trent locks) with instructions on how to access the lock safely – or contact the lock keeper. The lock accepts craft up a maximum size of 72' x 17' 6". The lock is keeper-operated (give as much prior notice as possible by telephoning 01427 890204) and passage can usually be made 2½ hours before to 4½ hours after high water. By coincidence, flood (when the tide ceases ebbing and turns to come back in) at Stockwith is the same time as high water at Hull. The flood runs for approximately 2½ hours and the direction of flow changes very rapidly. VHF radio frequencies: calling channel 16, working channel 74. The radio is not constantly manned. Commercial river traffic operates on channel 6 upstream of Keadby Bridge and it is useful for VHF users to monitor this channel to establish the whereabouts of large craft.
2. All subsequent locks on the waterway require a Watermate key to release the anti-vandal mechanism.
3. 'Smart Cards' are available from the lock keeper and are required to operate facilities at Shireoaks Marina and the electrical hook-up at Drakeholes.
4. The Trent Series Charts, published by The Boating Association (www.theboatingassociation.co.uk), are detailed charts of the tidal Trent (and the tidal Ouse and non-tidal Trent) and are available to buy online. Also from BW lock keepers. Charge.

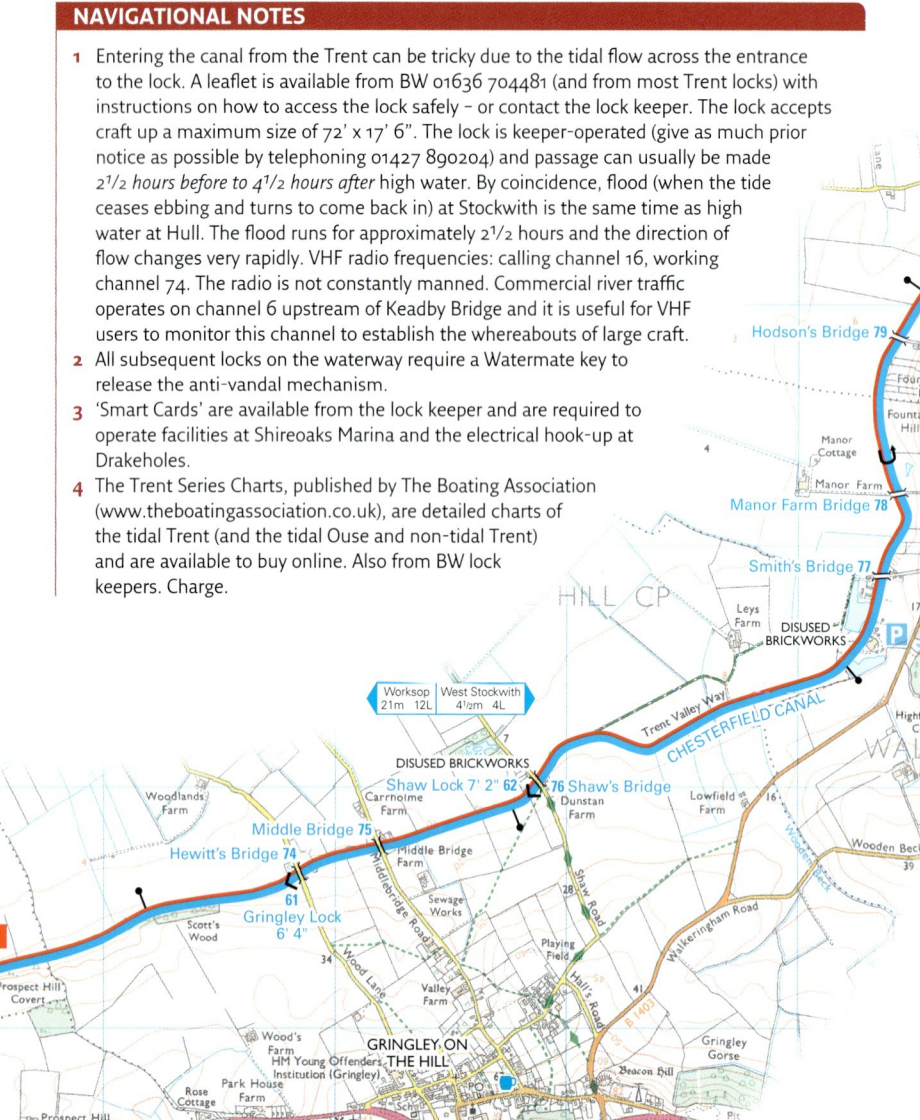

Pubs and Restaurants

- 🍺❌ **The Blue Bell Inn** High Street, Gringley on the Hill DN10 4RF (01777 817406). Well worth the walk up from the canal, this traditional village local serves real ales and excellent food *Thu-Sun*. Children welcome; garden seating. Open fires *in winter*, pub games and pool. *Open Mon-Wed 17.00-23.00 & Thu-Sun 12.00-23.00*.
- 🍺 **The Waterfront Inn** Canal Lane, West Stockwith DN10 4ET (01522 514774). Canalside at West Stockwith Basin. A good selection of real ales dispensed in a friendly pub together with excellent and inexpensive food available *L and E, daily. Sun L*. Children and dogs welcome. Decked seating area overlooking Stockwith Basin. Regular live music. B & B. *Open all day at weekends*.
- 🍺 **The White Hart** Main Street, West Stockwith DN10 4EY (01427 890176). By the junction of the rivers Idle and Trent. Friendly family country pub with a welcoming atmosphere, serving real ales (micro-brewery) and food *L and E until 21.00*. Children and dogs welcome. Garden.

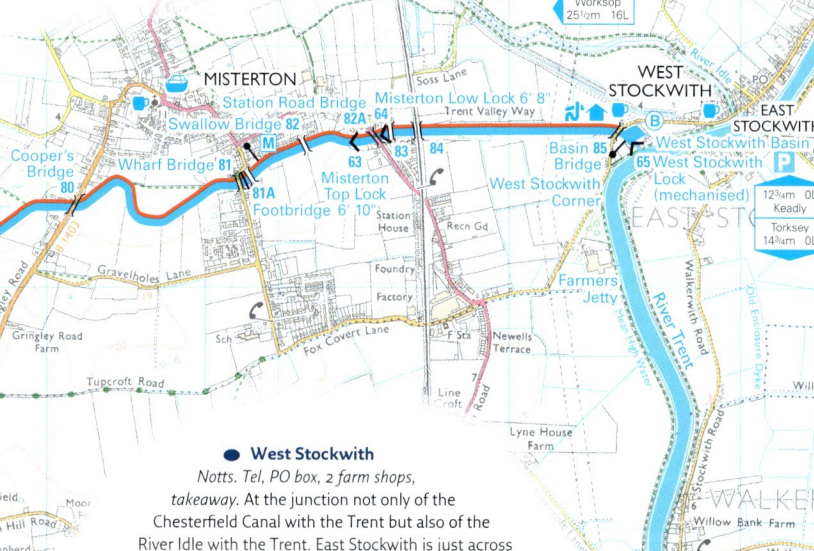

- ● **West Stockwith**
  Notts. Tel, PO box, 2 farm shops, takeaway. At the junction not only of the Chesterfield Canal with the Trent but also of the River Idle with the Trent. East Stockwith is just across the river, tantalisingly out of reach. The two communities used to be connected by a ferry. In a way, the total lack of communication with the other village, only 50yds away, serves to enhance the magical sense of remoteness that Stockwith possesses – especially when one sees big barges appearing round the bend, churning past the two villages and then as quickly disappearing again.
- ● **Misterton**
  Notts. PO, tel, stores, off-licence, takeaway, butcher, fish & chips, garage. The village has a thriving Methodist church, as do most of the places in this area. John Wesley came from nearby Epworth. The shop is *open daily 07.00-21.00*.
- ● **Gringley on the Hill**
  Notts. PO box, tel. The village is about a mile's walk up from the canal. A small rise on a level with the church tower gives a good view. On a clear day the pinnacles of Lincoln Cathedral can sometimes be seen, nearly 20 miles to the south east.

Boatyards

- Ⓑ **Chesterfield Canal Boat Company** West Stockwith Basin DN10 4ET (01522 514774). Narrowboat hire.
- Ⓑ The following facilities are available in the basin and are obtainable by telephoning the lock keeper on 01427 890204 or 07884 238780. 🎒🛒🚿 D Pump out, gas, short- and long-term mooring, winter storage, slipway, toilets, showers.

WILDLIFE ON THE CHESTERFIELD CANAL

Wildlife flourishes along the Chesterfield Canal, as this diverse selection of birds you might see on the canal demonstrates.

The *Canada Goose* is a large, unmistakable goose with an upright stance and a long neck, giving it a swan-like silhouette. The goose has white cheeks on an otherwise black head and neck. Its body is mainly grey-brown except for a white under stern; the juveniles are similar but the markings are less distinct. The canada goose nests beside wetlands and sometimes in nearby arable fields. Outside the breeding season, sizeable flocks of geese will be seen. In flight the geese utter a loud, disyllabic trumpeting call.

Mallard Ducks are widespread and familiar. The colourful male has a yellow bill and a green, shiny head and neck, separated from the chestnut breast by a white collar. Its plumage is otherwise grey-brown except for a black stern and white tail. The female has an orange bill and mottled brown plumage. In flight both sexes have a blue and white speculum (patch on trailing edge of inner wing).

Lapwing breed in open, flat country, including undisturbed farmland and coastal marshes, and nest on the ground. After nesting, flocks form and travel to find suitable feeding areas free of frost. In winter the British population is boosted by an influx of continental birds. The lapwing looks black and white at a distance but in good light has a green, oily sheen on the back; winter birds have buffish fringes to their feathers on the back. The spiky crest feathers are longer in male birds that the females. In flight the lapwing has rounded, black and white wings and a flapping flight. Their call is a loud 'peewit'.

The *Green Woodpecker*, despite its size and bright, colourful plumage, can be surprisingly difficult to see. It is usually rather wary and often prefers to hide behind tree trunks rather than show itself. Sometimes it is seen feeding on lawns or areas of short grass when the green back, greenish buff underparts and red and black facial markings can be seen. It uses its long tongue to collect ants. If disturbed the green woodpecker flies off revealing a bright yellow-green rump. The spiky tail gives support when climbing tree trunks. Its presence is often detected by a loud and distinctive yaffling call. The stout, dagger-like bill is used to excavate wood for insect larvae and to create nest holes. It favours open, deciduous woodland.

Redshank A fairly common resident breeding species, numbers being boosted by an influx of continental birds in winter. A nervous bird, the loud, piping alarm call alerts observers to its presence. It is easily recognised by its red legs and long, red-based bill. Plumage is mostly grey-brown above and pale below with streaks and barring; plumage is more heavily marked in the breeding season. In flight the redshank shows a characteristic broad, white trailing margin to the wing. During the breeding season, the bird favours flood meadows, salt marshes and moors, nesting among grasses; in winter, coastal habitats, especially mudflats and estuaries. Its food includes shrimps, snails and worms. The redshank has an even-paced, jerky walk as it hunts its prey.

The *Moorhen* is a widespread and familiar wetland bird: often wary, in urban areas they can become rather tame. The adult has brownish wings but otherwise mainly dark grey-black plumage. It has a distinctive yellow-tipped red bill and a frontal shield on its head, with white feathers on the sides of the undertail and a white line along the flanks. Juvenile birds have pale brown plumage. The moorhen's legs and long toes are yellowish. It swims with a jerky movement, with tail flicking. In flight the moorhen shows dangling legs.

The *Grey Heron* is a familiar large, long-legged wetland bird. The adult has a dagger-like, yellow bill and a black crest of feathers. The head, neck and underparts are otherwise whitish except for black streaks on the front of the neck and breast. The back and wings are blue-grey. In flight, the wings are broad and rounded with black flight feathers; the heron employs a slow, flapping wingbeat and holds its neck folded in a hunched 's' shape close to its body. The juvenile is similar to the adult but the markings are less distinct and the plumage more grubby in appearance. The heron is often seen standing motionless for hours on end on long, yellow legs, sometimes with its neck hunched up. It will occasionally actively stalk prey which comprise mainly amphibians and fish, especially eels. The heron's call is a harsh and distinctive 'frank'. The heron nests in loose colonies mainly in trees but sometimes seen on coasts in winter.

Goldfinch A beautiful, small finch, with bright yellow wingbars and a white rump. The adult has red and white on face, a black cap extending down the sides of the neck, buffish back and white underparts with buff flanks. The juvenile has brown, streaked plumage but yellow wingbars as in the adult. Goldfinch favour wasteground and meadows where the narrow, pointed bill is used to feed on the seeds of thistles and teasel in particular. The goldfinch builds a neat, deep nest towards the end of a branch. They are usually seen in small flocks which take to the wing with a tinkling flight call. The male's song is twittering but contains call-like elements.

The *Great Tit* is a common woodland and garden species, appreciably larger than the blue tit alongside which it is often seen at bird feeders. The great tit has bold black and white markings on its head and a black bib forming a line running down its chest, broader in the male than the female. The underparts are otherwise yellow and upperparts mainly greenish. Juveniles have sombre plumage with no white on the head. Their song is extremely variable but a striking 'teecha teecha teecha' is rendered by most males. In summer the birds feed mainly on insects.

The *Kingfisher* is a dazzlingly attractive bird, but its colours often appear muted when the bird is seen sitting in shade or vegetation. It has orange-red underparts and mainly blue upperparts; the electric blue back is seen to the best effect when the bird is observed in low-level flight speeding along a river. It is invariably seen near water and uses overhanging branches to watch for fish. When a feeding opportunity arises, the kingfisher plunges headlong into the water, catching its prey in its bill: the fish is swallowed whole. Kingfishers nest in holes excavated in the river bank.

The *Mute Swan* is a large and distinctive water bird, the commonest swan in Britain. The adult has pure white plumage, black legs and an orange-red bill. The black blob at the base of the bill is smaller in the female than the male. Young cygnets are often seen accompanying the mother. While swimming, the bird usually holds the neck in an elegant curve.

Chesterfield Canal

Wildlife on the Chesterfield Canal

49

Chesterfield Canal at Cinderhill, Shireoaks (see page 37)

RIVER DERWENT AND THE POCKLINGTON CANAL

RIVER DERWENT
Environment Agency, Coverdale House, Amy Johnson Way, Clifton Moor, York YO3 4UZ (08708 506506; www.environment-agency.gov.uk).

MAXIMUM DIMENSIONS (at Barmby Lock)
Length: 62'
Beam: 16' 6"
Headroom: 10' 6"
Draught: 4'

A certificate must be purchased from the Barrage Control Centre if you are joining the Derwent, to certify that your craft complies with anti-pollution requirements. Navigation through or above Sutton Lock without riparian owners' permission is a matter of contention.

MILEAGE
STAMFORD BRIDGE to:
Sutton Lock: 6½ miles
Junction with Pocklington Canal: 10½ miles, 1 lock
Bubwith: 15 miles, 1 lock
Wressle: 19 miles, 1 lock
RIVER OUSE: 22 miles, 1 lock

POCKLINGTON CANAL
MAXIMUM DIMENSIONS
Length: 56' 9"
Beam: 14'
Headroom: 8'
Draught: 4'

MANAGER
0113 281 6800;
enquiries.northeast@britishwaterways.co.uk

MILEAGE
RIVER DERWENT to:
Melbourne: 5 miles
Bielby: 7 miles
CANAL HEAD: 9½ miles

RIVER DERWENT
Prior to 1702 the River Derwent was navigable to Stamford Bridge. A 'publick' act in that year allowed locks to be built to make the river navigable to Scarborough Mills, although works were never carried out above Yedingham, and little trade developed above Malton. Following the repeal of the 1702 Act in 1935, the navigation fell into disrepair, although pleasure craft continued to use sections of the river. New lower gates were fitted to Sutton Lock in 1972, and these are now owned by the Yorkshire Wildlife Trust (1 St George's Place, York YO24 1GN; 01904 659570; www.ywt.org.uk). Consult them **before** making a passage through the lock, and also contact the Environment Agency on 01757 638579 for passage through the top gates of the lock. Entry into the lower part of the river from the River Ouse is by way of Barmby Barrage Lock, controlled by the Environment Agency. The whole of the waterway covered by this book is a Site of Special Scientific Interest (SSSI), being considered one of the finest examples of a lowland river in the country. The seasonally flooded meadows around the lower reaches, known as the Derwent Ings, are of international importance for traditionally managed grassland communities and the species of wildfowl and wading birds supported.

THE POCKLINGTON CANAL
This canal was promoted in a bill of 1814 by merchants in Pocklington and was originally intended to join the River Ouse at Howden. However Earl Fitzwilliam, then owner of the Derwent Navigation, intervened and the canal was connected with the River Derwent. The opening of the York & North Midland Railway in 1847 started the canal's demise, and traffic ceased in 1932. Restoration has been completed on structures as far as Coates Lock, although the canal is currently only navigable to the Melbourne Arm. The area surrounding Canal Head has also been put in good order. Virtually all of the route is designated an SSSI, and rich communities of aquatic plants and the invertebrates they support are well established in the disused section. The Pocklington Canal Amenity Society campaigns and works for its complete restoration.

Stamford Bridge

The presently navigable River Derwent leaves the moorings by Stamford Bridge, and approaches a large railway viaduct with a sturdy central iron span, built in 1846. Although the tracks have now been lifted, it has been preserved as an ancient monument, and you can walk across it for a splendid view. Access is from the old station in Stamford Bridge (in Church Road). Beyond the viaduct the river flows into a shallow valley amongst gentle rolling countryside, which persists until East Cottingwith. The village of Low Catton can be seen to the east, its Norman church standing quite close to the river.

WALKING & CYCLING

There is a path beside the Derwent from Stamford Bridge to Elvington. This is shared with The Minster Way, which starts at Beverley Minster (about 8 miles from Market Weighton) and follows a route across the Wolds for a distance of 51 miles to finish at York Minster. A guide, by Ray Wallis, published by the East Riding and Derwent Ramblers' Association, is available. Paths by the rest of the river are very patchy, although the last couple of miles from Loftsome Bridge can be walked. A towpath exists along the whole length of the Pocklington Canal.

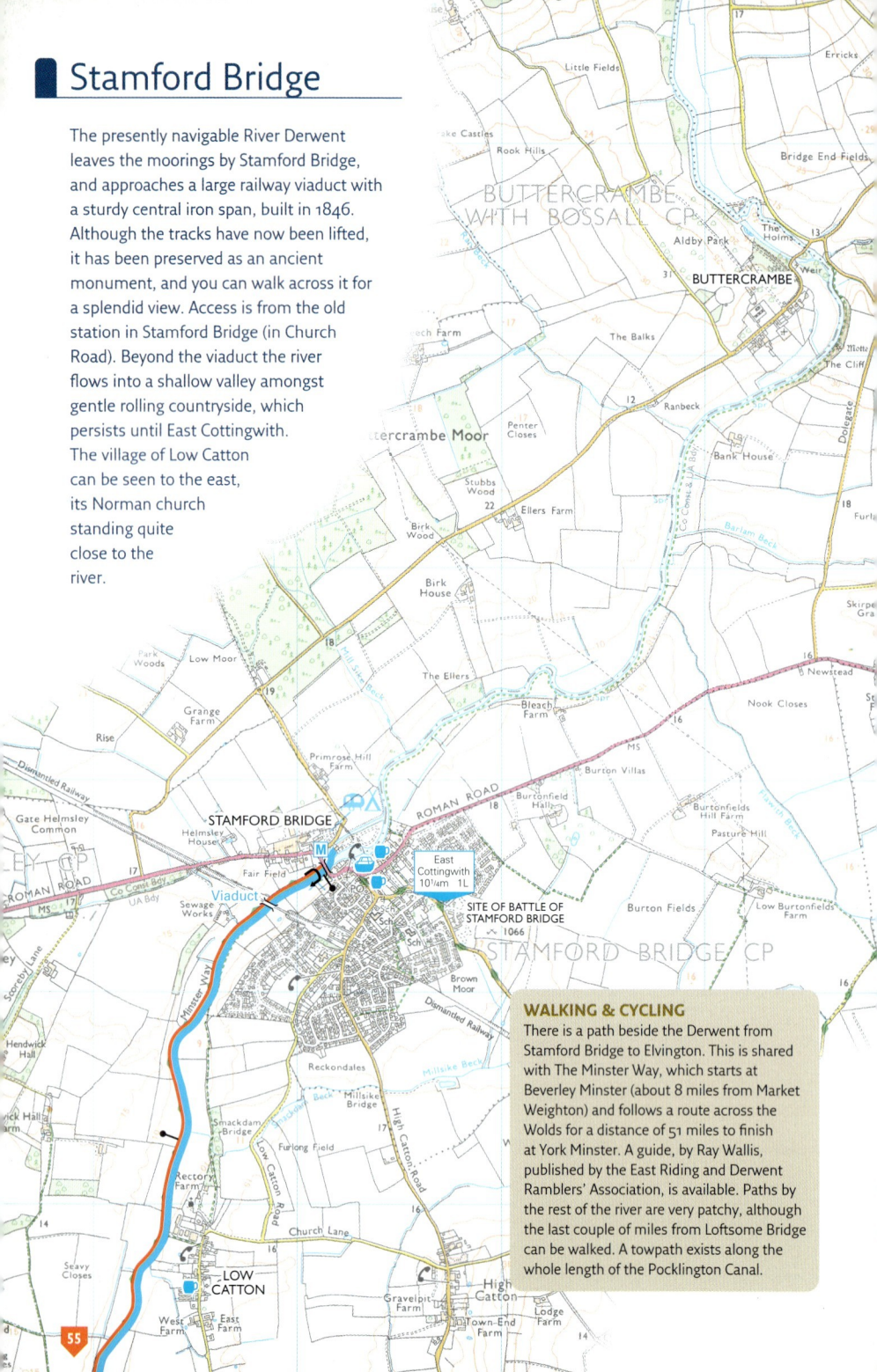

Stamford Bridge

N. Yorks. PO, tel, stores, chemist, takeaways, garage, bank. An unremarkable but pleasant village centred to the east of the bridge, which was built in 1727 by William Etty. There are several small pleasant pubs to visit, and a picnic area immediately downstream of the road bridge, on the east bank. This is also a popular area for camping and caravanning. In recent years it has suffered the effects of flooding.

Whiskys.co.uk 7 The Square, Stamford Bridge, York YO41 1AG (01759 371356; www.whiskys.co.uk). A truly amazing selection of over 400 single-malt whiskies, from a bottle to an ancient cask.

Battle of Stamford Bridge, 1066 Taking place on the morning of 25 September, this battle was to mark the end of Scandinavian influence over the politics of England. Harald Hardrada had joined forces with the King's brother Tostig and together they had taken York. In response King Harold's army marched the 185 miles from London, in an astonishing six days, to take Hardrada's forces by surprise. Attacking across the river, they broke through the Viking lines and killed Hardrada. Harold then offered a truce, but this was rejected and the fighting continued until Tostig was also killed. With the now-depleted English army in York, William of Normandy (William the Conqueror) seized his opportunity and landed unopposed on the south coast. The Battle of Hastings followed.

Low Catton

N. Yorks. PO box, tel. A plain village lying to the south east of All Saints Church. Originally Norman, later additions include the north aisle and south doorway, both built in the 13th C. The font also dates from this time. The stained-glass east window is worth a look. It depicts the crucifixion, dates from 1866, and is by Morris.

Pubs and Restaurants

The Swordsman The Square, Stamford Bridge, York YO41 1AJ (01759 371307). Large, rambling, comfortable and friendly riverside pub serving real ale, and substantial bar meals *L*, also *E Fri and Sat*. Traditional *Sun* lunch. Children welcome. There is a large garden and during the season there are frequent quiz nights *Sun*.

The Bay Horse Main Street, Stamford Bridge, York YO41 1AB. A handsome brick-built pub with a small garden, serving real ale. Fish & chip shop next door.

The Gold Cup Inn Low Catton, Stamford Bridge, York YO41 1EA. Traditional village inn with open fires, and booth seating and tables, all made from a single oak tree. Real ale. Bar and restaurant meals, all home-made with local ingredients, *l and E (not Mon L)*. Children welcome. Pretty garden.

AN ELECTION TAKES ITS TOLL

The Derwent Navigation was owned between 1782 and 1833 by Earl Fitzwilliam, and it became quite prosperous. But when, in 1807, the local electors did not return both of the Earl's nominees to Parliament, and voted instead for an independent, he gave vent to his displeasure by raising tolls on the river:

'Take Notice, That from and after the First Day of July next, you are hereby required to deliver ... to the lock keeper ... a full Account, in Writing, of all the Coals, Corn, Goods, Wares, Merchandize (sic) or Commodities, that shall be carried up or down the said River ... and to pay to the said lock keeper ... at Stamford Bridge, such sum of Money as shall be demanded, for every ton weight ... that shall be carried or conveyed in any such Boat, barge or Vessel, up the said River Derwent ... or down the said River Derwent ... not exceeding Eight Shillings ... *Dated this 16th Day of June, 1807*'

When the independent's election to Parliament was later declared to be invalid, he was replaced by the Earl's nominee. Tolls were then brought back to their original rates.

Elvington

Discreetly hiding away in its shallow valley, the River Derwent proceeds virtually due south, gently meandering and avoiding all settlements, which have sensibly been kept well away from the flood plain. The countryside is pleasantly old-fashioned, being divided into many small fields, each separated by a substantial hedge. The meadow known as the Mask, on the eastern bank, is particularly pretty. Hedges here are rich with hawthorn, crab apple, dog rose and oak.

- **Kexby**
N. Yorks. There is nothing much of note in this village. The church of St Paul, constructed in 1852, lies to the west of the river. The main road now bypasses the original bridge, which dates from the 17th C.
- **Elvington**
N. Yorks. PO, tel, stores, off-licence. There are moorings below Sutton Lock, so you can leave your boat here and walk up to the village, which is particularly pretty around the green. Holy Trinity Church, built in 1877, is well worth a look. It has a large nave and aisle, a substantial square tower with a clock, and a timber bell-stage. Sutton Bridge was built around 1700: just downstream is the lock, which was constructed in 1878 and more recently restored in memory of E.L. who was, apparently, 'a true gentlemen'. The water abstraction plant above the village, and another at Barmby on the Marsh, take as much as 20 per cent of Yorkshire's water supply from the river.
Yorkshire Air Museum Halifax Way, Elvington, York YO41 4AU (01904 608595; www.yorkshireairmuseum.co.uk). About 2 miles north west of Elvington, off the B1228. A fascinating and dynamic museum, authentically based on a World War II Bomber Command Station. The unique displays include the original Control Tower, Air Gunners' Collection, Barnes Wallis' prototype 'bouncing bomb' and a superb new Airborne Forces Display. The rapidly expanding collection of historical aircraft depicts aviation from its earliest days, to World War II with the awesome and unique Halifax rebuild through to postwar jets, including Lightning, Mirage and Hunter fighters, a Buccaneer bomber and a Victor tanker. The British land speed record was broken here in May 1999. *Open Apr-Oct 10.00-17.00, daily; Nov-Mar 10.00-15.30, daily.* Charge.
- **Sutton-upon-Derwent**
N. Yorks. PO, tel. The church of St Michael and All Angels stands above the lock on the east bank, and dates from the early Norman period. Indeed the organ arch, discovered in 1927, is the original arch of a church without aisles. The arches of the arcades are also Norman. Other details, and the aisle windows, date from the 14th C. The substantial remains of an 11th-C cross shaft is still to be seen, with carved beasts' heads, the Virgin and child and other Viking work. The rest of the village is scattered away from the river. *Part-time PO* in the village hall.
- **The Ings**
Wheldrake, York. By the river, and extending downstream past Wheldrake Ings Nature Reserve, these areas are a showpiece for local traditional farming methods – flooding in winter, never ploughed and never treated with artificial fertilisers.

NAVIGATIONAL NOTES

Please refer to the notes *on page* 51 **before** making a passage through Sutton Lock. The lower gates have substantial leaks.

Pubs and Restaurants

▶**The Grey Horse Inn** Main Street, Elvington, York YO41 4AG (01904 608335; www.thegreyhorse.com). A cosy and friendly village pub serving real ale. Food served *Sun* only, with carvery available *12.00-15.00*. Children welcome. Garden. Occasional entertainment.

▶**The St Vincent Arms** Main Street, Sutton-upon-Derwent, York YO41 4BN (01904 608349; www.stvincentarms.co.uk). Traditional village pub with no music or machines, serving real ale and meals *L* and *E*. Children welcome. Garden.

River Derwent and the Pocklington Canal

Elvington

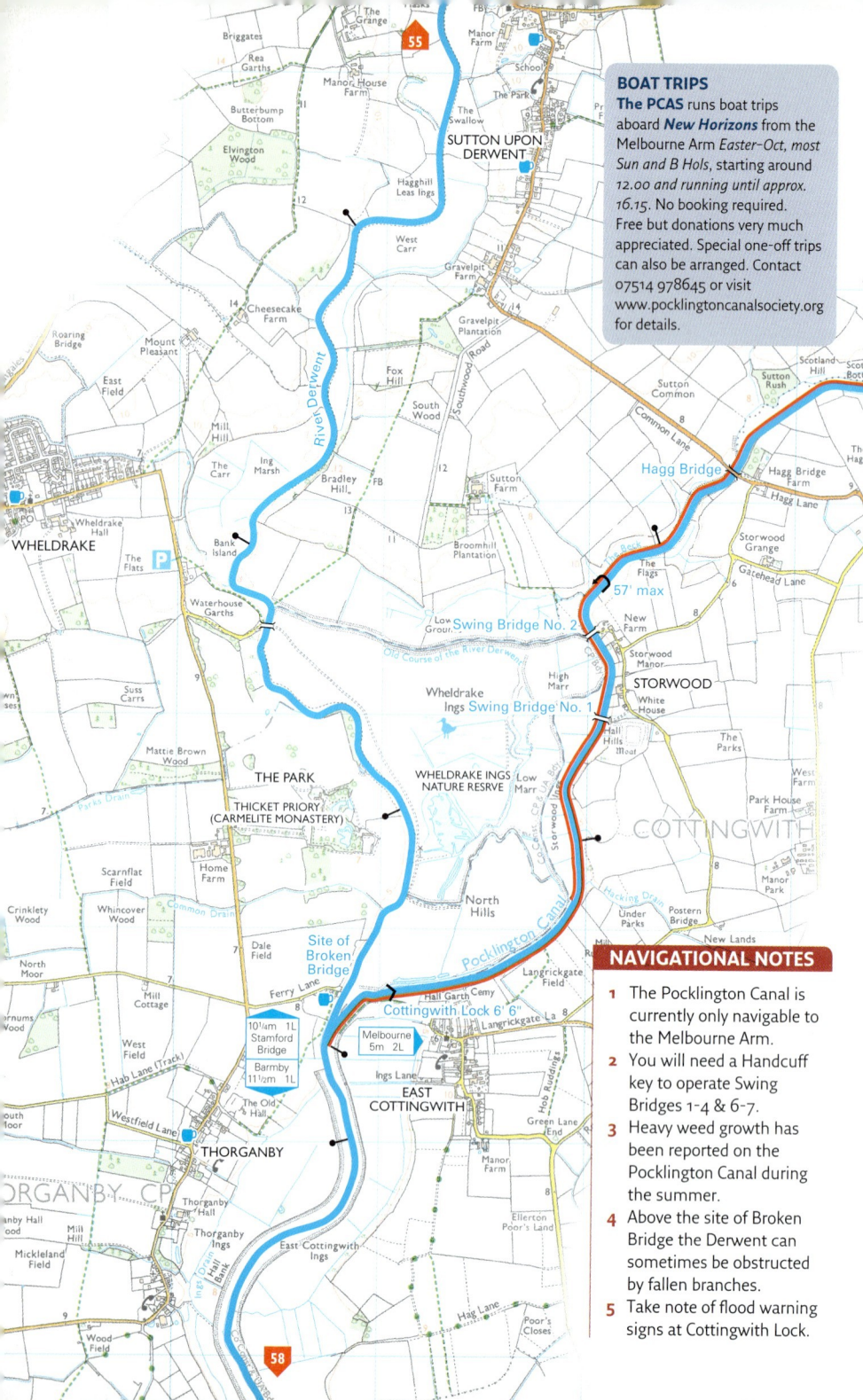

East Cottingwith

Just beyond a tiny and hardly recognisable riverside pub the river splits: the Beck heads north east and is joined by the Pocklington Canal at Cottingwith Lock. The towpath can be picked up to the north of East Cottingwith, via the path (Canal Lane) beside the village's old cemetery or via another path from the end of Church lane. Continuing through the flat farmland the canal reaches Melbourne, where there is an Arm with *services*, *toilets* and *moorings*. The canal beyond here has been restored as far as Coates Lock, although it is not currently navigable. You can, however, walk along the remaining stretch of waterway to Canal Head, to enjoy the scenery and view the restoration works. The terminus is especially attractive, with a *pub* close-by.

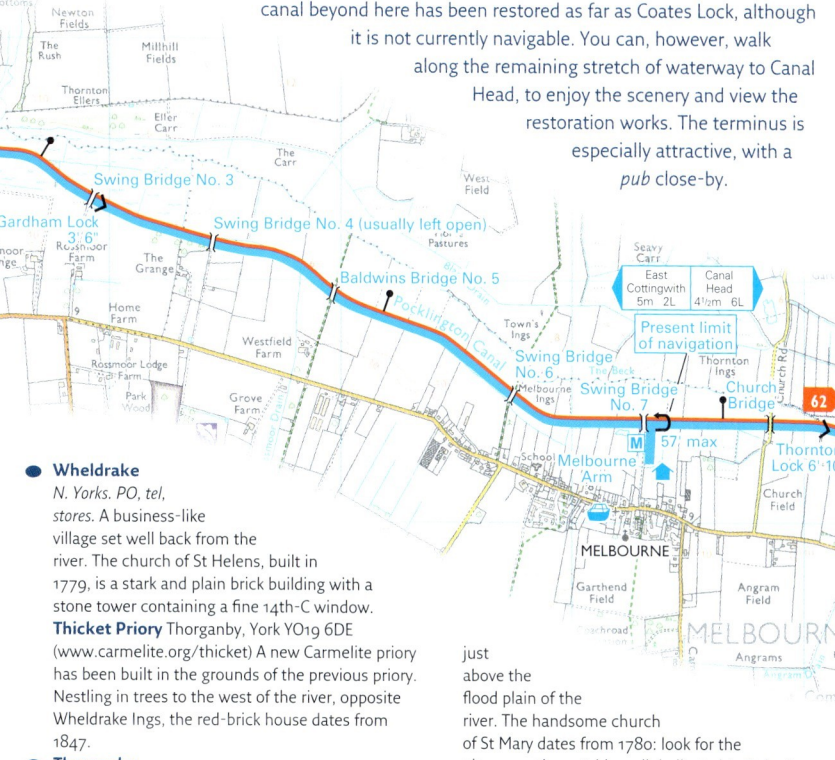

- **Wheldrake**
N. Yorks. PO, tel, stores. A business-like village set well back from the river. The church of St Helens, built in 1779, is a stark and plain brick building with a stone tower containing a fine 14th-C window.
Thicket Priory Thorganby, York YO19 6DE (www.carmelite.org/thicket) A new Carmelite priory has been built in the grounds of the previous priory. Nestling in trees to the west of the river, opposite Wheldrake Ings, the red-brick house dates from 1847.
- **Thorganby**
N. Yorks. PO box, tel. A pleasant village. The church of St Helens is brick-built with a stone tower, the base of which dates from the 12th C. The church registers date from 1653.
- **East Cottingwith**
E. Riding. PO box, tel. A simple red-brick village built just above the flood plain of the river. The handsome church of St Mary dates from 1780: look for the plaque on the outside wall dedicated to Robert Grey, full of lines of type which don't quite fit.
- **Melbourne**
E. Riding. PO, tel, stores, off-licence. Linked to the canal by an arm, the village is enlivened by handsome Georgian houses and a delightful corrugated-iron church, dating from 1882.

Pubs and Restaurants

The Ferry Boat Inn Ferry Lane, Thorganby, York YO19 6DD. Real ale is served in this riverside pub. Snacks available. Garden with willow trees and a jetty. Fishing, caravan site.
The Jefferson Arms Main Street, Thorganby, York YO4 6DB (01904 448376). A relaxed pub. Alongside the bar and restaurant areas, there is a lovely sitting room. Real ale. Excellent food is available *L and E*. Children welcome. Garden and barbecue area. B & B.

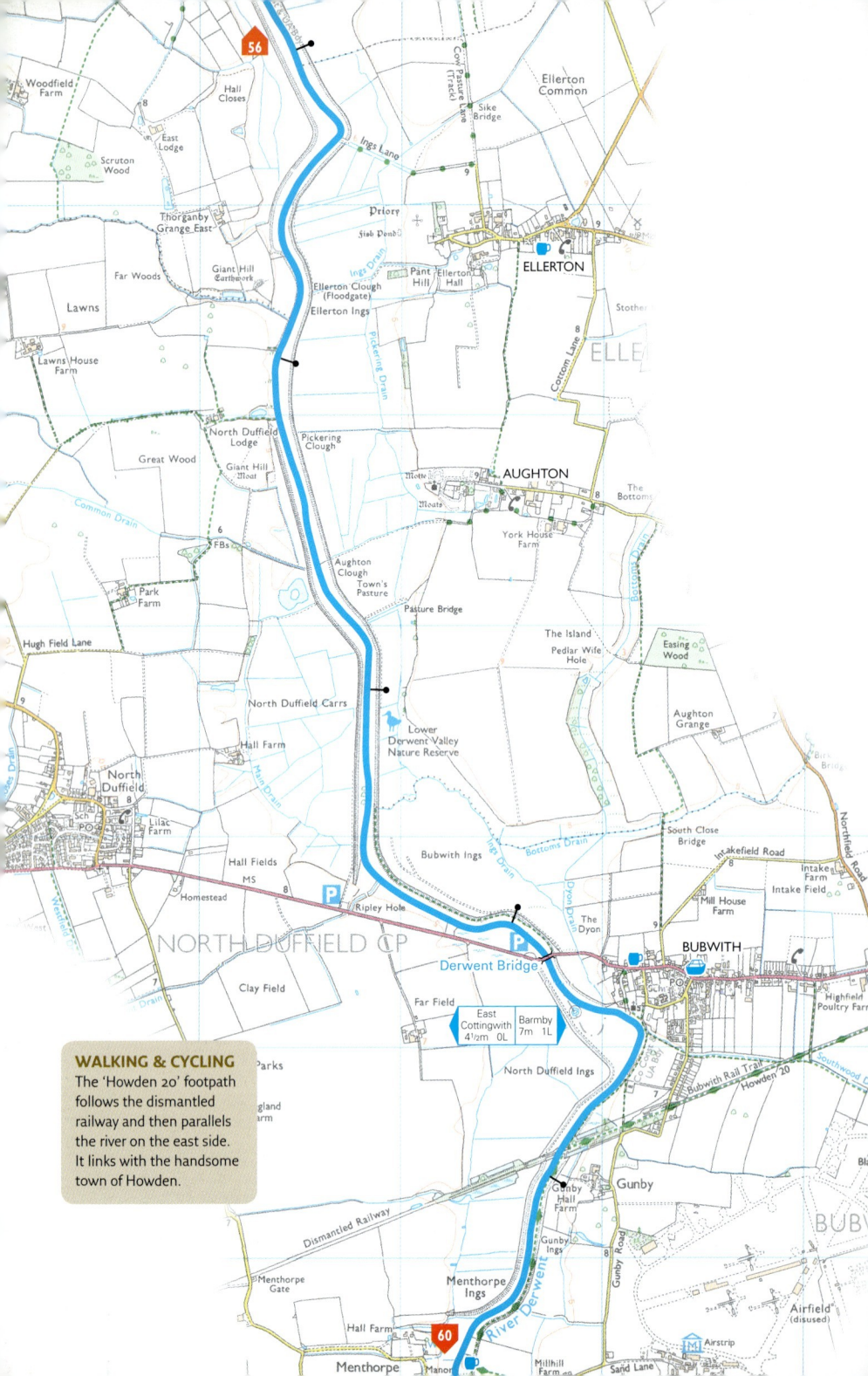

Bubwith

Firmly enclosed by floodbanks, the River Derwent, more substantial now, continues its business-like progress towards its junction with the Ouse. The countryside is quite flat, with the few buildings which are to be seen providing landmarks and an odd group of trees here and there giving a little colour. Just one road crosses on this section: the A163 between North Duffield and Bubwith.

- **Ellerton**
E. Riding. PO box, tel. A small village of old and new brick houses, with a pretty chapel and a duck pond. A windmill, standing separately to the east, has been converted into a dwelling. At the far west end of the village is the site of a priory, but little remains to be seen. The church of St Mary, built in 1848, stands nearby, once abandoned but now beautifully restored.

- **Aughton**
E. Riding. PO, tel. At the western end of this small farming village, beyond the substantial remains of a motte and bailey, is the splendid church of All Saints. Before you enter, it is worth having a good look from the outside: the tower slopes unreasonably and the chancel appears to have been sliced in half through a doorway, which is now bricked up. The Perpendicular tower has fine gargoyles and sinuous carvings of newt-like creatures crawling over the wall. These are the sign of the Aske family, who have long associations with the village. On the south side there is a sundial. The chancel arch is Norman, as is the south doorway. Brasses of Richard Aske and his wife date from 1466. Robert Aske, leader of the Pilgrimage of Grace, and executed in 1536, was born in the village.

- **Bubwith**
E. Riding. PO, tel, stores, off-licence, fish & chips. A pleasant village with several attractive Georgian houses facing the street, which is just a short walk along from the bridge, built in 1793. The large church of All Saints is tucked away right by the river. It is Norman in origin, with a chancel arch topped by a Norman gable end. The fine tower is Perpendicular. Fragments of Norman work can be seen built into the church, including a tiny winged figure, dating from c.1200.

Pubs and Restaurants

The Boot & Shoe Inn Main Street, Ellerton, York YO42 4PB (01757 288346). A pretty country pub near the chapel, serving real ale. Bar meals are served *L Sun and E Fri–Sat only*. Children welcome and there is a garden.

The White Swan 9 Main Street, Bubwith, Selby YO8 6LT (01757 282550). This pleasant village pub serves real ale. Food served *Fri 17.00–21.00 and Sun 12.00–15.30*. Children welcome and there is a garden.

A HALF-PRICE OFFER ON KELP AND LING – BUT FEW TAKERS

Much of the material used to construct the York & North Midland Railway's York & Scarborough line, opened in 1845, was carried on the Derwent – a last flush of trade on the river before an inevitable decline. Drastic toll cutting followed, but to little effect:

'On Coal, Slack and Cinders – 4d per Ton, *instead of 10d*

On Flour and Shelling – 4d per 20 Stone, *instead of 6d*

On Bones, Cobbles, Flints, Horns, Shoddy, Guano, Nitrate of Sods – 1s 6d per Ton, *instead of 2s 6d*

On Carrots, Potatoes, Fullers Earth, Kelp, Ling, Oil-Cake, Pipe-Clay – 1s 6d per Ton, *instead of 3s*

On Alum, Copperas, Fish, Iron of all descriptions, Woad, Chicory – 2s per Ton, *instead of 3s*'

The 70 or so barges which worked to Malton in 1855 had reduced to a single craft by 1894. Between 1921 and 1935 the London & North Eastern Railway took responsibility for the navigation, and administered its ultimate commercial decline.

Barmby on the Marsh

A few moored boats mark the presence of the pub at Breighton Ferry. Of course boating is a pleasure reserved just for the summer months, as during winter the situation can change radically, and high flood banks on the lower reaches of both the Derwent and the Ouse are a constant reminder of the potential power of these rivers. The Derwent finally enters the Ouse at the Barmby Tidal Barrage. There are moorings (available *daylight hours only*) here, so it is worthwhile stopping to explore. Boaters can either head upstream (right) *with the tide* towards York, or downstream (left) towards the North Sea, given a suitable craft.

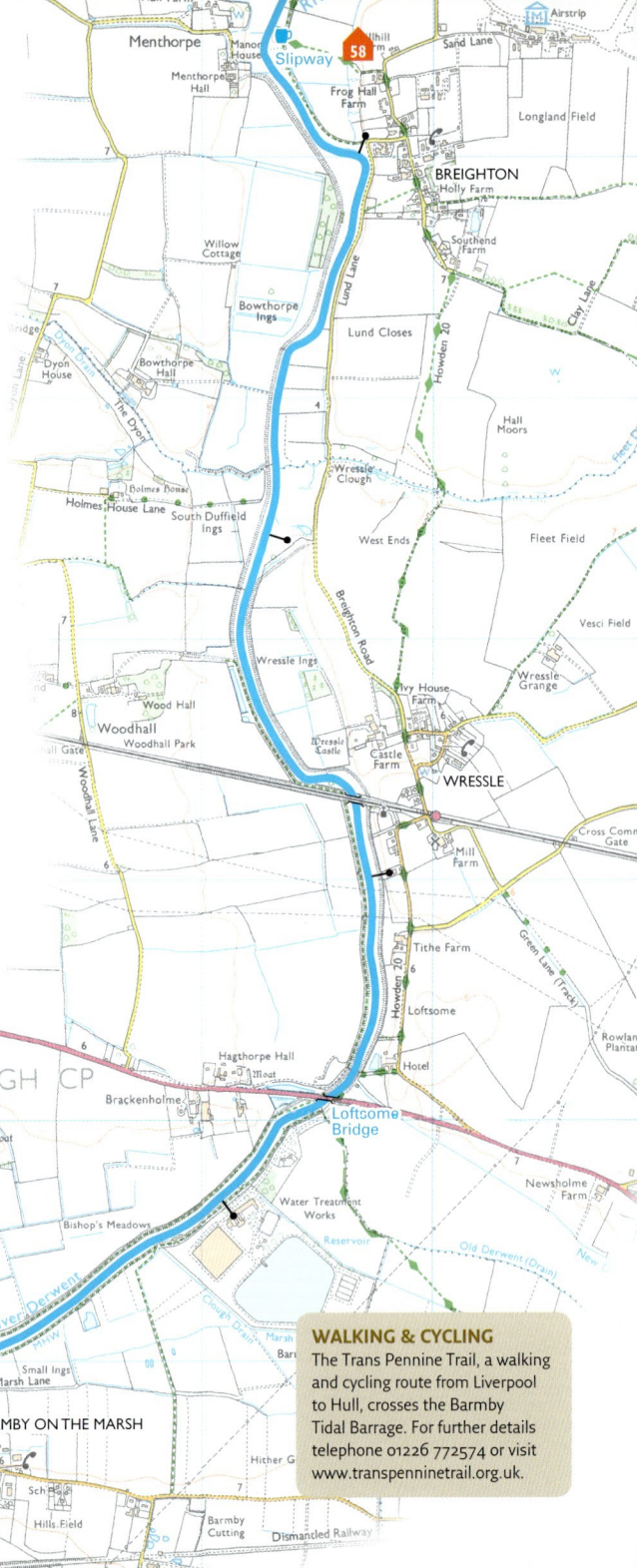

WALKING & CYCLING

The Trans Pennine Trail, a walking and cycling route from Liverpool to Hull, crosses the Barmby Tidal Barrage. For further details telephone 01226 772574 or visit www.transpenninetrail.org.uk.

NAVIGATIONAL NOTES

Entry to or exit from the River Derwent is through the lock at Barmby. Telephone and check your passage on 01757 638579/630072 – answerphone, or call on VHF Channel 74. Where possible give *24 hrs* notice. The maximum craft size is 62' x 16' 6" at Barmby and 60' x 14' at Sutton Lock. A certificate must be purchased from the Barrage Control Centre if you are joining the Derwent, to certify that your craft complies with anti-pollution requirements. High water Barmby is *approximately 1hr 40 mins after* HW Hull.

- **Breighton**
E. Riding. PO box, tel. A small, quiet agricultural settlement.
The Real Aeroplane Museum
The Aerodrome, Sand Lane, Breighton, Selby YO8 6DS (01757 289065; www.realaero.com). Entrance off Gunby Road. This enthusiastic working museum, airfield and runway has a splendid collection of aircraft, including a Supermarine Spitfire PR11, a Hawker Hurricane Mk12, a Messerschmitt Bf 109 and many others. There are plenty of exciting events during the summer where you will see, weather permitting, these planes, or others, in the air! Refreshments. *Open Sat and Sun 10.30-16.00 (or you can try on weekdays as well);* telephone or visit website for events calendar and for details of membership/season ticket required to airfield. Charge.

- **Wressle**
E. Riding. PO box, tel. A farming village scattered either side of the station and level crossing. Standing prominently to the north west, by the river, are the impressive towers of Wressle Castle, built for Sir Thomas Percy, Earl of Northumberland, around 1380. Beautifully constructed from fine stone, two of the four original towers still remain containing fragments of rooms, spectacular windows, fine fireplaces and, at the top, a stone crucifix. You can admire the remains of the castle from the river or the road, *but there is no public access.* Just to the south, over the railway crossing, is the handsome church of St John of Beverley. This was built wholly of brick in 1799. There is a pretty chapel house just down the road.

- **Barmby Tidal Barrage**
Barmby on the Marsh, Goole (01757 638579; answerphone 01757 630072). Constructed between 1972 and 1974 at a cost of £750,000, the barrage excludes the tide from the River Derwent, thus allowing more water to be extracted for domestic supply. The National Rivers Authority has, however, been quick to grasp the amenity value of the site, and there are excellent leisure facilities. Bird watching can be conducted from the wetland hide, which is *open daily 08.00-20.00.* Here you can expect to see the usual waders, plus herons, kingfishers, mallard, teal and swans, amongst others. Coarse fishing is free at the site and specially constructed platforms provide angling facilities for the disabled. There are several waterside picnic areas, toilets, and facilities for wheelchair users.

- **Barmby on the Marsh**
E. Riding. PO box, tel. A straggling red-brick village with some fine Georgian houses, hemmed in by the rivers Ouse and Derwent. St Helen's Church was built in the 18th C, and has a handsome brick tower, with some medieval work in the nave.

Pubs and Restaurants

- ✕ **The Breighton Ferry** Breighton, Selby YO8 6DH (01757 288407). In a fine riverside position, this homely pub serves bar meals, as well as more elaborate restaurant meals *L and E.* Children will enjoy the playthings in the large garden. Live music *Sat.* Camping and caravanning. Permanent moorings are maintained, there is launching for day boats, and fishing rights are held.

  ✕♉ **The Loftsome Bridge Coaching House** Loftsome Bridge Farm, Wressle, Selby YO8 6EN (01757 630070; www.loftsomebridge-hotel.co.uk). A modern riverside hotel and restaurant with a bar, south of Wressle. Restaurant meals are available *E Mon-Sat and Sun L.* Children welcome if eating. B & B.

- **The King's Head** High Street, Barmby on the Marsh, Goole DN14 7HT (01757 630705; www.thekingsheadbarmby.co.uk). Comfortable and friendly village pub serving real ale. Home-made meals, are served *L and E.* Children welcome.

Canal Head, Pocklington Canal

This last section of the Pocklington Canal is really very attractive, flanked on the east side by overhanging bushes and trees, and on the west by a low towpath hedge, through which rambling farms with grazing animals can be seen. The canal beyond Coates Lock is currently being restored: when this remaining section of the waterway is open, it will provide a worthy addition to the network (subject to a satisfactory agreement between British Waterways and Natural England). As the waterway turns towards Pocklington, the Bielby Arm, which would have once served the village and an old mill, is passed. To the north are the Wolds, low hills forming the horizon as the final locks are climbed and Canal Head is reached. The basin area here has been restored, and there are *picnic tables* overlooked by a canal warehouse, now tastefully converted into dwellings. A busy main road separates the basin from the Wellington Oak *pub*, where there is a *post box*. The Pocklington Canal Amenity Society (PCAS) was formed in 1969 with the objective of safeguarding and restoring the canal and today (amongst many other activities) they operate an Information Centre at Canal Head *on Sundays and bank holidays throughout the summer*. For more information contact 07514 978645; www.pocklingtoncanalsociety.org.

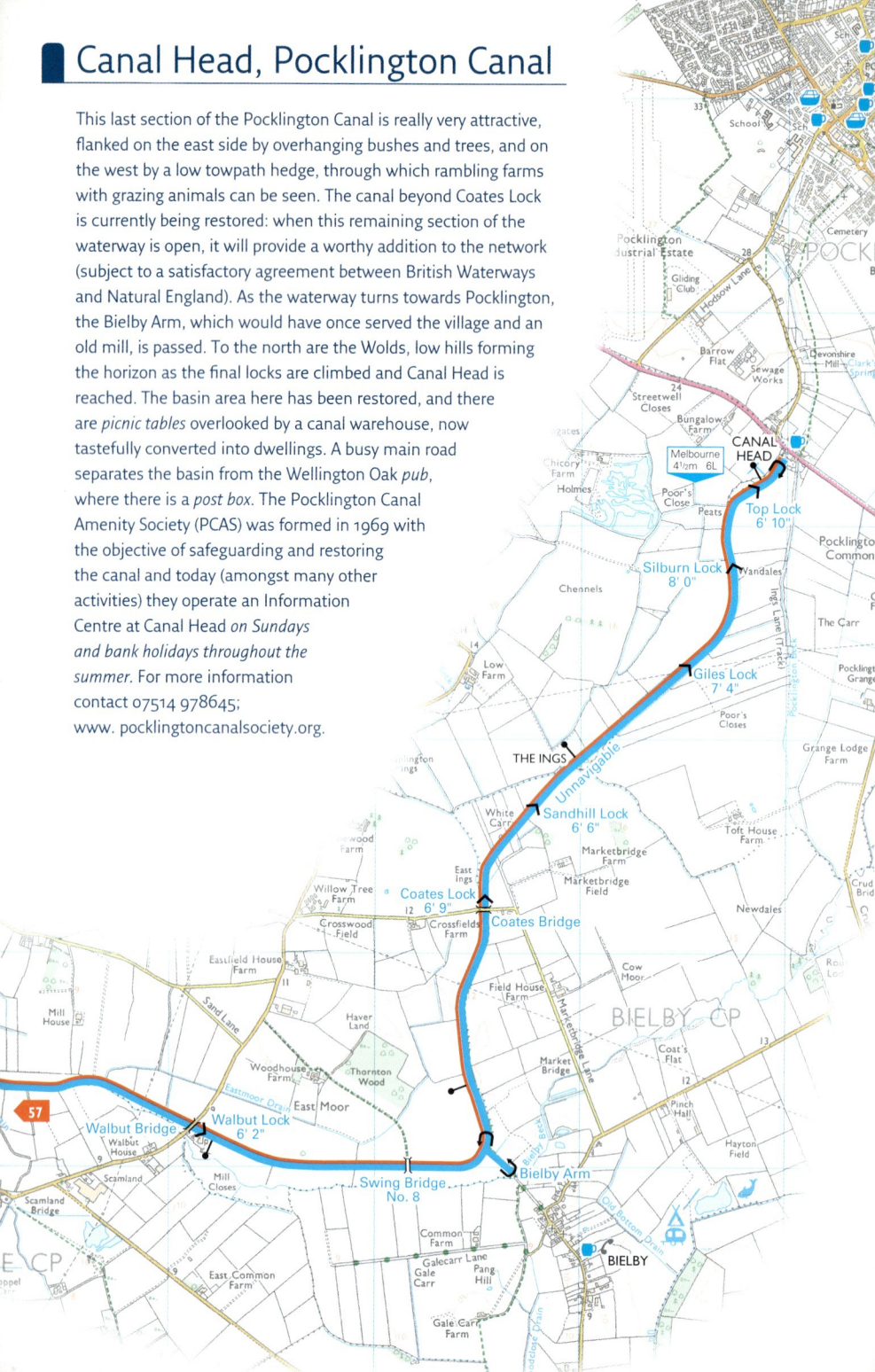

WALKING & CYCLING
There is a footpath from the east side of the Wellington Oak pub, Canal Head, which can be followed into Pocklington.

● **Bielby**
E. Riding. Tel. Quiet and attractive. The little church of St Giles dates from 1792, but has some far more ancient features. The Wesleyan chapel on the other side of the road dates from 1837, and is now a house, with an attractive sundial on the wall.

● **Pocklington**
E. Riding. PO, tel, stores, chemist, takeaways, banks, fish & chips. A mile to the north of Canal Head, but a worthwhile walk by road or footpath to explore this charming East Riding town. Prominent is the tall battlemented tower of All Saints Church, an endearing mixture of Early English and Perpendicular styles, with Norman fragments. By the pulpit is an engraved slab dating from the 13th C, but re-used to record the death of Margaret Easingwold, Prioress of Wilberfoss Priory in 1512. Kept inside is a churchyard cross dating from the 14th C: the crucifixion is depicted on one side, with the Virgin on the reverse. Readers of the inscription are asked to pray for John Sotheby. The Grammar School was founded in 1514 and proudly records the attendance of the philanthropist William Wilberforce (1759-1833), who was born in Hull. He led the parliamentary campaign against the slave trade, which was finally abolished in 1807.

Stewart's Burnby Hall Gardens and Museum Trust The Balk, Pocklington, York YO42 2QF (01759 307125; www.burnbyhallgardens.com). On the way into Pocklington from Canal Head. The gardens contain the finest collection of water lilies in Europe, with 80 varieties to be seen. The gardens and museum are open *Apr-Oct, daily 10.00-17.30, Oct-Christmas, Sat-Sun 10.00-15.00.* There is a café on site and good facilities, particularly for children, disabled and the elderly. Admission charge (parties of over 20 people *should telephone to book* and will get a discount).

Pubs and Restaurants

●**The College Arms** Main Street, Bielby, York YO42 4JW (01759 318361). A pleasant little village pub with a garden and children's play area. Real ale. As this is a quiet pub, food can be freshly prepared to order - telephone in advance. Children welcome.

●✕**The Wellington Oak** Canal Head, Pocklington, York YO42 1NW (01759 303854). Smart and pleasant brick and timber pub serving real ale. Bar and restaurant meals available *L and E*. Children and dogs welcome and there is a large garden, with a stream.

MISSING THE BOAT
What is now called the canal age was the short period from 1760 to 1840 - 80 years during which the population of England and Wales rose from 6½ million to 16 million. In 1760 Josiah Wedgwood founded his pottery works at Etruria, Stoke-on-Trent, and Clive left India. In 1840 the penny post was established.
Ideas for building the Pocklington Canal were first mooted in the 1770s: a public meeting was called, and agreed the canal would be a 'great utility'. In 1813 Lord Fitzwilliam, owner of the River Derwent Navigation, asked George Leather to make a survey, and this finally appeared in 1814. Subscriptions were opened and an Act of Parliament to enable the selling of shares was passed in 1815. Construction work began in August 1816, when it was agreed to 'let by ticket the cutting of the canal', and the 9½ mile route was finally completed in 1818, remarkably at less than the estimated cost. A mere 29 years after the initial celebrations it began its inevitable decline in the face of railway competition, slowly falling into disuse. The last commercial traffic used the canal in 1932.

Boston and the River Witham (see page 82)

FOSSDYKE & WITHAM NAVIGATIONS

MAXIMUM DIMENSIONS
Fossdyke Navigation (Torksey to Lincoln)
Length: 75'
Beam: 15' 3"
Headroom: 11' 3"
Draught: 5'

Witham Navigation (Lincoln to Boston)
Length: 75'
Beam: 15' 3"
Headroom: 9' 2"
Draught: 5'

MANAGER
01636 704481;
enquiries.eastmidlands@britishwaterways.co.uk

MILEAGE
TORKSEY to:
Saxilby: 5½ miles
Brayford Pool, Lincoln: 11 miles
Bardney: 20½ miles
Southrey: 23½ miles
Kirkstead: 26¾ miles
Dogdyke: 31¾ miles
Anton's Gowt: 40¼ miles

BOSTON Grand Sluice: 42¾ miles

Locks: 3

The Fossdyke Navigation was built about AD120 by the Romans, and is the oldest artificially constructed waterway in the country which is still navigable. It was designed to connect the River Witham (made navigable by the Romans) to the Trent and the Humber. The two navigations were used by the Danes when they invaded England, and later by the Normans to carry stone to build Lincoln Cathedral. Subsequently the Fossdyke and the Witham navigations became the responsibility of various riparian landowners, and of the church. The navigations gradually deteriorated and by the beginning of the 17th C were virtually impassable. King James I then transferred the Fossdyke to the Corporation of Lincoln, and from that time conditions improved. Acts of Parliament were passed in 1753 and 1762 for straightening and dredging both navigations, and in 1766 the Grand Sluice at Boston was built, to protect the Witham from the damaging effects of tides and floods. In the 18th and 19th C further improvements were made, many related to the extensive drainage systems carried out throughout the Fenlands. Thus over a period of centuries the two navigations came to assume the wide, straight course that is so characteristic of them today.

In 1846 the navigations were leased to the Great Northern Railway Company, and immediately their revenue began to fall. Railway competition continued, and by the end of the 19th C both navigations were running at a loss. After a period of dormancy the Witham & Fossdyke navigations became established cruising waterways, as pleasure boats replaced the last surviving commercial operators.

Today their isolation and total lack of development attracts many, while their survival preserves the pleasures of visiting Lincoln by boat; and Boston is one of the vital links between the inland waterways system and the open sea.

The newly constructed Fenland Waterways Link, connecting the South Forty Foot Drain with the Haven in Boston, opens up 150 miles of new and little used waterway, linking the cathedral cities of Lincoln, Ely and Peterborough with the towns of Spalding, Boston, Crowland and Ramsey.

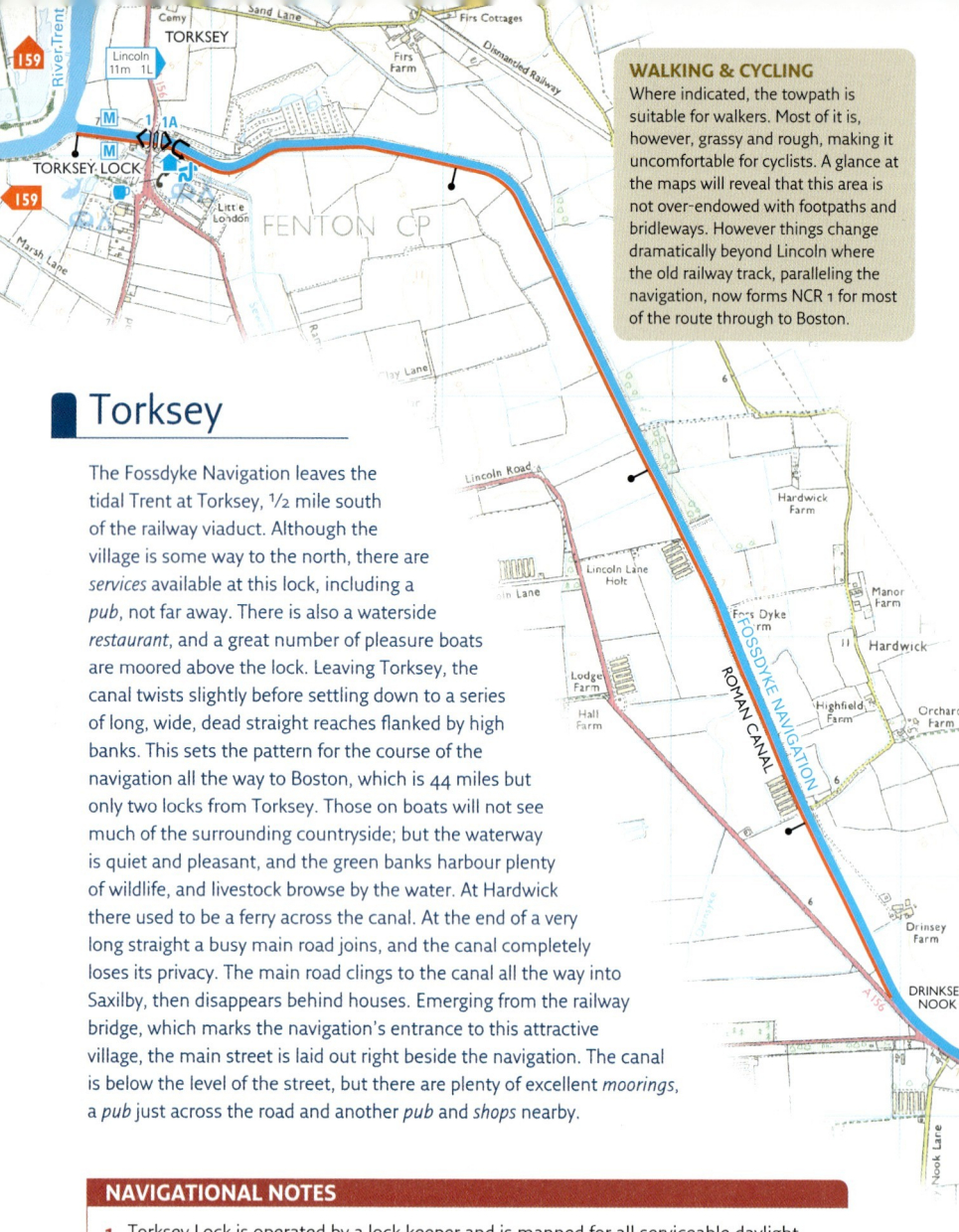

> **WALKING & CYCLING**
> Where indicated, the towpath is suitable for walkers. Most of it is, however, grassy and rough, making it uncomfortable for cyclists. A glance at the maps will reveal that this area is not over-endowed with footpaths and bridleways. However things change dramatically beyond Lincoln where the old railway track, paralleling the navigation, now forms NCR 1 for most of the route through to Boston.

Torksey

The Fossdyke Navigation leaves the tidal Trent at Torksey, ½ mile south of the railway viaduct. Although the village is some way to the north, there are *services* available at this lock, including a *pub*, not far away. There is also a waterside *restaurant*, and a great number of pleasure boats are moored above the lock. Leaving Torksey, the canal twists slightly before settling down to a series of long, wide, dead straight reaches flanked by high banks. This sets the pattern for the course of the navigation all the way to Boston, which is 44 miles but only two locks from Torksey. Those on boats will not see much of the surrounding countryside; but the waterway is quiet and pleasant, and the green banks harbour plenty of wildlife, and livestock browse by the water. At Hardwick there used to be a ferry across the canal. At the end of a very long straight a busy main road joins, and the canal completely loses its privacy. The main road clings to the canal all the way into Saxilby, then disappears behind houses. Emerging from the railway bridge, which marks the navigation's entrance to this attractive village, the main street is laid out right beside the navigation. The canal is below the level of the street, but there are plenty of excellent *moorings*, a *pub* just across the road and another *pub* and *shops* nearby.

NAVIGATIONAL NOTES

1. Torksey Lock is operated by a lock keeper and is manned for all serviceable daylight tides. The period of access to the lock is determined by the height of the tide and the amount of fresh water in the river. Contact the lock keeper on 01427 718202 or 07884 238781 – VHF Channel 74 – for further details.
2. See Navigational Notes, page 158. This also applies to Torksey Lock. Also note 4 on page 162.
3. During the winter months these navigations perform a vital drainage function. Bear in mind that *water levels can change rapidly*.
4. Commercial river traffic operates on VHF Channel 6 upstream of Keadby Bridge on the River Trent. It is useful for VHF users to monitor this channel to establish the whereabouts of large craft on the river.

Pubs and Restaurants

🍺 **The White Swan** Torksey Lock, Torksey, Lincoln LN1 2EJ (01427 718653). Near the lock. A local village pub, popular with boaters and fishermen. Real ale is served, along with food *L and E*. Children welcome, and there is a play area and garden. Quiz *Sun*. Moorings. Also caravan and camping site.

✗♆ **The Wheelhouse Restaurant** By Torksey Lock, Torksey, Lincoln LN1 2EH (01427 718301). Riverside restaurant, right by the moorings, serving English food *L and E (closed Mon)*. Families are welcome.

🍺✗ **The Hume Arms** Main Street, Torksey, Lincoln LN1 2EE (01427 718700; www.thehumearmstorksey.co.uk). Large, attractive old pub with bars and carvery restaurant, situated 300yds from the junction of the Fossdyke and Trent navigations. À la carte menu served *L daily*, carvery *Sun*. Garden. Children welcome. B & B.

🍺✗ **The Carpenters Arms** 22 Fenton Road, Fenton, Lincoln LN1 2EP (01427 718633). Restaurant and bar meals served. Children welcome, garden.

🍺✗ **The Bridge Inn** Gainsborough Road, Saxilby, Lincoln LN1 2LX. Traditional pub near the Fossdyke, with a large garden, decking, conservatory and play area. Food is available *L and E*. Children welcome *until 18.00*. Moorings.

🍺 **The Anglers** 65 High Street, Saxilby, Lincoln LN1 2HA (01522 702200; www.theanglerslincoln.co.uk). Real ale in a friendly local, with plenty of pub games each night. Stores nearby. Live music *B Hol weekends*.

✗ **Scrummies** 21-23 High Street, Saxilby, Lincoln LN1 2LN (01522 703528). Welcoming coffee shop and café in the centre of Saxilby.

🍺✗ **The Sun Inn** 20 Bridge Street, Saxilby, Lincoln LN1 2PZ (01522 702326; www.suninnsaxilby.co.uk). Canalside pub serving real ale, and haunted by the ghost of Tom Otter, who murdered his wife here during the 1800s. Meals *L & E Tue-Sun*, including *Sun* roasts. Children welcome. Garden. Regular live music.

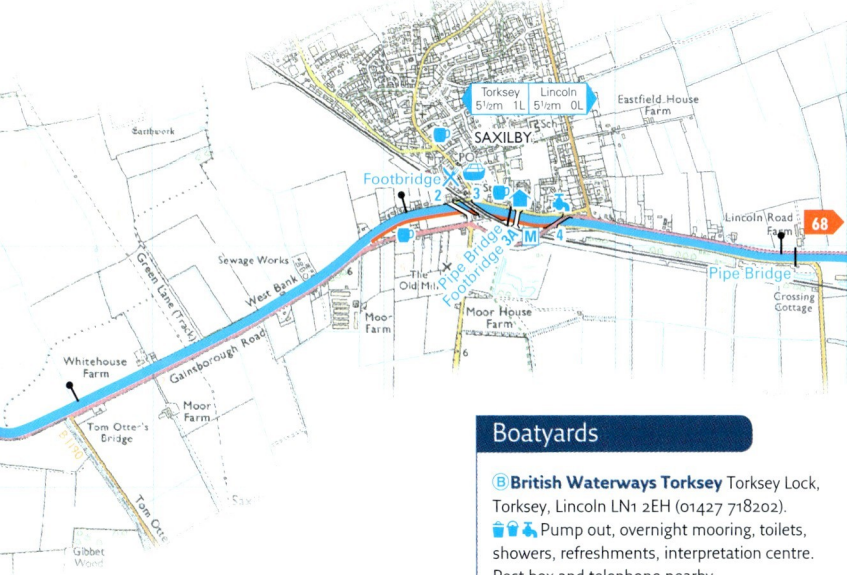

Boatyards

Ⓑ **British Waterways Torksey** Torksey Lock, Torksey, Lincoln LN1 2EH (01427 718202). Pump out, overnight mooring, toilets, showers, refreshments, interpretation centre. Post box and telephone nearby.

● **Torksey**
Lincs. PO, tel. Once an important Roman port, this was also a thriving settlement in the Middle Ages. It is now a small riverside village, a short walk north of the settlement centred upon the lock.

● **Saxilby**
Lincs. PO, tel, stores, garage, library, station, fish & chips. The presence of the Fossdyke has clearly determined much of the layout of the village, although the siting of the church over half-a-mile to the north has obviously provided another focal point, and as a result Saxilby extends between the two. Some of the buildings in the main street actually face the waterway, and a line of attractive cherry trees completes the scene. The church of St Boltolph is pretty, having an interesting mélange of building styles that may be the result of the west tower being at one time freestanding. There are excellent moorings on both sides of the waterway in the village and a barbecue for boaters' use (south west of the footbridge) as well as a DIY store nearby, selling gas.

Lincoln

As the road finally moves away from the navigation, the Gainsborough–Lincoln railway line moves in to take its place on the other bank, although separated from the canal for much of the way by a low hedge. After a few industrial works on the way out of Saxilby, the canal is entirely in countryside, green and flat. There then follows a fascinating stretch of waterway. The approach of Lincoln is marked by the magnificent towers of the cathedral on the hill. Passing the isolated Pyewipe *pub* on the canal bank, the Fossdyke bends briefly as it makes its final

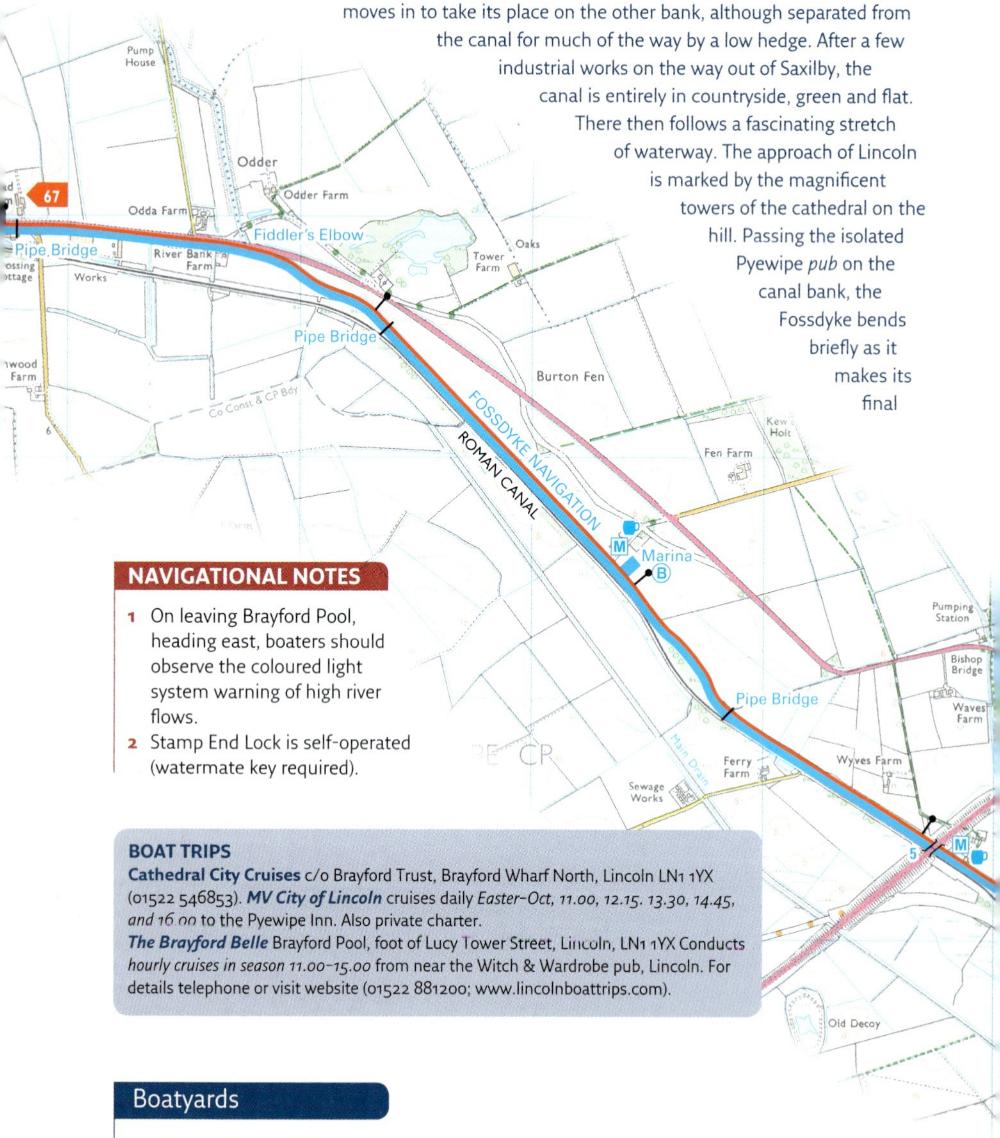

NAVIGATIONAL NOTES

1. On leaving Brayford Pool, heading east, boaters should observe the coloured light system warning of high river flows.
2. Stamp End Lock is self-operated (watermate key required).

BOAT TRIPS

Cathedral City Cruises c/o Brayford Trust, Brayford Wharf North, Lincoln LN1 1YX (01522 546853). *MV City of Lincoln* cruises daily *Easter–Oct*, 11.00, 12.15. 13.30, 14.45, and 16.00 to the Pyewipe Inn. Also private charter.
The Brayford Belle Brayford Pool, foot of Lucy Tower Street, Lincoln, LN1 1YX Conducts hourly cruises in season 11.00–15.00 from near the Witch & Wardrobe pub, Lincoln. For details telephone or visit website (01522 881200; www.lincolnboattrips.com).

Boatyards

B Burton Waters Marina Burton Lane End, Burton Waters LN1 2WN (01522 567404; www.burtonwaters.co.uk). **D** Pump out, moorings, servicing, repair, chandlery, toilets, showers, laundry.
B British Waterways Lincoln Yard Brayford Wharf, Fosse Bank, Lincoln LN1 1. Public telephone, toilets and showers.
B Lincoln Marina The Boatyard, Brayford Pool, Lincoln LN1 1RE (01522 526896). Overnight and long-term mooring.
B Brayford Trust Harbour Masters Office, Brayford Wharf North, Lincoln LN1 1YX (01522 521452). (**D** nearby) Pump out, overnight and long-term mooring, small slipway, telephone nearby, toilets, showers, café.

approach to Lincoln. Then a long line of moored pleasure boats, with new buildings behind, leads to a new road bridge. Beyond this the navigation widens out dramatically into the vast expanse of water known as Brayford Pool, overlooked by the university. There is a *boatyard* here, *boat clubs* and a floating *pub/restaurant*. Continuing through the pool, the River Witham can be seen flowing in as an unnavigable stream at the southern corner, and from here onwards (eastward) the Fossdyke Canal is replaced by the Witham Navigation. Leaving Brayford Pool, the channel becomes extremely narrow and goes straight through the heart of old Lincoln, passing under the famous and well-named Glory Hole, with an ancient half-timbered building concealing a busy street of shops astride the navigation. The arch dates from c.1160, and was once called the Murder Hole. In 1235 a chapel dedicated to St Thomas â Becket was built on the eastern side of the bridge, but it was destroyed during the Reformation. Houses on the bridge date from c.1540. East of the Glory Hole the navigation ducks under a striking new steel millennium sculpture and threads its way between a lively mélange of shops, pubs and cafés, where the waterway is overhung with trees, and a very large flock of swans lends an air of grace. The channel then once again widens and passes old flour mills which once used barges for shipping the grain, but have now found a new commercial life. Further on are Stamp End Lock and sluices. The top gate has no paddles, being simply raised *à la guillotine* into a steel framework to let the water in and boats pass underneath. Beyond the next railway bridge is another, larger bridge (with *moorings*): you are then back in an uncluttered, flat landscape, little different from that surrounding the Fossdyke Canal. To the west is Lincoln Cathedral, standing proudly on the hill above the town.

> **WALKING & CYCLING**
> The Tourist Information Centre is the place to buy a ticket for Lincoln's guided walking tours, including the ghost walks. Many of these tours are seasonal, so please check the dates and times.

- **Brayford Pool**
This expanse of water separates old Lincoln from industrial Victorian Lincoln. It joins the Fossdyke Canal to the Witham Navigation, and provides the navigator with a welcome relief from the long straight stretches of water either side of Lincoln. The modern building on the south bank is the campus of the University of Lincolnshire, opened by H M Queen on 11 October 1996. The annual Mayor's Regatta, held on Brayford Pool in *June*, is becoming a major event.

- **Lincoln**
All services. Lincoln is a fine city, with a vast amount for the visitor to see. Once the Celtic settlement of Lindon, it became Lindum Colonia, a Roman town; many Roman remains have been discovered. Plenty of these traces can be seen around the town. The old part of Lincoln is of course grouped around the cathedral, which sits on a hill to the north of the river, overawing the city and the surrounding countryside for miles. There are some splendid rows of houses in the Close and just outside it, where the steep and narrow cobbled streets have remained unchanged for centuries, and motor traffic can hardly penetrate. The Christmas market, held in the square in front of the cathedral in early December, is particularly atmospheric.

Lincoln Cathedral Lincoln LN2 1PX (01522 561600; www.lincolncathedral.com). This splendid building dominates the city and visitors to Lincoln should certainly find time for a visit. The original Norman cathedral was begun c.1074, but a fire and an earth tremor in the next century made two extensive restorations necessary. The present triple-towered building is the result of rebuilding in Early English style begun in 1192 by St Hugh of Avalon after the second disaster, although the magnificent central tower (271ft high) was not finished until 1311. The vast interior contains an abundance of fine stone monuments and wood carvings. In the Cathedral Treasury is one of the original copies of the Magna Carta. *Open Jul-Aug, Mon-Fri 07.15-20.00 and Sat, Sun 07.15-18.00; Sep-Jun, daily 07.15-18.00 (Sun 17.00).* Café and shop on site. Charge.

Lincoln Medieval Bishops Palace Minster Yard (01522 527468). Once the domain of the wealthy bishops of Lincoln, standing in the shadow of the cathedral. Banqueting halls, apartments and offices. *Open Apr-Oct 10.00-18.00 (Oct 17.00), Nov-Mar Sat and Sun 10.00-16.00; closed Tue and Wed.* Charge.

Lincoln Castle Castle Hill, Lincoln LN1 3AA (01522 511068; www.lincolnshire.gov.uk). Built as a stronghold for William the Conqueror in 1068, it stands on the crest of the hill close to the cathedral, where 166 houses were demolished to make the necessary space. Over 6 acres of lawns and trees are enclosed by the thick walls, the two towers and the Cobb Hall – a 14th-C addition. The Observatory Tower and the old keep were built on separate mounds on the south side of the castle. The keep is now a mere shell, but the Observatory Tower is in good repair and there is an excellent view of the surrounding area from the top. Cobb Hall, a lower battlemented tower, was built in the north east corner of the castle and was a place of imprisonment and execution. *Open all year daily from 10.00, except first Wed of month when 10.45; closing times vary dependent on season.* Café for refreshments. Charge.

The Collection Broadgate, Danes Terrace, Lincoln LN2 1LP (01522 550990). A permanent exhibition of Lincolnshire's rich archaeological heritage and a changing programme of exhibitions, events and education workshops *Open daily 10.00-17.00.* Free.

Tourist Information Centre 9 Castle Hill, Lincoln LN1 3AA (01522 545458; www.visitlincoln.com). Friendly and helpful. Guided walks and ghost walks are run *Easter, Whitsun, Spring and Aug B Hols; daily Jul-Aug; weekends Sep-Oct.* You can also obtain information on river trips and horse and carriage rides. Telephone for details of the City Cycle Race.

FLYING AROUND LINCOLNSHIRE

Finding yourself with some time to spare on the Fossdyke & Witham, you might like to make an excursion to see some of the county's RAF airfields. East of Tattershall Bridge is the Battle of Britain Memorial Flight Centre, where a Lancaster bomber, five Spitfires, a Hurricane and a Dakota are maintained at RAF Coningsby. These aircraft are not empty airframes filling a museum, but are fully maintained airworthy examples. You can visit *10.00-17.00 on weekdays* (01526 344041; www.bbmf.co.uk).

South of Lincoln is RAF Waddington, and here you can watch the activity from a public viewing area alongside the A15 road. This airfield came into service in 1916 as a training station for the Royal Flying Corps. It closed down in 1918 but re-opened in 1926, becoming a base for Hampdens, which attacked enemy shipping in the channel during the early part of World War II. The indomitable Lancaster first entered service at this base, on Christmas Eve 1941, flown by 44 Squadron. The long runway was built in 1953, assuring the airfield's future, and today AWACs (airborne early warning and control aircraft), with their prominent radar dishes mounted in front of the tail fin, and the last Nimrods, fly from here.

Trent Bridge, Newark (see page 148)

Pubs and Restaurants

The Woodcocks Burton Lane End, Saxilby Road, Lincoln LN1 2BE (01522 703460). Comfortable pub, serving real ale. Bar meals and from a wide ranging menu are available *12.00–22.00 daily (21.00 Sun)*. There is an outdoor play area for children. Garden.

The Pyewipe Inn, Lodge & Restaurant Fossebank, Saxilby Road. Lincoln LN1 2BG (01522 528708; www.pyewipeinnlincoln.co.uk). Two miles west of Lincoln. A comfortable, isolated and traditionally furnished pub first licensed in 1788 as an inn for the bargees. It has panoramic views over Lincoln, the cathedral and the Fossdyke as well as a helicopter landing pad in the grounds. Real ale, plus an extensive home-cooked menu with fresh vegetables and à la carte restaurant *all day*. Children welcome. Four-acre garden. Look out for the ghost floating along the navigation. Moorings.

The Horse & Groom 31 Carholm Road, Lincoln LN1 1RH. At the western end of Brayford Pool. Home-made food including takeaways is served *all day (until 17.00 Sun)*. Children welcome and there is outside seating in the large beer garden. Live music.

The Shed Lincoln Marina, Brayford Pool, Lincoln LN1 1RE (01522 526090). Well situated, with a terrace, this fine warm and friendly pub offers real ale and food *L and E daily*.

The Barge on the Brayford Brayford Wharf North, Lincoln LN1 1YW (01522 511448; www.bargeonthebrayford.com). A fine floating restaurant specialising in fresh fish and continental cuisine. Meals are available *L and E*. Children welcome. There is a sun terrace for warm days.

The Royal William IV Brayford Wharf North, Lincoln LN1 1YX (01522 528159). At the north east corner of Brayford Pool. A stylish old pub which is *open all day*. Real ale and food *L and E*. Children welcome.

The Witch and Wardrobe 21 Waterside North, Lincoln LN2 5DQ (01522 244385). Smart pub serving real ale and food *L daily*. Children welcome at meal times. Large garden.

The Green Dragon 31 Waterside North/Broadgate, Lincoln LN2 5DH (01522 567155). By the main road bridge, 300yds east of the Glory Hole. This pub beside the River Witham was once a 14th-C merchants house, known as the Great Garrett. These days it serves real ale and bar meals *L daily and E Fri-Sat*. Children *over fourteen* welcome at meal times only.

Stokes High Bridge Restaurant 207 High Street, Lincoln LN5 7AU (01522 512534). Above the Glory Hole. Established in 1902, they serve fine tea and freshly roasted coffee *09.00–11.30*. Also traditional luncheon *11.45–14.00*, light teas *14.00–16.30 (lunchtime only)*. Excellent ice cream.

Washingborough

Leaving Lincoln, the River Witham heads due east in a series of straight, wide reaches through landscape little different to that seen from the Fossdyke, following the bottom of a wide valley. To the west, the towers of Lincoln Cathedral remain visible from the river for about 10 miles to the east. Overhead, AWACs (airborne early warning and control aircraft) fly lazily away on their missions, having taken off from nearby Waddington airfield (www.raf.mod.uk/rafwaddington). There are several villages on the hills overlooking the Witham; to the south is Washingborough, all trees and chimneys, while opposite is Greetwell Hall and its little stone church. Further east is the unappealing sprawl of Cherry Willingham, and then Fiskerton. There is an *overnight stop jetty* at Washingborough.

● **Greetwell**
Lincs. About ½ mile west of Cherry Willingham is All Saints, a beautiful church of Norman origin, next to Greetwell Hall Farm. This was the site of a medieval village, with cultivation and post-medieval garden remains.

● **Washingborough**
Lincs. PO, tel, stores, chemist, fish & chips, off-licence, takeaways. The centre of this village on the south side of the Witham valley is quite pretty. There are some attractive stone terraced cottages, and many trees around the church of St John Evangelist,

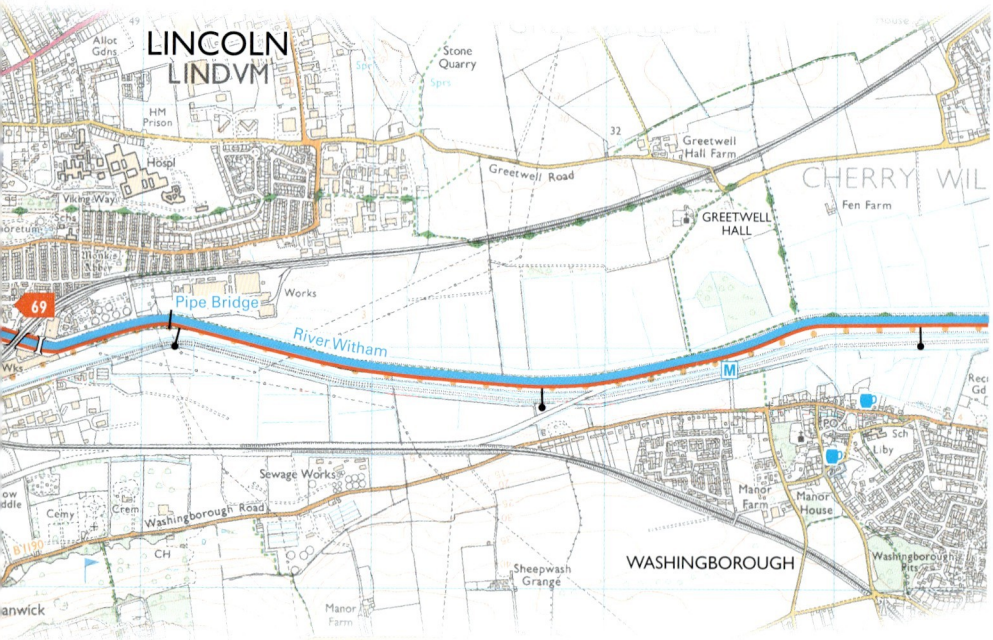

which contains an ornate Georgian chandelier, thought to have originated in Brighton. This has now become a smart commuter village but the shop is *open daily 07.00-22.00.*

- **Fiskerton**
Lincs. *PO, tel, stores, off-licence, garage.* The name of this village comes from 'fisher's town', since in the old days it was a fishing village, where boats could sail right up to the church on the tide. Later, the Fens here were drained and the river diverted into its present straight course.

Since then Fiskerton has stood back from the water. When the river breached its banks in 1962 however, the water once again reached the church. St Clement's itself is curious, as its Perpendicular west tower was built around the only circular tower in Lincolnshire. The rest of the building is a rich mélange of styles and parts, perhaps from the monastic houses at Bardney or Tupholme. The village itself is now full of new housing and the stores are *open Mon-Sat 08.00-20.00 & Sun 08.00-16.00.*

Pubs and Restaurants

- **The Royal Oak** Main Road, Washingborough, Lincoln LN4 1AU (01522 794312) Friendly village pub serving real ale. Children welcome, and there is a garden. Quiz night *Sun.*

- **The Carpenter's Arms** High Street, Fiskerton, Lincoln LN3 4HF. A black and white village pub serving real ale, and food *E daily, and L Fri-Sun.* Children welcome.

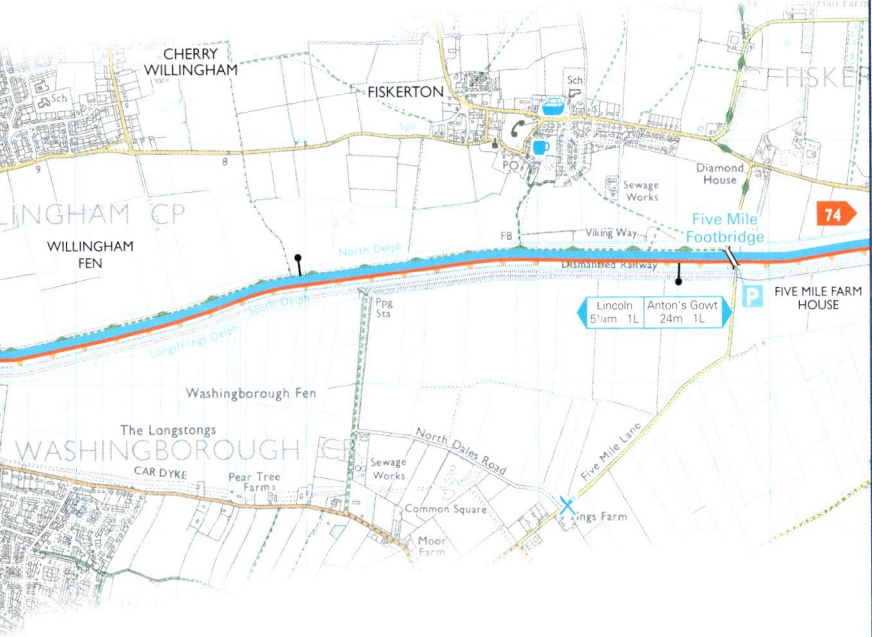

WALKING & CYCLING
There are footpaths down to the river from Greetwell, Fiskerton and the western end of Washingborough. You can walk from Fiskerton to Washingborough, crossing Five Mile Footbridge. National Cycle Route 1 uses the dismantled railway track alongside the navigation between Lincoln and Woodhall Spa and follows the waterway closely for the remainder of the journey into Boston.

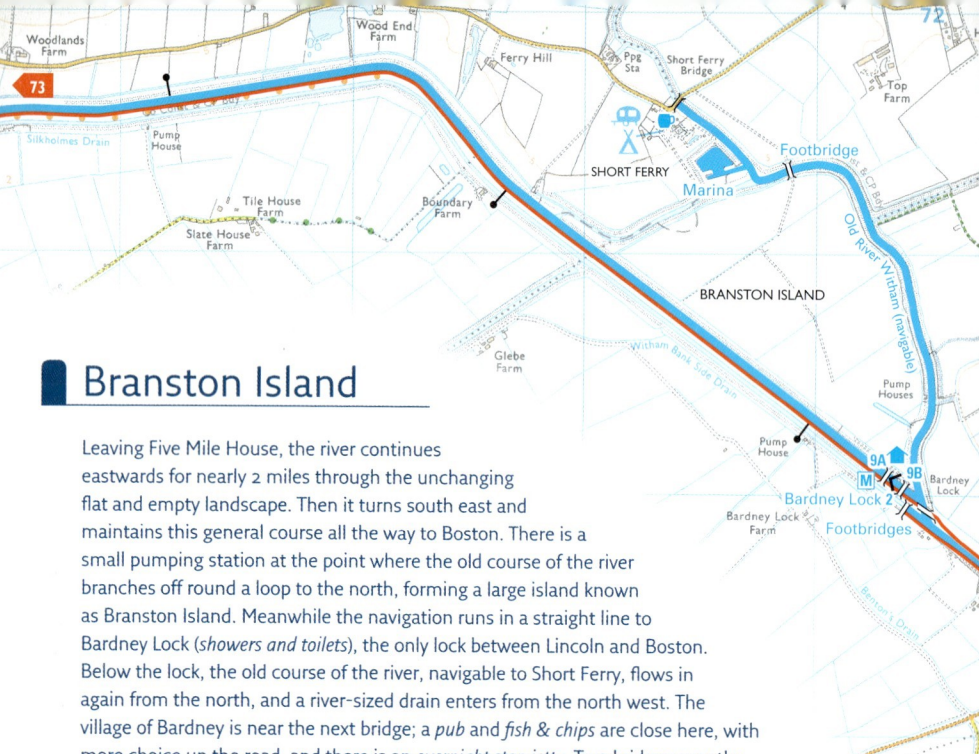

Branston Island

Leaving Five Mile House, the river continues eastwards for nearly 2 miles through the unchanging flat and empty landscape. Then it turns south east and maintains this general course all the way to Boston. There is a small pumping station at the point where the old course of the river branches off round a loop to the north, forming a large island known as Branston Island. Meanwhile the navigation runs in a straight line to Bardney Lock (*showers and toilets*), the only lock between Lincoln and Boston. Below the lock, the old course of the river, navigable to Short Ferry, flows in again from the north, and a river-sized drain enters from the north west. The village of Bardney is near the next bridge; a *pub* and *fish & chips* are close here, with more choice up the road, and there is an *overnight stop jetty*. Two bridges over the river connect the Bardney sugar-beet works with its associated settling ponds. The big ungainly buildings of this factory are conspicuous in the flat landscape, and continue to dominate the view for several miles. The river flows between high banks to Southrey, passing the drain (or field dyke) called Nocton Delph. At the village there is another brief flurry of buildings, including a converted station complete with name board. There are occasional farms on the south bank; the closed railway continues to hug the other side of the navigation all the way to Boston. Southrey has an *overnight stop jetty*.

Pubs and Restaurants

The Tyrwhitt Arms Ferry Road, Fiskerton, Lincoln LN3 4HU (01526 398460; www.shortferry.co.uk). Between Bardney and Fiskerton. A large rural pub adjacent to a caravan park. Food is served *L and E*. Children welcome, and there is a garden with play equipment and a children's room. Live entertainment *at weekends*. Access for boats is north from Bardney Lock up the old course of the Witham.

The Black Horse 16 Wragby Road, Bardney, Lincoln LN3 5XL (01526 398900; www.bardneyblackhorse.co.uk). A fully licensed guest house and restaurant in a 16th-C building with beams and low ceilings, serving home-cooked food *L. Garden*. B & B.

The Riverside Inn Ferry Road, Southrey, Lincoln LN3 5TA (01526 398374). Spacious and pretty pub serving real ale. Restaurant and bar meals are served *daily L and E (not Tue)*. Book ahead for weekends. Children and dogs welcome, and there is a garden. Closed *Mon L*. Hidden on the roof is a message to low flying pilots: 'If you can read this, you are too b****y low'.

NAVIGATIONAL NOTES

At Bardney Lock boats heading upstream towards Lincoln must turn right to pass under the railway bridge and then turn immediately left into the lock chamber (01636 704481).

● **Bardney**
Lincs. PO, tel, stores, chemist, butchers, off-licence, garage. A small village to the east of the river, on a slight rise, Bardney is attractive, with the mellow 15th-C church of St Lawrence and a pleasant village green. Inside the church is an incised slab to Abbot Richard Horncastle, 1508, taken from the abbey, together with many minor architectural features from the same source. The parish almshouses by the green were built in 1712. The remains of the Benedictine abbey lie to the north of the village. It was founded late in the 7th C and subsequently over-run by the Danes. Re-established in 1087 by Gilbert of Ghent as a cell of Charroux, the abbey buildings were begun again in 1115. The whole site was excavated 1909-14 and reported on by Sir Harold Brakspear in 1922, but much of what was found then has once again disappeared. Bardney has become well known in recent years as the scene of music festivals; in fact the site is to the south east of the village, towards Southrey. The shop is *open Mon-Sat 09.00-20.00 & Sun 10.00-16.00*.

● **Southrey**
Lincs. PO box, tel. A small village of little intrinsic interest, but with reasonable river access. The little white wooden church of St John the Divine, with its belfry, is delightful. It was built by the villagers in 1898 and is clearly cherished. A mile to the north, in undulating countryside, are the ruins of Tupholme Abbey, founded in 1160. The station platforms and name board survive – the track has long since disappeared.

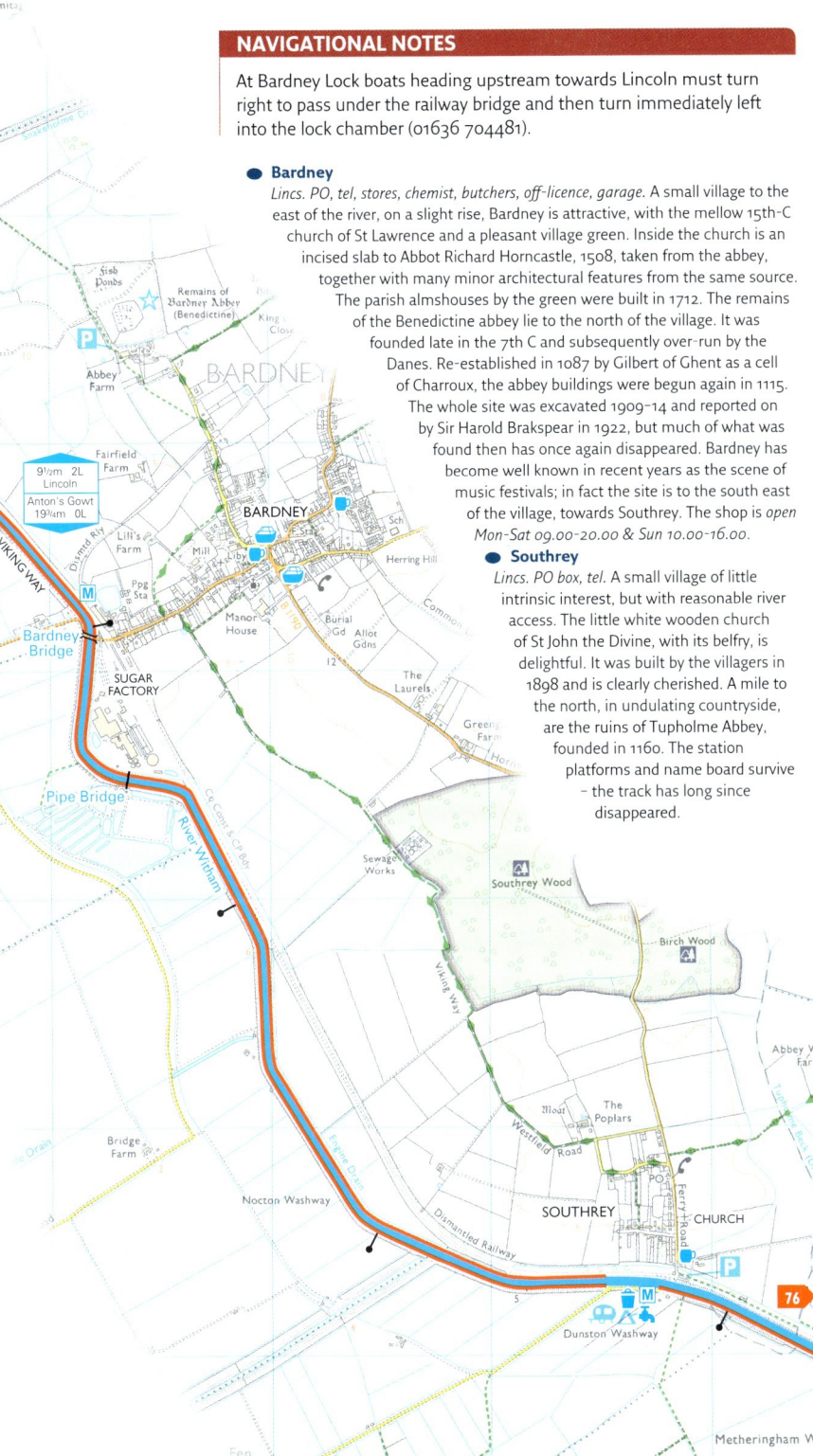

Fossdyke & Witham Navigations Branston Island

75

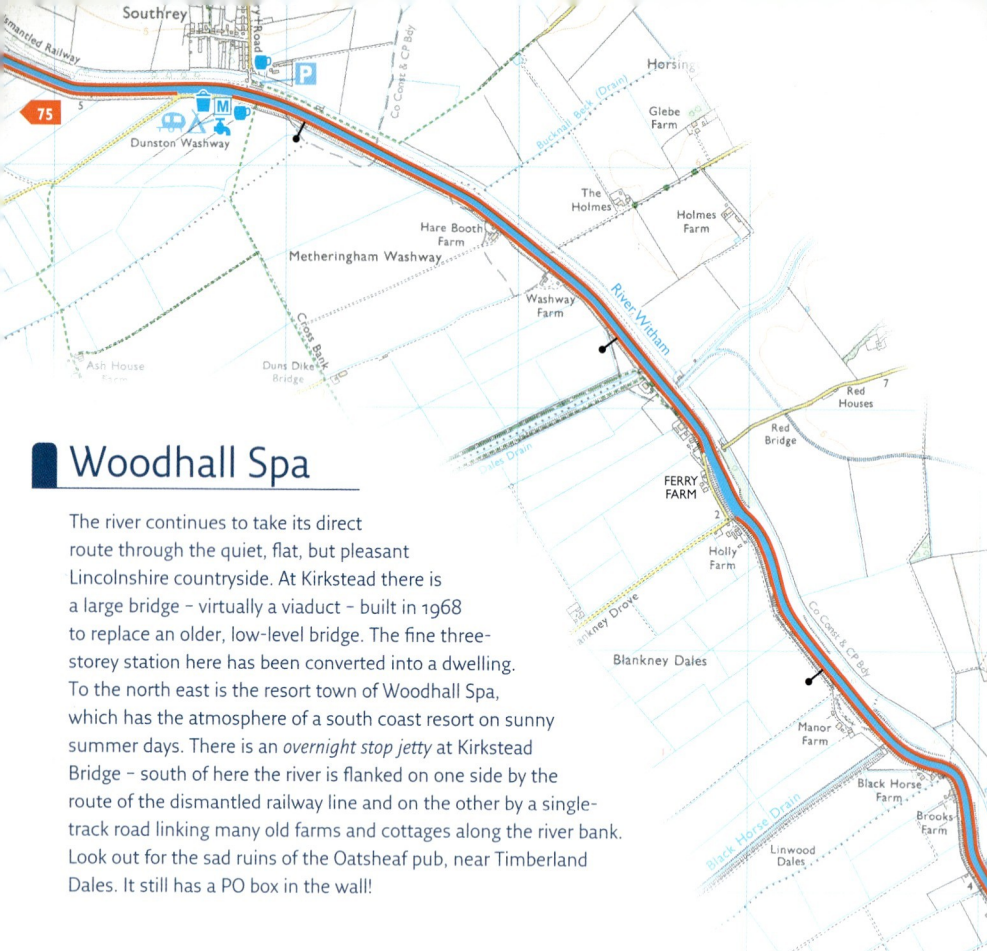

Woodhall Spa

The river continues to take its direct route through the quiet, flat, but pleasant Lincolnshire countryside. At Kirkstead there is a large bridge – virtually a viaduct – built in 1968 to replace an older, low-level bridge. The fine three-storey station here has been converted into a dwelling. To the north east is the resort town of Woodhall Spa, which has the atmosphere of a south coast resort on sunny summer days. There is an *overnight stop jetty* at Kirkstead Bridge – south of here the river is flanked on one side by the route of the dismantled railway line and on the other by a single-track road linking many old farms and cottages along the river bank. Look out for the sad ruins of the Oatsheaf pub, near Timberland Dales. It still has a PO box in the wall!

WALKING & CYCLING
There is a 5-mile circular cycle route through Ostler's Plantation, to the east of Woodhall Spa. Start from the car park off Kirkby Lane (B1191). It is an easy ride through a managed woodland established on the site of a World War II airfield which was the base of 617 Squadron, the famous 'Dambusters'. One of the old buildings is now a hibernaculum for long-eared bats. The Spa Trail is a traffic-free route for walkers and cyclists which starts just off the B1191 at Martin Moor, to the east of Woodhall Spa, and extends to Thornton Lodge Farm, near Horncastle.
For more walk and cycle trails, visit www.woodhallspa.org.

Pubs and Restaurants

The King's Arms Church Road, Martin Dales, Woodhall Spa N10 6XZ (01526 352633). On the west bank of the river. A sociable and comfortable pub. Bar meals available *L and E*. Children's room. B & B.
The Railway Hotel 195 Witham Road, Woodhall Spa LN10 6QX (01526 352580). On the east bank near the station, this is a traditional pub with open fires, in a railway house. Real ale. Food is served *L and E (not Mon in winter)*, with special *Sun* lunches. Children welcome.
The Mall Hotel Station Road, Woodhall Spa LN10 6QL (01526 352342). The only pub in the town, and thankfully it serves real ale. Bar and restaurant meals available *L and E*. Children welcome if you are dining. There is outside seating.

- **Kirkstead Abbey** Abbey Lane, Kirkstead, Woodhall Spa LN10 6QZ. 3/4 mile east of Kirkstead Bridge. A solitary finger of masonry about 30ft high is all that remains of the enormous Cistercian monastery founded in 1139, and moved here in 1187. A trained eye can recognise the former fishponds attached to the monastery grounds.
- **St Leonard's Church** Abbey Lane, Kirkstead, Woodhall Spa LN10 6QZ. Originally an extramural chapel of the abbey, it was built in the mid 13th C and survives largely intact as one of the finest examples of its kind. Beautifully decorated, it was sensitively restored in 1913-14. The 13th-C wooden screen is one of the oldest in the country, and an effigy of a knight, dating from c.1250, must also be one of the earliest in the country. The church is just a few hundred yards north east of the bridge.
- **Woodhall Spa**
Lincs. PO, tel, stores, takeaways, bank, butchers, chemist, fish & chips, off-licence, cinema, garage. A resort town in the woods a mile north east of Kirkstead Bridge, and which would not look out of place on the south coast of England. Perhaps you will notice also that the town sign features a fine railway engine, although regrettably the line to Woodhall Spa is no more. In 1811, while drilling for coal, iodine mineral water was found at a depth of 511ft. An inn was built beside the shaft, and a new well was sunk in 1824. The town then grew and it still has the characteristic Victorian atmosphere of many English spa towns. Jubilee Park has a heated outdoor swimming pool, open in the *summer*. There is a very popular and curious Kinema, complete with Compton organ, tucked away in the woods near to the spa building. It was built in the 1920s, and is unusual in that it uses back-projection (01526 352166; www.thekinemainthewoods.co.uk). Petworth House, now a hotel, served as the officers' mess for 617 Squadron, the 'Dambusters', stationed nearby. One-and-a-half miles north east of the town is the Wellington Monument, by Waterloo Wood, which was planted from acorns 'sown immediately after the memorable Battle of Waterloo'. The stores are *open Mon-Sat 08.00-22.00 & Sun 10.00-16.00* and there is a *part-time PO* at Kirkstead, between the river and the town.
- **The Cottage Museum** Iddesleigh Road, Woodhall Spa LN10 6SH (*see below*) (01526 353775; www.cottagemuseum.co.uk). Contains a variety of historical information about the village and a changing display of local history. *Open Easter to end Oct, daily, 10.30-16.30.* Charge.
- **Tourist Information Centre** Seasonal at the Cottage Museum, Iddesleigh Road, Woodhall Spa LN10 6SH (01526 353775; www.poachercountry.co.uk). Friendly and helpful. *Open daily 10.30-16.30.* There are a series of 10 walks based on the TIC.

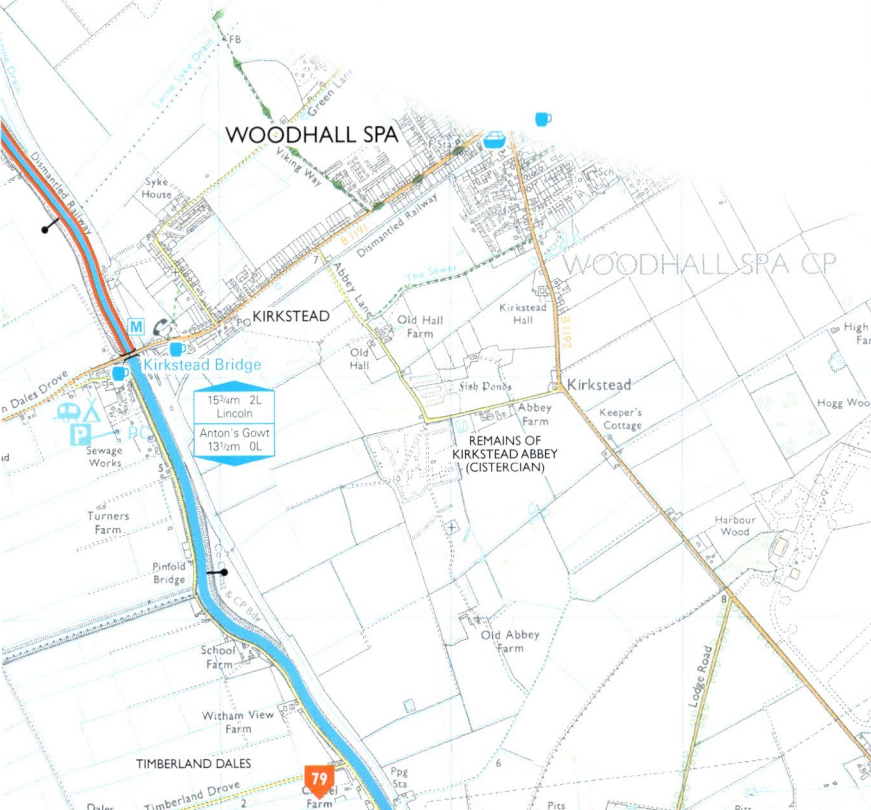

Dogdyke

The river continues southward, now on a pretty and winding course which provides a pleasant contrast to the former straight navigation. Along the Kesteven bank are a number of farm cottages served by a minor road. The old junction with the Horncastle Canal can still just be seen as a slight dent in the east bank. Less than a mile from Tattershall Bridge is Dogdyke, just a short way beyond the old steam pump. It is an attractive place with a *marina* and a riverside *pub*. Coningsby Airfield is close by: one end of the runway is near the river, so navigators may find aircraft screaming over them at a height of perhaps 100ft. This can be disconcerting on an otherwise quiet summer's afternoon. South of Dogdyke there is a small landing stage (charge) on the west bank; this marks a caravan site with facilities useful to those on boats (*shop, shower, gas,* 🛒 *etc*). Beyond it are the houses of Chapel Hill, where the Kyme Eau or Sleaford Navigation joins *(see below)*. Beyond here the river becomes straight and wide once again, with piling to protect and strengthen the bank on one side, and reeds on the other. Boston Stump, the tower of the church, can be seen from here, some 9 miles away beneath breezy open skies. There is an overnight stop jetty at Tattershall Bridge.

Tales of the River Bank Visitor Centre Telephone Horncastle TIC for opening times (*see* below). An exhibition explaining how the fen was formed, and is now drained and used.

Timberland Pumping Station Telephone Horncastle TIC for opening times (*see* below). This pumping station was built in 1839 to drain 2500 acres of Timberland and Thorpe Tilney fens It is a splendid working example, and once featured a scoop wheel over 26ft in diameter, lifting water from Walton Delph into the River Witham. The present pump was installed by Gwynnes of London in 1924.

Tattershall Castle Tattershall, Lincoln LN4 4LR (01526 342543; www.nationaltrust.org.uk). *NT*. 1 mile north east of Tattershall Bridge. The original castle was built by Sir Robert de Tateshall in 1231, and rebuilt in brick in the 15th C for Ralph Cromwell, Treasurer of England 1434-5. Rescued by Lord Curzon between 1911 and 1914, only the keep of this superb building remains. It is 110ft high, and the bricks, 322,000 of them, were supplied from Edlington Moor, 9 miles to the north. *Open Mar-Oct, Sat-Wed 11.00-17.00; Nov-Dec, weekends only 11.00-16.00; closed Jan-Feb*. Charge. Shop, teas.

Horncastle Canal This navigation, 10 miles long, was built 1792-1802 to serve the small country town of Horncastle. The remains of the first lock are about 300yds from the river. Nearer Horncastle parts of the canal are still in water, and the town basin survives. It was abandoned in 1885.

Tourist Information Centre Wharf Road, Horncastle LN9 5HL (01507 601111;

horncastleinfo@e-lindsey. gov.uk). Out of season, contact Louth TIC (01507 609289; louthinfo@e-lindsey.gov.uk).

● **Dogdyke**
Lincs. *PO box, tel*. 'A ditch where docks grow', and now a riverside settlement close to a signpost which indicates 2½ miles to New York and 12 miles to Boston – nice for a photograph.

Dogdyke Pumping Station Tattershall LN4 4JG (01636 707642; www.dogdyke.com). Between Tattershall Bridge and Dogdyke off the A153 at Bridge Farm. Home of the two remaining land drainage engines: a 1855 steam beam-engine driving a scoop-wheel and a Ruston Oil engine driving a pump. Although superseded by an electric pump, the pumps are still maintained in case the electric set fails. *Open days throughout the year*; visit the website for details. Charge.

● **Chapel Hill**
Lincs. *PO box, tel, stores, garage*. A pleasantly compact and tiny village.

Kyme Eau (01522 689460; sleaford.navigation@ntlworld.com; www.sleafordnavigation.co.uk). Navigable through Kyme Lock (BW Watermate key needed) for over 7½ miles to Cobblers Lock, where it is possible to wind. Maximum dimensions are 70' 0" x 14' 0" with a headroom of 5' 6" and a draught of 2' 0". Progress can be slow on this navigation. From *Oct-Mar* the gates at Lower Kyme Lock are chained back for flood prevention reasons, and navigation is difficult in winter. Full restoration to Sleaford is planned.

Boatyards

Ⓑ **Belle Isle Marina** Dogdyke, Coningsby LN4 4UU (01526 342124; www.belleislemarina.co.uk). ⛽ 🛒 Gas, overnight and long-term mooring, winter storage, slipway, crane, boat and engine sales and repairs, toilets, showers.

Ⓑ **Orchard Caravan Park** Witham Bank, Chapel Hill, Coningsby LN4 4PZ (01526 342414). 🛒 ⛽ Overnight mooring, swimming pool, toilets, showers, laundrette, bar.

Ⓑ **Chapel Hill Marina & Holiday Park** Chapel Hill, Lincoln LN4 4QB (01526 342750). At the entrance to the Kyme Eau. ⛽ 🛒 D Gas, overnight and long-term mooring, boat sales, restaurant nearby.

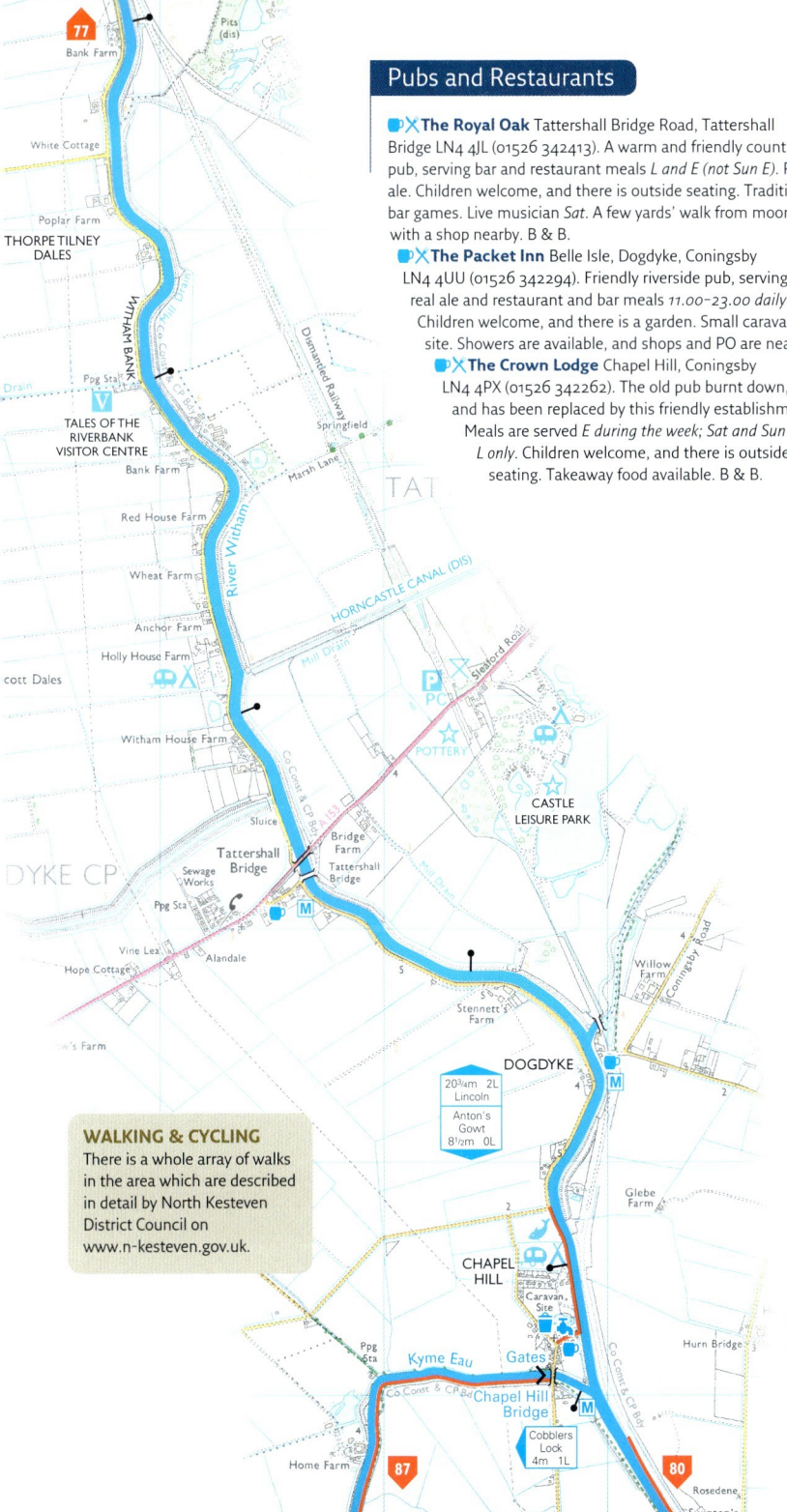

Pubs and Restaurants

🍺✕ **The Royal Oak** Tattershall Bridge Road, Tattershall Bridge LN4 4JL (01526 342413). A warm and friendly country pub, serving bar and restaurant meals *L and E (not Sun E)*. Real ale. Children welcome, and there is outside seating. Traditional bar games. Live musician *Sat*. A few yards' walk from moorings with a shop nearby. B & B.

🍺✕ **The Packet Inn** Belle Isle, Dogdyke, Coningsby LN4 4UU (01526 342294). Friendly riverside pub, serving real ale and restaurant and bar meals *11.00–23.00 daily*. Children welcome, and there is a garden. Small caravan site. Showers are available, and shops and PO are nearby.

🍺✕ **The Crown Lodge** Chapel Hill, Coningsby LN4 4PX (01526 342262). The old pub burnt down, and has been replaced by this friendly establishment. Meals are served *E during the week; Sat and Sun L only*. Children welcome, and there is outside seating. Takeaway food available. B & B.

> **WALKING & CYCLING**
> There is a whole array of walks in the area which are described in detail by North Kesteven District Council on www.n-kesteven.gov.uk.

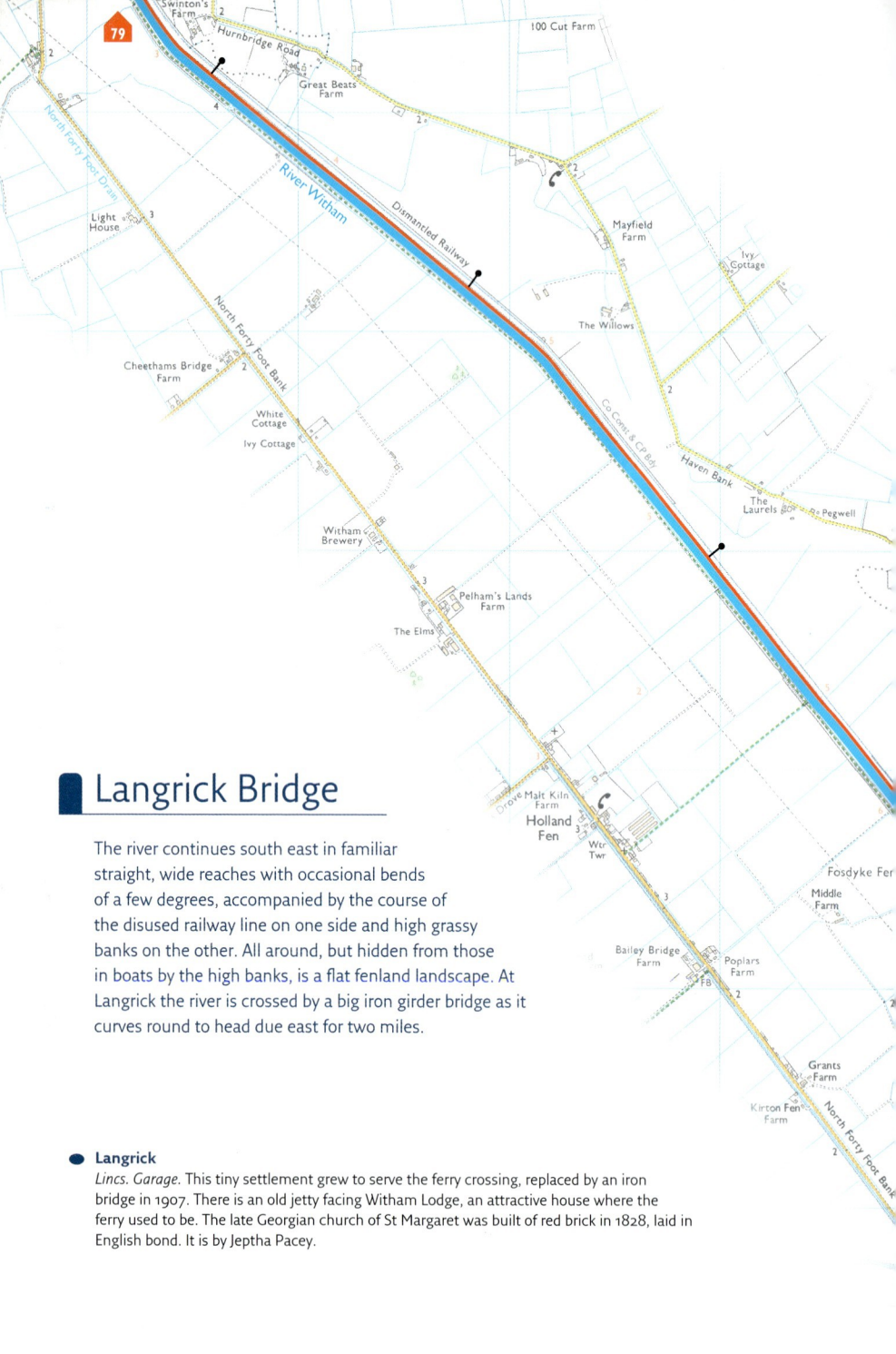

Langrick Bridge

The river continues south east in familiar straight, wide reaches with occasional bends of a few degrees, accompanied by the course of the disused railway line on one side and high grassy banks on the other. All around, but hidden from those in boats by the high banks, is a flat fenland landscape. At Langrick the river is crossed by a big iron girder bridge as it curves round to head due east for two miles.

● **Langrick**
Lincs. Garage. This tiny settlement grew to serve the ferry crossing, replaced by an iron bridge in 1907. There is an old jetty facing Witham Lodge, an attractive house where the ferry used to be. The late Georgian church of St Margaret was built of red brick in 1828, laid in English bond. It is by Jeptha Pacey.

Boatyards

ⓑ **Geordie's Boat Sales** Main Road Garage, Brothertoft, Boston PE20 3SW (01205 280311). 🚻🚿⛽D Pump out, long-term mooring, overnight mooring, gas safe engineering service, boat sales, Calor gas, boat safety examinations, new and second-hand chandlery, well-stocked grocery shop, ice creams, newspapers, stamps, postbox, chip & pin service. New ownership, with the site under development. *Open Mon-Fri 08.00-18.00, Sat 08.00-13.00.*

Pubs and Restaurants

🍺✕🍷 **Witham & Blues** Main Road, Langrick, Boston PE22 7AJ (01205 280546; www.withamandblues.com). A licensed New York style bar and grill, with separate café, serving light refreshments and meals *daily, L and E*. Also canalside ice cream parlour. Children and dogs welcome. Easy disabled access. Large garden with play area.

✕🍷 **Langrick Café** Main Road, Langrick, Boston PE22 7AH (01205 280023). Serves food *Mon-Sat 06.00-15.00*. Fully licensed.

HE WHO LAUGHS LAST . . .

The line of a dismantled railway closely follows the north bank of the River Witham – it was opened on 17 October 1848 following an agreement between the proprietors of the navigation and the Great Northern Railway company, which leased the river for 999 years at £10,545 per annum. The competition between steam packet boats and railway trains was intense, with the railway ultimately providing *fourth-class* carriages at the fare of a halfpenny per mile, undercutting anything the boats could do, and finally putting them out of business in 1863. Railway trains also took freight from the river – 19,535 tons of coal passed through the Grand Sluice at Boston in 1847 but, after the railway opened, this had fallen to 3,780 tons in 1854. A large railway warehouse was built in 1897 alongside Brayford Pool in Lincoln, with a branch dock to provide shipment facilities. But swans now occupy what was the dock, and the railway is no more. The River Witham, made navigable by the Romans, flows quietly on.

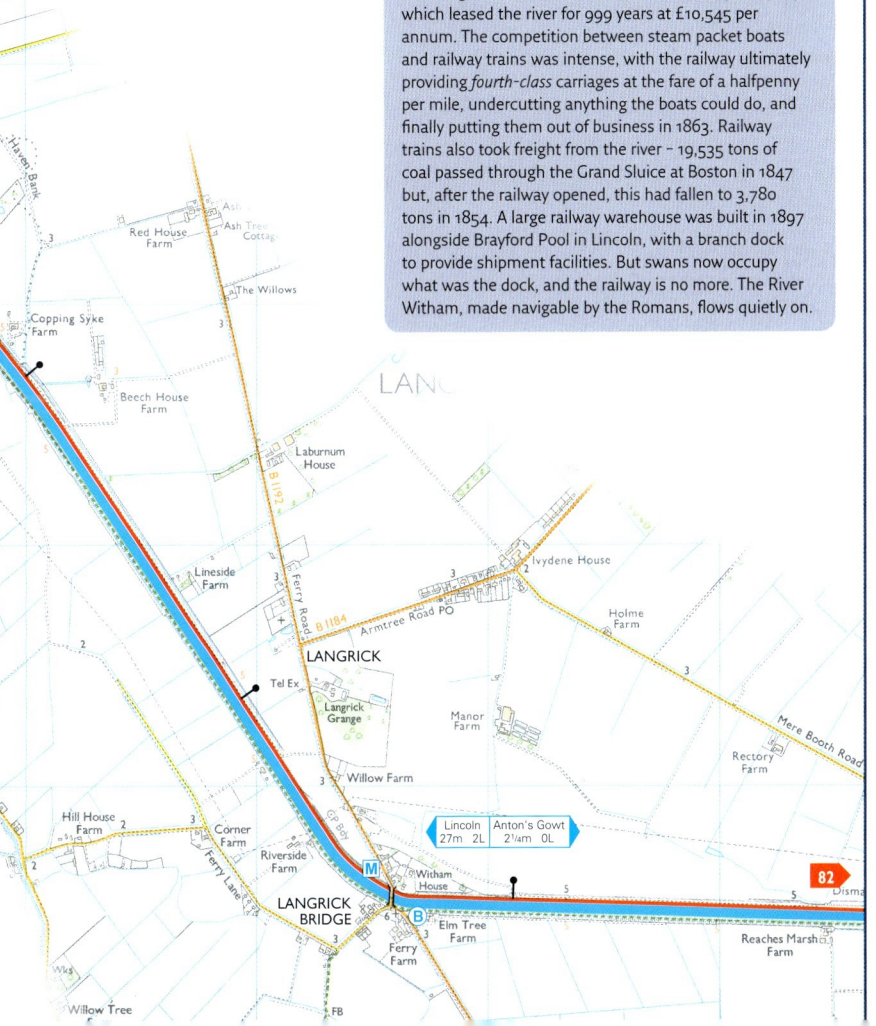

Fossdyke & Witham Navigations — Langrick Bridge

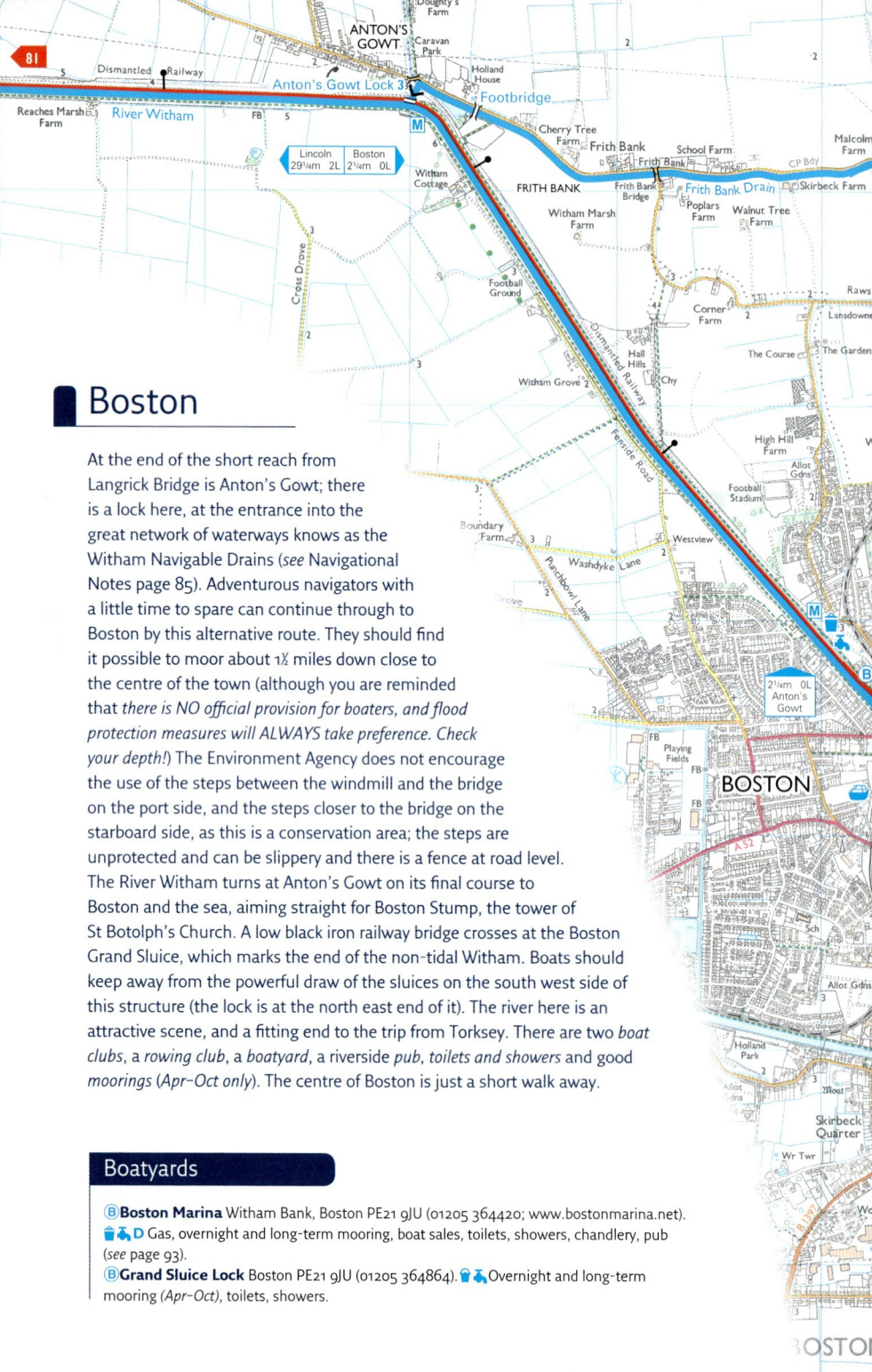

Boston

At the end of the short reach from Langrick Bridge is Anton's Gowt; there is a lock here, at the entrance into the great network of waterways knows as the Witham Navigable Drains (see Navigational Notes page 85). Adventurous navigators with a little time to spare can continue through to Boston by this alternative route. They should find it possible to moor about 1¼ miles down close to the centre of the town (although you are reminded that *there is NO official provision for boaters, and flood protection measures will ALWAYS take preference. Check your depth!*) The Environment Agency does not encourage the use of the steps between the windmill and the bridge on the port side, and the steps closer to the bridge on the starboard side, as this is a conservation area; the steps are unprotected and can be slippery and there is a fence at road level. The River Witham turns at Anton's Gowt on its final course to Boston and the sea, aiming straight for Boston Stump, the tower of St Botolph's Church. A low black iron railway bridge crosses at the Boston Grand Sluice, which marks the end of the non-tidal Witham. Boats should keep away from the powerful draw of the sluices on the south west side of this structure (the lock is at the north east end of it). The river here is an attractive scene, and a fitting end to the trip from Torksey. There are two *boat clubs*, a *rowing club*, a *boatyard*, a riverside *pub*, *toilets and showers* and good moorings *(Apr-Oct only)*. The centre of Boston is just a short walk away.

Boatyards

ⓑ **Boston Marina** Witham Bank, Boston PE21 9JU (01205 364420; www.bostonmarina.net). Gas, overnight and long-term mooring, boat sales, toilets, showers, chandlery, pub (see page 93).

ⓑ **Grand Sluice Lock** Boston PE21 9JU (01205 364864). Overnight and long-term mooring *(Apr-Oct)*, toilets, showers.

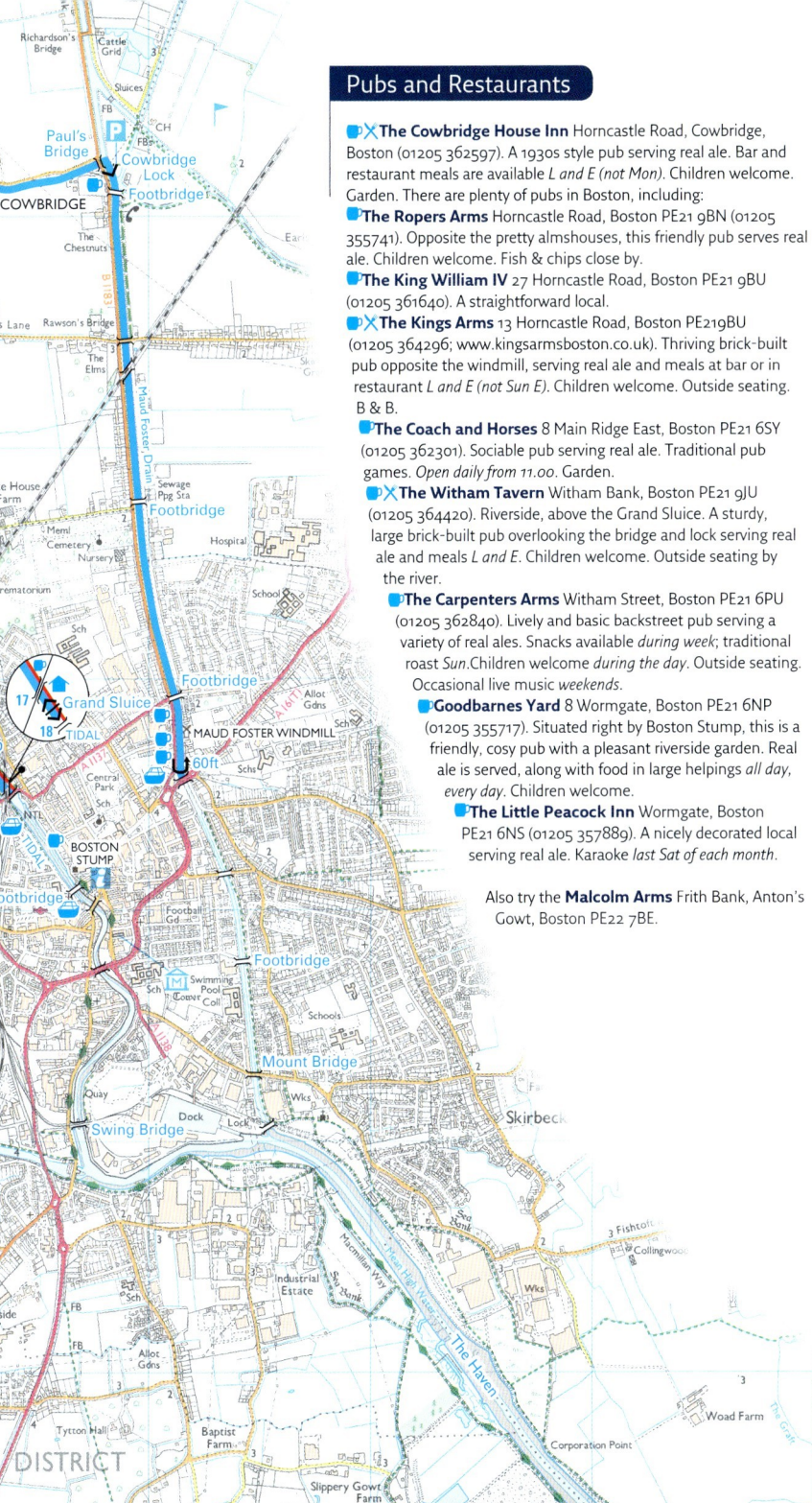

Pubs and Restaurants

🍺✖ **The Cowbridge House Inn** Horncastle Road, Cowbridge, Boston (01205 362597). A 1930s style pub serving real ale. Bar and restaurant meals are available *L and E (not Mon)*. Children welcome. Garden. There are plenty of pubs in Boston, including:

🍺 **The Ropers Arms** Horncastle Road, Boston PE21 9BN (01205 355741). Opposite the pretty almshouses, this friendly pub serves real ale. Children welcome. Fish & chips close by.

🍺 **The King William IV** 27 Horncastle Road, Boston PE21 9BU (01205 361640). A straightforward local.

🍺✖ **The Kings Arms** 13 Horncastle Road, Boston PE219BU (01205 364296; www.kingsarmsboston.co.uk). Thriving brick-built pub opposite the windmill, serving real ale and meals at bar or in restaurant *L and E (not Sun E)*. Children welcome. Outside seating. B & B.

🍺 **The Coach and Horses** 8 Main Ridge East, Boston PE21 6SY (01205 362301). Sociable pub serving real ale. Traditional pub games. *Open daily from 11.00*. Garden.

🍺✖ **The Witham Tavern** Witham Bank, Boston PE21 9JU (01205 364420). Riverside, above the Grand Sluice. A sturdy, large brick-built pub overlooking the bridge and lock serving real ale and meals *L and E*. Children welcome. Outside seating by the river.

🍺 **The Carpenters Arms** Witham Street, Boston PE21 6PU (01205 362840). Lively and basic backstreet pub serving a variety of real ales. Snacks available *during week*; traditional roast *Sun*. Children welcome *during the day*. Outside seating. Occasional live music *weekends*.

🍺 **Goodbarnes Yard** 8 Wormgate, Boston PE21 6NP (01205 355717). Situated right by Boston Stump, this is a friendly, cosy pub with a pleasant riverside garden. Real ale is served, along with food in large helpings *all day, every day*. Children welcome.

🍺 **The Little Peacock Inn** Wormgate, Boston PE21 6NS (01205 357889). A nicely decorated local serving real ale. Karaoke *last Sat of each month*.

Also try the **Malcolm Arms** Frith Bank, Anton's Gowt, Boston PE22 7BE.

- **Witham Navigable Drains**
This remarkable network of waterways north of Boston exists to drain and irrigate a flat and highly vulnerable tract of fenland. The network is a vital part of the local economy and of the defence of the area against the encroachment of the North Sea. Castle Dyke Drain, Houghbridge Drain, Newham Drain, Frith Bank Drain, Medlam Drain, Stonebridge Drain, West Fen Catchwater Drain, East Fen Catchwater Drain, Maud Foster Drain (these last three are classified as 'main river'), are only navigable *May–Sep*. Craft of 75' x 18' can pass through Anton's Gowt Lock, and the limiting size at Cowbridge is 70' x 10', but note there are no formal turning points on the Maud Foster Drain. *Information regarding water levels* can be obtained from the gauging board fitted to the tail wing of Anton's Gowt Lock (a zero reading indicates sufficient water for navigation). Access to Cowbridge Lock is by BW Watermate key or by telephoning 01205 310099 *during office hours*, or 01205 353758 *evenings and weekends*. However, it should always be remembered that navigation is NOT the top priority of the drainage authority, and sometimes a navigator is brought up sharply by a low bridge, often in a place where the channel is no wider than 30ft for several miles. Anton's Gowt Lock is the only entrance to these waterways. The best (widest) course is to head east from this lock, along Frith Bank Drain for 2 miles, to the great junction of waterways at Cowbridge Lock. From here you can go north towards the Lincolnshire Wolds, or south for about 1½ miles to the outskirts of Boston along the Maud Foster Drain. You can visit the centre of Boston via this non-tidal route. Such a visit should only be made between *May–Sep*, and be prepared to be flexible regarding your mooring. BE WARNED that levels on ALL the drains can rise or fall rapidly – moor cautiously, allowing plenty of slack in your warps. NOTE: THERE IS NO CONNECTION WITH THE TIDAL WITHAM VIA THE MAUD FOSTER DRAIN.

- **Boston**
Lincs. All services. An immensely attractive town at the mouth of the Witham, Boston has been an important seaport for over 800 years – indeed in 1205 it was second only to London. There are many splendid buildings in the town, but of course the most conspicuous among them is the famous Boston Stump – the 272ft tower of the parish church. There are two large market places, virtually contiguous. This area is the scene of much revelry in the spring, when the May Fair takes place. Under a charter of Elizabeth I dated 1573, the fair is held *3–10 May*.
St Botolph's Church beside the Witham. This enormous building, the largest parish church in England, is a magnificent example of the late Decorated architecture, and reflects the prosperity of Boston following the rise of its wool trade in the 13th C. The thriving guilds paid for the church, into which were built their respective chapels. Inside, the church is immensely spacious, the tall roof carried by slender quatrefoil columns. There are plenty of interesting things to look at here. The main south door is a remarkable piece of dovetailing, the pulpit is an elaborate Jacobean affair and the choir stalls are an excellent example of 14th-C carving. There are some good brasses and other monuments. The 272ft tower may be ascended, at a small charge; with 365 steps up a claustrophobic narrow turret, this can be hard going, but one may walk right around a balcony near the top and of course the view over the fenland is unbeatable – on a clear day Lincoln, 32 miles away, is visible. The openness of the work at the top of the tower has led to speculation that it perhaps at one time carried a light for the benefit of shipping; speculation also suggests that it was intended to carry a tall spire – otherwise why call it the stump? Whatever plans there may have been, the church is much loved by the inhabitants of Boston, Massachusetts, who have largely financed its structural repairs this century.
Boston Guildhall Museum South Street, Boston PE21 6HT (01205 365954). Near the river, south of the Market Place. An ancient and fascinating building constructed in 1450 for the Guild of St Mary, and now a museum illustrating Boston's history. It contains the cells then in 1607 held William Brewster and his friends after their unsuccessful attempt to leave the country. They were tried in the courtroom above. On the ground floor of this dark but historic building is the original kitchen. The roasting spit is self-propelled; the heat rising from the fire drives simple fans connected to a chain that operates the turning gear. This remarkably useful device is over 500 years old. There is also a Banqueting Hall, a Council Chamber and a Maritime Room to be visited. *Open Wed–Sat 10.30–15.30, Apr–Sep.*
Fydell House next to the Guildhall, South Square, Boston PE21 6HU (01205 351520). A superb town house built in 1726 by William Fydell, a successful wine merchant who was three times Mayor of Boston. The building was saved from demolition in 1935 by the pioneering Boston Preservation Trust, who have fully restored this and many other venerable buildings hereabouts. *Open Mon–Fri 10.00–16.00.*
Maud Foster Mill Willoughby Road, Boston PE21 9EG (01205 352188; www.maudfoster.co.uk). A beautifully preserved windmill, built in 1819. Organic stoneground flour is sold here. *Open all year Wed 10.00–17.00, Sat 10.00–17.00, B Hol Mons 10.00–17.00. Also Thu and Fri Jul–Aug, and all B Hol Mons 11.00–17.00. Charge.*
Tourist Information Centre Boston Guildhall Museum, South Street, Boston PE21 6HT (01205 365954; www.boston.gov.uk). The usual friendly and helpful service.

BOAT TRIPS
Maritime Leisure Cruises Jolly Sailor Café, Sluice Bridge, Boston PE21 9JU (07776 251878; www.maritimecruises.co.uk), offer public sea and river cruises and private charters aboard *Mystere* and *Boston Belle*.

NAVIGATIONAL NOTES

1. At Boston Grand Sluice the River Witham becomes tidal, leading down through Boston past the docks and into the Wash. It is most inadvisable to venture along the tideway unless you have a suitable, seagoing boat and are familiar with the currents and shallows in the Wash. The Grand Sluice is of course a sea lock, operated and manned at tide times by British Waterways, with gates facing both ways, but what is particularly interesting about it is that, unlike most tidal locks, the sea gates (referred to locally as doors) here are actually used at every tide. In other words the North Sea at high water is always above the level of the non-tidal Witham, and the sea gates close automatically twice a day to keep out the tide. This makes locking through the Grand Sluice somewhat complicated as far as times are concerned. It is not possible to lock up into the tide, since there is only one pair of outward facing gates, but on the other hand the tidal river practically dries out at low water. The only time to lock through is 2½ hrs prior to high water and 2½ hrs after high water. The lock will take boats up to 41' long by 14' wide by 14' height – below 12' height beam increases to 20', and larger craft can pass straight through when the tidal and non-tidal Witham 'make a level'. Draft to Bardney is 5'. A lock keeper is on duty in the nearby office: telephone 01205 364864/07712 010920 (or VHF Channel 74 – *only manned during tidal operations*) and you should *give as much notice as possible (minimum 24 hrs for craft wishing to use the lock 06.00-21.00 & 48 hrs for night passage 21.00-06.00)*. There is an answerphone for messages. The sluice is not automatically manned during the night. Telephone BW Emergency Helpline (0800 47 999 47) in an emergency. There is also overnight and long-term mooring *Apr–Oct* available for up to 50 boats here, with 🚻♿ and access ramps for the disabled. For access to Boston via the Maud Foster Drain, *see* Witham Navigable Drains opposite.
2. Passage across The Wash (which is classified as 'Tidal – Rough' for insurance purposes) is not deemed suitable for most inland craft and you may well not be able to obtain cover for the voyage.
3. When you have cleared the railway swing bridge, on the tidal side of the Witham, you should switch to VHF Channel 12 to monitor Boston Port information.
4. The footbridge on the Maud Foster Drain, close to the cemetery, is very low.
5. Mooring at Grand Sluice and on the Witham Navigable Drains is not allowed *Nov–Mar*.
6. No attempt should be made to navigate beyond Bargate Bridge, which is immediately south of the Maud Foster Mill.

WALKING & CYCLING
A series of leaflets describing walks around Boston, along the river and out to Freiston Shore and Frampton Marsh are available from local libraries. Visit www.boston.gov.uk or telephone 01205 354320 for more information.
Contact Sustrans (0845 113 00 65; www.sustrans.org.uk) for details of cycle routes and maps in the area, including NCR 1: the main traffic-free section of the route is the Water Rail Way and follows the River Witham.

INSECT LIFE
The *Banded Demoiselle* is an attractive damselfly, often found resting among waterside vegetation: it is commonly seen on the River Witham. Males are seen in small, fluttering groups hovering over water; the flight of the female is rather feeble. The body of the male is blue with a metallic sheen; the smoky wings show a conspicuous blue 'thumbprint' mark. The female has a green body, with metallic sheen, and greenish brown wings. Flies May–August.

Kyme Eau

This remarkable navigation leaves the Fossdyke & Witham at Chapel Hill (*see* page 79), slipping through flood gates and beginning its journey across the flat fenlands, hemmed in by high banks and seeming at times to be impossibly narrow. Turning sharply south the nicely restored Bottom Lock is soon reached, opened in November 1986, standing alone amidst the fields. After passing Terry Booth Farm the navigation turns to the west and makes a pretty passage through South Kyme, where there is a pub, Kyme Tower and the remains of a priory. Once again the waterway enters open farmland, although those in boats will see only the high grassy banks. There is a brief flurry of interest at Ferry Bridge, where the navigation makes a sharp turn to head towards the present limit of navigation at Cobblers Lock. Those who fancy a challenge can then undertake to walk the remaining unrestored section into Sleaford (beware, the towpath is, in places, blocked), passing what appear to be the disproportionately large and, as yet, unrestored locks.

● **Kyme Eau** (01522 689460; sleaford.navigation@ntlworld.com; www.sleafordnavigation.co.uk). This 13-mile-long navigation leaves the Witham at Chapel Hill to reach Sleaford to the south west, through seven locks. Slea is taken from the old English sleow, meaning a slimy, muddy stream. Plans for a commercially viable waterway were mooted as early as 1343, and Gilbert d'Umfraville, one of the Lords of Kyme, received royal assent for charging tolls on a part of the river. It was not until 1773, however, that local businessmen initiated plans to make the river navigable. Their scheme was not accepted, and it was not until 1792 that a new plan by Creasey and Jessop was put forward and accepted. The Sleaford Navigation Company was formed, supported by local people and the City of Boston. William Jessop was appointed as engineer, and local funds were made available. The navigation opened in 1794 amidst great celebration, and the eagerly anticipated boom in local prosperity duly followed. At one point plans were even mooted to extend the navigation westwards to Grantham thereby connecting back into the main waterways system. A builders, a coach-makers, a brickworks, an iron foundry, a mill and a brewery were all founded near Navigation Wharf in Sleaford. Navigation House, in Carre Street, still stands as a testimony to the waterway's early prosperity. However, as with all such local navigations, the coming of the railways brought about a rapid decline in prosperity. Tolls were lowered but to no avail, and navigation finally ceased around 1880. The opening in 1857 of the Boston, Sleaford and Midland Counties Railway had reduced the importance of the town of Sleaford, since it now became a mere stop on the line between Boston and Grantham. The Navigation Society was formed in 1976 and their restoration achievements have been considerable. Kyme Eau is now navigable through Kyme Eau Lower Lock (BW

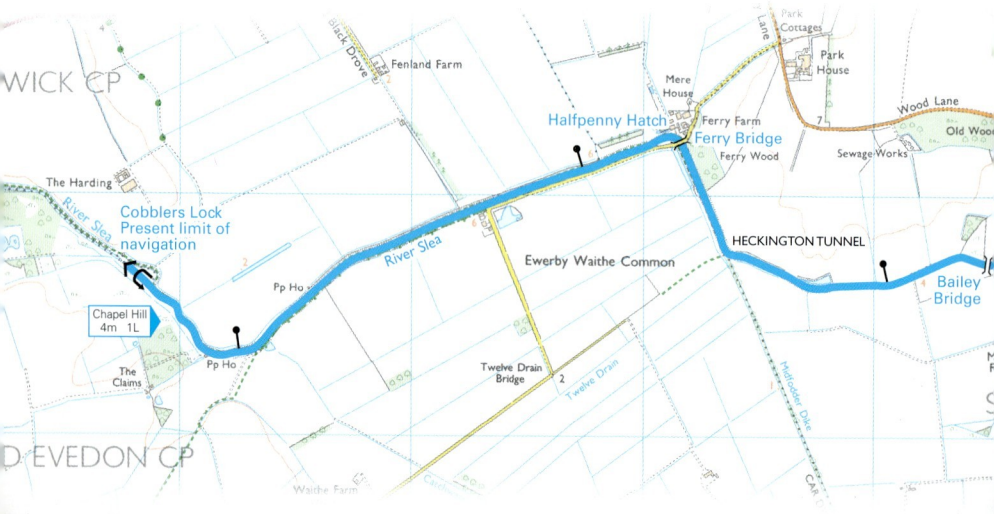

Watermate key needed) for over 7½ miles to Cobblers Lock, where it is possible to wind. Maximum dimensions are 70' 0" x 14' 0" with a headroom of 5' 6" and a draught of 2' 0". Progress can be slow on this navigation. From *Oct–Mar* the gates at Lower Kyme Lock are chained back for flood prevention reasons, and navigation is difficult in winter. Full restoration to Sleaford is planned.

- **South Kyme**
Lincs. *PO box, tel*. A quiet, remote and inauspicious fenland settlement, enlivened by the fine wooden sculpture of a kingfisher made by Simon Todd in 1990, and a handsome schoolhouse dated 1843. However, just to the west, and enclosed by the road and the navigation, are the timeless remains of a tower and priory, standing starkly amidst the fields. South Kyme Tower is a very impressive four-storey battlemented turret which dominates the surrounding flat landscape. It was built sometime between 1338 and 1381 by Sir Gilbert d'Umfraville, and was probably at one time part of a larger house, dismantled around 1720. It now stands desolate and empty, with no floors above the second which, due to its pattern, was known as the Chequer Chamber. The nearby church was built in 1890 onto the surviving fragments of a grand priory of Augustinian Canons, founded in 1169. A handsome Norman doorway survives, decorated with lions and other beasts, together with some fine Anglo-Saxon carving dating from the 7th or 8th C, at the east end of the north wall. It depicts trumpet spirals and foliage, and is reminiscent of early manuscripts.

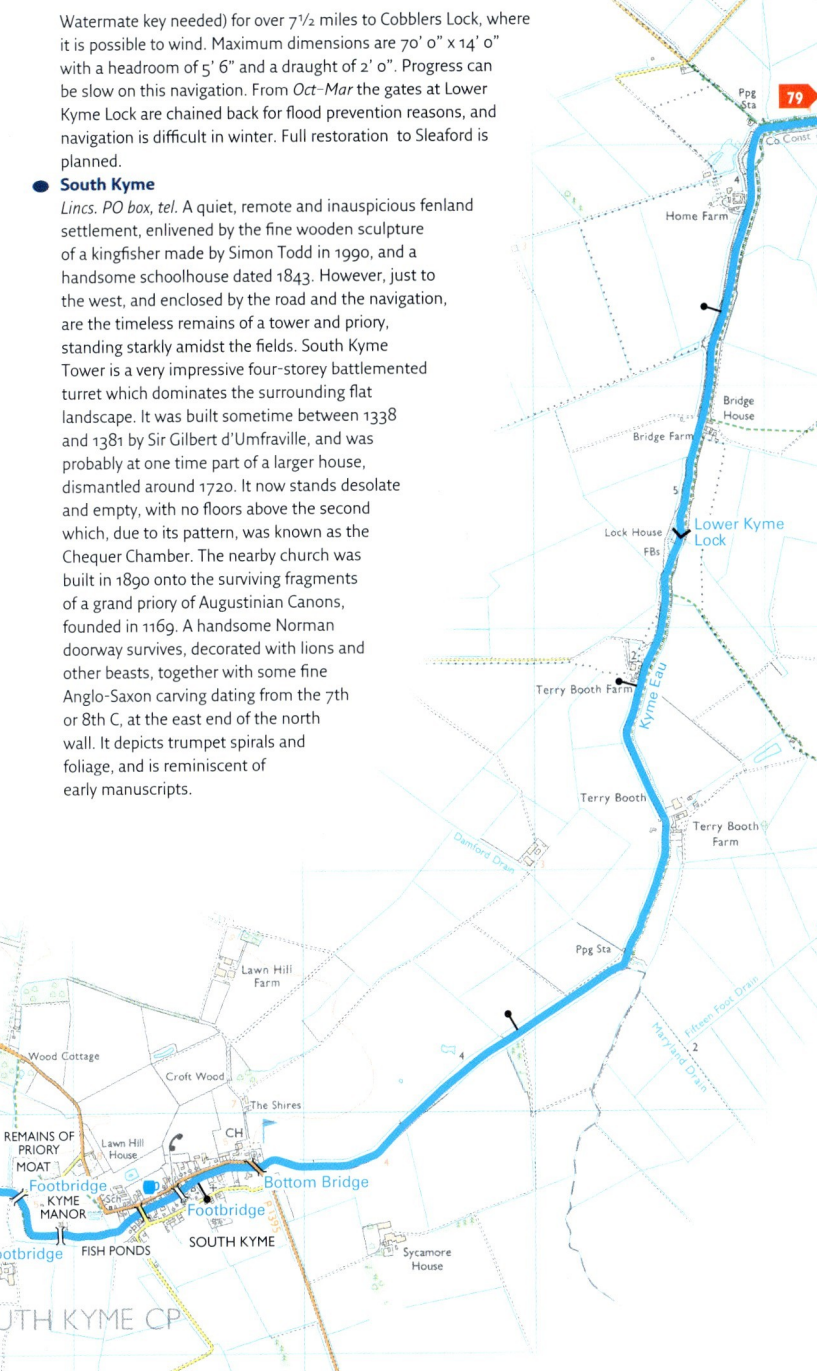

RIVER OUSE, RIVER URE AND RIPON CANAL

MAXIMUM DIMENSIONS

River Ouse

Goole to tail of Naburn Locks:
Length: 134'
Beam: 24' 6"
Headroom: 59' 11"

Naburn to Scarborough Bridge, York:
Length: 134'
Beam: 24' 6"
Headroom: 21' 6"
Draught: 8'

Scarborough Bridge, York to Swale Nab:
Length: 57' 6"
Beam: 15' 3"
Headroom: 19' 6"
Draught: 3' 6"

River Ure
Length: 57' 6"
Beam: 15'
Headroom: 10'
Draught: 3' 6"

Ripon Canal
Length: 57'
Beam: 14' 3"
Headroom: 8' 6"
Draught: 3' 6"

MILEAGE

RIPON to:
Boroughbridge: 7½ miles
York: 28¼ miles
Selby: 47¼ miles
GOOLE: 63 miles

Locks: 7

MANAGER

0113 281 6800
enquiries.northeast@britishwaterways.co.uk

The Rivers Ure and Ouse are prone to flooding. Ring British Waterways Customer Services at Leeds for further information – contact details as above.

The River Ouse, flowing as it does through the flat lands of north east England, has long been navigable to York, and has provided a natural transport artery for that city. Indeed, at one time, coal was brought in from Newcastle: a 200-mile journey involving a trip by keel down the Tyne, then by ship to the Humber and then on by barge up the Ouse, rather than undertake an overland journey of 20 miles from the coalfields of the West Riding. In 1766 it was decided to extend navigation along the River Ure and then by a short canal as far as Ripon. Proposals for this scheme were submitted by John Smeeton. Royal assent was granted in 1767 and work began. Milby Lock and Cut were completed in 1769 and a cast iron bridge, one of the first in the country, was built over the canalised section at Boroughbridge. This was replaced in 1946. This northerly section of the inland waterways network was immediately prosperous, with Boroughbridge serving as the port for Knaresborough, one of England's greatest linen manufacturing towns.

On the lower Ouse the Aire & Calder Navigation Company obtained an Act of Parliament in 1820 to extend to Goole, where a brand new port was to be created. When it opened in 1826, the population was 450: this increased to more than 20,000 over the following 100 years. The canal company built the grand and stately church of St John here in 1843–8.

The River Ouse escaped nationalisation in 1948, and until recently there was commercial traffic as far as Selby. Above York the river is quieter and more suited to pleasure boats; beyond Boroughbridge the surroundings are particularly attractive with the added bonus of a short section of canal into Ripon. Restoration of this navigation was completed in 1996. Cruising Notes for the Ripon Canal and the Rivers Ure and Ouse are available from British Waterways at Leeds (0113 281 6800) or downloadable from www.waterscape.com/boatersguides.

Ripon

The demure, yet pretty Ripon Canal terminates in a fine basin overlooked by a handsomely restored warehouse, tasteful and sympathetically designed new dwellings, along with some fine older houses. The navigation, having lain derelict for years, now provides good moorings, excellent *facilities* including *showers* and *toilets* and easy access to Ripon. Leaving the city, the initial half-mile or so is closely accompanied by a main road. This is soon left behind, however, as the waterway swings to the south and descends Rhodesfield and Bell Furrows locks, passing to the west of Ripon Marina and the racecourse through quiet, open countryside. Ripon Boat Club's marina occupies a pretty spot near Littlethorpe, where the canal makes its approach to the River Ure, falling through Oxclose Lock. Entering the river, the character of the navigation is immediately less demure as it snakes towards Westwick Cut and Lock, set amidst flat farmland, with trees by the river. This unremarkable but pretty countryside makes Newby Hall and its attractively landscaped gardens stand out; its jetty beckons the passing boater, and its miniature railway makes quite a startling impression. At Cherry Island Wood there is another sharp turn as the handsome village of Roecliffe is approached.

- **Ripon**
N. Yorks. PO, tel, stores, chemist, garage, bank, takeaways. The horn you will hear blown at 9 o'clock each evening is that of the City Wakeman, dressed in traditional clothes and fulfiling the 1000-year-old custom of setting the watch. This traditionally signified that the town was under the Wakeman's care for the night. If there was then a robbery, he was obliged to make good the loss! Alas this is no longer the case today. His two-storey 14th-C half-timbered house, standing in the square, was used as a museum but unfortunately the building became unsafe for visitors and the museum and Tourist Information Centre were moved to new premises. The centre of Ripon remains elegant and well preserved, with narrow winding streets enclosed by buildings of many periods, mostly brick built. The fine open square is dominated by a tall obelisk erected in 1781, which commemorates William Aislabie of Studley Royal's 60-year membership of Parliament. On the south side of the square is the imposing town hall, built in 1801 by James Wyatt.
Ripon Cathedral Minster Road, Ripon HG4 1QS (01765 603462; www.riponcathedral.org.uk). The central tower of this imposing building stands over a Saxon crypt, believed to have been built by St Wilfred c.670. Wilfred's original church was destroyed in 950 by King Edred of Northumberland, and rebuilding did not begin again until about 1180. It was Archbishop of York Roger de Pont l'Évêque who began the reconstruction, with the superb west front being completed around 1230. Further substantial work was carried out by Christopher Scune, who built the Gothic nave around 1520. The building was restored in 1832, with the re-creation of the diocese and elevation to cathedral status. Look out for the splendidly carved choir stalls 1489-94, the work of the Bromflets, a local family of wood carvers, and an interesting 1896 Arts & Crafts pulpit associated with William Morris. Admission by donation.

Yorkshire Law and Order Museums (01765 690799; www.riponmuseums.co.uk). Three award-winning museums. The **Prison & Police Museum** St Marygate, Ripon HG4 1LX is housed in part of the former House of Correction and Liberty Gaol which also housed the West Riding Constabulary for a while. The history of policing is traced through collections of police and prison memorabilia; visitors can also experience prison life as it was in Victorian times. The **Workhouse Museum** Sharon View, Allhallowgate, Ripon HG4 1LE, features the original Workhouse Kitchen Garden which has been restored and features vegetables and fruit from the 1890s. The museum itself provides an insight into the reality of life in a Victorian workhouse.
The **Courthouse Museum** Minster Road, Ripon HG4 1QS, is housed the original, restored Georgian museum and includes a 19th-century court room scene. The museums are child-friendly and designed for all the family. Regular special events. *Open Mon-Sun 13.00-16.00, extended during school holidays.* Charge.
Tourist Information Centre Minster Road, Ripon HG4 1QT (01765 604625). *Open Apr-Oct, Mon-Sat 10.00-17.00 & Sun 13.00-16.00; Nov-Mar, Thu & Sat 10.00-16.00* for a friendly and helpful service. You can purchase head of canal plaques and walking trail leaflets from here.
Fountains Abbey & Studley Royal Water Garden Fountains, Ripon HG4 3DY (01765 608888; www.fountainsabbey.org.uk). Three miles south west of Ripon (bus service from the city). *NT*. The glorious ruins of a 12th-C Cistercian abbey and monastic waterwheel set amidst 100 acres of beautiful grounds. Founded in 1132, this was one of the most complete survivors of the dissolution. The superb water garden was designed by John Aislabie and his son William in the 1700s. Enjoy the Temple of Fame, the Octagon Tower and Serpentine Tunnel. Look out for the ghosts of a choir of monks. *Open Mar-Oct, daily 10.00-16.00, Nov-Feb, daily 10.00-16.00. Closed Nov-Jan, Fri.* St Mary's Church is *open Apr-Sep, daily 12.00-16.00.* Charge. Café and shop.

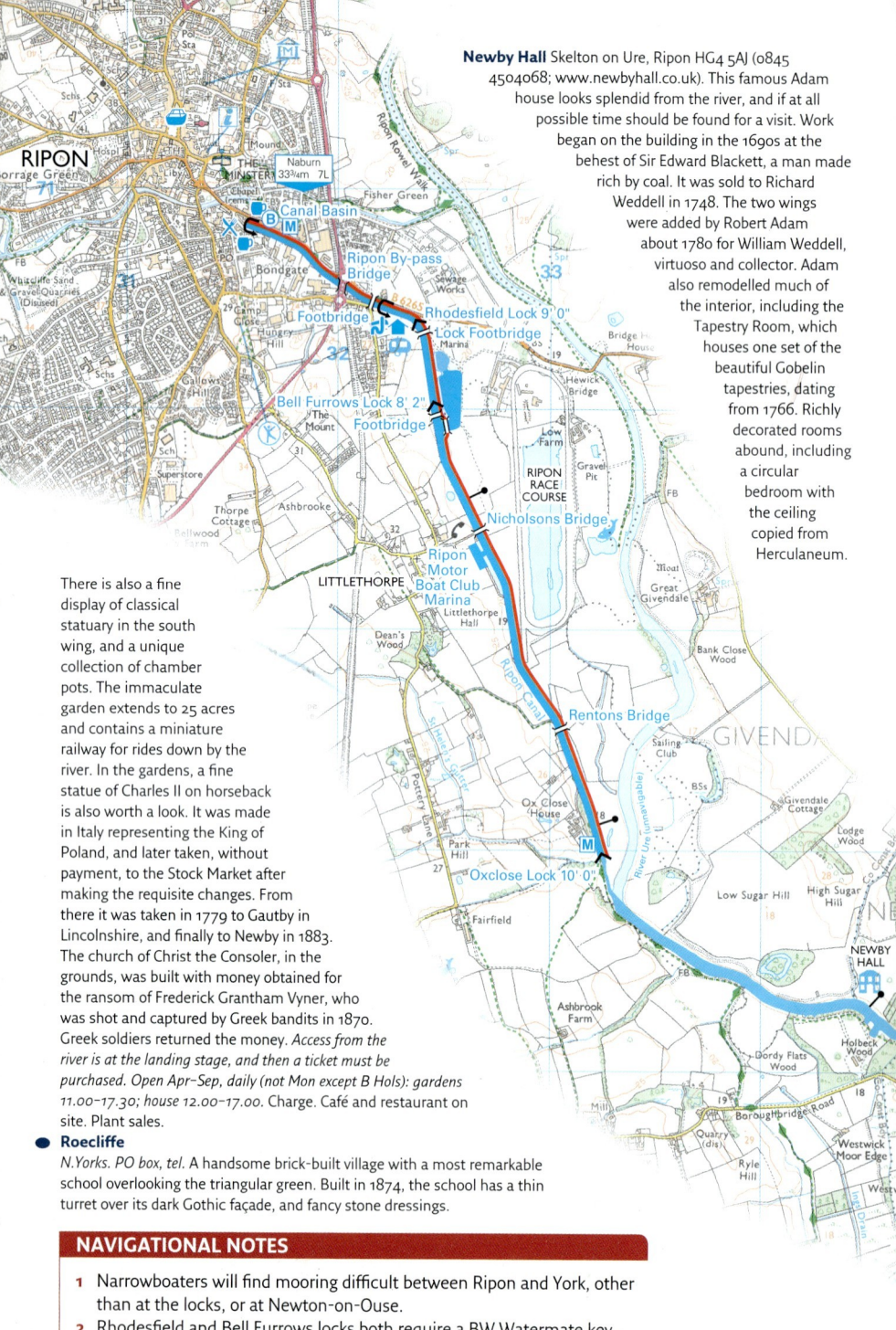

Newby Hall Skelton on Ure, Ripon HG4 5AJ (0845 4504068; www.newbyhall.co.uk). This famous Adam house looks splendid from the river, and if at all possible time should be found for a visit. Work began on the building in the 1690s at the behest of Sir Edward Blackett, a man made rich by coal. It was sold to Richard Weddell in 1748. The two wings were added by Robert Adam about 1780 for William Weddell, virtuoso and collector. Adam also remodelled much of the interior, including the Tapestry Room, which houses one set of the beautiful Gobelin tapestries, dating from 1766. Richly decorated rooms abound, including a circular bedroom with the ceiling copied from Herculaneum. There is also a fine display of classical statuary in the south wing, and a unique collection of chamber pots. The immaculate garden extends to 25 acres and contains a miniature railway for rides down by the river. In the gardens, a fine statue of Charles II on horseback is also worth a look. It was made in Italy representing the King of Poland, and later taken, without payment, to the Stock Market after making the requisite changes. From there it was taken in 1779 to Gautby in Lincolnshire, and finally to Newby in 1883. The church of Christ the Consoler, in the grounds, was built with money obtained for the ransom of Frederick Grantham Vyner, who was shot and captured by Greek bandits in 1870. Greek soldiers returned the money. *Access from the river is at the landing stage, and then a ticket must be purchased. Open Apr-Sep, daily (not Mon except B Hols): gardens 11.00-17.30; house 12.00-17.00. Charge. Café and restaurant on site. Plant sales.*

● **Roecliffe**
N.Yorks. PO box, tel. A handsome brick-built village with a most remarkable school overlooking the triangular green. Built in 1874, the school has a thin turret over its dark Gothic façade, and fancy stone dressings.

NAVIGATIONAL NOTES

1 Narrowboaters will find mooring difficult between Ripon and York, other than at the locks, or at Newton-on-Ouse.
2 Rhodesfield and Bell Furrows locks both require a BW Watermate key. There are moorings above Rhodesfield and Oxclose Locks.

WALKING & CYCLING
The towpath on the Ripon Canal is excellent, however cycling is not allowed. The towpath on the river is only approachable in parts.

Pubs and Restaurants

🍺**The Navigation** 1 Canal Road, Ripon HG4 1QN (01765 605676). Spacious and friendly pub just across the road from the pretty canal basin. Real ales. Outside seating at the front.

🍺**The Water Rat** 24 Bondgate Green, Ripon HG4 1QW (01765 602251; www.thewaterrat.co.uk). Just across the main road from the basin, this attractive and friendly pub serves real ale, along with bar meals *L and E, and all day Sat and Sun*. Children welcome. Conservatory and benches outside overlook the River Skell and Alma weir.

✗**Forge Farm Shop & Café** The Old Smithy, Canal Wharf, Ripon HG4 1AQ (01765 698249). Popular farm shop and sandwich bar by the canal.

🍺✗**The Crown Inn** Roecliffe, Boroughbridge YO51 9LY (01423 322300; www.crowninnroecliffe.co.uk). A pretty end-of-terrace hotel, restaurant and bar, with real fire for the winter and outdoor seating for summer. Real ale and bar and restaurant meals *L and E*. Children welcome. Disabled access. The inn has its own smokehouse and sells kippers and smoked salmon. B & B.

WORKING ON SHIFTING SANDS

Our roads are now overcrowded – everyone who uses them knows this. In a region where there is much heavy industry, and good access to water transport, it makes sound sense to move bulk goods by barge. Acaster's Water Transport, Swinefleet, Goole DN14 8DR, who, amongst other activities, once transported newsprint from Goole to the Yorkshire Evening Press in York (regrettably, this now goes by road), is a small family business which manages to survive in an uncertain world. Graham Acaster and his wife might work in Goole Docks on *Little Shifta* and *Little Shuva*, or on the Trent with their son Karl, who shifts bulk loads of gravel to Goole. Acaster's have also adapted their boats *River Star*, *Twite* and *Poem 24* at Waddington's yard to create a 600-ton barge, taking the name *River Star*, to move aggregates efficiently from Besthorpe Quarry, near Cromwell Lock.

In spite of our national reluctance to use modern water transport, Acasters remain stoically cheerful and optimistic, and totally devoted to the cause. For the sake of the environment, let us hope they remain in business, and that others join them.

Boatyards

ⓑ**Ripon Racecourse Marina** Boroughbridge Road, Ripon HG4 1UG (01482 609960; www.bwml.co.uk). Pump out, toilets, showers, long-term mooring.

ⓑ**Wharf Services Ripon** 12 Canal Wharf, Bondgate Green, Ripon HG4 1AQ (01765 609777; www.wharfservices.co.uk). Crane, washing, sandblasting, repainting, blacking, sign writing, storage.

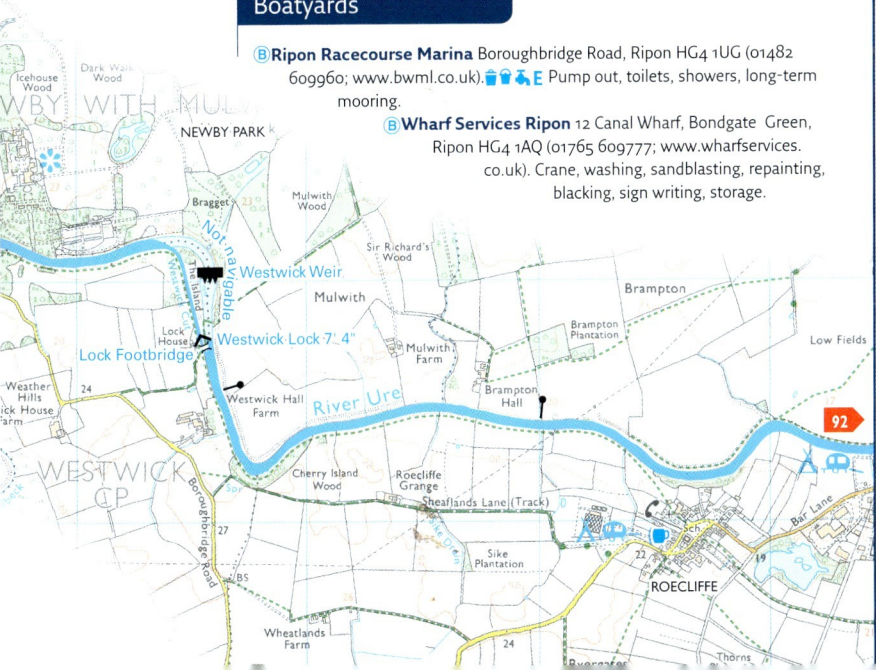

Boroughbridge

The navigation swings under Arrows Bridge and the busy A1 as it makes its approach to Boroughbridge, passing the marina and finally entering Milby Cut, leaving the weir stream to the south. The town lies beyond the weir stream, and imposes little, but there are good moorings, a *sanitary station, showers and toilets*, so a stop to explore is worthwhile. Beyond the town is open country as the river gently winds through pleasant farmland.

Pubs and Restaurants

The Fox and Hounds Langthorpe, York YO51 9BZ (01423 322717; www.foxandhoundslangthorpe.co.uk). Originally a cottage with an adjacent granary. Pub and restaurant serving real ale. Children welcome if eating. Outside seating. Regular entertainment. *Open Mon–Fri E and all day Sat–Sun*. Meals served *Tue–Sat E, Sun 12.00–15.00*.

The Grantham Arms Milby, Boroughbridge, York YO51 9BW (01423 322261; www.granthamarms.com). Canalside pub serving real ale and freshly prepared bar meals *L and E (all day Sat & Sun)*. Children welcome, and there is outside seating. B & B.

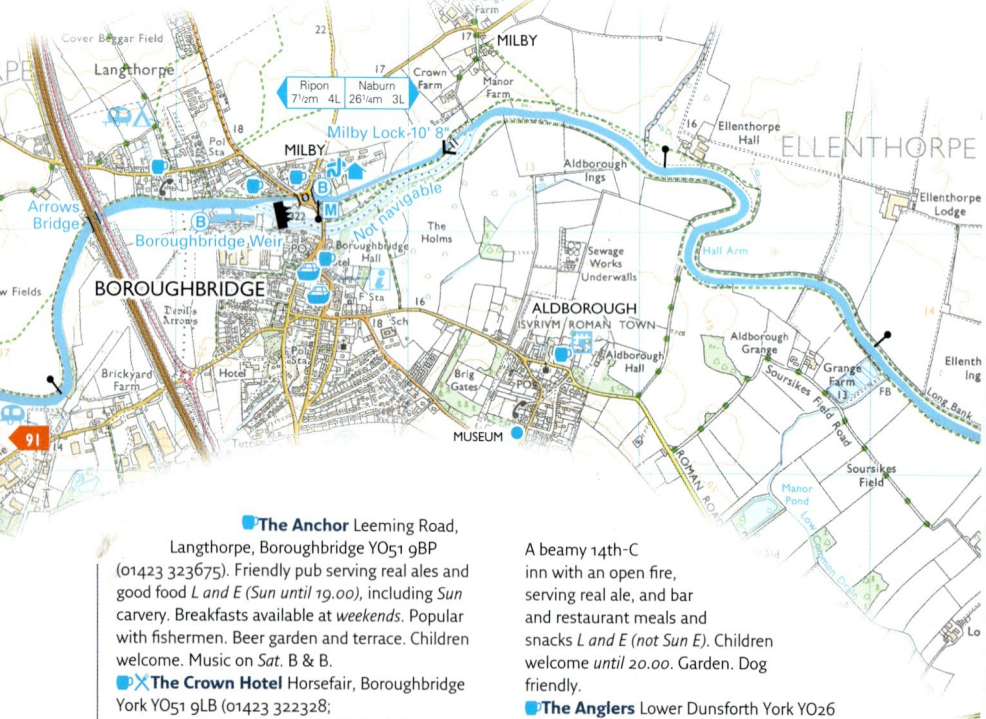

The Anchor Leeming Road, Langthorpe, Boroughbridge YO51 9BP (01423 323675). Friendly pub serving real ales and good food *L and E (Sun until 19.00)*, including *Sun* carvery. Breakfasts available at *weekends*. Popular with fishermen. Beer garden and terrace. Children welcome. Music on *Sat*. B & B.

The Crown Hotel Horsefair, Boroughbridge York YO51 9LB (01423 322328; www.crownboroughbridge.co.uk). Real ale. Bar meals *all day, every day*, and restaurant meals *L and E*. Children welcome. The courtyard is a leisure club with a sauna, gym and indoor pool. B & B.

The Ship Inn Low Road, Aldborough, Boroughbridge, York YO5 9ER (01423 322749).

A beamy 14th-C inn with an open fire, serving real ale, and bar and restaurant meals and snacks *L and E (not Sun E)*. Children welcome *until 20.00*. Garden. Dog friendly.

The Anglers Lower Dunsforth York YO26 9SA (01423 322537). Large and welcoming country inn, with open fires, mainly catering for fishermen, golfers, walkers and race-goers. Real ales. Children welcome, and there is a garden and a games room. *Open daily except Wed*.

Boatyards

B Boroughbridge Marina Valuation Lane, Boroughbridge YO51 9LJ (01423 323400). 🎁🚻♿
E (Pump out at BW facility 300yds away). Long-term and visitor moorings, slipway, gas, chandlery, toilets, showers, fuel available nearby, laundrette, marine engineering, facilities for narrowboat lifting, dry dock, BBQ and picnic area.

B Canal Garage Milby, Boroughbridge YO519BL (01423 322318). D Gas, engine repairs and service.

• **Boroughbridge**
N. Yorks. PO, tel, stores, bank, butcher, chemist, takeaways, garage. The Crown Hotel, just up the road from the bridge, used, when the town sat astride the Great North Road, to have stabling for 100 horses. The first mail coach passed through in 1789, but now the A1 thankfully bypasses the town. Boroughbridge was the 44th of some 400 settlements established by the Normans and their successors between 1066 and 1348 as part of a plan to unite their new kingdom, and served as the port for Knaresborough, 7 miles away. The present river bridge dates from between 1562 and 1784, having been continually repaired during that period. It replaced an earlier wooden structure, which in turn had replaced a ford downstream near Milby. The well, in the Market Place, is 250ft deep.

Tourist Information Centre 1 Hall Square, Boroughbridge, YO51 9AN (01423 323373; www.boroughbridge.org.uk). *Open Easter-Oct, Mon-Fri 10.00-16.00, Sat 10.00-12.00; winter Sat only.*

Battle of Boroughbridge 1322 Rebel barons led by the Earl of Lancaster struggled with Edward II's supporters for control of the bridge over the River Ure. Eventually Lancaster was taken to his own castle at Pontefract, where he was executed.

Battle of Myton 1319 North of Swale Nab. Known as the white battle from the number of churchmen who were involved. While Edward II was holding Berwick-upon-Tweed under siege, an army of Scots infiltrated into the north of England. They met a hastily assembled English force at Myton and defeated them. Heavy losses were incurred on the English side with some 3000 killed, including 300 priests.

• **Aldborough**
N. Yorks. Tel. A Georgian village less than a mile from Boroughbridge, with a May pole, restored in 1999, on the green. It was once the walled Roman town of *Isurium Brigantum*, and before that *Iseur*, built by the ancient Britons. It functioned for the Romans as the civitas, or civilian capital of the Brigantes, a tribe who occupied most of what is now Yorkshire and Lancashire. Once enclosed by mighty red sandstone walls, perhaps 20ft high, the remains are modest but interesting.

Aldborough Roman Site Aldborough, Boroughbridge, York YO51 9ES (01423 322768; www.english-heritage.org.uk). Relics gathered from the Roman town. Museum and grounds *open early Apr-Sep, daily 10.00-13.00 and 14.00-18.00.* Charge. Telephone or visit website to confirm winter opening. Suitable for picnics.

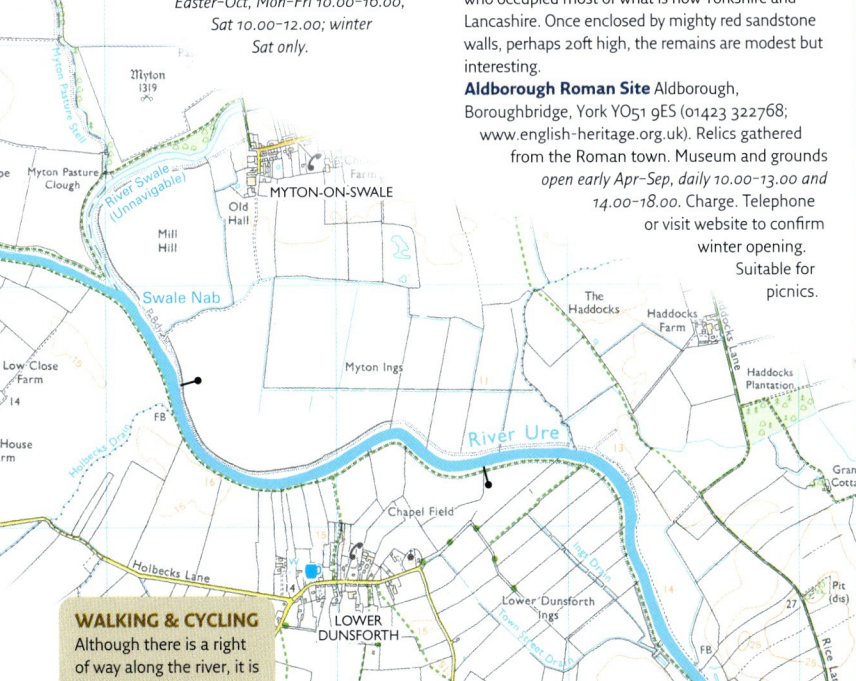

WALKING & CYCLING
Although there is a right of way along the river, it is often obstructed.

Linton Lock

The river continues to meander gently through quiet, unprepossessing countryside with villages scattered alongside, but never actually on its banks. The rickety toll bridge at Aldwark provides the only river crossing on this stretch, emphasising its remote nature. Just before the river turns east at Cuddy Shaw Reach its name changes from Ure to Ouse, where the Ouse Gill Beck joins. To the north is Linton-on-Ouse RAF airfield, where training aeroplanes come and go noisily during the week, shattering the peace of an otherwise quiet area. The navigation falls through Linton Lock, leaving a fine large weir and salmon leap to the south. There are useful *boater services*, plus a *pub/restaurant*, here. The river then turns sharply to the west of Newton-on-Ouse to pass the extensive and well-tended grounds of Beningbrough Park and Hall, rich with trees and beautifully landscaped. As the river widens to accept the River Nidd, the outstandingly attractive and interesting village of Nun Monkton, and its splendid church, is passed.

NAVIGATIONAL NOTES

Keep right over to the north bank below Linton Lock, using the buoyed channel, to avoid shoals.

WALKING & CYCLING

The towpath is virtually non-existent on this stretch, apart from through Beningbrough Park.

Pubs and Restaurants

●**The Bay Horse Inn** Aldwark, Alne, York YO61 1UB (01347 838324). Village inn serving real ale and bar meals *L and E*. Children welcome and there is a garden.

●✕**The Lockhouse Café** Linton-on-Ouse, York YO30 2AZ (01347 848844; www.thelockhousecafeyork.co.uk). Riverside, in the lock house. Licensed pub/café serving freshly made food using locally sourced ingredients *summer, daily 09.00–21.00, winter E (breakfast and lunches available winter if pre-booked)*; fish and chips available for take away. Children welcome. Sports TV and wifi.

●**The Dawnay Arms** Newton-on-Ouse, York YO30 2BR (01347 848345; www.thedawnayatnewton. co.uk). In an 18th-C listed building, restaurant meals *L and E*. Children welcome. Large riverside garden, and moorings for patrons. *Closed Mon.*

●**The Blacksmiths Arms** Cherry Tree Avenue, Newton-on-Ouse, York YO30 2BN (01347 848249; www.blacksmiths-newton.co.uk). Opposite the church, this warm and friendly pub offers real ale. Home-cooked food is served *L (Fri-Sun) and E (all week)*. Children welcome, garden.

●✕**The Alice Hawthorn Inn** The Green, Nun Monkton, York YO26 8EW (01423 330303). Real ale is available in this handsome village inn, and food is served in the bar, dining room or restaurant *L and E*. Children welcome and there is a garden. Camping by arrangement.

River Ouse, River Ure and Ripon Canal — Linton Lock

- **Aldwark**
N. Yorks. PO (at the Bay Horse Inn), tel. The pretty pebble and brick church was built to an original design in 1846–53 by E. B. Lamb.
- **Linton-on-Ouse**
N. Yorks. PO, tel, stores. A village totally overwhelmed by the adjoining RAF airfield.
- **Newton-on-Ouse**
N. Yorks. The church of All Saints was built in 1849 for Miss Dawnay by G. T. Andrews. The base of the tower dates from the 12th C: the top is finished with a fine recessed spire.
Beningbrough Hall Beningbrough, York YO30 1DD (01904 470666; www.nationaltrust.org.uk). NT. A very fine Georgian house built in 1716, where most of the rooms have no electric light. With one of the most impressive baroque interiors in England, the room settings are atmospheric with over 100 portraits and wood-carvings on loan from the National Portrait Gallery. Also on view is a glimpse of life 'downstairs', in the Victorian laundry. Art exhibitions, children's play area, beautiful gardens. Beningbrough Hall was featured as 'Biddenborough Hall' in an episode of the Darling Buds of May TV series. Open Mar–Oct, Sat–Wed 11.00–17.30, also Thu and Fri during school holidays, check website or telephone for winter opening. Charge. Restaurant.
- **Nun Monkton**
N. Yorks. PO box, tel. Following the Norman conquest the village, together with other surrounding estates, was given to the Norman knight Osbern de Arches. It was one of Osbern's descendants, William de Arches, who chose this site at the junction of the rivers Nidd and Ouse to found a priory of Benedictine nuns dedicated to the Blessed Virgin Mary. Today only the nun's chapel survives as the church of St Mary. Built 1153–80 in Early English style, there is a late Norman porch and some very fine arcading above plain lower windows, access to which is gained via a staircase in the north west angle. Between the windows are 12 niches, which probably once contained effigies of the apostles. Set into the floor beneath the present altar is the pre-Reformation stone altar, with five crosses cut into it, thought to represent the five wounds of Christ. The church is quite properly considered to be one of the finest in Yorkshire, and will amply repay a visit. The village green has a splendid May pole, and a fine duck pond.

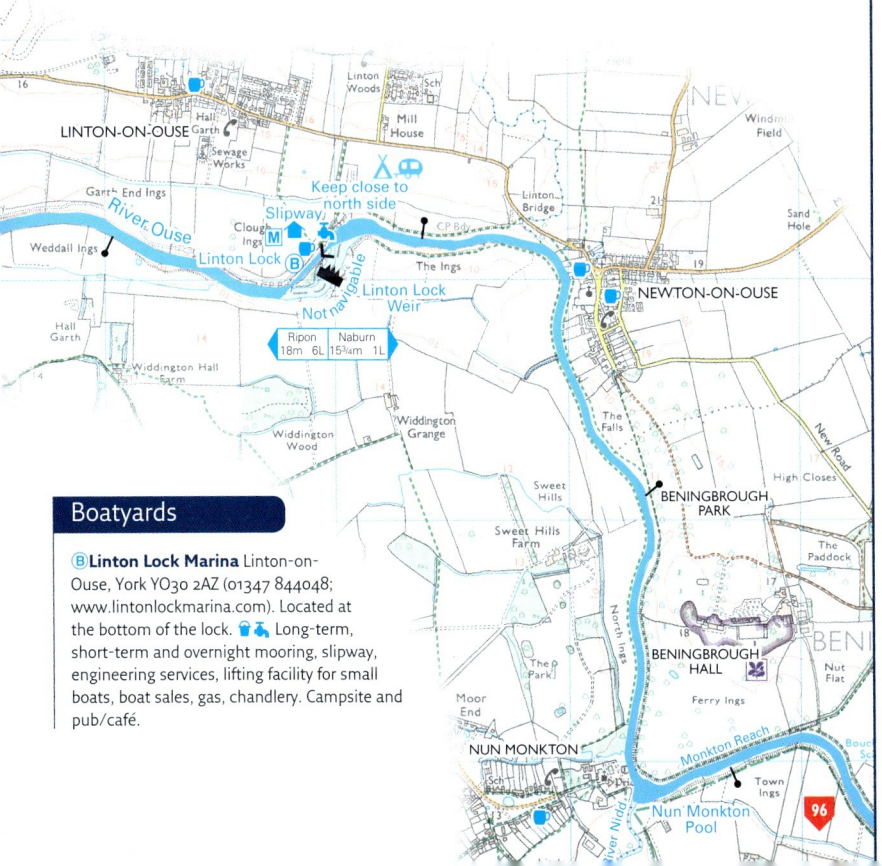

Boatyards

- **Ⓑ Linton Lock Marina** Linton-on-Ouse, York YO30 2AZ (01347 844048; www.lintonlockmarina.com). Located at the bottom of the lock. Long-term, short-term and overnight mooring, slipway, engineering services, lifting facility for small boats, boat sales, gas, chandlery. Campsite and pub/café.

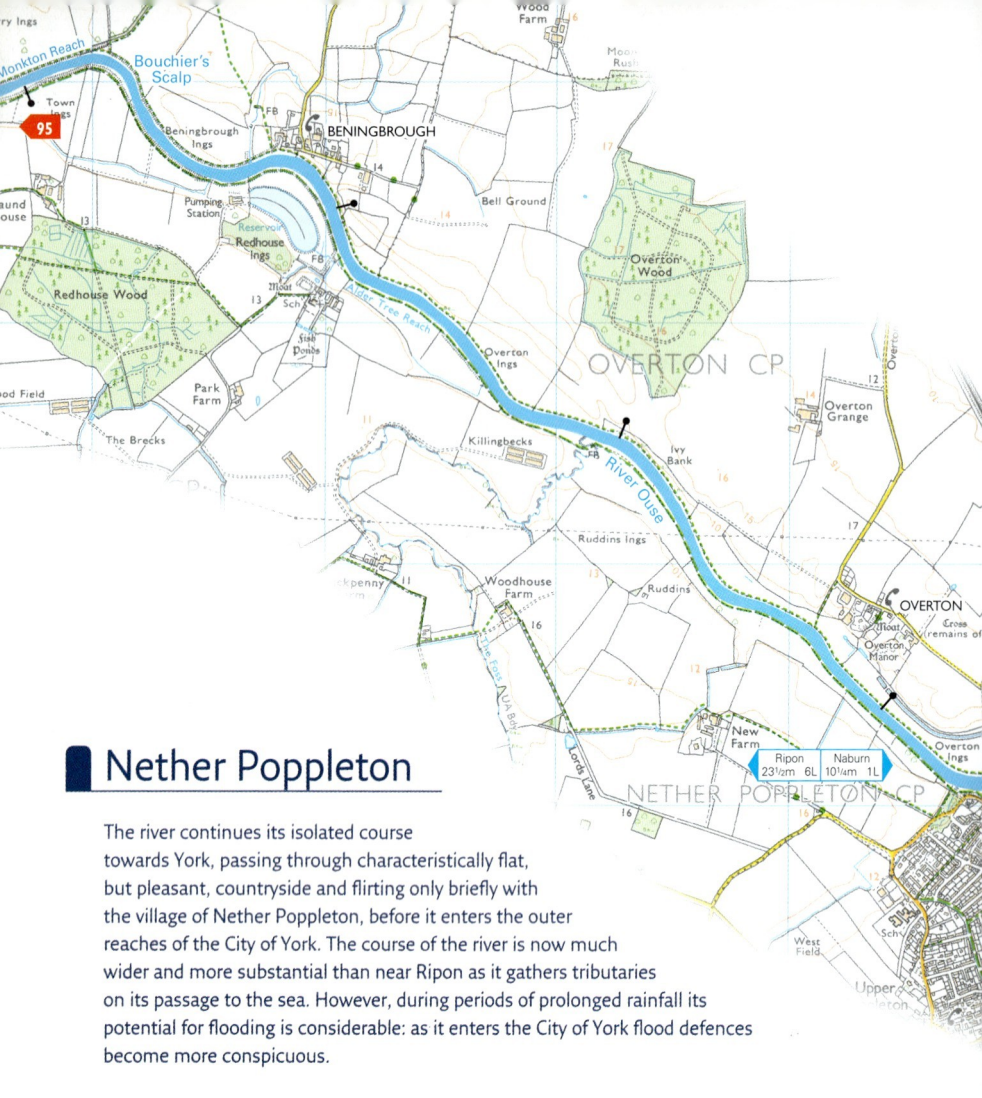

Nether Poppleton

The river continues its isolated course towards York, passing through characteristically flat, but pleasant, countryside and flirting only briefly with the village of Nether Poppleton, before it enters the outer reaches of the City of York. The course of the river is now much wider and more substantial than near Ripon as it gathers tributaries on its passage to the sea. However, during periods of prolonged rainfall its potential for flooding is considerable: as it enters the City of York flood defences become more conspicuous.

- **Beningbrough**
  N. Yorks. PO box, tel. A remote farming settlement by the river.
- **Overton**
  N. Yorks. A tiny settlement around Overton Manor, which the abbots of St Mary, York once used as their major country house. The moat can still be traced, at the north end of the village, and a farmhouse near the church re-used the stones.
- **Nether Poppleton**
  N. Yorks. PO, tel, stores. A commuter village for York, most attractive by the river. The small church of St Everilda, at the far eastern end, is of Norman origin, with relics of 14th- and 15th-C glass in the east window. There are also some fine monuments to the Huttons: Sir Thomas, 1620, is depicted kneeling; Ursula, her husband and another woman, c.1640, are smaller but also kneel; Anne, 1651, is less formal, with more movement in the figure.
- **Skelton**
  N. Yorks. PO, tel. The church of St Giles is a superb example of Early English work, built c.1240, by the masons who had worked on York Minster, for Walter de Gray, Archbishop of York. Neatly constructed from magnesian limestone, there is no tower – just a bellcote separating the nave from the chancel. Toolmarks left by the masons can be seen inside, together with their marks. It was restored 1814–18 by Henry Graham, who was nineteen when the work started.

Pubs and Restaurants

🛈 **The Lord Nelson** 9 Main Street, Nether Poppleton, York YO26 6HS. A handsome brick-built pub serving real ale. Food is available L and E. Children are welcome and there is a garden with a bouncy castle and play area to amuse them. Caravan site to the rear of the pub.

WALKING & CYCLING
There is a right of way on the north bank from Beningbrough to Rawcliffe.

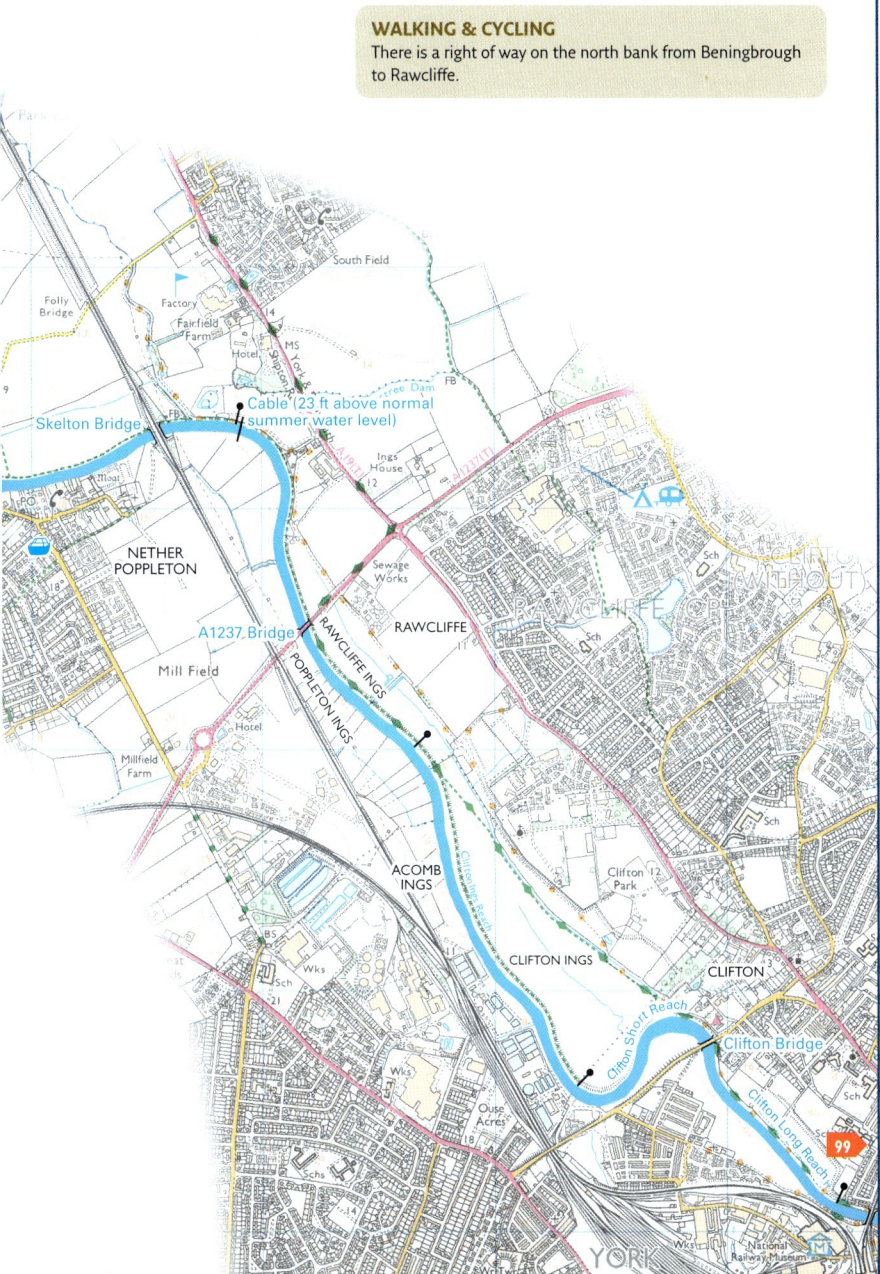

River Ouse, River Ure and Ripon Canal — Nether Poppleton

York

The River Ouse makes its passage through York, where all the major sights are tightly enclosed within the city walls, and none are more than a short walk away from the moorings. Trip boats ply back and forth, their commentaries adding to the general hub-bub of a working city and popular tourist venue. To the south of Skeldergate Bridge the River Foss joins from the east, and, whilst the entrance seems inviting and the first mile-and-a-half is navigable, there are no official moorings on the Foss, and the passage through the lock is very expensive. The riverside to the south of the city is extremely pleasant as you pass under the attractive Millennium Bridge, its cable-stayed structure inspired by bicycle spokes. Look out, on the east bank, for the Roman Well, then swing round under the A64 and pass the extremely pleasant Bishopthorpe Palace and grounds. Enjoy what view there is to the west as you leave behind a very large sewage works on the east bank, then pass under Naburn Bridge to once again enter open countryside.

RIVER FOSS

York City Council, 9 St Leonard's Place, York YO1 2ET (01904 551550). The river is navigable for just over 1½ miles from Blue Bridge, until the depth disappears before a low pipe bridge. The lock size is 112' x 20'. Craft over 36' long will be unable to wind. Do not enter the lock unless the flood lights are showing green. IWA volunteers are also operating the lock *during summer months* (without charge). A *minimum of 4 days notice* is required; boaters must have valid insurance documents on board and, as water levels are crucial, lock sharing is preferred. Contact 07588 236597 leaving your name, name of boat and mobile telephone number on the *24 hr* answering service, or email tonymartin451@yahoo.co.uk. There are no official moorings on the River Foss in York.

Boatyards

Ⓑ**York Marina** Naburn, York YO19 4RW (01904 621021; www.yorkmarina.co.uk). 🏠 🚻 🔑 P D Pump out, gas, overnight and long-term mooring, winter storage, slipway, hoist, boat sales and repairs, engine repairs, chandlery, toilets, showers.

NAVIGATIONAL NOTES

Water, elsan disposal, refuse disposal and moorings are available at Museum Gardens in York - just upstream of Lendal Bridge on the north bank – *Apr-Sep*. A BW watermate key is required..

● **York**
N. *Yorks. All services*. Everything you will wish to see is packed within the square mile or so contained by the limestone medieval city walls which, if you are feeling energetic, you can walk around. Or you can climb the 275 steps to the top of the Minster for a superb panorama of this fine walled city and its surroundings. You will see the river passing through its centre, crossed by three handsome bridges: the stone-built Ouse Bridge, designed by Peter Atkinson; and the decorous cast iron constructions of Lendal Bridge and Skeldergate Bridge. Just how much of this fine city you can enjoy will depend upon how long you plan to stay, but the Minster should be a high priority on everyone's list. Then perhaps wander south through the maze of 'snickleways', including the impossibly narrow and picturesque Shambles, to enjoy the Jorvik Centre and the museums to its south. York finds its origins in the Roman base of Eboracum, established during the first century AD. If you walk a short way along Museum Street from Lendal Bridge and turn into Museum Gardens, you can see the substantial remains of the Multangular Tower, the western corner of the original Roman fortress. When the Romans left, York became a Saxon settlement, and it was they who built a wooden church on the spot where the cathedral now stands. The Saxons were overrun by the Vikings in 867, and the damp soils surrounding the river thankfully preserved substantial remains of their stay here, which can now be seen in a spectacular presentation at the Jorvik Centre. Following the Norman conquest in 1066, William the Conqueror built two wooden towers to guard the Ouse. The present cathedral was begun by Archbishop Walter de Gray during the early part of the 13th C, and was completed some 250 year later. After Charles I made York his northern headquarters in 1639, the Parliamentarians laid it siege in 1644 and, following the Battle of Marston Moor fought 6 miles to the west, Charles' garrison capitulated on the understanding that none of the city's fine religious buildings be desecrated. York's 19th-C history is centred upon the birth of the railways and the prosperity this new means of transport brought to the city. George Hudson, three times mayor of York, successfully cashed in on this boom and although he fell from grace for a while due to some doubtful business deals, he was returned to favour this

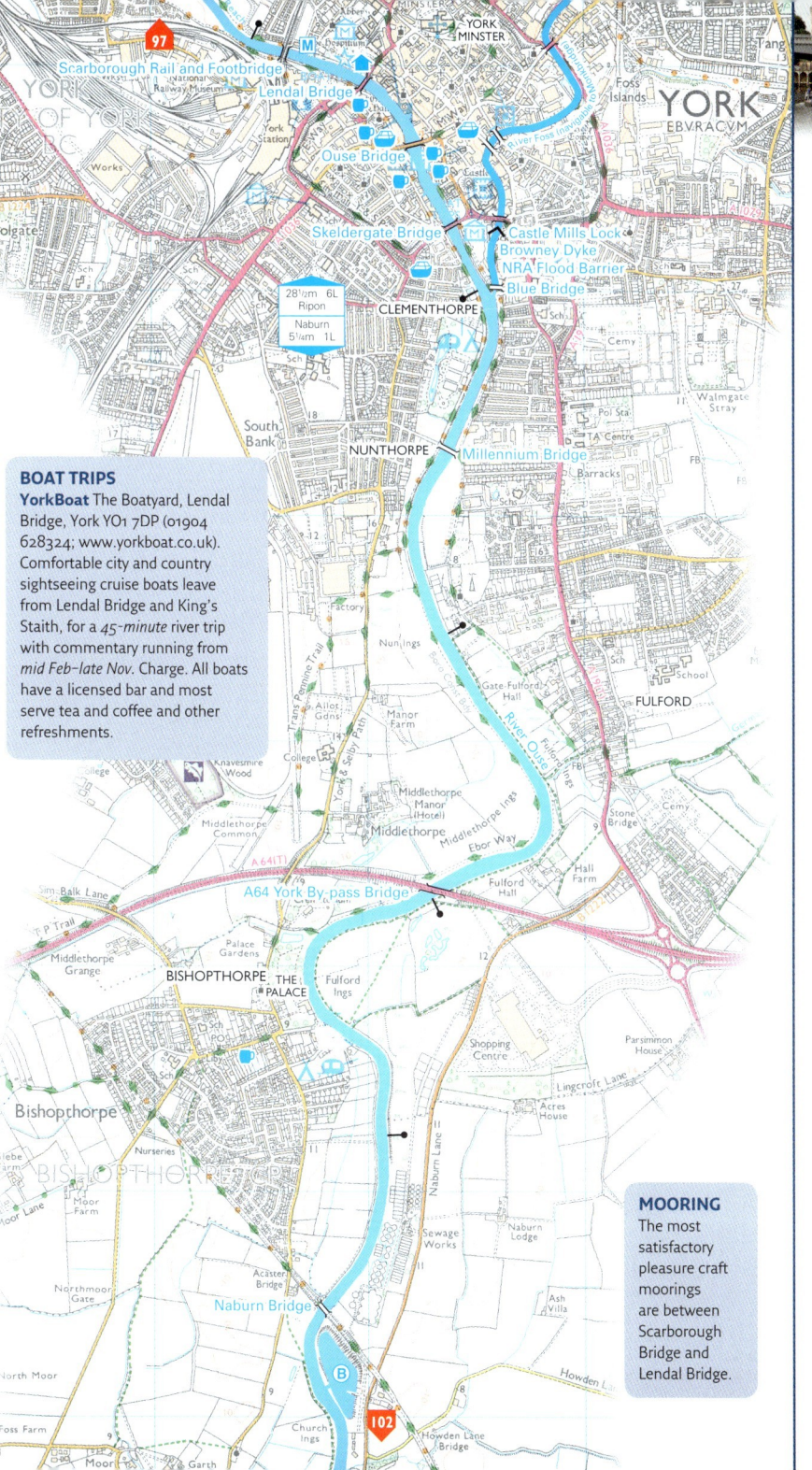

River Ouse, River Ure and Ripon Canal — York

BOAT TRIPS
YorkBoat The Boatyard, Lendal Bridge, York YO1 7DP (01904 628324; www.yorkboat.co.uk). Comfortable city and country sightseeing cruise boats leave from Lendal Bridge and King's Staith, for a *45-minute* river trip with commentary running from *mid Feb–late Nov*. Charge. All boats have a licensed bar and most serve tea and coffee and other refreshments.

MOORING
The most satisfactory pleasure craft moorings are between Scarborough Bridge and Lendal Bridge.

century, and his portrait now hangs in the fine 18th-C Mansion House. Shoppers can enjoy the vast array of shops in the streets by the Minster, and of course everyone will want to visit the Shambles, a narrow cobbled street which was once filled with butchers, but is now a good place for souvenirs. The university opened in 1963, reviving the city's reputation as a seat of learning.

Bar Convent Museum 17 Blossom Street, York YO24 1AQ (01904 643238; www.bar-convent.org.uk). The country's oldest active convent, founded in 1686. The dome of the chapel was remarkably hidden under a pitched roof. The present buildings are Georgian. *Museum open Mon–Sat 10.00–16.00. Free. Also café (open from 07.45)*, shop, guest house and conference rooms. Café, shop.

Cliffords Tower Tower Street, York YO1 9SA (01904 646940; www.cliffordstower.com). There is a good view of the city from the top of this tower, the last remaining part of York Castle, which once stood in Jewbury, where the city's Jews lived. In 1190 they were attacked by townsfolk complaining about loan repayments, and took refuge in the tower. There they committed mass suicide rather than convert to Christianity. Telephone or visit website to confirm opening times. Charge.

Fairfax House Castlegate, York YO1 9RN (01904 655543; www.fairfaxhouse.co.uk). Built in 1762, this superb town house houses the Terry collection of furniture and clocks. Special 18th-C Christmas exhibition each year. *Open Tue–Sat 10.00–16.30, Sun 12.30–15.30, B Hol Mons 10.00–16.30 otherwise admission Mon by guided tour only 11.00–14.00.* Charge.

Jorvik DIG St Saviour's Church, St Saviourgate, York YO1 8NN (01904 615505; www.digyork.com). This attraction offers a unique archaeological adventure, as visitors excavate Roman, Viking, medieval and Victorian finds themselves. All visits are accompanied by archaeologists and are timed. Pre-booking (telephone or online) is advised, although you can just turn up and join a tour. *Open daily 10.00–17.00.* Charge.

Jorvik Viking Centre Coppergate, York YO1 9WT (01904 643211; www.jorvik.co.uk). The superbly re-created Viking town of Jorvik, discovered whilst excavating the Coppergate Shopping Centre and now superbly displayed. Sit in a time-car to journey back in time through 1000 years of English history, culminating at the Viking port discovered on this site. Journey along a Viking street surrounded by the smell of wood smoke and pigs, listening to the sounds of herring being unloaded, together with an informative commentary. *Open Easter–Oct, daily 09.00–17.00; Nov–Easter daily 10.00–16.00.* Visitors are advised to call 01904 615505 or visit the website to pre-book. Charge.

The York Dungeon 12 Clifford Street, York YO1 9RD (01904 632599; www.thedungeons.com). Branding, boiling, roasting and beheading of people are just a few of the attractions of this startling place, which is definitely *not recommended for the squeamish*. The story of Guy Fawkes is also vividly re-told including, of course, his torture and execution. Telephone or visit website for opening times and details of special events. Charge.

National Railway Museum Leeman Road, York YO26 4XJ (01904 686286; www.nrm.org.uk). Near York railway station. This is reputedly the world's largest railway museum, housed in two vast hangars, and whilst there are of course many superb locomotives, the exhibits illustrate rail travel in its broadest sense. Here you will see photographs, paintings, ceramics, models, ticket displays and the reproduction of a section of the Channel Tunnel. Locomotives on display include the *Agenoria*, which hauled coals in Staffordshire from 1829, and the splendid *Mallard*, which reached a speed of 126mph in 1938, still the world record for a steam locomotive. In the South Hall a replica station includes Queen Victoria's royal carriage, plus the carriage used by Queen Elizabeth II until 1977. Background recordings keep the railway atmosphere at a peak. Tours, demonstrations and rides. *Open daily 10.00–1800.* Free. Restaurant, gift shop.

Treasurer's House Minster Yard, York YO1 7JL (01904 624247; www.nationaltrust.org.uk). *NT.* A Jacobean façade on a house of which much was built in the 17th C, on the site of a Roman road. It was at one time owned by Frank Green, an industrialist and obviously intensely practical man: he put nails into the floor to remind servants where the furniture should stand. Walled garden, tearoom, art gallery and ghosts of Roman soldiers. *Open mid Feb–Oct, Sat–Thu 11.00–16.30 by guided tour only.* Charge. Tea room.

Merchant Adventurers' Hall The Hall, Fossgate, York YO1 9XD (01904 654818; www.theyorkcompany.co.uk). One of York's finest timbered buildings, with a fine undercroft and a beautifully panelled hall. Museum. *Open Mar–Oct, Mon–Thu 09.00–17.00, Fri–Sat 09.00–15.30, Sun 11.00–16.00; Nov–Feb Mon–Fri 09.00–16.00, Sat 09.00–15.30.* The Hall is occasionally closed for private functions.

York Minster Deangate, York YO1 7HH (01904 621756; www.yorkminster.org). Earliest records of a religious building near this site relate to a wooden church, recorded by the Venerable Bede as being built by the Saxons in AD627. The present Minster was begun by Archbishop Walter de Gray, and completed in 1472, after 250 years' work. Built on a truly grand scale, it is 524ft long and 249ft wide (by volume, it is the largest cathedral in the country), topped by a central tower 234ft tall, completed about 1730. This tower needed remedial work in 1967, when serious weaknesses were found. The work, however, revealed a rich hoard of Roman and Saxon treasures, many of which are now displayed in the Undercroft Museum, along with all other aspects of the Minster's history. There are over 100 stained-glass windows spanning a period of 800 years, making the interior surprisingly light and airy. The earliest glass is in the second window on the left from the west door of the nave, and dates from c.1150. There is also a funeral procession of monkeys to look out for. Fine carvings around the capitals, the east window with Old and New Testament illustrations, and the stone choir screen, carved with England's rulers from William I to Henry VI, are other delights. In 1984, following some controversial statements made by the Bishop of

Durham, the roof of the south transept was struck by lightning, causing considerable damage and invoking comment about the wrath of God. This was repaired incorporating designs submitted by *Blue Peter* viewers. Every hour a priest asks visitors to stop their sightseeing and pray. Excellent free tours can be taken, leaving from the information desk. *Open Jan-Mar & Oct-Dec, Mon-Sat 07.00–18.00; closes Apr 18.30, May 19.30, Jun-Aug 20.30, Sep 20.00 (Sun opens for visitors 13.00).*
York Castle Museum The Eye of York, York YO1 9RY (01904 687687; www.yorkcastlemuseum.org.uk). A fascinating array of objects and displays kept in two 18th-C prisons, one of which includes the cell where Dick Turpin spent his last night. Reconstructions of a Victorian pub, Kirkgate, a Fancy Repository and a toyshop are packed full of fascinating artifacts. Many visitors will remember similar 1950s front rooms, complete with a television. *Open year round, daily 09.00–17.00. Closed Xmas and New Year.* Charge. Gift shop, coffee shop.
Theatre Royal St Leonard's Place, York YO1 7HD (01904 623568; www.yorktheatreroyal.co.uk). Shakespeare, ballet, opera and large popular productions. Café and restaurant.
Tourist Information Centre Exhibition Square, York YO1 7HB (01904 621756; www.visityork.org).

Boatyards

ⓑYork Marine Services Ferry Lane, Bishopthorpe, York YO23 2SB (01904 704442; www.yorkmarine.co.uk). 🚽 ⛽ 🚤 Pump out, gas, boat hire, overnight and long-term mooring, winter storage, slipway, crane, boat and engine sales and repairs, chandlery, toilets, showers, DIY facilities, caravan and camping.

WALKING & CYCLING
There is no continuous towpath on this section, although there is a fine riverside walk through York. The walk around the longest city wall in Britain should be undertaken if at all possible. Allow about 4 hours, and be prepared to make the link from Skeldergate Bridge to Monk Bar by road, via the Castle Museum, Coppergate, The Shambles and Goodramgate. You will also have to link Bootham Bar and Lendal Bridge. You will see many of the city's finest sights on the journey. Details of several walks around the city can be obtained from: Walking in the Countryside Around York, City of York Council, 9 St. Leonard's Place, York YO1 7ET (01904 551338; walking.cycling@york.gov.uk). In York 15 per cent of the population cycle to work compared with a national average of 3 per cent, so you can feel at home here on a bicycle. Maps detailing all of York's cycle routes are available from cycle retailers, libraries and City of York Council *(details above)*. The York to Beningbrough cycle route is a 9-mile ride from the city centre, initially traffic-free and with the last 5 miles along quiet lanes. It is part of the National Cycle Network route from Hull to Middlesbrough. Start from the railway station side of Lendal Bridge. You can also ride the old railway path to Selby, passing the old Terry's chocolate factory. Start from the railway station side of the Ouse Bridge at the junction of Skeldergate and Micklegate.

Pubs and Restaurants

There are many fine pubs in York, including:
🍺The Maltings Tanners Moat, near Lendal Bridge, York YO1 1HU (01904 655387; www.maltings.co.uk). An atmospheric small pub, voted Cask Ale Pub of Great Britain twice, and which runs its own beer festivals each year (telephone for details). Real ales and draught ciders. Bar meals are available *Mon-Fri 12.00–14.00, Sat and Sun 12.00–16.00.* Children welcome if eating. Folk on *Tue.*
🍺The York Arms 26 High Petergate, by the Minster, York YO1 7EH (01904 624508). Real ale, and bar meals *Thu-Mon 12.00–16.00.* Children welcome if you are eating.
🍺Yates's Wine Lodge Church Lane, Low Ousegate, York YO1 9QT (01904 613569). Riverside wine bar where meals are available *all day 09.00–21.00.* Some outside seating in the courtyard and DJ *Thu-Sun.*
🍺The Kings Arms Kings Staith, York YO1 9SN (01904 659435). The last surviving remnant of the Water Lanes, this is also York's famous flooding pub, with water levels over the last 100 years recorded. Stone floors, brick walls, exposed beams and open fires (when the water level drops). Bar meals *L.* Outside seating. Moorings.
🍺The Bluebell 53 Fossgate, York YO1 9TF (01904 654904). Over 200 years old, this pub is reputed to have the smallest and oldest interior in York. Six real ales are usually available.
🍺The Cock & Bottle 61 Skeldergate, York YO1 6DS (01904 654165). Reputedly York's most haunted pub, and it serves real ale. Bar meals are available *all day Fri-Sun.* Children welcome.

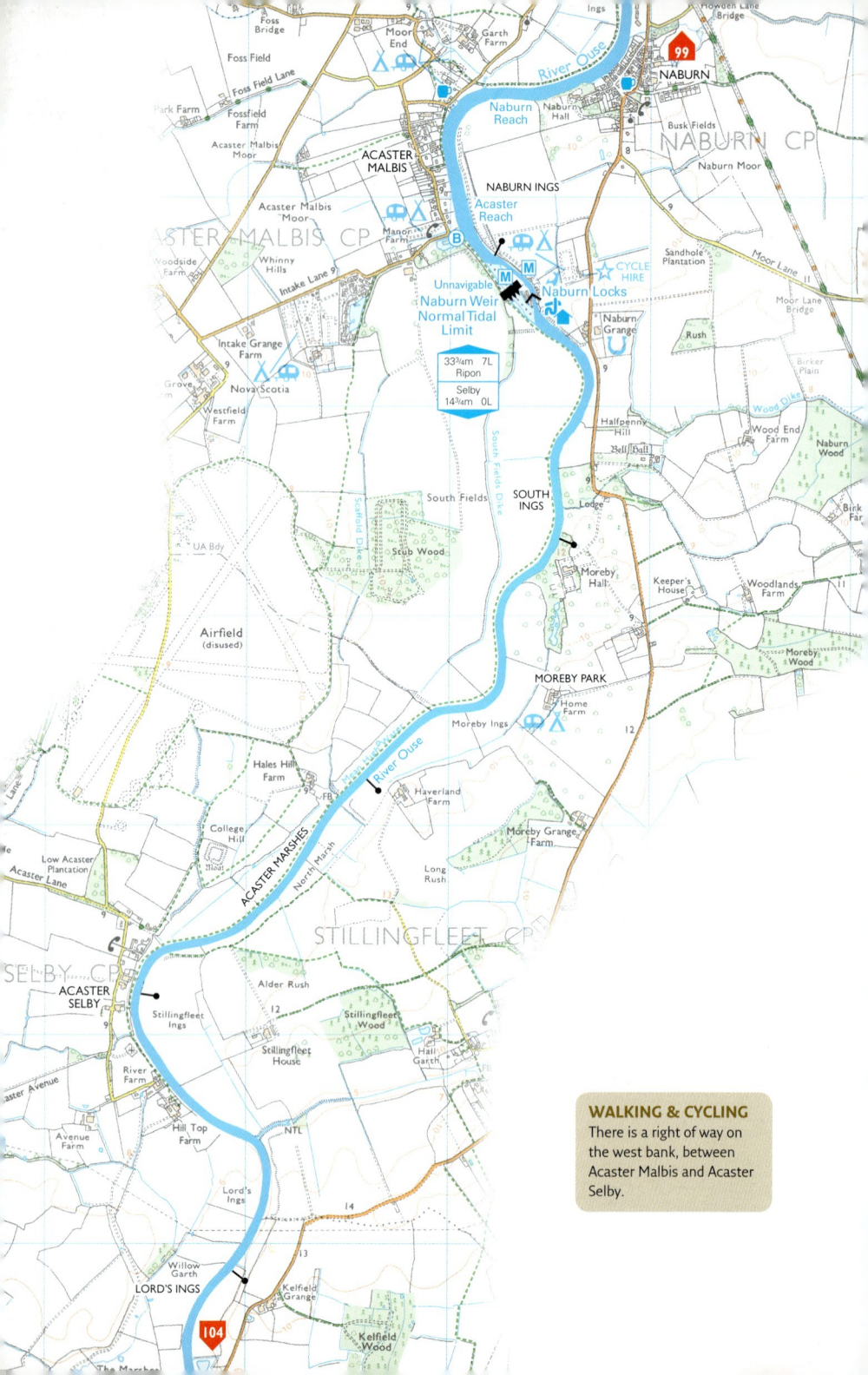

Naburn Locks

Having left the excitement of York, the river resumes its quiet passage through unassuming countryside, passing Naburn and Acaster Malbis on its way to Naburn Locks. Here the elegant British Waterways buildings, swing bridges and crane create a fine riverside scene, marking the start of the tidal river and a gradual change in surroundings. There are also *toilets* and *showers* and a full range of *boater services*. Now the intimacy of the upper river is slowly replaced by bare banks and more open countryside around the tidal waters. Bell Hall, just half a mile south of the lock, was built in 1680, and is a fine example of its period. Moreby Park, also on the east bank, provides almost a mile of pleasing parkland and relief from the generally flat countryside. Acaster Selby, a small farming settlement, lies inconspicuously behind a bend as the river continues its languorous route south.

NAVIGATIONAL NOTES

1 The River Ouse is tidal below Naburn Lock so craft can only pass through the lock on a flood tide. Where possible please give the lock keeper *24 hrs notice* on 01904 728500.
2 The Trent Series Charts, published by The Boating Association (www.theboatingassociation.co.uk; info@theboatingassociation.co.uk), are detailed charts of the tidal Ouse (and the tidal and non-tidal Trent) and are available to buy online. Also from BW lock keepers. Charge.

● **Naburn**
N. Yorks. Tel. A charming and compact brick-built village nestling on a bend in the river. The church of St Matthew, built in 1854, stands separately to the south, with the famous locks a mile further on. The large Banqueting House, by the lock, was built 1823–4 as a meeting place for members of the Ouse Navigation Company.

● **Acaster Malbis**
N. Yorks. PO box, tel. A pretty but nondescript village, with caravan parks at each end. A half-mile to the north is the large 14th-C church of the Holy Trinity, with its fine weatherboarded Victorian bell turret and spire. Look for the pretty stained glass in the east window, c.1320, and the effigy of John Malbis, from about the same time, in the south chapel. The pulpit is an elaborate 17th-C piece.

● **Acaster Selby**
N. Yorks. A small farming settlement around what is left of Acaster Hall, built c.1670.

Boatyards

ⓑ **Waterline Leisure** Acaster Airfield, Acaster Malbis, York YO23 2UY (01904 702049; www.waterlineleisure.co.uk). Riverside yard just upstream of Naburn Locks. Long-term mooring, winter storage, slipway, 10-ton crane, boat and engine sales and repairs, toilets, showers, DIY facilities.

Pubs and Restaurants

●**The Blacksmiths Arms** Main Street, Naburn, York YO19 4PN (01904 623464). Very comfortable and friendly pub, which for over 300 years was a blacksmith's shop. The bar has a fine collection of plates and teapots, and you can enjoy a pint here, or retreat into a cosy alcove. Real ales, and good bar meals *all day, everyday, including Sun* carvery. Children welcome. There is a large garden. Moorings.

●✕**The Ship Inn** Moor End, Acaster Malbis, York YO23 2UH (01904 703888). A large, stylish and haunted 17th-C coaching house, once used by Oliver Cromwell's men, and now a popular venue for visitors by road and river. Real ales and bar meals *L and E*. Children welcome, and there is a garden. River trips leave from here.

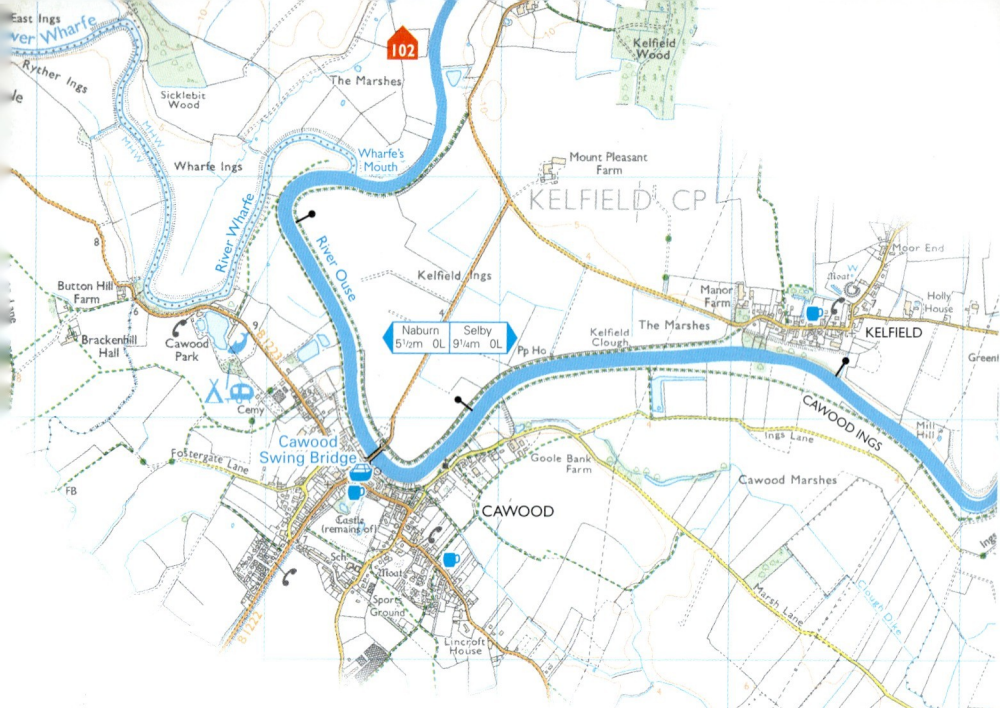

Cawood

The Ouse now starts to gather momentum as the River Wharfe, coming down from Tadcaster, joins from the west *(see below)*. Sweeping eccentrically past Cawood, the Ouse passes under the only river crossing on this section. Enclosed by flood banks and surrounded by rich farmland, the river now pursues an isolated course, with towns and villages showing a healthy respect by keeping their distance.

- **Cawood**
  N. Yorks. PO, tel, stores. A pretty red brick and tile village, with narrow streets, nestling on the south bank and joined to the north by the swing bridge. A castle owned by the Archbishops of York once stood here, dating from AD930. Cardinal Wolsey visited, and was arrested here in 1530 for high treason. His fate is recalled in the nursery rhyme 'Humpty Dumpty'. All that now remains is a white stone gate house, dating from the first half of the 15th C. It has been renovated by the Landmark Trust and is available for lets (01628 825925). The Church of All Saints stands to the east of the village, and has a fine Perpendicular tower containing a monument to George Mountain, Archbishop of York, who died in 1623.

- **Kelfield**
  N. Yorks. Tel. Seeming to ignore the river totally, this village contains a chapel dated 1852, beautifully converted into a house.

- **Riccall**
  N. Yorks. PO, tel, stores, butcher, fish & chips. The church of St Mary has a Norman doorway, dating from 1160, and Norman arcading from the 13th C. The south door is 12th C.

NAVIGATIONAL NOTES

River Wharfe
Although in theory navigable for just over 9 miles to Tadcaster Weir, this is not advisable without local knowledge. The lower reaches are not particularly attractive and shallows around Ulleskelf, known locally as huts, are one of the problems you may encounter.

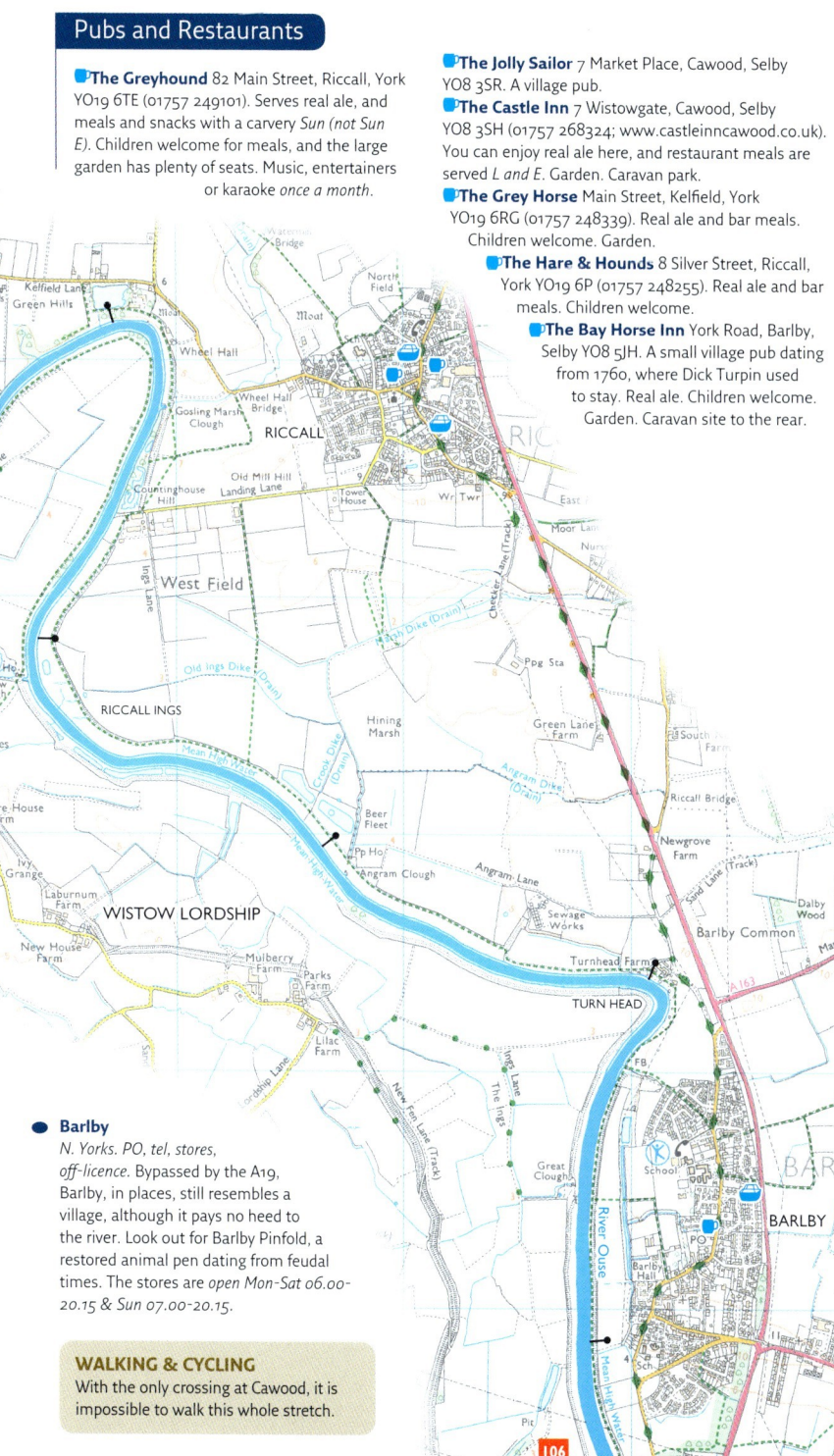

Pubs and Restaurants

The Greyhound 82 Main Street, Riccall, York YO19 6TE (01757 249101). Serves real ale, and meals and snacks with a carvery *Sun (not Sun E)*. Children welcome for meals, and the large garden has plenty of seats. Music, entertainers or karaoke *once a month*.

The Jolly Sailor 7 Market Place, Cawood, Selby YO8 3SR. A village pub.

The Castle Inn 7 Wistowgate, Cawood, Selby YO8 3SH (01757 268324; www.castleinncawood.co.uk). You can enjoy real ale here, and restaurant meals are served *L and E*. Garden. Caravan park.

The Grey Horse Main Street, Kelfield, York YO19 6RG (01757 248339). Real ale and bar meals. Children welcome. Garden.

The Hare & Hounds 8 Silver Street, Riccall, York YO19 6P (01757 248255). Real ale and bar meals. Children welcome.

The Bay Horse Inn York Road, Barlby, Selby YO8 5JH. A small village pub dating from 1760, where Dick Turpin used to stay. Real ale. Children welcome. Garden. Caravan site to the rear.

Barlby

N. Yorks. PO, tel, stores, off-licence. Bypassed by the A19, Barlby, in places, still resembles a village, although it pays no heed to the river. Look out for Barlby Pinfold, a restored animal pen dating from feudal times. The stores are *open Mon-Sat 06.00-20.15 & Sun 07.00-20.15*.

WALKING & CYCLING

With the only crossing at Cawood, it is impossible to walk this whole stretch.

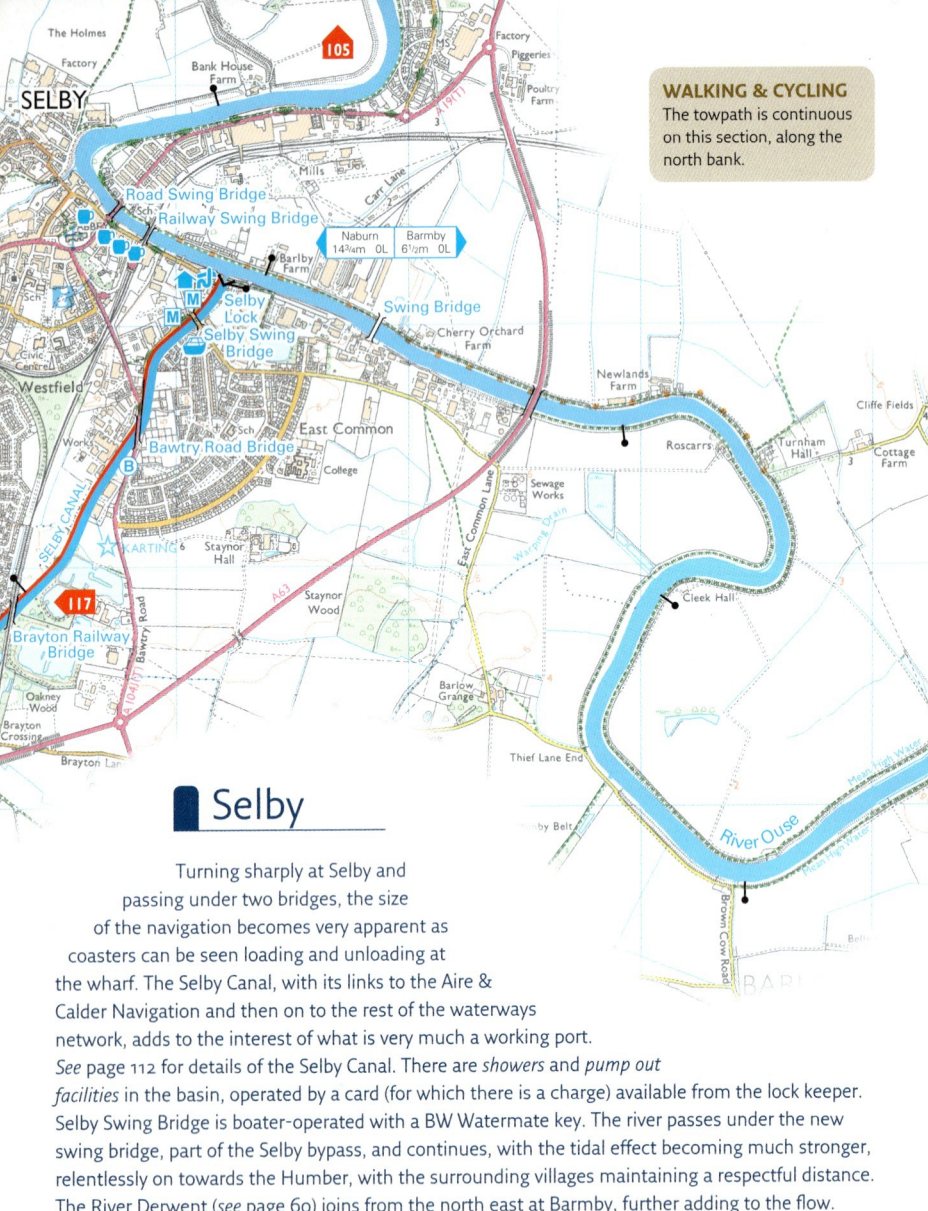

WALKING & CYCLING
The towpath is continuous on this section, along the north bank.

Selby

Turning sharply at Selby and passing under two bridges, the size of the navigation becomes very apparent as coasters can be seen loading and unloading at the wharf. The Selby Canal, with its links to the Aire & Calder Navigation and then on to the rest of the waterways network, adds to the interest of what is very much a working port. See page 112 for details of the Selby Canal. There are *showers* and *pump out facilities* in the basin, operated by a card (for which there is a charge) available from the lock keeper. Selby Swing Bridge is boater-operated with a BW Watermate key. The river passes under the new swing bridge, part of the Selby bypass, and continues, with the tidal effect becoming much stronger, relentlessly on towards the Humber, with the surrounding villages maintaining a respectful distance. The River Derwent (*see* page 60) joins from the north east at Barmby, further adding to the flow.

NAVIGATIONAL NOTES

1. The Ouse is now a working river, with large craft and a strong tidal effect. Navigation should not be attempted without the requisite experience and a suitable craft.
2. Selby Lock is tidal and mechanised, so the lock keeper works a flexible week around the tidal fluctuations to provide maximum usage of the canal during daylight hours. Where possible *24 hours notice* should be given of your arrival in either direction by telephoning the lock keeper on 01757 703182.
3. Visitor moorings are available in Selby Basin. A transit licence is available for craft on River Registration to use the canals between Selby and Keadby on the Trent (missing Trent Falls).

River Ouse, River Ure and Ripon Canal — Selby

● **Selby**
N. Yorks. All services. Away from the River Ouse, this is a handsome market town, dominated by its sparkling abbey. The present road bridge was built in 1970, and became toll-free in 1991: it replaced an earlier structure which had stood since 1791.
Selby Abbey The Crescent, Selby YO8 4PU (01757 703123; www.selbyabbey.org.uk). Founded for the Benedictines, as a result of Benedict's vision of three swans landing on a river coming to fruition here. The east window shows the family tree of the Kings of Israel and dates from the 14th C. Below the south east window is the grave slab of Laurence Selby, abbot from 1486-1504. Notice that the three swans seen by Benedict are featured in a shield by his shoulder. *Open daily 10.00-16.00, although* if there is a ceremony taking place some of the abbey will be cordoned off to visitors.
Selby Park Selby. A very pleasant 5 acres of trees and plants, with a children's play area, picnic tables, mini-golf and bowls. *Open Mon-Fri 10.00-21.00, Sat and Sun 10.00-17.00.*
Selby Market Selby. Over 150 stalls, food and entertainment in front of the Abbey. *Every Mon 08.00-15.30 and a smaller market takes place on Sat.*
Abbey Leisure Centre Scott Road, Selby YO8 4BL (01757 213758; www.selbyleisure.co.uk). *Open Mon-Fri 07.00-23.00, Sat 07.00-19.30, Sun 08.00-21.00.* Charge.
Visitor Centre 52 Micklegate, Selby YO8 4EQ (0845 0349543). Located in Selby Library.

● **Hemingbrough**
N. Yorks. PO, tel. The very tall slender spire of the church of St Mary can be seen for miles across the flat Yorkshire countryside, standing fully 189ft high.
Drax Power Station Drax, Selby YO8 8PH (01757 618381; www.draxpower.com). This is Europe's largest coal-fired power station, producing 10 per cent of England's electricity. Opened in 1973 it dominates the area for miles around. Guided tours for groups only, by prior arrangement.

● **Barmby on the Marsh**
N. Yorks. PO box, tel. Village with some Georgian houses hemmed in by the rivers Ouse and Derwent.

Pubs and Restaurants

● **The Cricketers** Market Place, Selby YO8 4PB (01757 702120). Excellent real ale, and food *L daily.*
●✕ **The Londesborough Arms Hotel** Market Place, Selby YO8 4NS (01757 707355). Bar and restaurant meals are available *L and E, daily.* Garden. Children welcome when eating. Nightclub with *late night opening Thu-Sun.* B & B.
● **The Albion Vaults** New Street, Selby YO8 4PT (01757 213817). Cosy traditional corner house serving real ale. Children welcome, garden. Quiz night *Tue.*
● **The Fox & Pheasant** Main Street, Hemingbrough, Selby YO8 6QE. Friendly pub, where children are welcome. There is a large garden. *Monthly karaoke.*
● **The Crown Inn** Main Street, Hemingbrough, Selby YO8 6QE (01757 638434). Traditional country pub serving real ale, along with food *L and E.* Children welcome, and there is a large garden.

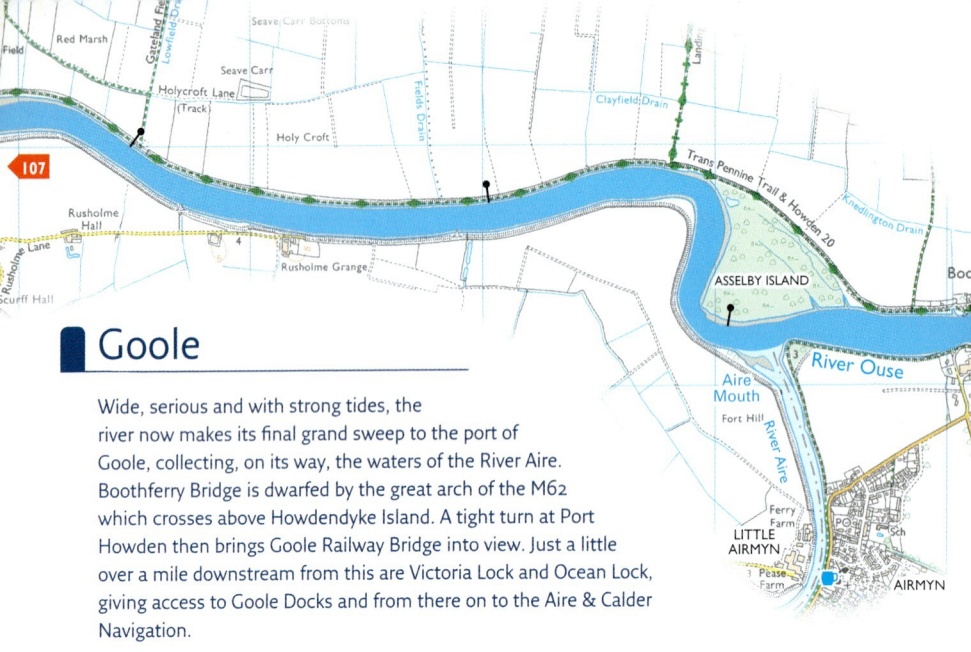

Goole

Wide, serious and with strong tides, the river now makes its final grand sweep to the port of Goole, collecting, on its way, the waters of the River Aire. Boothferry Bridge is dwarfed by the great arch of the M62 which crosses above Howdendyke Island. A tight turn at Port Howden then brings Goole Railway Bridge into view. Just a little over a mile downstream from this are Victoria Lock and Ocean Lock, giving access to Goole Docks and from there on to the Aire & Calder Navigation.

NAVIGATIONAL NOTES

1. The Ouse is now a working river, with large craft and a strong tidal effect. Navigation should not be attempted without the requisite experience and a suitable craft. Cruising notes are available free of charge from Selby Locks (01757 703182) and Naburn Locks (01904 728500). The lock keeper at Goole will willingly offer advice and information on navigating the tideway. For their part boaters must inform Associated British Ports (ABP) that they are on the river and make their position known (see note 2). ABP maintain a continuous watch on channel 14.
2. At the west end of South Dock, Goole, the navigation is under the jurisdiction of ABP. Contact them on VHF radio channel 14 – call *Goole Docks* – or by telephoning 01482 327171. Boats using Ocean Lock and the tideway **must carry VHF radio and have at least two people on board**.
3. To the west of this point ocean-going shipping is manoeuvring and contact must be made with Ocean Lock Control before entering the docks.
4. Overnight mooring will incur a substantial charge and temporary mooring, whilst awaiting a lock or bridge swing, is only permitted if the crew are in attendance. Mooring on any pier whilst on the tideway (unless awaiting a lock) will also incur a charge.
5. Lock operating times are 2½ *hours before high tide and 1 hour after* for which no charge is made. Outside these times special pens are always available on payment of a fee.
6. The Trent Series Charts, published by The Boating Association (www.theboatingassociation.co.uk; info@theboatingassociation.co.uk), are detailed charts of the tidal Ouse (and the tidal and non-tidal Trent) and are available to buy online. Also from BW lock keepers. Charge.
7. It is about 7 miles from Swinefleet to Trent Falls. *See* notes on page 172.

Pubs and Restaurants

▶**The Percy Arms** 89 High Street, Airmyn, Goole SN14 8LD (01405 780792; www.thepercyarmsairmyn.co.uk). Cosy village pub with open fires. Real ale. Meals *L and E*. Children welcome. Conservatory and large garden. Quiz night *Tue*.

▶**The Victoria Hotel** Hook Road, Goole DN14 5JB (01405 763839). Real ale in a typical homely northern pub, built in 1794, with dark wooden panelling and cream paintwork.

▶**The Ferryboat Inn** Boothferry Road, Howden, Goole DN14 7ED (01430 430300). Overlooking the river, this pub serves food *L and E*, *daily*. Children welcome, and there is a riverside garden.

Boatyards

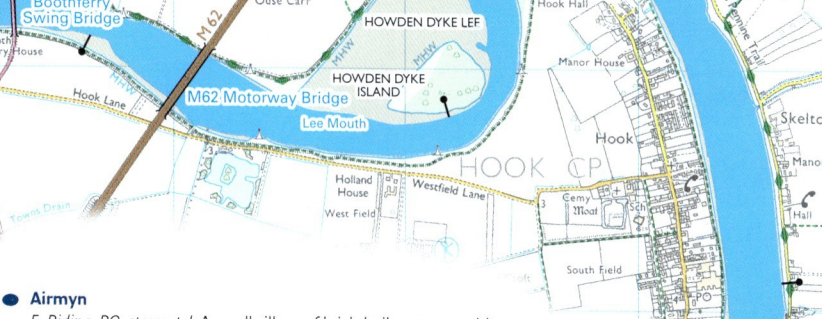

B Goole Boathouse The Timber Pond, Dutch Riverside, Goole DN14 5TB (01405 763985). ⚓ **D E** Gas, overnight & long-term mooring, storage, slipway, crane, dry dock, repairs, chandlery, toilets, showers, groceries, solid fuel, laundry.
B Viking Marine Albert Street, Goole DN14 5SY (01405 765737; www.vikingmarine.co.uk). **D** Mooring, gas, hoist, drying standing, maintenance & repairs, approved Honda marine sales and service, chandlery. Closed *Sun*.

● **Airmyn**
E. Riding. PO, stores, tel. A small village of brick-built cottages with a sturdy clock-tower, facing the raised banks of the River Aire.

● **Goole.**
E. Riding. All services. When the Aire & Calder Navigation applied for an Act to build a canal from Knottingley to Goole in 1819, Goole was no more than a few cottages scattered around the marshes on the banks of the Ouse. Work commenced on cutting the canal in 1822 and by 1828 foreign trade had begun with Hamburg; the local people entertained themselves by going down to the docks in the evening to await the arrival of foreign vessels on the spring tides. The docks are still very much the focal point, handling cargoes from Europe and Scandinavia.

Goole Museum and Art Gallery Carlisle Street, Goole DN14 5AA (01405 768963). The museum houses an interesting exhibition depicting the development of Goole and the surrounding area, with an emphasis on the docks and shipping. *Open Tue, Thu and Fri 10.00–17.00, Wed 10.00–19.00, Sat 09.00–16.00.* Free.

Yorkshire Waterways Museum Dutch Riverside, Goole DN14 5TB (01405 768730; www.waterwaysmuseum.org.uk). Museum displays, boat tours of Goole docks (*weekends*). Café. *Open Mon-Fri 09.00–16.00; Sat, Sun and B Hols 10.00–16.00.* Free.

River Ouse, River Ure and Ripon Canal — Goole

109

Rhodesfield Lock, Ripon (see page 90)

SELBY CANAL

MAXIMUM DIMENSIONS
Bank Dole Junction, Knottingley, to junction with the River Ouse, Selby
Length: 78' 6"
Beam: 16' 6"
Draught: 4'
Headroom: 8'

MANAGER
0113 281 6800
enquiries.northeast@britishwaterways.co.uk

MILEAGE
Bank Dole Junction, Knottingley to:
Haddlesey Flood Lock: 6½ miles
Selby, junction with the River Ouse: 11¾ miles

Locks: 4

Bank Dole and West Haddlesey locks give access to river sections of the navigation. River level gauge boards indicate conditions as follows:

GREEN BAND – Normal river levels safe for navigation.

AMBER BAND – River levels are above normal. If you wish to navigate the river section you are advised to proceed on to and through the next lock.

RED BAND – Flood conditions unsafe for navigation. Lock closed.

In 1774 the Aire and Calder Navigation Company obtained an Act to construct a navigation from the River Aire at Haddlesey to the Ouse at Selby. This was not, however, the first attempt to improve communication by navigable waterways in the area. During the 17th C local industry had transported goods by packhorse along the Hambleton Causeway to Selby Dock from where they were shipped to their destination. When the Aire was eventually made navigable to small vessels, Selby's trade declined. For some 70 years the traders battled with the difficulties that navigating the Aire presented until, in 1770, there were rumours that there was to be a new canal created, covering some 23½ miles and linking Leeds directly to Selby. The proprietors of the Aire & Calder Company soon realised the gravity of this threat. In making a connection with a tidal waterway at each end of its navigation, the Leeds and Liverpool Canal Company could very soon put the Aire & Calder Canal Company out of business. The latter employed the services of John Smeaton and William Jessop in the hope of eliminating the tideway on the river. Instead an Act was finally secured in 1774 which took the shortest and cheapest option. That was a direct route from the Aire's lowest lock at Haddlesey to Selby, a mere 5½ miles. The navigation opened on 29 April 1778. It was built to Jessop's design and cost £20,000. As a result Selby flourished. The town was in the enviable position of being at the junction of two great waterways and at a point where river, canal and road met. The manufacturers of the West Riding were able to send goods directly to Hull and London as well as being within more easy access of York and Leeds. By 1821 one-third of the people living in Selby were making their living from the waterways. The town was busy with ship and boat building, rope and sail making, flax dressing and linen manufacture. Industries in Leeds, Castleford and Knottingley improved, to all of which Selby had direct access. The building of a customs house at Selby enabled traffic to go straight out into the North Sea without having to stop at Hull to complete the necessary paperwork. The 8 acres of land around the lock were thriving with a counting house, rigging house, tarring house and sailmaker's shop. A small cut was made parallel with the Ouse where smaller vessels could be kept for transhipment of goods from larger vessels on the river. (This land is now mostly filled in and is the site of Rigid Paper Products.) A sailing packet left Selby every Monday for Hull, returning Thursday if weather conditions permitted. The fare was two shillings return, with food available on board at a cost of sixpence for men and fourpence for ladies. As trade increased, so did the amount of traffic and the size of loads carried on the navigation. The one shortcoming of the quick and cheap construction of the canal, namely the shallow draught of only 3' 6", proved to be its downfall. The Aire & Calder Canal Company was under fire from merchants and traders, all dissatisfied by the lack of capacity that the navigation offered for larger vessels. The rise in the production of coal from the Selby coalfield highlighted a serious deficit in the capacity of larger vessels and soon the company was under pressure to provide an alternative course. By 1826 the new and deeper canal from Knottingley to Goole was in operation and trade on the Selby Canal, although not entirely abandoned, suffered greatly as a consequence.

Today the canal is used solely for leisure and recreational purposes. The acquisition of the River Ouse by British Waterways has resulted in the Selby Canal being promoted as a through-route to the city of York. Since 1988 boating numbers have doubled, with nearly 1000 boats now passing through Selby Lock each year. The towpath now forms part of the Selby Horse Shoe Walk. A recent Canal Corridor Study has recognised the potential of the canal in creating a linear urban park. At present the industries which line its banks are turning their backs on the water, but an imaginative scheme set to reverse this trend promises to inject some life and create a valuable recreational resource along the banks of the canal. It is hoped that before too long Selby's canal will once again be recognised for the important role it once played in the life of the town.

Beal

The navigation from Knottingley provides a welcome escape from the intensive industry of the area. However, the concentration required to navigate safely on the commercial waterways cannot be abandoned, as the Aire adopts a fairly tortuous course as it meanders across more open countryside towards Haddlesey. Care needs to be taken on the countless bends until the navigation changes course at Haddlesey Lock.

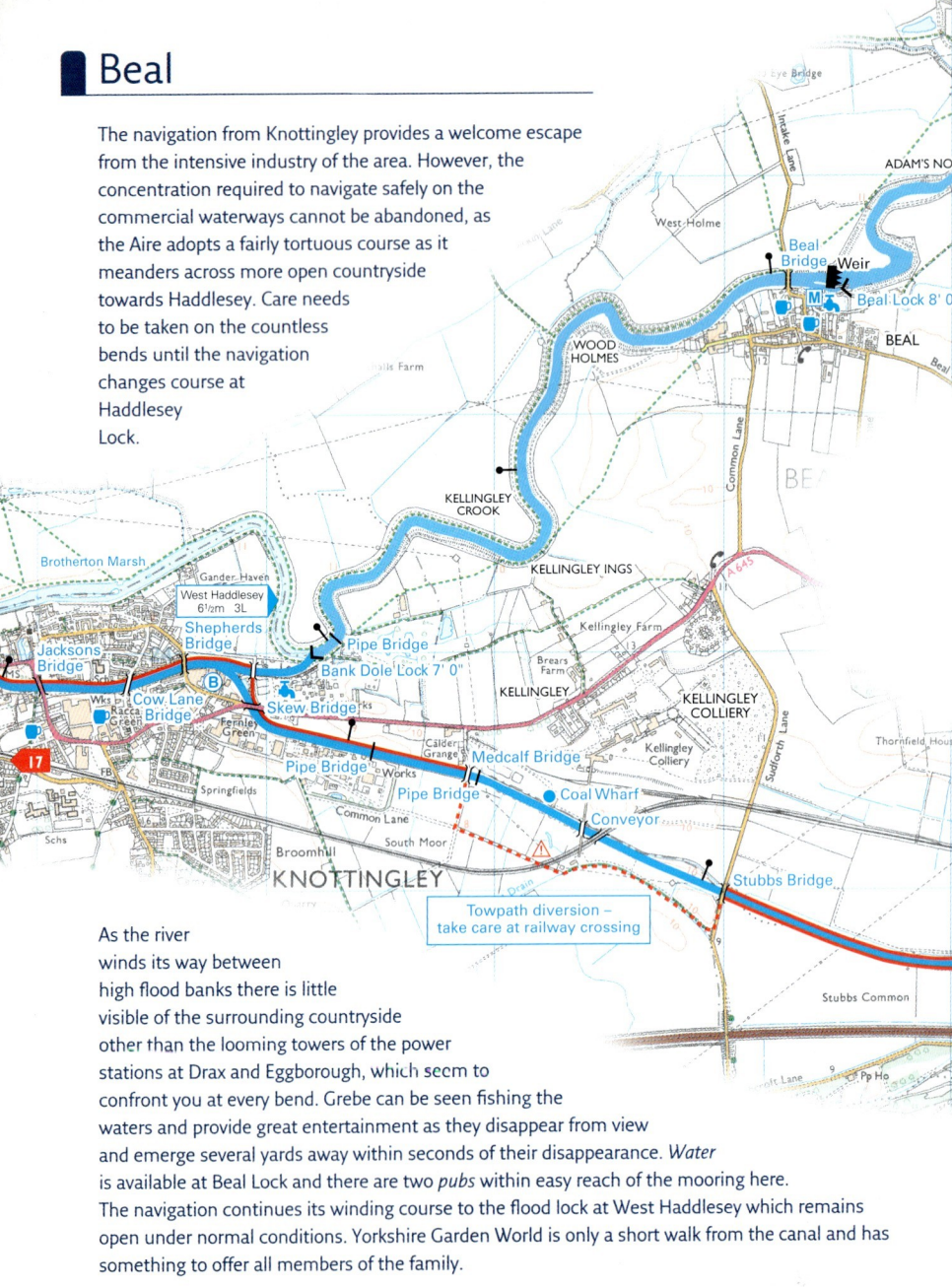

As the river winds its way between high flood banks there is little visible of the surrounding countryside other than the looming towers of the power stations at Drax and Eggborough, which seem to confront you at every bend. Grebe can be seen fishing the waters and provide great entertainment as they disappear from view and emerge several yards away within seconds of their disappearance. *Water* is available at Beal Lock and there are two *pubs* within easy reach of the mooring here. The navigation continues its winding course to the flood lock at West Haddlesey which remains open under normal conditions. Yorkshire Garden World is only a short walk from the canal and has something to offer all members of the family.

NAVIGATIONAL NOTES

Bank Dole Lock is unmanned. Temporary mooring is available on the river alongside all locks, although the landing stages should be approached with care. Care is needed locking up as the paddles are quite fierce. Caution should also be exercised on entering the lock at West Haddlesey as the wind can easily catch the boat, forcing it against the approach wall.

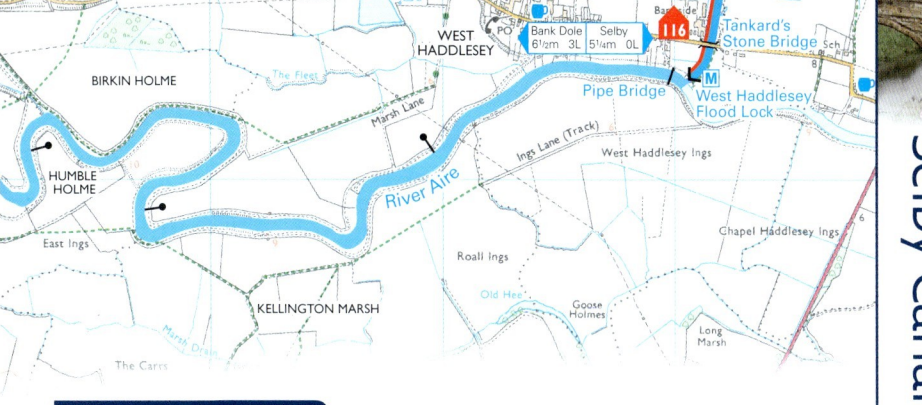

Selby Canal — Beal

Pubs and Restaurants

🍺 **Jenny Wren** Main Street, Beal DN14 0SS (01977 673487). A selection of real ales is served in the old taproom, unchanged for 50 years. Food is available *Sun L, and E (not Wed)*. Quiz nights *Wed*. Children and dogs welcome. Patio.

🍺✕ **Hungry Fox** Marsh Lane, Beal DN14 0SS (01977 607180; www.hungryfox.co.uk). Bar and restaurant serving well-kept real ale. Generous portions of home-made food, with special rates for pensioners, are available *L and E* . Booking advised *at weekends*. Children welcome. Games room. Outside patio. Facilities for disabled. Quiz *Tue*.

🍺 **George and Dragon Inn** West Haddlesey (01757 228198). One mile to the west of the lock. Real ale is served from the bar where you can enjoy a real fire and home-cooked food *Tue-Sat E and Sun L*. Children welcome. There is an outside patio. Quiz *Tue* and live music *Wed*.

🍺 **The Jug** Chapel Haddlesey, Selby YO8 8QQ (01757 270718; www.juginn.com). A regular choice of real ale is dispensed in this traditional village country pub with heavily beamed ceilings and open fires. Freshly prepared, home-made food is available *daily, L and E*. Children and dogs welcome. Large riverside beer garden accessible from the Aire. Pub games.

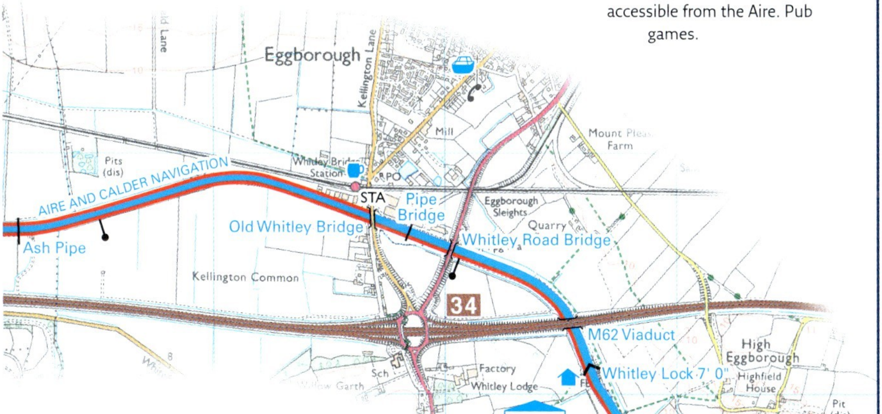

● **Beal**
N.Yorks. *Tel, stores*. A small settlement to the south of the river.

● **West Haddlesey**
N.Yorks. A pretty village with some very well-kept houses backing onto the river. The village inn dates back to the early 1800s and has the original village well.
Yorkshire Garden World Main Road, West Haddlesey, Selby YO8 8QA (07584 637486). Six acres of display and nursery gardens including over 500 varieties of herbs and an aromatherapy garden. Gift shop, dried flowers, tearoom, pets corner, a collection of larger animals (including llamas, Soay sheep, pot-bellied pigs and rare breeds of poultry), old farming implements. *Open daily 09.30–17.30 (17.00 Sun and B Hols). Closed Mon (except B Hols) and Oct-mid Mar.* Charge for gardens and animals.

Selby

Leaving West Haddlesey and the River Aire behind, the navigation now enters the Selby Canal, whose course provides a welcome contrast. The rich vegetation on both banks changes with the seasons but is never without interest. The towpath, which follows the north bank, is popular with the local people and the banks are well-populated with fishermen, particularly during competition time when the short stretch to Selby may attract as many as 1000 competitors! Several old milestones can be seen along the bank marking the distance from the River Ouse. Just to the north of Burton Bridge is Burton Hall, built on the site of a medieval manor, and beyond it the wooded hill of Brayton Barff which provides excellent views over the Vale of York to Selby. Barff is an ancient British name for barrow or burial place. There is a *pub* and also *mooring* at Burn Bridge, providing access to Brayton to the north, where there are further *pubs*, two *stores*, a *post office* and a *butcher*. The graceful 15th-C spire of St Wilfrid's Church at Brayton can be seen across the fields. Passing under Brayton Railway Bridge, which carried the old east coast line, the canal enters the short industrial corridor into Selby basin. The railway, which once headed directly north from Selby, had to be diverted to the west to avoid subsidence due to the newly opened deep mines to the north east of the town. Selby Swing Bridge is boater-operated with a Watermate key and can only be used during *daylight hours*. There are *toilets*, *showers* and *pump out facilities* in the basin operated by a Smart card available from the lock keeper.

WALKING & CYCLING
The towpath is in excellent condition for both walking and cycling between Selby Lock and Burn Bridge but is better suited to walking beyond here.

NAVIGATIONAL NOTES

1 Selby is a tidal lock, now mechanised, and can only be used at flood tide so the lock keeper here works a flexible week around the tidal fluctuations to provide maximum usage of the lock during daylight hours. Where possible *24 hours* notice should be given of your arrival in either direction by telephoning the lock keeper on 01757 703182.

2 *See* also note 6 on page 108.

Selby Canal — Selby

● **Brayton**
N.Yorks. Tel, PO, stores, garage.
Brayton's handsome church is well worth a look. Some parts of it date back to Norman times and there is some elaborate carving around the doorway and chancel arch.

● **Selby**
See page 106.

Boatyards

Ⓑ **Selby Boat Centre** Bawtry Road, Selby YO8 8NB (01757 212211; www.selbyboatcentre.co.uk). **D E** Pump out, gas, gas installations, narrow boat hire, overnight moorings, long-term moorings, winter storage, slipway, engine repairs (including outboards), crane, boat and engine sales, boat repairs and fitting out, DIY facilities, solid fuel, chandlery, books, maps and gifts. *Emergency call out.*

Pub

🍺 **The Wheatsheaf Inn** Main Road, Burn, Selby YO8 8LJ (01757 270614; www.wheatsheafburn.co.uk). Perfect place to stop for refreshment. Real ale and home-made food *L (daily) and E (Thu–Sat only)*. Beer garden. Children and dogs welcome.

There are many pubs in Selby. *See page 101 for details.*

BURSTING AT THE SEAMS

It is difficult to conceive whilst cruising quietly around the waterways of Yorkshire that underground there was the biggest coal mining complex in Europe. Only the effects of subsidence remind us of the extensive activity which took place below. The mines which comprised the Selby coalfield extracted some 11 million tons of coal, and provided work for 4000 people. Shafts sunk in the 1960s and 1970s at a cost of £1 billion extend eastwards towards the North Sea at a depth of 700ft, some seams measuring two or three miles in length. In spite of it once being the most modern and productive complex in Europe, this high tech operation still chose to employ the cleanest and most environmentally-friendly mode of transport at one of its collieries – the canal. In 1996 Kellingly Colliery celebrated the transportation of the 35-millionth ton of coal by barge to Ferrybridge Power Stations. However, since the demise of Hargreaves (who operated the highly efficient tugs and coal carrying pans) it would appear that coal will be transferred onto the road and rail system at a significant environmental cost.

Drakeshole Tunnel (see page 45)

SOUTH YORKSHIRE NAVIGATIONS

MAXIMUM DIMENSIONS

Sheffield to Rotherham
Length: 60' 0"
Beam: 15' 1"
Headroom: 10'
Draught: 4' 3"
Locks from Rotherham to the bottom of the Tinsley Flight are longer and will pass narrowboats up to approximately 70'

Rotherham to Sykehouse
Length: 198'
Beam: 20'
Headroom: 10' 6"
Draught: 8' 2"

Bramwith to Keadby
Length: 61' 8"
Beam: 17'
Headroom: 10' 6"
Draught: 7' 3"

New Junction Canal
Length: 215'

Beam: 22' 6"
Headroom: 10' 10"
Draught: 9'

MANAGER

0113 281 6800;
enquiries.northeast@britishwaterways.co.uk

MILEAGE

SHEFFIELD Basin to:
Rotherham: 6 miles, 15 locks
Swinton Junction: 12 miles, 18 locks
Doncaster Lock: 21½ miles, 23 locks
Bramwith Junction: 28 miles, 24 locks
Thorne: 33 miles: 26 locks
Crowle Wharf: 39½ miles, 26 locks
KEADBY, junction with River Trent: 43 miles
Locks: 27

SOUTHFIELD JUNCTION, junction with Aire & Calder Canal: 33½ miles
Locks: 25

Four separate waterway developments combine to make up the South Yorkshire Navigations. Prior to their improvement, trade with the industrial heartland of South Yorkshire was by horse and cart to Bawtry, and then by the natural line of the River Idle into the Trent and on into the Humber estuary. The River Don was largely given over to powering water wheels along its upper length, whilst its lower reaches split into two channels west of Thorne and drained into the Trent. In 1627 Cornelius Vermuyden was employed to drain Hatfield Chase and the Isle of Axholme. His scheme involved blocking one of the River Don's outlets into the Trent, thereby forcing all its waters into the tidal River Aire. This was unsuccessful and resulted in flooding, making what had been an already difficult river navigation into a hazardous one. A new channel, the Dutch River, was cut east from the River Don into the Ouse. This improved drainage, but not navigation.

Upstream, the river between Doncaster and Mexborough had, by 1729, been considerably improved, with complete navigation to Tinsley, four miles from Sheffield, a reality by 1751. All goods to and from Sheffield for shipment by water travelled by road between a river wharf at Tinsley and the city. It was not until 1815 that an Act of Parliament was obtained to build a canal into the city centre. The Sheffield Canal was opened on 22 February 1819. For the first time the city was linked directly to the sea, via the Trent and Humber. The Trent link had in fact been made 17 years earlier, with the construction of the Stainforth & Keadby Canal, which bypassed the tidal reaches of the old Dutch River.

The navigation declined until 1888, when the Sheffield & South Yorkshire Navigation Company was formed, and improvements made. The Straddle Warehouse built over Sheffield Basin dates from this period, as did the negotiations with the Aire & Calder Navigation to link Sheffield directly to the port of Goole and the more northerly coalfields. These negotiations resulted in the opening of the New Junction Canal on 2 January 1905. In 1983 the navigation was upgraded to the 700-tonne Eurobarge standard as far as Rotheram. Unfortunately, with no established traffic, the annual tonnage of goods carried is now just a fraction of the record one million tonnes achieved in 1951 and the navigation's future now seems to be firmly in the area of leisure and recreation.

Sheffield

The restored Sheffield Basin is dominated by the impressive Straddle Warehouse, built on columns over the water in 1895 by the South Yorkshire Navigation Company. Immediately behind this stands the Grain Warehouse, beyond which is the original Terminal Warehouse of 1819, standing an imposing seven storeys high. Leaving the basin *(showers and toilets)* the canal initially curves away beneath a railway bridge. Bridge 6, Bacon Lane, built in 1819, was also known as Needle's Eye, due to the problems its narrow width posed. The sharp-eyed will be able to spot evidence of boats having been forced through with a crowbar. It is now renowned as the place where the *Full Monty* was filmed. Staniforth Road Bridge provides useful access to pubs, *cafés, restaurants and shops* on Attercliffe Road. At Darnall Road Aqueduct – known locally as 'T'Acky Dock' – the landscape is dominated by stadia built to accommodate the Universiade, or World Student Games, in 1991. Access to the Hallam Stadium, *shops*, *pubs* and *cafés* can be made by leaving the towpath at the aqueduct. At Greenland Road Bridge the towpath crosses to the north side of the canal. The water here was once polluted, but this has now been eliminated and wildlife has recovered well. Fishermen can be seen along the banks, as can clumps of Michaelmas daisies, toadflax and valerian. Ahead the canal enters the top lock of the Tinsley Flight *(toilets* and *showers* here), and descends under the shadow of a massive steel viaduct carrying the M1 across the valley. A total of 11 locks, with tranquil wide pounds and open views, lower the navigation from its summit level, with the bright-green domed roofs of the Meadow Hall shopping centre dominating the outlook to the west. The canal joins the River Don at Halfpenny Bridge, and bends sharply right after passing the head of a large weir. Three locks, almost equally spaced, continue the descent towards Rotherham. The chamber of Rotherham Lock is quite tiny – retaining the original keel length of 61' 6" – and looks very pleasant in front of the court house, where barristers and defendants alike can be seen crossing the canal to the car park. There then follows a very tight right turn before the waterway seems almost to burrow underground and snake through the heart of the town.

Boatyards

ⓑ Jonathan Wilson Boatbuilders Victoria Boatyard, Sussex Street, Sheffield S4 7YY (0114 278 1234). Long-term mooring, slipway, crane, boat building, boat and engine sales and repairs, chandlery, toilets, DIY facilities.

South Yorkshire Navigations — Sheffield

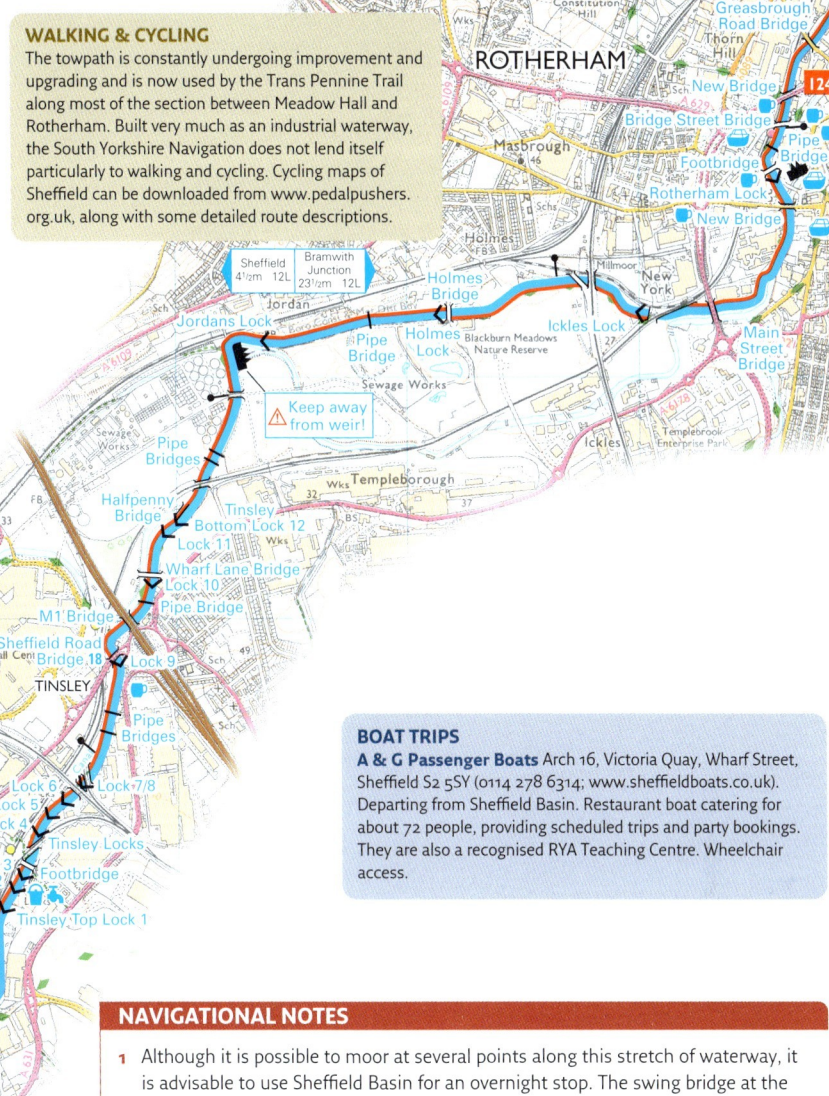

WALKING & CYCLING

The towpath is constantly undergoing improvement and upgrading and is now used by the Trans Pennine Trail along most of the section between Meadow Hall and Rotherham. Built very much as an industrial waterway, the South Yorkshire Navigation does not lend itself particularly to walking and cycling. Cycling maps of Sheffield can be downloaded from www.pedalpushers.org.uk, along with some detailed route descriptions.

BOAT TRIPS

A & G Passenger Boats Arch 16, Victoria Quay, Wharf Street, Sheffield S2 5SY (0114 278 6314; www.sheffieldboats.co.uk). Departing from Sheffield Basin. Restaurant boat catering for about 72 people, providing scheduled trips and party bookings. They are also a recognised RYA Teaching Centre. Wheelchair access.

NAVIGATIONAL NOTES

1. Although it is possible to moor at several points along this stretch of waterway, it is advisable to use Sheffield Basin for an overnight stop. The swing bridge at the entrance to the Basin requires a Watermate key and a windlass.
2. Passage through the Tinsley Flight requires assistance from one of the lock keepers who are on duty *daily 08.00-16.00 throughout the year*. No boat longer than 60' 0" may now use these locks. Telephone 07710 175488 (or 0113 281 6800 if no reply) *and ensure that you give 24 hours notice*.
3. From Tinsley to Doncaster Town Lock you are entering a river navigation with a series of artificial cuts. Many of the locks are accompanied by large weirs, so keep a sharp lookout for signs which direct you safely into the locks.
4. Once the river level rises 2ft above normal (gauging sticks are fixed at the top and bottom of all locks) pleasure craft may well experience difficulty due to the current, floating debris and the pull at weirs. Seek advice from BW staff before proceeding.
5. All locks require a Watermate key for operation; Holmes and Ickles Locks require a windlass. Obey the traffic light signals.
6. All weirs are protected by weir booms – keep well away.

Sheffield

S. Yorks. All services. Sheffield is England's fourth largest city and owes its world-famous reputation to the manufacture of steel, cutlery and silverware. The unique landscape into which Sheffield was built, steep hills sliced by deep-cut valleys, contributed to its importance during the Industrial Revolution. Five rivers facilitated the operation of water wheels, and hills rich in iron ore made Sheffield a natural pioneer of the steel industry. Today the city bustles with life, and new shopping complexes merge with the existing Georgian and Victorian architecture to give a lively mix. Overhead the two-car units of the Supertram shuttle back and forth, and the station close to the Canal Basin makes access to this excellent means of transport quite easy. Tudor Square brings together the internationally famous Crucible Theatre with the Lyceum Theatre, restored to its former Victorian splendour (from Park Square, by the Canal Basin, walk along Commercial Street, then turn left into Arundel Gate to find them). Also nearby are the award-winning Ruskin Gallery and Graves Art Gallery. Just across Exchange Street an open market is useful for supplies.

Town Hall Pinstone Street, Sheffield S1 2HH. Built in 1897 and designed by Mountford, the town hall has a clock tower, 210ft high, crowned with a statue of Vulcan, Roman God of Fire. There is a sculptured frieze outside depicting the industries of Sheffield.

Cutlers' Hall Church Street, Sheffield S1 1HG (0114 276 8149; www.cutlers-hall-sheffield.co.uk). Built in 1832, the Cutlers' Hall houses the Cutlers' Company collection of silver. Tours for parties. Telephone for details.

Millennium Galleries Arundel Gate, Sheffield S1 2PP (0114 278 2600; www.museums-sheffield.org.uk). A venue for art and design, bringing major exhibitions to the city. Paintings, drawings and prints of John Ruskin, plus a craft and design gallery. *Open Mon-Sat 10.00–17.00, Sun 11.00–16.00. Free (charge to some special exhibitions).*

Weston Park Western Bank, Sheffield S10 2TP (0114 278 2600; www.museums-sheffield.org.uk). The museum contains the largest collection of Sheffield Plate in the world and has a unique section devoted to cutlery. Also Bronze Age antiquities, local geology and wildlife gallery. *Open Mon-Sat 10.00–17.00, Sun 11.00–16.00. Closed 25, 26 December and 1 January. Free.* Touch sessions available for visually impaired people.

Cathedral of St Peter & St Paul Opposite the Cutlers' Hall in Church Street, Sheffield S1 1HA (0114 275 3434; www.sheffieldcathedral.org). A largely 15th-C church with 12th-C foundations and an interesting extension incorporating a new glass and steel porch, elevated to cathedral status in 1914. Five years later it was decided to enlarge the building, whilst retaining much of the original, to designs by Sir Charles Nicholson. Visitors will enjoy the stained-glass windows depicting local history and the Chaucer window in the Chapter House. *Open daily.* Guided tours can be arranged.

Kelham Island Museum Alma Street, Sheffield S3 8RY (0114 272 2106; www.simt.co.uk). Set upon an island in the River Don, this museum takes you through Sheffield's industrial past, with a chance to see craftsmen at work. A trail takes you past the only surviving Bessemer Converter, George Stephenson's first reversing-link engine, a grand-slam bomb, a Spitfire crankshaft and a 150hp Crossley gas engine. The River Don Engine (a 12,000bhp engineering wonder) is usually in steam twice a day. *Open Mon-Thu 10.00–16.00, Sun 11.00–16.45. Charge.* Café and shop.

Abbeydale Industrial Hamlet Abbeydale Road South, Sheffield S7 2QW (0114 272 2106; www.simt.co.uk). Four miles south west of the city centre. A superb example of industrial archaeology which displays a restored community, built around a water-powered scythe and steel works on a site used for iron forging for at least 500 years. *Open Apr–Sep Mon–Thu 10.00–16.00, Sun 11.00–16.45. Charge.* Café and shop. Bus from the High Street (continuation of Commercial Street, off Park Square).

Bishop's House Norton Lees Lane, Sheffield S8 9BE (0114 278 2600; www.museums-sheffield.org.uk). A timber-framed Bishop's house of 15th-C origins with 16th- and 17th-C additions. Other displays include Sheffield in Tudor and Stuart times and changing local history exhibitions. *Open Mon-Fri for pre-booked groups only. Charge.* Bus from the Transport Interchange, opposite the BR station in Pond Street, south of Park Square.

Crucible Theatre 55 Norfolk Street, Sheffield S1 1DA (0114 249 6000; www.sheffieldtheatres.co.uk). Studio theatre. The World Snooker Championships are held here each year.

Tourist Information Centre 14 Norfolk Row, Sheffield S1 2PA (0114 2211900; www.sheffield.gov.uk/out--about/tourist-information/).

Rotherham

S. Yorks. All services. An attractive town set amidst the industrial heartland of South Yorkshire where the buildings, although dating from a variety of periods, integrate well to form a coherent town centre. A part of the medieval town plan remains while the old town hall, in its new guise of an arcade, presents a fine renovation. In ancient times Rotherham was an important seat of learning, the College of Jesus being founded in 1482 by Archbishop Thomas and surviving until the Dissolution. The pinnacled tower of All Saints Church dates from 1409, and the remainder was almost entirely constructed during the same century. Its position, whilst maintaining an intimate contact with the town, is nevertheless imposing. Standing on the remaining four arches of the bridge which spans the River Don, the Chapel of Our Lady was built in 1483 and again fell victim to the Dissolution, after which it variously became an almshouse, a prison and a tobacconist's. It was finally restored and re-consecrated in 1924 and forms a very attractive feature in the lower part of the town. The key is available from the verger of All Saints, nearby.

Rotherham's modern growth dates from 1746 when Samuel Walker, a former schoolmaster, established its first ironworks. Coal mining developed, as well as the production of brass, steel, rope and glass, yet it is probably for the production of quality steels, in the form of fine-edge tools, that the town is best known.

Clifton Park Museum Clifton Lane, Rotherham S65 2AA (01709 336233; www.rotherham.gov.uk). A collection containing gemstones and examples of Rockingham and other local pottery can be seen here, in a house dating from 1783. Loan exhibitions of paintings. Roman remains from Templeborough can be seen in the park, opened by the Prince of Wales in 1891 and which covers an area of 56 acres. *Open Apr-Sep Mon-Thu and Sat 10.00-17.00, Sun 13.30-16.30 (Oct-Mar Sun 13.30-16.30). Closed Fri. Free. Café.*

Magna Science Adventure Centre Sheffield Road, Templeborough, Rotherham S60 1DX (01709 720002; www.visitmagna.co.uk). Housed in a former steelworks, this is an interactive centre, where you can experience the full power of the natural elements: air, water, fire and earth. Shoot with a water cannon, dodge lightning, feel what it is like to fly, use water power to launch a rocket, control a JCB and explode a rock face. *Open Mar-Oct daily 10.00-17.00, Nov-Feb Tue-Sun 10.00-17.00. Charge. Restaurant, café, shop.*

Meadowhall Shopping Centre Above Lock 9 on Tinsley Flight, Sheffield S9 1EP (0845 600 6800; www.meadowhall.co.uk). An immense indoor shopping mall accessible from above Lock 9 on the Tinsley Flight. *Open Mon-Fri 10.00-21.00, Sat 09.00-20.00, Sun 11.00-17.00. Restaurants and bars.*

Elsecar Heritage Centre Wath Road, Elsecar, Barnsley S74 8HJ (01226 740203; www.barnsley.gov.uk). Access by train from Sheffield. Follow the signs from Elsecar Station. These Victorian engineering workshops dating from the early 1800s have been transformed into an exciting centre, containing the Darwin Iron Works, the Elsecar Power House, The National Bottle Collection and the Elsecar Steam Railway. *Open daily 10.00-17.00. Closed Xmas and New Year. Charge. Tearooms.*

Tourist Information Centre 40 Bridgegate, Rotherham S60 1PQ (01709 835904; www.rotherham.gov.uk).

ART GALLERIES IN SHEFFIELD

Graves Third floor, Central Library Building, Surrey Street, Sheffield S1 1XZ (0114 278 2600; www.museums-sheffield.org.uk). A fine collection of English watercolours, drawings and prints, European paintings and Old Masters (16th-C to present). *Open Mon-Sat 10.00-17.00. Free. Coffee bar.*

Ruskin Collection Millennium Gallery, Arundel Gate, Sheffield S1 2PP (0114 278 2600; www.museums-sheffield.org.uk). A fine collection of minerals, plaster casts and architectural details, paintings, watercolours, illuminated manuscripts and books collected by John Ruskin for the people of Sheffield. Craft gallery. *Open Mon-Sat 10.00-17.00 and Sun 11.00-17.00. Free. South west of Park Square.*

Pubs and Restaurants

There are many pubs and restaurants in Sheffield, but few are close to the navigation.

The Quays 1819 Arches 1819, Victoria Quay, Wharf Street, Sheffield S2 5SY (0114 276 3031; www.sheffieldboats.co.uk). Operated by A & G Passenger Boats (*see page 121*). Friendly continental café and licensed bar serving real ale, tea, coffee, homemade meals and breakfasts. Children and dogs welcome. Outside seating. *Open Mon-Thu 10.00-18.00, Fri 10.00-19.30, Sat 11.00-early evening, Sun 13.00-16.00 (telephone or check website for details). Wifi.*

Yate's Wine Lodge 767 Domine Lane, Rotherham S60 1QA (01709 839349). A typically sociable wine lodge, serving food *L and E*. Children welcome *until 18.00*, and there is a garden. *Closed Sun.*

The Phoenix Hotel 1 College Road, Rotherham S60 1EY (01709 511121). West of Bridge Street Bridge. A town-centre pub serving real ale.

Nellie Denes at the Bridge Inn Greaseborough Road, Rotherham S60 1RB (01709 836818). Real ale is served here. *Closed Sun.*

123

Swinton

The exit from Rotherham is marked by a very large expanse of water before Rawmarsh Road Bridge, beyond which the Rotherham Cut eventually rejoins the River Don. When Eastwood Locks were combined on the upper site the river was re-aligned along the old canal bed. The new lock, opened on 1 June 1983 by the then Chairman of BWB (now BW), and called Sir Frank Price Lock in his honour (it is now Eastwood Lock), completed the modernisation to the 700-tonne barge standard of the South Yorkshire Navigations. There are good *moorings* here, with *toilets, showers and electricity*. It is worth noting, however, that from Sheffield the navigation has remained virtually unchanged since its original construction, a lasting tribute to its designers. At Aldwarke Lock a short channel bypasses the weir and a new concrete flyover has taken over from Wash Lane Bridge. Built in 1834, this listed structure bears the marks of much abuse from both barges and road traffic alike. The navigation now follows the course of the River Don, twisting and turning between high and often tree-lined banks, passing gaunt modern factory complexes, largely engaged in specialist steel manufacture. All discharges from these works are now carefully monitored for purity and to this end brightly coloured booms surround each outfall, containing their emissions for regular testing by the Environment Agency. Within recent memory the Don was fast becoming one of the most polluted rivers in Europe, but stringent control measures have reversed this trend and fishing on this stretch of water is now quite popular. Overlooked to the east by Thrybergh Park, it is not at all unpleasant. Kilnhurst Cut is entered at Kilnhurst Flood Lock, where the towpath crosses the river – without the benefit of a bridge, barge horses were obliged to use flat-decked chain ferries. At Hooton Road Bridge there is a reasonable *mooring*, a *grocer (open daily 05.00-22.00) off-licence* and *fish & chips*, together with a *takeaway and a pub*. To the east Hooton Common, criss-crossed with hedges and trees, rises to a more distant skyline. Once a tar works and a colliery lined the left bank, the former receiving the bulk of its deliveries by barge from local town gas works, before natural gas made these plants redundant. At Swinton Junction, the remains of the Dearne & Dove Canal climbs the locks off the mainline towards Barnsley. Waddington's boats throng the junction in a jumble of boilers, pipes and cranes, using the first pounds of the closed canal as a dock. The lock on the main line here was renamed Waddington Lock in recognition of the contribution that E.V. Waddington's barges once made to the life of the navigation. Let us hope they will contribute again.

NAVIGATIONAL NOTES

There is currently regular oil traffic on the South Yorkshire Navigations to Rotherham, operating two to three times a week, together with less frequent steel deliveries. Stone, loaded from Cadeby Quarry (*see* map page 127) is also transported along the waterway. Therefore, moor only at recognised mooring sites, using fixed rings or bollards, and keep a good lookout when underway.

Boatyards

Ⓑ**Tulley Marine Services** Boatyard, Northfield Road, Rotherham S60 1RR (01709 836743). 🚻 🛒 🔧 D Gas, overnight and long-term mooring, winter storage, slipway, hoist, boat building, boat and engine sales and repairs, toilets, DIY facilities.

Ⓑ**Waddingtons of Swinton** Boatyard, Broomwille Street, Swinton, Rotherham S64 8AT (01709 582232). In existence for 200 years, this proud and famous water freight company now finds operating conditions onerous, and some af the considerable fleet has either been broken up or sold. There are still many Waddingtons vessels to be seen around their boatyard.

● **Eastwood**
S. Yorks. PO, tel, stores. A suburb of Rotherham, with an excellent variety of corner shops dotted throughout the streets.

● **Kilnhurst**
S. Yorks. PO, tel, stores. A nondescript village merging into the conurbation linking Mexborough with Rotherham. Once the site of an ironworks and, more recently, a colliery, both now closed down. It was also known for the production of earthenware pottery.

● **Swinton Junction**
Swinton, Rotherham (www.bddct.org.uk). Here the Dearne & Dove Canal left the mainline and provided a route to Barnsley and thence via the Barnsley Canal to Wakefield. Together they made up the southern loop for the so-called Yorkshire Ring. Both waterways have long since fallen into disrepair but ambitious plans have been mooted to re-open them. Once a busy waterway junction and boat building centre, it still forms an interesting canal settlement, worthy of exploration.

Pubs and Restaurants

🍺**The Canal Bar** Swinton. A handy pub by the Dearne & Dove Canal.

Conisbrough

The fruits of EU land reclamation grants have been in evidence between Sheffield and here, in the form of both landscaping and tree planting, as the concept of waterways as linear parks comes close to reality. Cadeby Quarry makes regular use of the waterway to transport stone and boaters should be on the look out for barges unloading and manoeuvring immediately to the north of the railway bridge. The canal then passes Sprotbrough Flash, with woodland on the opposite bank. There are attractive *moorings* above Sprotbrough Lock which, being on the river, are prone to flooding after heavy rain.

- **Mexborough**
S. Yorks. All services. The tiny church of St John the Baptist has a 13th-C tower arch. Gardens and a fine reconstructed archway face the canal.
- **Conisbrough**
S. Yorks. All services. A relatively attractive town.
Conisbrough Castle Castle Hill, Conisbrough, Doncaster DN12 3BU (01709 863329; www.conisbroughcastle.org.uk). A Norman castle – c.1185 – with a circular keep capped by a conical wooden roof, superbly sited 90ft above the River Don. Excellent visitor centre. *Open Apr-Sep, daily 10.00-17.00 (Oct-Mar closes 16.00). Charge. Shop.*
- **Sprotbrough**
S. Yorks. PO, tel, stores, chemist, butcher, takeaways, off-licence. A useful source of provisions as the stores are open Mon-Sat 06.00-22.00 & Sun 07.00-21.00. Sir Walter Scott is reputed to have written part of *Ivanhoe* here. The church of St Mary dates from the 13th C, and is well worth a visit. In the chancel floor are brasses to William Fitzwilliam, 1474, who left £40 towards the building of the church tower.

Boatyards

Ⓑ **Waddingtons of Swinton** Boatyard, Broomville Street, Swinton, Rotherham S64 8AT (01709 582232). In existence for 200 years, this proud and famous water freight company now finds operating conditions onerous, and some af the considerable fleet has either been broken up or sold. There are still many Waddingtons vessels to be seen around their boatyard

Pubs and Restaurants

- **The Ferryboat** Church Street, Mexborough S64 0ER. Close to the canal, north of Mexborough Top Lock. A spacious 400-year-old pub serving real ale. Children welcome. Outside seating area and children's play area.
- **The George & Dragon** Church Street, Mexborough S64 0HE. Near to the Ferryboat. Serves real ale. Garden and children's play area.
- **Pastures Hotel** Pastures Road, Mexborough S64 0JJ (01709 577707; www.pastureshotel.co.uk). Beside the canal with Pastures Lodge, a pub and restaurant serving meals L and E. Children's play area.
- **The Cadeby Inn** Main Street, Cadeby, Doncaster DN5 7SW (01709 864009). Fine village pub, with open fires, in a converted farmhouse. Serves real ale and bar food L and E. Children welcome, and there is a garden. Quiz Wed.
- **Boat Inn** 1 Nursery Lane, Sprotbrough, Doncaster DN5 7NB (01302 858500; www.vintageinn.co.uk). Off Boat Lane, on the north bank of the canal above the lock. Former coaching house where Sir Walter Scott reputedly wrote *Ivanhoe*. Since 1652 this building has regularly alternated between farmhouse and pub. After lying derelict for 20 years, it was renovated to the present high standard and now serves real ale. Bar meals, all freshly prepared, available L and E. Children welcome. Open fires for winter, courtyard for the summer.
- **The Ivanhoe** Melton Road, Sprotbrough, Doncaster DN5 7NS (01302 853130). ½ mile from the river at the top of the village. Lively, comfortable pub overlooking the cricket pitch. Real ale is served, together with bar meals L and E (not Sun or Mon E). Children welcome. Garden.

> **BOAT TRIPS**
> **Alan Oliver (Cruises)** Tall Pines, Cadeby Road, Doncaster DN5 7SD (01302 853556; www.riverboatcruises.co.uk). Waterbus service from above Sprotbrough Lock on *Sun and B Hols* aboard ex-Clyde ferry *Wyre Lady*. Also private charter and special events.

South Yorkshire Navigations — Conisbrough

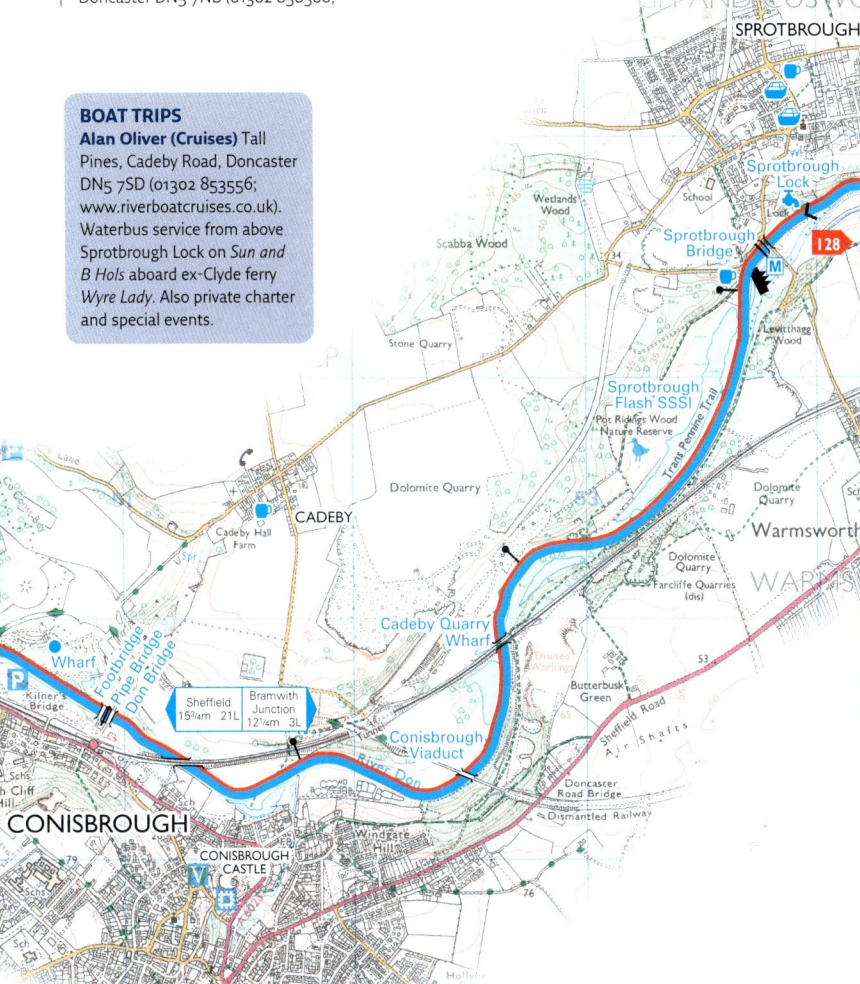

Doncaster

The waterway now enters a pleasant tree-lined valley, only briefly intruded upon by the noise of motorway traffic crossing overhead on the slender Don viaduct. Passing beneath two iron-girdered railway bridges, the waterway sweeps around wide bends towards Doncaster. Just before Doncaster Town Lock the navigation finally parts company with the River Don, although the river is never far away for many miles to come. Ahead lies a jumble of transport systems as road crosses railway, which in turn crosses the canal, all just beyond Doncaster Town Lock. Then the navigation is in Doncaster, widening out opposite the church. The town centre is a short walk to the east, where there is a large *market place*, with some excellent seafood stalls, and the expansive Frenchgate Shopping Centre and a *supermarket*. There is a *laundrette* in Beckett Road, 5 minutes' walk to the west. As you leave the town, factories sprawl around the outside sweep of a wide bend, while all the time the River Don hugs the left-hand bank, obscured by flood embankments.
There is little of interest between the centre of Doncaster and Long Sandall Lock, with its tower-shaped control cabin looking down on manicured lawns and neat flower beds. There is a *picnic site* and a self-operated *pump out* here. Dickens stayed in Long Sandall in 1857 and described nearby Doncaster as being thronged with 'horse-mad, betting-mad, drunken-mad, vice-mad crowds'. Some say the area is quieter now.

Pubs and Restaurants

- **The Black Bull** 12 Market Place, Doncaster DN1 1LQ (01302 361661). Food is served from *11.30–17.00*, along with real ale. Garden. Discos and karaoke.
- **The Red Lion** 37–38 Market Place, Doncaster DN1 1NH (01302 732120). A wide choice of real ale and food *all day, every day*. Children welcome.

WALKING & CYCLING
Details of the annual Doncaster Walking Festival can be found at www.doncaster.gov.uk. There are usually more than 20 organised walks, such as the 4-mile Sprotbrough and Cusworth Millennium Walk, a stroll round Highfields Country park and the more challenging Beating the Bounds walk. From Long Sandall Lock walkers and cyclists should follow the waymarked signs to complete their journey into Doncaster.

NAVIGATIONAL NOTES
Long Sandall Lock: When locking upstream keep away from the top gates to avoid excessive turbulence. Similarly, boats below the lock should keep well clear of the bottom gates when it is emptying. This applies to Sykehouse Lock as well.

● **Doncaster**
S. Yorks. All services. Once the site of a Roman station – Danum – the town became an important industrial centre in the 19th C; the home of a large railway and carriage works and ringed by a girdle of mining villages. Exploited for almost a century, the pits of the South Yorkshire Coalfield yielded open-cast coal to the west, whilst to the east of a dividing ridge of magnesian limestone, deep mines were sunk. In the early part of the 19th C, when the town was largely an agricultural community straddling the Great North Road, its High Street was regarded as the finest along the route between London and Edinburgh. Alas, most of the buildings of the last 50 years pay little regard to the original character. One consistent link with the past is, however, provided by the annual St Leger horse race, first run in 1776, and pre-dating the Derby by two years. There is a large market to the east of the canal.

Parish Church of St George (Doncaster Minster) Church Street, Doncaster DN1 1RD (01302 323748; www.doncasterminster.co.uk) Built to a design by Gilbert Scott in 1858 on an almost cathedral scale (the crossing tower is fully 170ft tall), it replaced a medieval church burnt down in 1853. A very fine example of Victorian Neo-Gothic. *Open to visitors Mon–Sat 10.30–15.30, and Sun for service.*

Mansion House High Street, Doncaster DN1 1BN (01302 737600; www.doncaster.gov.uk). An impressive civic building designed by James Paine and finished in 1748. *Open by appointment only.*

Museum and Art Gallery Chequer Road, Doncaster DN1 2AE (01302 734293; www.doncaster.gov.uk). Opened in 1964, it contains relics from the Roman station, early town documents, costumes, paintings, ceramics and silver, archaeological and natural history displays, and the regimental collection of the King's Own Yorkshire Light Infantry. *Open Mon–Sat 10.00–17.00. Free.*

Cusworth Hall Museum Cusworth Park, Cusworth Lane, Doncaster DN5 7TU (01302 782342; www.doncaster.gov.uk). The Georgian house (rebuilt and then altered by James Paine in the 1740s) set in landscaped parkland, contains a museum which illustrates South Yorkshire's history, industries, agriculture and social life. Check online or telephone to confirm opening times. Charge. Shop, teas.

Brodsworth Hall Brodsworth, Doncaster DN5 7XJ (01302 722598; www.english-heritage.org.uk). About 5 miles north west of Doncaster, off the A635, and worth the effort. A rare example of a Victorian country house which has survived, largely unaltered, with much of its original furnishings and decorations intact. It was built during the 1860s, and retains a faded grandeur which speaks of an opulent past. The gardens are delightful. *Open Apr–Oct, Tue–Sun 13.00–16.30. Gardens open 10.00–17.00; winter gardens only 11.00–16.00.* Charge. Tearoom and shop. Telephone 01709 515151; or visit www.travelsouthyorkshire.com for details of buses from Doncaster.

Tourist Information Centre 38–40 High Street, Doncaster DN1 1DE (01302 734309; www.visitdoncaster.com. gov.uk). *Open Mon–Fri 09.00–17.00, Sat 10.00–15.30.*

Stainforth

At Sandall Grove there is a tiny, though delightful, hotch potch of a church, nestling beside a farmyard, beyond which Barnby Dun comes into view. There is a *shower block* with facilities for the disabled at this pretty village.

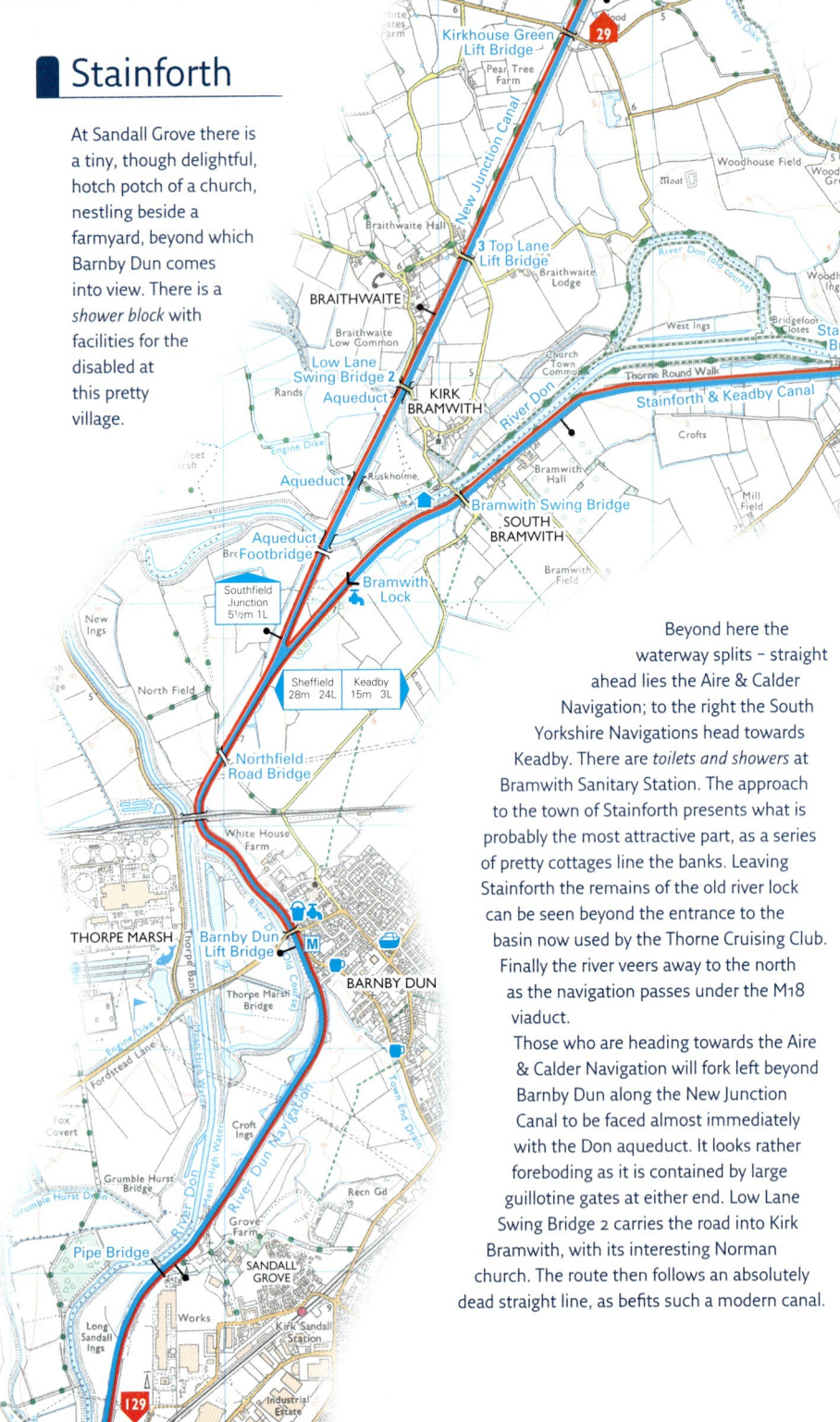

Beyond here the waterway splits – straight ahead lies the Aire & Calder Navigation; to the right the South Yorkshire Navigations head towards Keadby. There are *toilets and showers* at Bramwith Sanitary Station. The approach to the town of Stainforth presents what is probably the most attractive part, as a series of pretty cottages line the banks. Leaving Stainforth the remains of the old river lock can be seen beyond the entrance to the basin now used by the Thorne Cruising Club. Finally the river veers away to the north as the navigation passes under the M18 viaduct.

Those who are heading towards the Aire & Calder Navigation will fork left beyond Barnby Dun along the New Junction Canal to be faced almost immediately with the Don aqueduct. It looks rather foreboding as it is contained by large guillotine gates at either end. Low Lane Swing Bridge 2 carries the road into Kirk Bramwith, with its interesting Norman church. The route then follows an absolutely dead straight line, as befits such a modern canal.

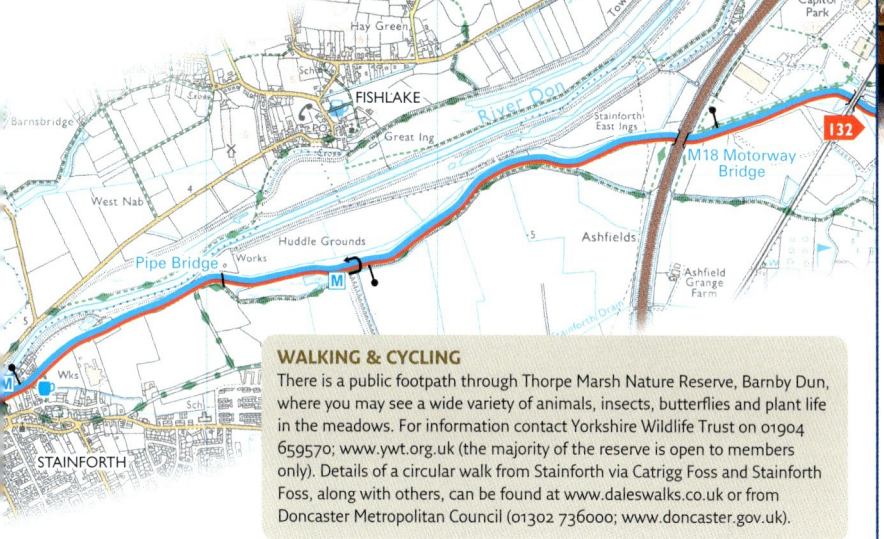

South Yorkshire Navigations — Stainforth

WALKING & CYCLING
There is a public footpath through Thorpe Marsh Nature Reserve, Barnby Dun, where you may see a wide variety of animals, insects, butterflies and plant life in the meadows. For information contact Yorkshire Wildlife Trust on 01904 659570; www.ywt.org.uk (the majority of the reserve is open to members only). Details of a circular walk from Stainforth via Catrigg Foss and Stainforth Foss, along with others, can be found at www.daleswalks.co.uk or from Doncaster Metropolitan Council (01302 736000; www.doncaster.gov.uk).

Barnby Dun
S. Yorks. PO, tel, stores, chemist, butcher, off-licence, takeaways, fish & chips, garage. An attractive village laid out along one side of the canal on slightly rising ground. Once a picturesque mix of old cottages, more recent infilling threatens to overpower the original village and turn it into a Doncaster suburb. It is reported that the once boggy marshland around the village yielded a surprising find: the vertebrae of a whale. From the Lift Bridge (*toilets and showers*) a walk along the street, which almost parallels the canal, will be rewarded by an excellent farm shop selling fresh local produce, two pubs and a Chinese restaurant. The church of St Peter and St Paul is a virtually intact example of 14th-C work, with some remarkable gargoyles. It is well worth a visit. The shop is open *daily 06.00–23.00*.

Stainforth
S. Yorks. All services – station 1 mile distant. An unprepossessing town strung out along the main road south of the canal.

NAVIGATIONAL NOTES
1. All locks and moveable bridges can be boater-operated using a BW Watermate key.
2. A windlass is needed to operate Bramwith Lock.
3. Bramwith Lock has two chambers. Check to see whether in fact the lock is in use before operating.

Pubs and Restaurants

The White Hart Top Road, Barnby Dun, Doncaster DN3 1DB (01302 882959). Real ale is dispensed in this cosy and welcoming local pub. The bar and seating area are liberally decorated with antiques, particularly china, while the portions of food are generous in the extreme, and an extensive menu is offered *L and E (not Sun E)*. Children welcome. Outside seating. Quiz *Sun and Wed*, karaoke *Thu*.

The Star High Street, Barnby Dun, Doncaster DN3 1DY (01302 882571). East of the canal, this friendly pub serves bar food *L and E (not Wed)*. Children welcome. Garden. Quiz *Tue*.

NEW JUNCTION CANAL
This waterway, completed in 1905, provides a link between the South Yorkshire Navigations and the Aire & Calder Navigation. It is 5½ miles long and completely straight all the way, the monotony being broken only by a series of swing and lift bridges. There are aqueducts at each end of the long corridor formed by the navigation, the one in the south carrying the canal over the River Don. Both aqueducts are equipped with tall guillotine gates, which serve either to isolate the canal in times of flood, or to facilitate repairs. Moorings are available beside Sykehouse Lock and Sykehouse Lift Bridge but there are no facilities. (*see page 29*).

Thorne

Stanilands Marina, immediately beyond the railway bridge, provides both safe *moorings* and a range of *services*, Thorne town centre being only ¼ mile away. Beyond Thorne Bridge there are further *moorings*, available to visitors, at the marina. Leaving Thorne the landscape again opens up and a rich, fertile plain borders the navigation. Boaters will no doubt enjoy operating Wykewell Lift Bridge, which, together with the road barriers and flashing red lights, is controlled by pressing the appropriate buttons in the grey box. At Moores Swing Bridge a line of farms can be seen to the north of the canal. Here there is still evidence of the old strip system of farming, where each dwelling is backed by a long narrow strip of land. These units of land would vary in size according to the type of soil and the lie of the land. The one-acre strip (220yds long by 22yds wide) was a rarity in most parts of the country, farms generally possessing strips much smaller than this. Much of the land along the length of the navigation from Stainforth to Keadby was prone to seasonal flooding and consequently benefited greatly from

● **Thorne**
S. Yorks. All services. A small brick-built market town with an attractive pedestrian precinct around Finkle Street. Thorne's early industries were rope making, sacking and weaving with a canal traffic of coal, pig iron and stone. The town was in fact dependent on the river and the canal for its water supply, the only boreholes supplying Darley's brewery and the workhouse. Regettably the brewery ceased to function as such in 1986. St Nicholas' church displays a variety of 13th-C work, including the south doorway and an unbuttressed west tower.

Pubs and Restaurants

There are many pubs in Thorne. The following is right by the navigation:

●✕ **The Canal Tavern** South Parade, Thorne, Doncaster DN8 5DZ (01405 813688). North of Thorne Bridge. A lively canalside pub with a beer garden, serving real ale. Bar and restaurant meals available *L and E daily*. Children welcome in the restaurant. Canalside garden and mooring for patrons. Regular music and quiz nights, plus pool, darts and TV.

the drainage schemes established during the 17th C. Herons abound in this area, and grebe can also be seen along the more overgrown sections of the waterway, where their floating nests are anchored to the reeds. Only 100 years ago these birds had been all but exterminated in England due to fashionable Victorian ladies wishing to display not just the odd feather, but occasionally the entire plumage, in their hats. At Maud's Bridge, again boater-operated, instructions for its operation are to be found on the white box. Now the railway adds some excitement by joining the canal and running along the north bank to Medge Hall and Crook o'Moor Swing Bridge, where it moves briefly away only to rejoin the line of the navigation at Godnow Bridge.

BOAT TRIPS
The Ethel Trust Staniland Marina, Lock Lane, Thorne, Doncaster DN8 5EP (0114 2536725/ 07722 678168; www.etheltrustcommunitybarge.co.uk). Sailing barge *Ethel* is available for day or weekend charter, and can cater for wheelchair users.

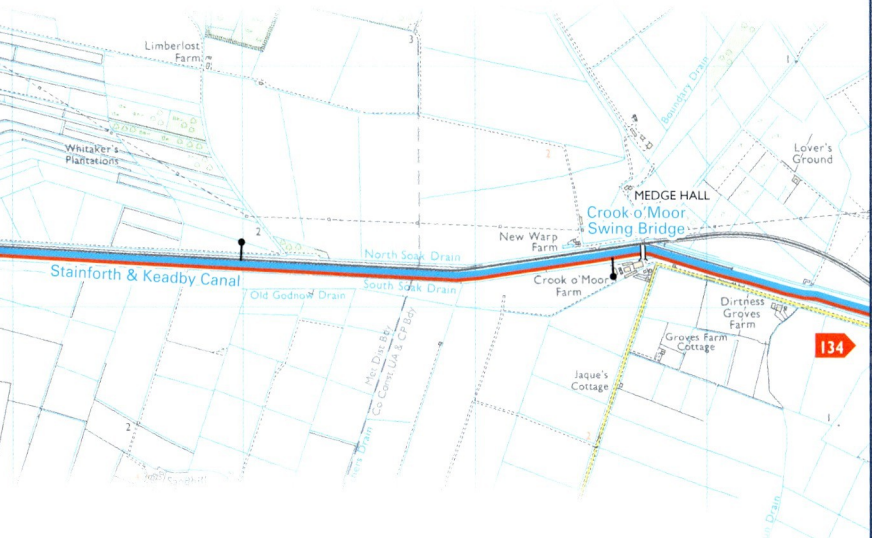

Boatyards

Ⓑ✕ 🏆 **Stanilands Marina** Lock Lane, Thorne, Doncaster DN8 5EP (01405 813150; www.staniland-marina.co.uk). 🎁🚻⛽D Pump out, gas, overnight and long-term mooring, winter storage, slipway, hoist, boat sales and repairs, engine repairs, chandlery, toilets, showers, laundrette, DIY facilities. Clubhouse bar with restaurant.

Ⓑ**Thorne Boat Services** South Parade, Thorne, Doncaster DN8 5DZ (01405 814197). 🎁🚻⛽

toilets and showers next door) **D** Pump out gas, boat repairs, engine sales and repairs, chandlery, books and maps. *Emergency call out service.*

Ⓑ 🏆 **Blue Water Marina** South End, Thorne, Doncaster DN8 5QR (01405 813165; www.bluewatermarina.co.uk). 🎁🚻⛽D Pump out, gas, overnight and long-term mooring, slipway, boat sales, toilets, showers, limited chandlery. Visitors welcome.

Keadby

The village of Crowle can be reached from either Godnow Swing Bridge or Crowle Bridge. It is a mile to the north, and is worth the walk since it has a selection of *shops* and *pubs*, and an interesting church. In 1747 the body of a woman was found nearby in the peat moor, buried upright at a depth of 6ft. From her sandals it appeared that she had been there for several centuries, but was remarkably well preserved. Just beyond Crowle Station there is evidence of the site of the old Axholme Joint Railway Bridge, demolished in 1972. The bridge must have proved an impressive landmark, consisting of four brick archways and a circular brick abutment upon which the railway pivoted through 90 degrees, thus allowing the passage of the tall-sailed keels. Ahead lies the long straight to Keadby. It is not without excitement, however, as immediately beyond Vazon Swing Bridge there is a remarkable railway bridge, skewed across the canal only a couple of feet above the water. Built in 1915, the bridge is supposedly one of only three of its kind in Europe. In order to allow the passage of boats, winches slide the bridge deck sideways, so clearing the navigation and, by a further series of wire cables and pulleys, winch the deck back into place. The entire operation is controlled from the nearby signal box. Once beyond the bridge the canal passes the rebuilt Keadby Power Station, which dominates the north bank. A wind farm is due to be constructed on land adjacent to the power station and a new bridge will be built, crossing both canal and railway, to facilitate access. Ahead is Keadby Swing Bridge and Lock, allowing entry into the tidal Trent. There are two *pubs* nearby, *showers* and *toilets* in the services block, and *moorings* are available before the swing bridge.

NAVIGATIONAL NOTES

1. Keadby Lock is 77' 8" x 22' 6" although longer craft can be admitted when the tide makes a level. Draught may be limited by the build up of silt at the mouth of the lock.
2. Commercial river traffic operates on VHF Channel 6 upstream of Keadby Bridge on the River Trent. VHF users should monitor this channel to establish the whereabouts of large craft on the river. Keadby Lock operates on channel 74.
3. See notes 4 and 5 on pages 168 and note 4 on page 162.
4. Toot your horn when approaching Vazon Sliding Railway Bridge. Operational *24 hrs a day*.
5. The lock keeper at Keadby should be contacted on 07733 124611 or 01724 782205 giving at least 24 hours notice. If unattended, contact BW 0113 281 6800.
6. In order to secure your boat safely whilst using Keadby Lock, bow and stern ropes should be at least 25' in length.

- **Crowle**
Humberside. All services - station 1 mile distant beside the waterway. A straggling village one mile north of the canal. There are some attractive Georgian houses in the vicinity of the church. The Market Square retains some of its character and is dominated by the elaborate Victorian façade of the old ballroom, now used for discos. The church of St Oswald is a handsome structure containing much Norman work, and some fine incised doorways. During the restoration of the tower in 1840 an Anglo-Saxon cross shaft, probably inspired by the Vikings and some 7ft in length, was found over a doorway. It is believed to date from the 11th C and now stands at the back of the church.

- **Ealand**
Humberside. PO, tel, stores. A small settlement next to the canal. There are some pretty cottages in the village, and a station. Gas is available from the stores.

- **Keadby**
Humberside. Tel. PO, stores, fish & chips and station in Althorpe to the south of the village. A dull settlement which has declined since the Stainforth & Keadby Canal ceased to carry commercial traffic. The only real activity is provided by craft entering the tidal Trent, the commercial vessels unloading at the river wharf, and the two pubs.

South Yorkshire Navigations — Keadby

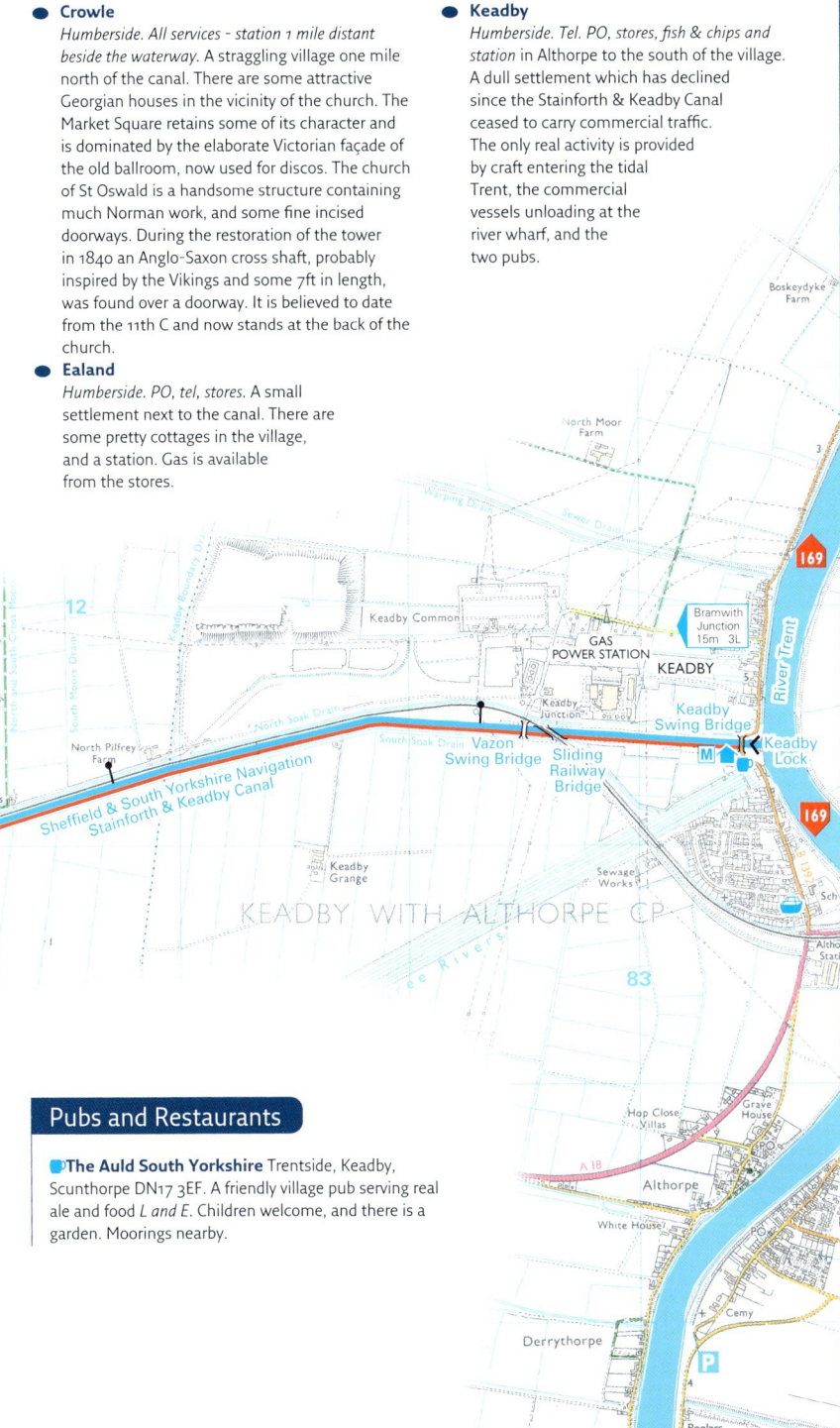

Pubs and Restaurants

The Auld South Yorkshire Trentside, Keadby, Scunthorpe DN17 3EF. A friendly village pub serving real ale and food *L and E*. Children welcome, and there is a garden. Moorings nearby.

RIVER TRENT

MAXIMUM DIMENSIONS
Shardlow to Meadow Lane Lock, Nottingham
Length: 81'
Beam: 14' 6"
Headroom: 8'

Meadow Lane Lock to Gainsborough
Length: 165'
Beam: 18' 6"
Headroom: 13'

MANAGER
01636 704481; enquiries.eastmidlands@britishwaterways.co.uk

MILEAGE
DERWENT MOUTH to:
Cranfleet Lock: 2 3/4 miles
Beeston Lock: 7 miles
Meadow Lane Lock, Nottingham: 12 miles
Gunthorpe Bridge: 22 miles
Fiskerton: 29 3/4 miles
Newark Castle: 35 1/2 miles
Cromwell Lock: 40 1/2 miles
Dunham Bridge: 53 miles
TORKSEY Junction: 57 miles
Littleborough: 60 1/4 miles
GAINSBOROUGH Bridge: 67 miles
WEST STOCKWITH: 71 3/4 miles
KEADBY Junction: 84 1/4 miles
TRENT FALLS: 93 3/4 miles

Locks: 12

The River Trent is a historic highway running for about 100 miles from the Midlands to the Humber ports and the North Sea, and has long been of prime economic and social importance to the areas through which it flows. It is thought that as long ago as the Bronze Age the Trent was part of the trade route from the Continent to the metal-working industry in Ireland. The Romans recognised the value of the river as a route to the centre of England from the sea. In about AD 120, in the time of Emperor Hadrian, they built the Foss Dyke canal to link the Trent valley with Lindum Colonia (now Lincoln), the River Witham and the Wash. The Trent later acted as an easy route for the Danish invaders, who penetrated as far as Nottingham. In about AD 924 Edward the Elder expelled the Danes from Nottingham and built the first bridge there. The second bridge at Nottingham was built in 1156 (some 20 years earlier than Old London Bridge) and lasted 714 years. Its remains can still be seen. The third bridge was built in 1871 and forms the basic structure of today's Trent Bridge. The first Act of Parliament to improve the Trent as a navigation was passed in 1699. In 1783 an Act authorised the construction of a towpath, thus allowing for the first time the passage of sail-less barges. Ten years later the Trent Navigation Company's engineer drew up a comprehensive scheme to build locks and weirs, to increase the depth in certain reaches and build a number of training walls to narrow and thus deepen the channel. In 1906, the Royal Commission on Inland Waterways adopted it as the official future plan, authorising locks at Stoke Bardolph, Gunthorpe, Hazleford and Cromwell. The works were completed in 1926. Trade soon increased fourfold.
At its peak in the 19th C and early 20th C, the Trent formed the main artery of trade for the East Midlands, connecting with the South Yorkshire Navigations, the Chesterfield Canal, the Fossdyke, the Grantham Canal, the Erewash Canal, the River Soar Navigation and the Trent & Mersey Canal. Although it remains connected today to all but the Grantham Canal, the large trade between these waterways dwindled away with railway competition and in particular as a result of railway ownership of most of those connecting waterways. Today most of the commercial carrying is from gravel pits at Besthorpe and Girton to Hull, Goole and Whitwood with sporadic traffic as far upstream as Gunthorpe.
The Trent remains a useful through route for pleasure craft, easy to navigate and with many interesting connections. British Waterways has improved facilities for pleasure craft with landing stages at locks, moorings and easier lock operating systems.

Thrumpton

Downstream from Derwent Mouth *(see Books 3 and 4)*, the navigation goes through Sawley Cut, avoiding the weir to the north, by the M1 bridge. Near the head of the cut is a flood lock, which under most conditions is open. Beyond this lock and the main road bridge is a wide stretch of waterway, where both banks are crowded with moored boats. Just at the tail of Sawley Locks (a pair – both now mechanised with a keeper – 0115 973 5234) is a large railway bridge over the river; this line carries oil and coal trains to Castle Donington and Willington power stations. To the east the cooling towers of the huge Ratcliffe Power Station are clearly visible, but they are discreetly tucked away behind Red Hill and their intrusion into the landscape is thus minimised. Trent Lock marks the junction of the Erewash Canal with the River Trent, while at the wooded Red Hill is the mouth of the River Soar. It is important not to get lost here, for there is a large weir just downstream of the railway bridges. Boats aiming for Nottingham should bear left at the big sailing club house, entering Cranfleet Cut. A pair of protective flood gates will be passed, then another railway bridge (the line disappearing into the decorative tunnel portal through Red Hill), another long line of moored motor cruisers (many belonging to the Nottingham Yacht Club) and an attractive white accommodation bridge. At the end of the cut is Cranfleet Lock; from here one may enjoy a view of the woods hiding Thrumpton Park. The old lock house at Cranfleet is now the headquarters of the Nottingham Yacht Club. Steep wooded slopes rise behind Thrumpton, while the towers of the power station still overlook the whole scene. Below Thrumpton, the river winds through flat land, passing the village of Barton in Fabis.

Pubs and Restaurants

Chandlery Restaurant Sawley Marina, Long Eaton NG10 3AE (0115 946 0300). Part of the marina complex this café/restaurant serves food *L (not Mon)*, specialising in large portions at low prices. Children and dogs welcome.

Plank & Leggit Tamworth Road, Sawley, Long Eaton NG103AE (0115 972 1515). 200yds south of Sawley Cut, behind the marina, serving real ale. A wide ranging, inexpensive menu, majoring on healthy eating, is available *all day* as are inexpensive children's and special menus (wide V choice). Indoor and outdoor children's play areas, outside seating and summer barbecues. Dogs welcome on outdoor patio area.

Harrington Arms Tamworth Road, Sawley Long Eaton NG10 3AU (0115 973 2614; www.harringtonarms-longeaton.co.uk). North of the flood lock. 400-year-old, heavily beamed pub, ¼ mile from Sawley Marina, serving an extensive selection of meals *available all day*. Excellent real ale selection. No children or dogs. Large garden and heated patio area. Real fires. Beer festival and occasional special events.

Nag's Head Old Wilne Road, Sawley, Long Eaton (0115 973 2983). Village local serving real ale and bar meals. No children or dogs. Darts and skittles. *Monthly* quiz.

White Lion Sawley, Long Eaton NG10 3AT (0115 973 3961). North of the flood lock. Skittles, darts, pool, real ale and food. Children welcome. Garden. Karaoke *Sat*.

The Trent Lock Trent Lock, Long Eaton NG10 2FY (0115 972 5159; www.vintageinn.co.uk). Formerly the Navigation Inn. Large, popular, family pub with a garden and play area. Real ales and a wide range of reasonably priced food available *L and E, daily*. Moorings.

Steamboat Inn Trent Lock, Long Eaton NG10 2FY. (0115 946 3955). On the Erewash Canal. Built by the canal company in 1791, when it was called the Erewash Navigation Inn, it is now an upmarket canalside pub and restaurant. Real ale available. Food served *all day* from bar and à la carte restaurant. Children welcome *until 20.00*. Live music *Thu* and *regular* quiz nights.

- **Sawley**
  Notts. PO, tel, stores, garage. The tall church spire attracts one across the river to Sawley, and in this respect the promise is fulfiled, for the medieval church is beautiful and is approached by a formal avenue of lime trees leading to the 600-year-old doorway. Otherwise Sawley is an uninteresting main road village on the outskirts of Long Eaton.

- **Sawley Cut**
  In addition to a large marina and a well-patronised mooring site, the Derby Motor Boat Club have a base on the Sawley Cut. All kinds of boats are represented here: canal boats, river boats and even seagoing vessels. It is certainly no place to be passing through on a summer Sunday late-afternoon, for there will be scores of craft queuing up to pass through the locks after spending the weekend downstream. There are windlasses for sale at Sawley Lock, as well as the more conventional facilities.

- **Trent Lock**
  A busy and unusual boating centre at the southern terminus of the Erewash Canal (see Book 3). There are two boatyards and two pubs here.

- **Thrumpton**
  Notts. Tel. This little village beside the Trent is, like so many other places on the river, a dead end. Motorists only go there if they have good reason to. Hence Thrumpton is a quiet and unspoilt farming village, with new development only up at the far end. Although the impressive Hall is hidden away at the west end of the village, its large uncompromising gateway serves to remind the villagers what they are there for. The tiny church, with its narrow nave and a tower, was built in the 13th C but restored in 1872 by the well-known architect G.E. Street, at the expense of Lady Byron. The single street winds past it down to the river – there used to be a ferry here.

  Thrumpton Hall Thrumpton NG11 0AX (07590 818045; www.thrumptonhall.com). Basically a James I mansion built around a much older manor house. The Hall is famous for its oak staircase, which dates from the time of Charles II. The ground-floor rooms are well-used, and elegantly decorated; the grounds are delightful, encompassing a backwater off the River Trent. The house is private and used as a

  wedding location. Gardens open Wed 11.00–15.00 but telephone in advance to confirm.

- **Barton in Fabis**
  Notts. Tel. A small and isolated village, composed mainly of modern housing and set well back from the river. The 14th-C church seems unbalanced in several respects; it has a great variety of styles. The building has, however, considerable charm, being light, and attractively irregular. It contains several monuments to the Sacheverell family.

River Trent — Thrumpton

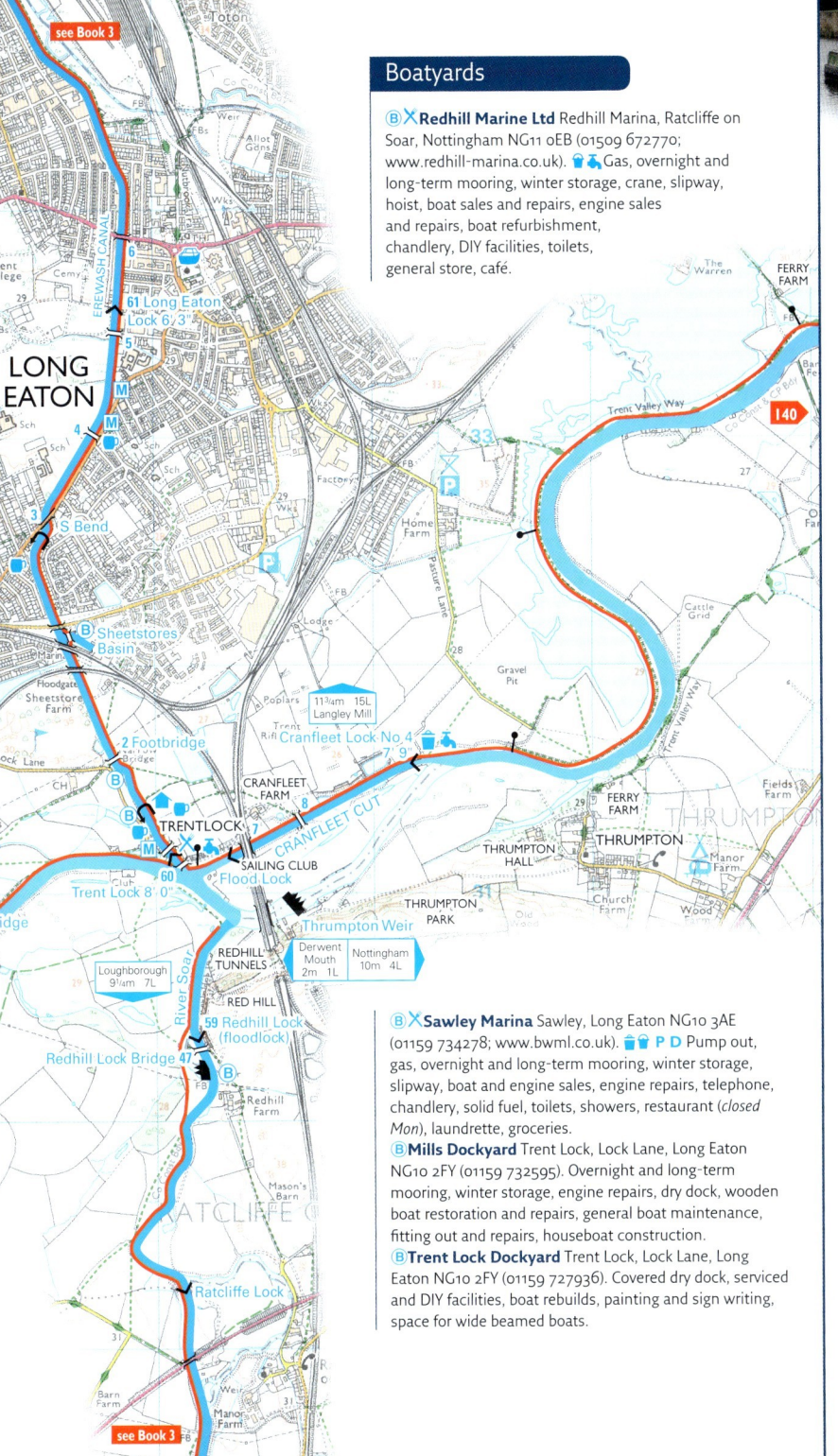

Boatyards

ⒷⓍ **Redhill Marine Ltd** Redhill Marina, Ratcliffe on Soar, Nottingham NG11 0EB (01509 672770; www.redhill-marina.co.uk). Gas, overnight and long-term mooring, winter storage, crane, slipway, hoist, boat sales and repairs, engine sales and repairs, boat refurbishment, chandlery, DIY facilities, toilets, general store, café.

ⒷⓍ **Sawley Marina** Sawley, Long Eaton NG10 3AE (01159 734278; www.bwml.co.uk). P D Pump out, gas, overnight and long-term mooring, winter storage, slipway, boat and engine sales, engine repairs, telephone, chandlery, solid fuel, toilets, showers, restaurant (*closed Mon*), laundrette, groceries.

Ⓑ **Mills Dockyard** Trent Lock, Lock Lane, Long Eaton NG10 2FY (01159 732595). Overnight and long-term mooring, winter storage, engine repairs, dry dock, wooden boat restoration and repairs, general boat maintenance, fitting out and repairs, houseboat construction.

Ⓑ **Trent Lock Dockyard** Trent Lock, Lock Lane, Long Eaton NG10 2FY (01159 727936). Covered dry dock, serviced and DIY facilities, boat rebuilds, painting and sign writing, space for wide beamed boats.

139

Nottingham

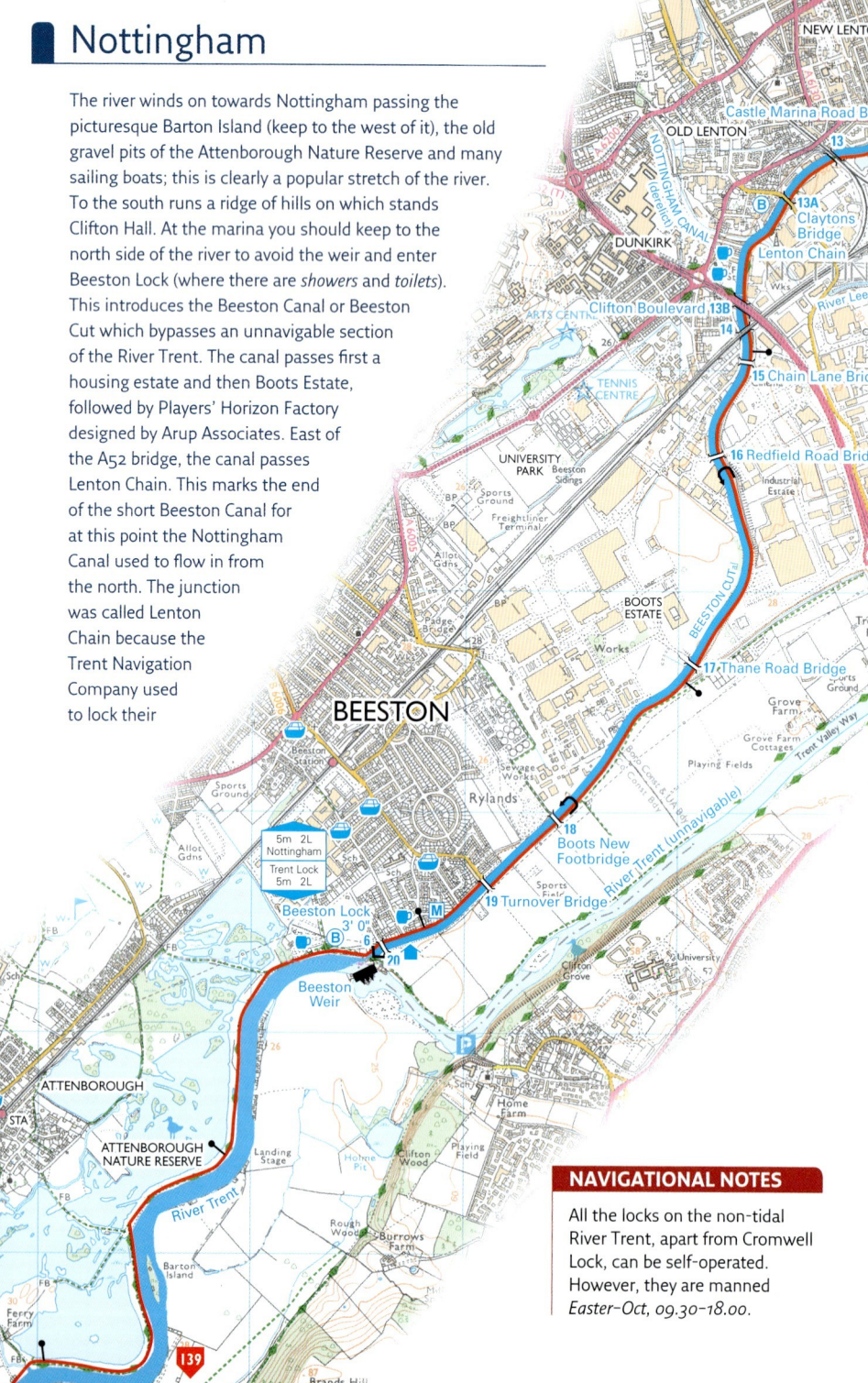

The river winds on towards Nottingham passing the picturesque Barton Island (keep to the west of it), the old gravel pits of the Attenborough Nature Reserve and many sailing boats; this is clearly a popular stretch of the river. To the south runs a ridge of hills on which stands Clifton Hall. At the marina you should keep to the north side of the river to avoid the weir and enter Beeston Lock (where there are *showers* and *toilets*). This introduces the Beeston Canal or Beeston Cut which bypasses an unnavigable section of the River Trent. The canal passes first a housing estate and then Boots Estate, followed by Players' Horizon Factory designed by Arup Associates. East of the A52 bridge, the canal passes Lenton Chain. This marks the end of the short Beeston Canal for at this point the Nottingham Canal used to flow in from the north. The junction was called Lenton Chain because the Trent Navigation Company used to lock their

NAVIGATIONAL NOTES

All the locks on the non-tidal River Trent, apart from Cromwell Lock, can be self-operated. However, they are manned *Easter–Oct, 09.30–18.00.*

River Trent

Nottingham

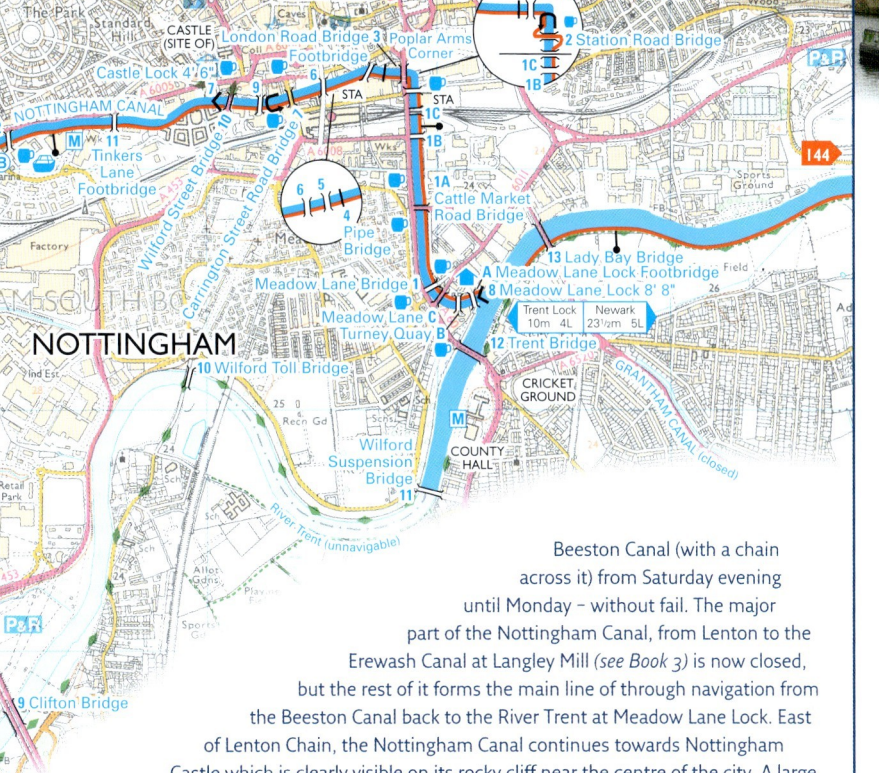

Beeston Canal (with a chain across it) from Saturday evening until Monday – without fail. The major part of the Nottingham Canal, from Lenton to the Erewash Canal at Langley Mill *(see Book 3)* is now closed, but the rest of it forms the main line of through navigation from the Beeston Canal back to the River Trent at Meadow Lane Lock. East of Lenton Chain, the Nottingham Canal continues towards Nottingham Castle which is clearly visible on its rocky cliff near the centre of the city. A large *marina*, houses and a *Sainsbury's superstore* cheer up what was once a gloomy aspect. There are moorings beyond the shallow Castle Lock, bounded by an area of vibrant new building and centrally placed for the railway station and city centre. Approaching Poplar Arms corner, once hemmed in by massive stone viaducts: a memorial to the Great Central Railway, the waterway opens out and makes a sharp turn at what was once a junction and progresses in a cutting, grassed and tidied up, towards Meadow Lane Lock and the River Trent. Upstream the river is navigable for a short distance above Trent Bridge (good moorings on County Hall steps) but the main navigation is to the east. Near Meadow Lane Lock is the Notts County football ground, while on the opposite side of the river is the Trent Bridge cricket ground with Nottingham Forest football stadium next to it. Below the latter is the entrance to the now-derelict Grantham Canal.

Boatyards

ⒷBeeston Marina Riverside Road, Beeston, Nottingham NG9 1NA (0115 922 3168; www.beestonmarina.com). 🚽⛽🔧 D E Gas, overnight mooring, long-term mooring, winter storage, slipway, 7-tonne crane, chandlery, engine sales and repairs (including outboards), books, maps and gifts, groceries, solid fuel, café, bar, telephone.

ⒷTrevethicks Boatyard Canal Wharf, Gregory Street, Old Lenton, Nottingham NG7 2NP (0115 978 3467). Traditional boat builders, boat repairs, welding, dry dock, boat restoration, painting and sign writing.

ⒷNottingham Castle Marina Marina Road, Castle Marina Park, Nottingham NG7 1TN (0115 941 2672; www.nottinghamcastlemarina.co.uk). 🚽⛽🔧 D Pump out, gas, overnight and long-term mooring, winter storage, slipway, wet dock, chandlery, books, maps and gifts, boat sales, solid fuel, toilets, launderette and drying room.

141

- **Attenborough Nature Reserve** Barton Lane, Attenborough, Nottingham NG9 6DY (0115 972 1777; www.attenboroughnaturecentre.co.uk). Worked out gravel pits, once derelict and unsightly, are now providing an interesting habitat for plant and animal life. There are comprehensive nature trails and a wooden observation hide. Designated SSSI. Café. *Visitor centre open Mon-Fri 10.00-16.00, weekends 09.00-16.00; access to reserve 07.00-dusk.* Free.
- **Beeston Lock**
Nottingham (0115 925 4946). A splendidly kept lock where facilities are available for boats. The pretty cottages and the little backwater off the canal are a hint of its past importance; until some years ago there used to be a lock down into the river here, at right angles to the present lock. The river channel used to be navigable – by shallow-draught vessels – from here down to Trent Bridge, the Beeston Canal being cut to connect with the Nottingham Canal and to afford access into the middle of the town. But now the river is unnavigable as a through route and the canal is the only way.
- **Nottingham**
Notts. All services. The city's prosperity derives largely from the coal field to the north, and the long-established lace industry. John Player & Son made all their cigarettes here and Raleigh turned out bicycles for the world. The city centre is busy and not unattractive – there is an imposing town hall in Slab Square – but little of the architecture is of note. Modern developments are encouraging, however, notably the superb Playhouse Theatre and the appearance of a variety of theme festivals spread throughout the year.
Nottingham Contemporary High Pavement, Nottingham NG1 2GB (0115 948 9750; www.nottinghamcontemporary.org). One of the largest contemporary art spaces in the UK. *Open Tue-Fri 10.00-19.00, Sat 10.00-18.00, Sun 11.00-17.00.* Café bar.
Brewhouse Yard Museum Castle Boulevard, Nottingham NG7 1FB (0115 915 3600; www.nottinghamcity.gov.uk). Re-created shops, period rooms and a shopping street from between the wars. *Open Apr-Sep Fri-Sun 10.00-17.00; Oct-Mar Fri-Sun 10.00-16.00.* Charge. Limited disabled access.
Caves of Nottingham Drury Walk, Upper Level, Broadmarsh Shopping Centre, Nottingham (0115 952 0555; www.cityofcaves.com). A unique honeycomb of caves temporarily closed until 2012 (at the time of writing). Charge.
The Galleries of Justice High Pavement, Lace Market, Nottingham NG1 1HN (0115 952 0555; www.galleriesofjustice.org.uk). A major crime and punishment experience. Visitors assume the identity of real 19th-C criminals, take part in a trial, visit the cells and finally the gallows. New civil law and children's activity centres. *Open daily, 10.00-17.00. Last admission 1 hour before closing.* Charge.

Lakeside Arts Centre University Park, Nottingham NG7 2RD (0115 846 7777; www.lakesidearts.org.uk). Attractive lakeside walks, two cafés, affordable craft items and a broad spectrum mix of theatre, dance, exhibitions and concerts. *Open Mon-Sat from 10.00 and Sun from 12.00.*
Nottingham Castle Friar Lane, Off Maid Marian Way, Nottingham NG1 6EL (0115 915 3700; www.nottinghamcity.gov.uk). William the Conqueror's castle, which was notorious as the base of Robin Hood's unfortunate enemies while King Richard I was away crusading, has been destroyed and rebuilt many times during its tumultuous history. (It was a Yorkist stronghold in the Wars of the Roses and it was here that Charles I raised his standard in 1642, starting the Civil War.) Though the original secret caves beneath the castle still exist and can be visited on a guided tour, the present building dates only from 1674. It now houses the city's **Museum and Art Gallery** which includes fine displays of English pottery, silver and glass together with a collection of 17th-, 18th- and 19th-C paintings by artists including Rosetti, Le Brun and Nottingham artists Bonington and Sandby. Also the exciting interactive Circle of Life gallery. Café. *Open Tue-Sun and B Hols 10.00-17.00. Last admission 16.30. Closed 25-26 Dec, and Fri Nov-Feb.* Charge. Disabled access except caves.
Nottingham Goose Fair Forest Recreation Ground, outskirts of Nottingham City Centre, just off Mansfield Road/A60, Nottingham (www.nottinghamgoosefair.co.uk). The Goose Fair is now a conventional funfair but on a gigantic scale. It features traditional entertainments like boxing bouts (challengers invited to fight the house champ) as well as the usual mechanical fairground delights. The fair's original site was in the town centre but now it is out on the Forest Recreation Ground, a mile to the north east (served by buses). The fair takes place in the *first week of Oct* and it is advisable to get there before the Saturday, when the prices are doubled.
Nottingham Playhouse Wellington Circus, Nottingham NG1 5AF (0115 941 9419; www.nottinghamplayhouse.co.uk). Box office *open Mon-Sat 10.00-20.00; Sun and B Hols 2 hours before a performance.* Wide variety of theatre, a stunning Sky Mirror sculpture by Anish Kapoor in the forecourt, exhibitions. Bar.
Nottingham Tourism Centre 1-4 Smithy Row, Nottingham NG1 2BY (08444 775678; www.experiencenottinghamshire.com). *Open Mon-Sat 09.30-17.30, Sun until 15.00.*
- **Grantham Canal**
A long-disused but delightful canal from Trent Bridge, Nottingham, to Grantham. The canal was built purely to serve the agricultural communities of eastern Nottinghamshire, so it pursues a remarkably circuitous course through pleasant farmland, including the Vale of Belvoir (pronounced 'beever'). Belvoir Castle, seat of the Duke of Rutland, is only about a mile from the canal at one point. A tramway was constructed to connect canal and castle, in order

to carry coal up to the castle using wagons drawn by horses. Traces can still be seen of this, one of Nottinghamshire's earliest railways. The Grantham Canal still feeds water down from secluded reservoirs at Knipton and Denton to the Trent and large sections of the towpath are available for walking and cycling – visit www.granthamcanal.com for more information. There are well-advanced plans for its complete restoration and re-connection to the River Trent.

WILDLIFE
The River Trent has historically been heavily polluted: water taken directly from the Trent has not been used as a drinking supply in living memory. However, as money is invested in the quality of the river water, the situation is changing. After becoming all but extinct in England (particularly the Midlands) since the late 1990s, the number of *otters* around the Trent and its tributaries has been steadily increasing. Otters are superbly adapted to an amphibious lifestyle and their dives can last for several minutes. They feed mainly on fish.

Pubs and Restaurants

The Boat & Horses Trent Road, Beeston NG9 1LP. North of Beeston Lock. Once a changeover station for barge horses. Fine traditional pub serving real ale. Food available *L and E (not Sun E)*. Children welcome if eating; dogs when food is not being served. Large garden.

The Johnsons Arms 59 Abbey Street, Dunkirk, Nottingham NV7 2NZ (0115 978 6355; www.johnsonarms.co.uk). West of Lenton Chain. Friendly real ale establishment. Food available *Mon-Fri L and E, Sat E, Sun L*. Large garden. Regular beer festivals, live music. Petanque and board games. Quiz night *Tue*.

The Boat Inn Priory Street, Nottingham NG7 2NX (0115 978 0267; www.theboatinnlenton.co.uk). West of Lenton Chain. A 'proper' pub dispensing real ales surrounded by naval memorabilia. Food available *L*. Children and dogs welcome in the garden.

The Navigation 6 Wilford Street, Nottingham NG2 1AA (0115 808 7280). Canalside by Castle Lock. Real ale. Bar food available *all day*, including American burgers. Canalside seating and mooring below the lock. Live music. Quiz in *winter*.

Ye Olde Trip to Jerusalem 1 Brewhouse Yard, Nottingham NG1 6AD (0115 947 3171; www.triptojerusalem.com). Set into the cliff face below the castle, this is allegedly the oldest inn in England and is not without atmosphere. Real ale together with food served from an extensive menu *12.00-22.00*. Children welcome if eating *until 19.00*. Story telling *last Thu of month*. Outside seating. Pub games.

F.M.C. 54 Canal Street, Nottingham NG1 7EH (0115 950 6795; www.fellowsmortonandclayton.co.uk). Set in the old Fellows, Morton & Clayton warehouse, this establishment has its own real ales which are served together with a selection of guest ales. Good value, traditional pub food available *L and E until 20.00 (18.00 Sun)*. Children welcome in family area. Large-screen TV. Patio and terrace seating. Regular live music. *Open all day*.

The Vat & Fiddle 12-14 Queens Bridge Road, Nottingham NG2 1NB (0115 985 0611; www.castlerockbrewery.co.uk). Close to the railway station. Traditional pub serving a wide selection of real ales, malt whiskies and real cider. Bar meals served *L*. Children welcome *until 21.00*. Outside seating. Live music *weekly*. *Open all day*. Wifi.

Stoke Bardolph

Downstream from the railway bridge, the wide river soon leaves Nottingham behind and enters pleasant countryside. On the north bank are many boating centres and the Colwick racecourse. On the south side an exploration of the landscaped area will reveal the magnificent rowing course at Holme Pierrepont. Downstream are Holme Lock and sluices; the lock is on the south side (0115 981 1197). This section serves to establish the Trent's attractive rural character as it continues to sweep along through Nottinghamshire. Passing under a railway bridge (the Nottingham-Grantham line), one sees a very steep escarpment of tree-covered hills, effectively cliffs, rising out of the water. Radcliffe on Trent is concealed in the woods by the bend, but access is difficult. It is better to move on, down to the delightfully secluded Stoke Lock (0115 987 8563/07887 787353), where there are *full boater facilities* and *toilets*. The lock island is covered with trees. Below the lock, the river bends northwards and crosses over to the other side of the valley, leaving behind the woods and cliffs. At Burton Joyce the river rebounds from the side of the valley and turns east again. The water meadows that accompany the river serve to keep at bay any inroads by modern housing.

Pubs and Restaurants

The Manvers Arms Main Road, Radcliffe on Trent, Nottingham NG12 2AA (www.themanversarmsinradcliffe.co.uk). Real ale together with traditional pub food available *L and E (not Sun E)*. Children's play area and beer garden. Pub games and quiz *Sun*.

The Royal Oak Main Road, Radcliffe on Trent, Nottingham NG12 2FD (0115 933 5659; www.royaloakpubandkitchen.co.uk). Cosy, village local dispensing a selection of real ales. Good bar food available *L and E daily*. Children welcome. Outside seating and real fires.

The Ferry Boat Inn Stoke Bardolph, Nottingham NG14 5HX

(0115 987 1232). Riverside. Good temporary mooring (ask permission). Bar food available *all day, every day*. Large heated courtyard popular with families with its outdoor children's play areas.

The Earl of Chesterfield Manor Lane, Shelford, Nottingham NG12 1EQ (0115 933 2227). Real ale and bar snacks served *L (not Sun)*. Children welcome, outside seating. Occasional entertainment.

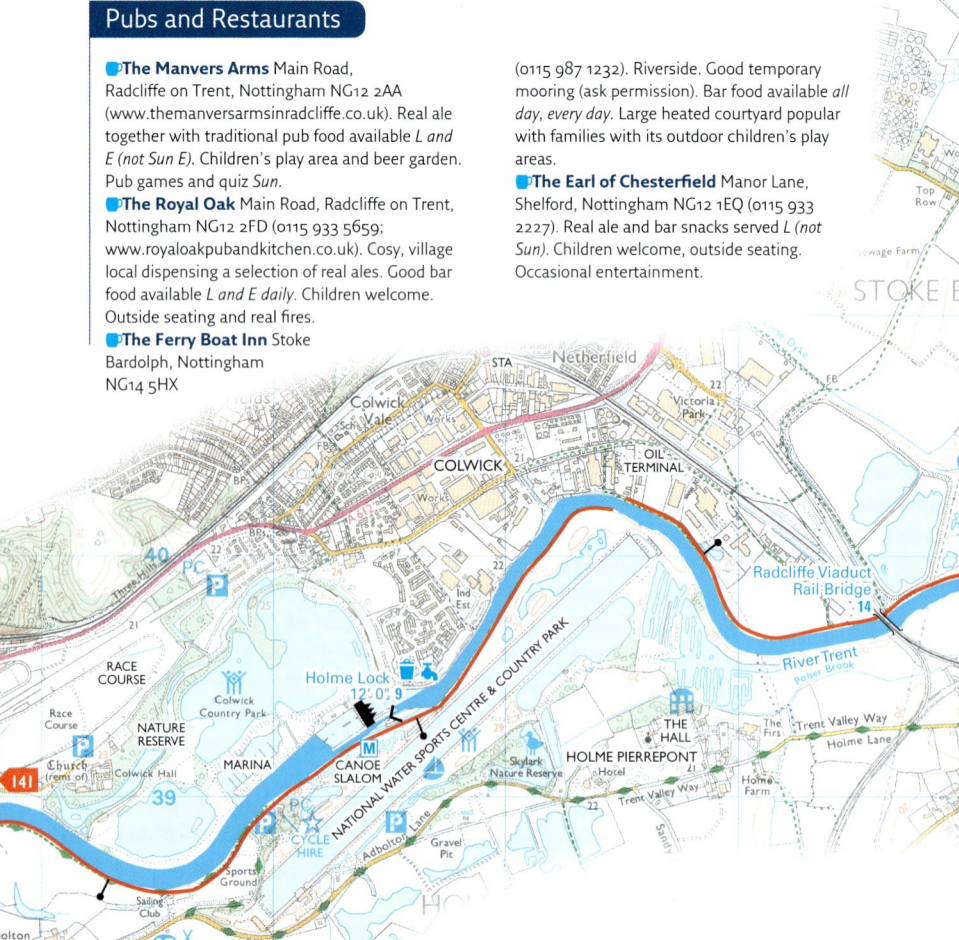

River Trent

Stoke Bardolph

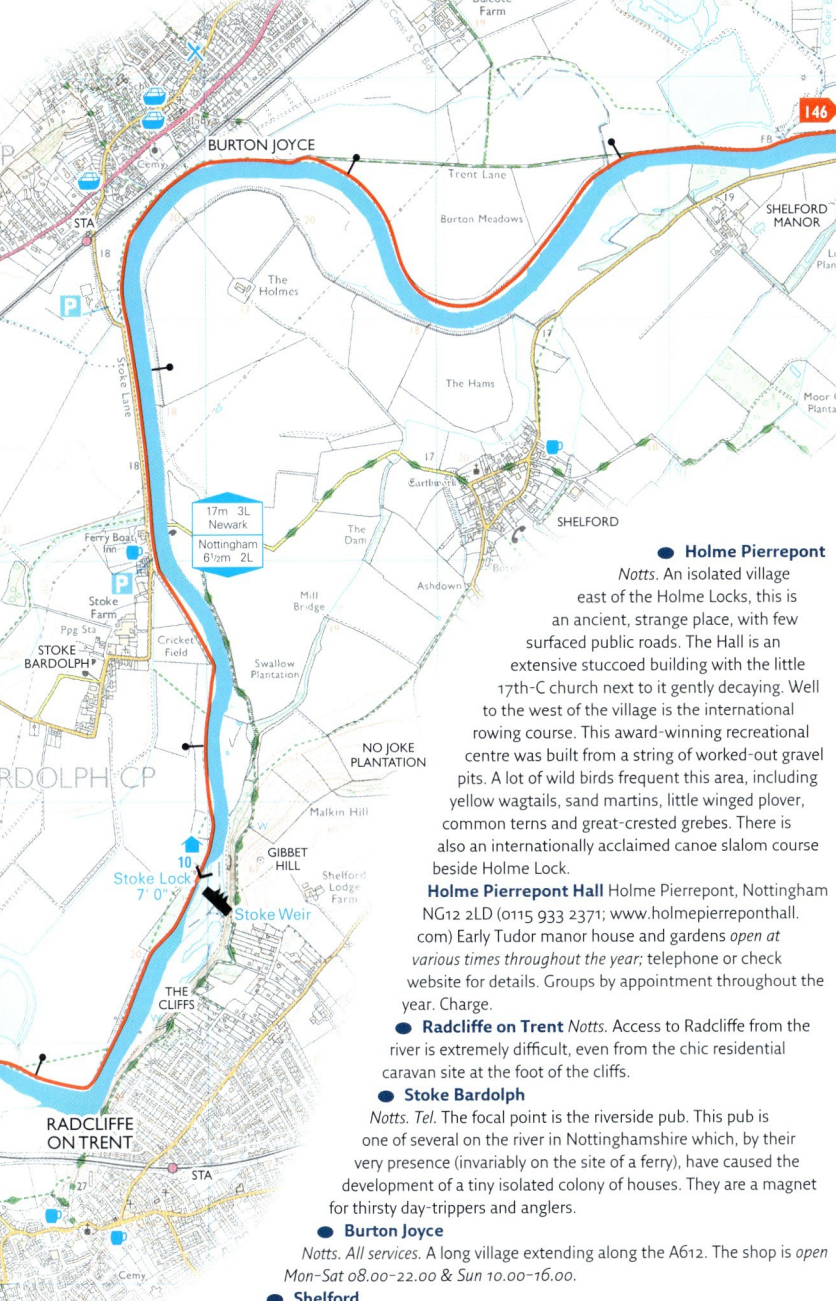

● **Holme Pierrepont**
Notts. An isolated village east of the Holme Locks, this is an ancient, strange place, with few surfaced public roads. The Hall is an extensive stuccoed building with the little 17th-C church next to it gently decaying. Well to the west of the village is the international rowing course. This award-winning recreational centre was built from a string of worked-out gravel pits. A lot of wild birds frequent this area, including yellow wagtails, sand martins, little winged plover, common terns and great-crested grebes. There is also an internationally acclaimed canoe slalom course beside Holme Lock.

Holme Pierrepont Hall Holme Pierrepont, Nottingham NG12 2LD (0115 933 2371; www.holmepierreponthall.com) Early Tudor manor house and gardens *open at various times throughout the year*; telephone or check website for details. Groups by appointment throughout the year. Charge.

● **Radcliffe on Trent** *Notts.* Access to Radcliffe from the river is extremely difficult, even from the chic residential caravan site at the foot of the cliffs.

● **Stoke Bardolph**
Notts. Tel. The focal point is the riverside pub. This pub is one of several on the river in Nottinghamshire which, by their very presence (invariably on the site of a ferry), have caused the development of a tiny isolated colony of houses. They are a magnet for thirsty day-trippers and anglers.

● **Burton Joyce**
Notts. All services. A long village extending along the A612. The shop is *open Mon-Sat 08.00-22.00 & Sun 10.00-16.00.*

● **Shelford**
Notts. Tel. A flood bank protects this quiet and isolated village from the Trent. The old church has a wide Perpendicular tower which commands the Trent valley. There is a pub, but there is no obvious mooring place for boats to be left on the river.

145

Hoveringham

This is a stretch in which the presence of big old riverside *pubs* has far more effect on the river scene than do the villages that they represent. Passing Shelford Manor, one arrives at the sleek arches of Gunthorpe Bridge – the only road bridge over the river in the 24 miles between Nottingham and Newark. To the east of the bridge are the grand houses up on the hills of East Bridgford. Boats heading downstream should keep left to enter the mechanised Gunthorpe Lock (0115 966 3821/07887 787353) and avoid the foaming weir. On the west bank, just below the bridge, there is a BW *mooring pontoon*, while above the lock there are the full range of *facilities* including *showers and toilets*. The next 5 or 6 miles below Gunthorpe are probably the most beautiful and certainly the most dramatic on the whole river. On the east side, the wooded cliffs rise almost sheer from the flat valley floor to a height of 200ft, allowing here or there the presence of a strip of fertile land on which cattle graze. Only at two places does a track manage to creep down the perilous slope to the river; otherwise, access is impossible. On the west side, by contrast, the ground is flat for miles, across to the other side of the valley. The river continues along its superb isolated course, with the forested cliffs of the Trent Hills striding along the river's east bank, while on the other side the flat plain of the valley rolls away through green fields and quiet Nottinghamshire villages. Unseen up on the plateau to the east is the big Syerston Airfield, now little used.

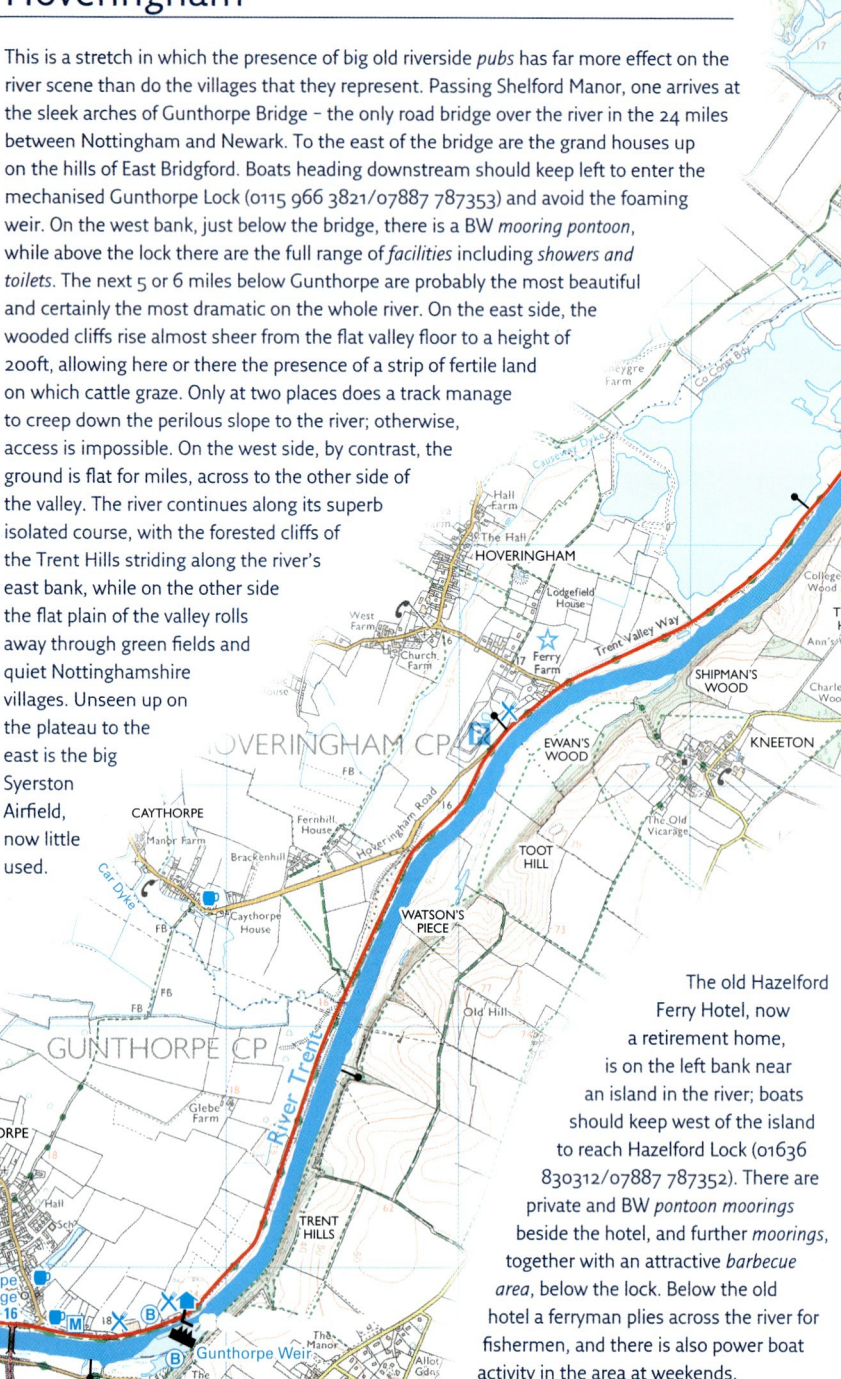

The old Hazelford Ferry Hotel, now a retirement home, is on the left bank near an island in the river; boats should keep west of the island to reach Hazelford Lock (01636 830312/07887 787352). There are private and BW *pontoon moorings* beside the hotel, and further *moorings*, together with an attractive *barbecue area*, below the lock. Below the old hotel a ferryman plies across the river for fishermen, and there is also power boat activity in the area at weekends.

River Trent — Hoveringham

- **Shelford Manor**
Shelford, Nottingham NG12 1ER. Near the river just west of Gunthorpe Bridge. The old manor was burnt down in 1645 after 2000 Roundheads attacked this Royalist stronghold. They massacred 140 of the 200 men inside. The manor was rebuilt in 1676. *Not open to the public.*

- **Gunthorpe**
Notts. Tel, garage. Gunthorpe has been an important river crossing point for over 2,000 years. The bridge built in 1875 was replaced by the present one in 1927. Prior to this a ferry was here.

- **East Bridgford**
Notts. PO, tel, stores, garage. Accessible via a shady lane up the hill from the river. The church is pleasantly light. Rector Oglethorpe, one-time incumbent of this parish, crowned Queen Elizabeth I.

Margidunum Castle Hill, East Bridgeford NG13 8 (www.roman-britain.org). 1½ miles south east of East Bridgford is the site of Margidunum, a Roman town on the Fosse Way (the straightest road in England). Margidunum was probably located here to guard the ford at East Bridgford. The shop is *open Mon-Fri 08.30-19.30, Sat 09.00-19.30, Sun 09.00-12.00.*

- **Hoveringham**
Notts. PO box, tel.. A village intimately linked with the gravel extraction industry.

- **Bleasby**
Notts. PO, tel, stores, station. Gas available at the caravan site approximately 500 yds up the lane from the old Hazelford Ferry Hotel. The village shop is *open Mon-Fri 06.30-19.30, Sat 07.00-19.30, Sun 08.00-13.00.*

Pubs and Restaurants

The Anchor Inn 80 Main Street, Gunthorpe, Nottingham NG14 7EU. Lively riverside pub, *open all day*. Real ales. Bar food available *12.00-20.00 daily*. Children welcome *until 20.30* when dining. Indoor children's play area. Outside seating. Quiz *Thu*. Caravan site.

Tom Brown's The Old School House, Trentside, Gunthorpe, Nottingham NG14 7FB (0115 966 3642; www.tombrowns.co.uk). Restaurant/bar serving real ales and an imaginative range of excellent food *L and E, daily*. This establishment is set in an old Victorian schoolhouse. There are some good value 'Early Bird' meal deals for both *L and E* on an otherwise fairly expensive menu. Outside seating.

The Unicorn Hotel Trentside, Gunthorpe, Nottingham NG14 7FB (0115 966 3612; www.marstonsinnsandtaverns.co.uk). This riverside hotel serves real ales and food *all day, every day*. Children welcome. Outside seating. Quiz *Mon in winter only*. B & B.

The Gunthorpe Lock Tearoom Gunthorpe Lock, Gunthorpe, Nottingham NG14 7 (0115 966 4833). Set in the old waterways workshops, the tearoom is *open daily 10.00-17.00* (opens earlier and closes later in season) serving breakfasts, tea, coffee, rolls and baking. Children and dogs welcome. Patio area and pet ducks. *Limited opening during the winter.*

Ferry Farm Park and Restaurant Boat Lane, Hoveringham, Nottingham NG14 7JP (0115 966 4512; www.ferryfarm.co.uk). Quality lunches, snacks and cream teas in conjunction with a farm park featuring rare breeds, animals to pet, children's adventure playground; assault course and slides for all ages and large indoor soft play area. Telephone for *opening times*.

The Waggon & Horses Gypsy Lane, Bleasby NG14 7GG (01636 830283). ½ mile north of Hazelford Ferry. Real ales and inexpensive home-made bar food available *L and E (not Sun E or all day Mon)*. Children and dogs welcome. Outside seating.

Boatyards

Trentside Marina Trentside, Gunthorpe, Nottingham NG14 7FB (0115 966 4283). Pump out, gas, narrowboat hire, long-term mooring, winter storage, café, maps and gifts. *See page 144.*

Newark-on-Trent

Beyond Hazelford Lock the steep Trent Hills dwindle away and the river leaves the woods (near the battlefield of East Stoke) for Fiskerton. Downstream of Fiskerton, the river sweeps round past the parkland at Stoke Hall. The site of a 4-acre Roman fort is on the nearby Fosse Way. At Farndon, a pleasant riverside village with sailing clubs on either side and a small ferry, there is a BW *mooring pontoon*. The boat population is further increased by the use of some old gravel pits just north of Farndon as a mooring site for pleasure boats. Navigators must be especially careful to avoid the large Averham Weir which takes the main channel of the Trent to Kelham and round the north side of Newark. Boats heading downstream should keep right, steering by the 240ft spire of Newark church. The waterway immediately becomes narrower east of this weir. This is the Newark Branch which takes boats straight into the middle of the town. On the way into Newark, the navigation passes an old windmill, a boatyard at the mouth of the River Devon (pronounced 'Deevon'), some extensive old maltings, and a restored warehouse (now a museum and brasserie) with the words Trent Navigation Company in faded lettering on the side. Opposite is the British Waterways repair yard, followed by Newark Town Lock (01636 702226/07887 754487) and then below is the Waterways Office. Alongside the town lock are the remains of the old lock, half of which is now used as a mooring for pleasure boats while the rest is a covered dry dock (01636 704106). The townscape at this point is dominated by the north west wall of the ruined Newark Castle. Nearby is a splendid old seven-arched stone bridge. The size of the arches limits the width of boats which can use the navigation but this bridge is listed as an ancient monument and so cannot be altered to accommodate bigger vessels.

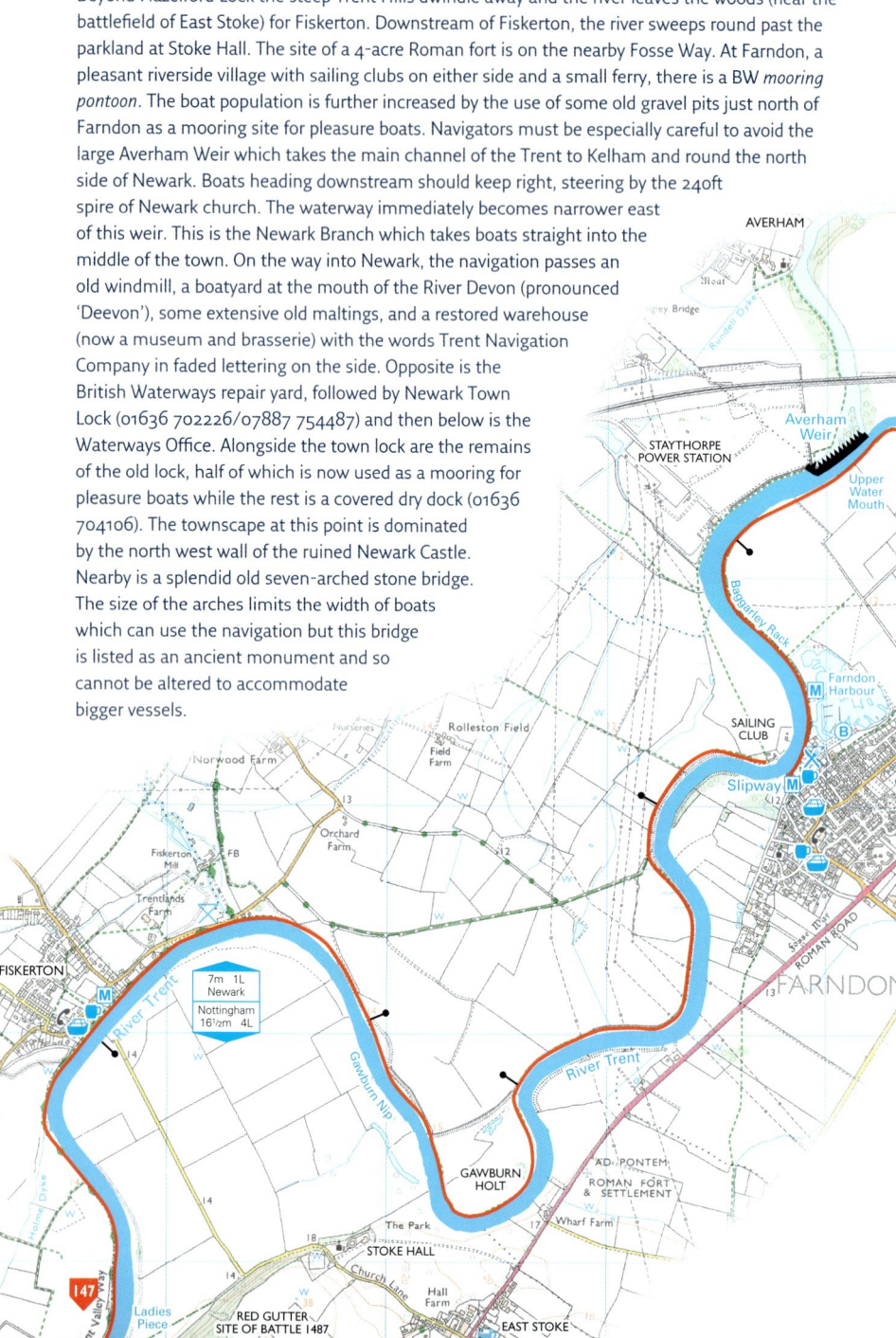

River Trent

Newark-on-Trent

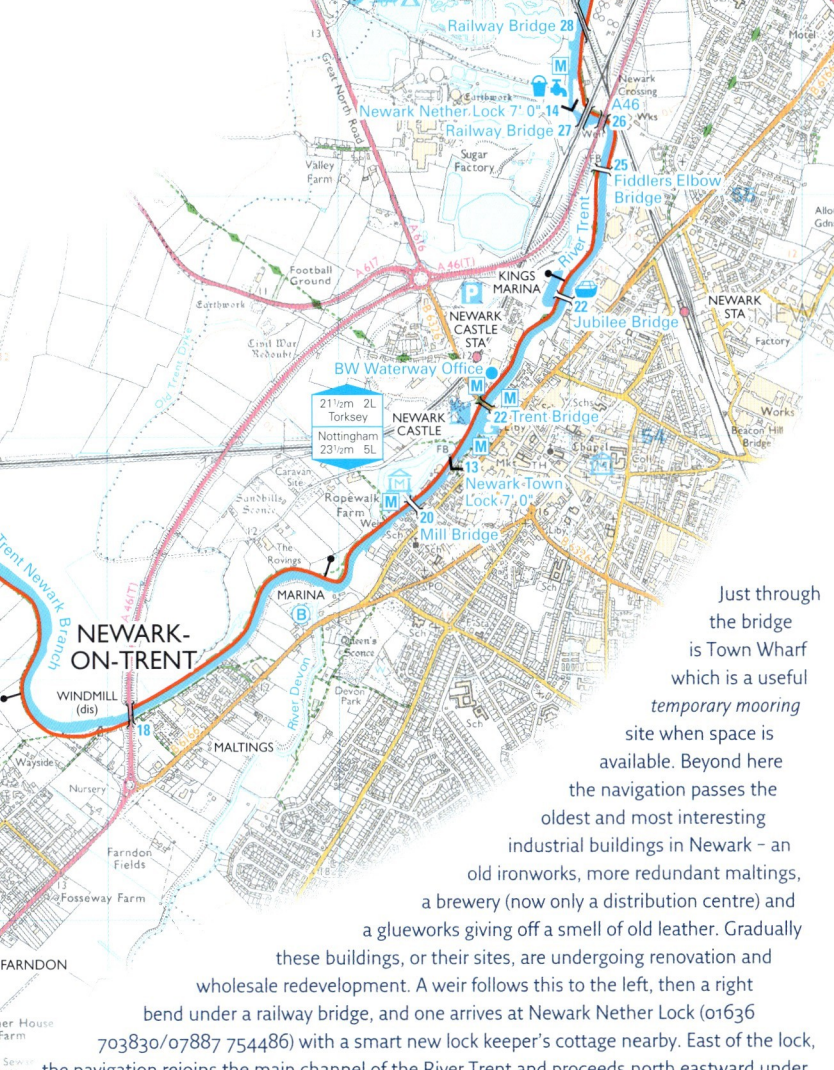

Just through the bridge is Town Wharf which is a useful *temporary mooring* site when space is available. Beyond here the navigation passes the oldest and most interesting industrial buildings in Newark – an old ironworks, more redundant maltings, a brewery (now only a distribution centre) and a glueworks giving off a smell of old leather. Gradually these buildings, or their sites, are undergoing renovation and wholesale redevelopment. A weir follows this to the left, then a right bend under a railway bridge, and one arrives at Newark Nether Lock (01636 703830/07887 754286) with a smart new lock keeper's cottage nearby. East of the lock, the navigation rejoins the main channel of the River Trent and proceeds north eastward under the graceful modern road bridge carrying the Newark bypass.

BOAT TRIPS
Newark Line River Cruises Cuckstool Wharf, Castle Gate, Newark NG5 1HR (01636 706479). Departs from just below Newark Town Lock. Pleasure and charter trips *each weekend Easter–Oct* plus *weekdays during peak periods* on *Sonning*. Drinks and snacks available. Also *fortnightly* jazz cruises.

- **Fiskerton**
Notts. PO, tel, stores, off-licence, station. Charming riverside village with excellent access for boats. Although the normal river level is well below the wharf, all the buildings along the splendid front are carefully protected from possible flood by stone walling or a bank of earth. The shop is *open Mon–Fri 06.30–19.00, Sat 07.00–18.00, Sun 08.00–17.00*.

- **Southwell**
Notts. Three miles north west of Fiskerton, this very attractive country town is well worth visiting in order to see its minster. The minster was founded at the beginning of the 12th C by the Archbishop of York, and is held by many to be one of the most beautiful Norman ecclesiastical buildings in England. Its scale is vast for Southwell, but it is set well back from the houses and is in a slight dip so it does not overawe the town centre, in spite of the two western towers and the massive central tower. Chief among the treasures inside the building are the naturalistic stone carvings in the late 13th-C chapter house, and the wooden carvings of the choir stalls.

- **Farndon**
Notts. PO, tel, stores, off-licence. A local ferry still transports the fishermen to the far side of the river in this attractive village. The pub makes it a popular spot in summer as do the sailing boats. Extensive renovation of the 14th-C church in 1891 revealed a stone coffin containing a Saxon bronze sword. The shops are *open Mon–Sat 06.00–21.00, Sun 07.00–21.00*.

- **Newark**
Notts. All services. Two stations. Newark is magnificent, easily the most interesting and attractive town on the Trent, and it is very appealing from the water. Situated at the junction of two old highways, the Great North Road and the Fosse Way, the town is of great historical significance. During the Civil War it was a Royalist stronghold which was besieged three times by the Roundheads between March 1645 and May 1646. The defensive earthworks or sconces constructed by the Royalists are still visible. Today Newark, like everywhere else, is large, busy and surrounded by industry and modern housing. But the town centre is intact and still full of charm. Elsewhere antique stalls, markets and warehouses attract a steady flow of bargain hunters and collectors to the town. However, it is only the decaying, riverside maltings that give a hint of its past significance within the brewing industry.
British Horological Institute Upton Hall, Upton, Newark NG23 5TE (01636 813795; www.bhi.org.uk). Library, training and educational centre for all those interested in matters horological together with a fascinating museum open to the public. Housed in Upton Hall, built in 1828, the museum displays the original 'Six Pip' generator and the actual watch worn by Captain Scott on his final, disastrous expedition, amongst many other gems. Tearoom. *Open to members during office hours; group visits by appointment; open day when clocks change*. Charge. Partial disabled access. Regular bus service from Newark.
Church of St Mary Magdalene Market Place, Newark NG24 1JS (01636 704513). The enormous spire is all that one can see of this elegant church from the market place, for the buildings on one side of the square hide the body of the structure. Inside, the church is made light and spacious by soaring columns and a magnificent 15th-C east window in the chancel. The building was begun in 1160 and completed about 1500. It is rich in carving, but one of the church's most interesting features is a brass made in Flanders to commemorate Alan Fleming, a merchant who died in 1375. The monument is made up of 16 pieces of metal and measures 9ft 4ins by 5ft 7ins - one of the biggest of its type in England.
Market Place Newark. It is worth making a point of visiting Newark on market day to view the scene in the colourful old market. In opposite corners of the square once stood two ancient pubs: one of them, the White Hart, now resited elsewhere in the town, was built in the 15th C and is the oldest example of domestic architecture in the town; the other is the Clinton Arms where W. E. Gladstone made his first speech in 1832. He later became Prime Minister.
Millgate Museum 48 Millgate, Newark NG24 4TS (01636 655730; www.newark-sherwooddc.gov.uk). Depicts the bygone social life of Newark, its trade and industry. Reconstruction of its streets, shops and house interiors set in an old waterside warehouse. *Open Mon–Fri 10.00–17.00, weekends and B Hols 13.00–17.00. Last admission 16.30*. Free.
Newark Castle Castlegate, Newark NG24 1BG (www.newark-sherwooddc.gov.uk). Only a shell remains, the one intact wall overlooking the river. The first known castle on this site was constructed c.1129, probably for Alexander, Bishop of Lincoln. The present building was started in 1173, with various additions and alterations in the 14th, 15th and 16th C - notably the fine oriel windows. King John died here in October 1216, soon after his traumatic experience in the Wash. The castle was naturally a great bastion during the Civil War sieges and battles that focused on Newark. When the Roundheads eventually took the town in 1646, they dismantled the castle. The ruins and the grounds are *open daily*. Free.
Newark Gilstrap Centre Castlegate, Newark NG24 1BG (01636 655765; www.newark-sherwooddc. gov.uk). Castle exhibition and information centre. *Open all year except 25-26 Dec and New Year. Summer hours 10.00–17.00; winter hours 10.00–16.00*. Free.
Newark Town Hall Museum Town Hall, Market Place, Newark NG24 1DU (01636 680333; www.newarktownhallmuseum.co.uk). Newark town's treasures, which include paintings,

furniture and ceramics, ceremonial items, civic gifts and the town's charters. *Open all year Mon–Sat 10.30–15.30.* Free.
Weston Mill Pottery Units 8–9, Old Great North Road, Sutton on Trent, Newark NG23 6QS (01636 822795; www.wmpot.co.uk). Terracotta ware in a working pottery. Telephone to enquire about visiting.

Tourist Information Centre Gilstrap Centre, Castlegate, Newark NG24 1BG (01636 655765; www.newark-sherwooddc.gov.uk). *Opening times as per Newark Gilstrap Centre.*

Boatyards

Ⓑ**Farndon Marina** North End, Farndon, Newark NG24 3SX (01636 705483; www.farndonmarina.co.uk). 🛅 🛟 ♿ D E Pump out, gas, overnight mooring, long-term mooring, winter storage, slipway, crane (25 tonnes), chandlery, books, boat repairs, boat fitting out, DIY facilities, electrical repairs, boat sales, engine sales and repairs (including outboards), toilets, showers, laundrette. BW licensing. Boat transport by road. *24 hr emergency call out.*
Ⓑ**Newark Marina** 26 Farndon Road, Newark NG24 4SD (01636 704022; www.newark-marina.co.uk). 🛅 ♿ D Gas, overnight mooring, long-term mooring, winter storage, crane (40 tonne), chandlery, books and maps, gifts, boat building and fitting out, DIY facilities, boat sales and repairs, inboard and outboard engine sales and repairs, toilets and showers.
Ⓑ**Kings Marina** Mather Road, Newark NG24 1FW (01636 678549; www.bwml.co.uk). 🛅 🛟 ♿ D E Pump out, gas, overnight mooring, long-term and visitor mooring, chandlery, toilets, showers, laundry. Grocery shop close by.

Pubs and Restaurants

●**The Bromley Arms** Main Street, Fiskerton NG25 0UL (01636 830789; www.thebromleyarmsfiskerton.co.uk). An attractive riverside pub, set beside the old wharf, with superb country views and serving real ale. Inexpensive bar meals available *L and E (not Sun E)*. Children and dogs (on a lead inside) welcome. Outside seating overlooking the river. Pub games. Telephone in advance to use moorings outside. The pub runs their own trip-boat, the *Captain Cods*, daily in the summer. Overnight accommodation (no breakfast).
●✕**The Riverside Pub and Kitchen** Wyke Lane, Farndon NG24 3SX (01636 710990; www.riversidefarndon.co.uk). Popular riverside pub, serving real ale. Fresh, modern British cuisine served *all day, everyday*. Children welcome if dining. Moorings and patio. There is a slipway available in front of the pub (charge).
✕♇**Farndon Boathouse** Riverside, Farndon, Newark NG24 3SX (01636 676578; www.farndonboathouse.co.uk). Previously the New Ferry Restaurant. Bar and restaurant serving fresh food, sourced locally where possible *L and E*. Also real ales and continental beers. Live music *Sun*. Outside seating for the summer; open fires for winter. Moorings, free for patrons (book in advance).
●**The Rose and Crown** Main Street, Farndon, Newark NG24 3SA (01636 704334; www.everards.co.uk). Local pub dispensing real ale and home-made bar meals *L and E (not Sun E or Mon L)*. Children welcome. Beer garden and pub games. Occasional live music.
●**The Castle Barge** The Wharf, Newark NG24 1EU (01636 677320; www.castlebarge.co.uk). Floating pub in a 94ft former Spiller's grain barge. The lower deck provides an atmospheric bar with lots of polished wood and an interesting display of pictures. However, many prefer to sit outside in the summer and enjoy the river. Real ales and reasonably priced bar snacks with seasonal specials available *L and E until 20.00*. Morning coffee *from 11.00* and *daily* special offers. Karaoke *Wed and Sun*. Top deck facilities for children.
●**The Old Malt Shovel** 25 Northgate, Newark NG24 1HD. Cosmopolitan establishment, host to a wide-ranging clientele, serving real ale from a bar set up in a one-time bakery. Food from a varied menu is served *L and E (Mon E)*. Children welcome in garden and restaurant; dogs in garden only. Pub games and outside seating.

Cromwell Lock

From Newark, the Trent follows a generally northerly course towards the Humber, which is still over 50 miles away owing to the very sweeping and tortuous line of the river. The villages of North Muskham and Holme face each other across the water and used to be connected by ferry. A mile or more below Holme is Cromwell Lock and Weir. On 28 September 1975 ten volunteers of the 131 independent parachute squadron of the Royal Engineers lost their lives here whilst taking part in Expedition Trent Chase. Cromwell has always been a significant place on the river; in the 8th C a bridge was built at this point. The lock here marks the beginning of the tidal section of the Trent, so navigation north of it requires a very different approach.

NAVIGATIONAL NOTES

1. Cromwell Weir is the largest on the Trent. It is buoyed and has a safety boom. All boats should keep to the west side of the river. The lock too is truly enormous; it is mechanised, and there is a lock keeper on duty daily *06.00–21.00 during the summer and 08.00–16.00 in winter. Hours may be extended Fri-Sun and on B Hols* (01636 821213/07887 754485). Boaters can also book free passage through the lock outside these hours, to coincide with suitable tide envelopes, by giving *48 hours* notice.
2. Boaters intending to break their passage to Torksey Lock, by staying on the pontoon mooring at Dunham, are requested to inform the lock keeper at Cromwell to avoid alarm at their non-arrival at Torksey. Similarly should you change your plans and subsequently stop at Dunham please contact a lock keeper to avoid unnecessary concern for your safety.
3. Commercial river traffic operates on channel 6 upstream of Keadby Bridge and it is useful for VHF users to monitor this channel to establish the whereabouts of large craft.

Navigating the tidal Trent

A suitable boat is essential: proper navigation lights (compulsory on all the navigable Trent) and safety equipment (including an anchor and cable) is also compulsory. Navigation Notes are available from www.waterscape.com. The Trent Series Charts, published by The Boating Association, are detailed charts of the tidal Trent (and the tidal Ouse and non-tidal Trent) and are available from www.theboatingassociation.com; info@theboatingassociation.com. Also from BW (above) and lock keepers – charge. Deep-draughted boats should beware of shoals at low water and should avoid the inside of bends. The river banks are unsuitable for mooring and there are few wharves; those that remain are largely for commercial craft. There are excellent, though limited, pontoon moorings north of Gainsborough Arches. Navigators who are more used to canals and non-tidal rivers will be more likely to treat the tidal Trent as a link route with the Fossdyke & Witham Navigation, the Chesterfield Canal, the South Yorkshire Navigations or the Humber Estuary. They should plan their trip with an eye to the tide table. The best approach is either to use a Hull tide table (available from local boatyards, fishing shops and newsagents) bearing in mind that the Trent floods for only about 2¼ hours and ebbs for the remainder of the 12-hour period or, if in doubt, to ask the BW lock keepers at the various junctions along the river. The relevant telephone numbers are: Cromwell Lock 01636 821213/07887 754485; West Stockwith Lock 01427 890204/07884 238780; Torksey Lock 01427 890204/07884 238781; Keadby Lock 01724 782205/07733 124611. In most cases it is advisable to plan your journey so that the tide is running with you, but bear in mind the lock operating times.

Pubs and Restaurants

The Lord Nelson Gainsborough Road, Winthorpe, Newark NG24 2NN (01636 703578; www.lordnelsonwinthorpe.co.uk). Real ales. Home-cooked bar and restaurant meals available *daily, L and E*. Children welcome in garden and restaurant. Log fires, leather sofas and exposed beams.

The Muskham Ferry Ferry Lane, North Muskham, Newark NG23 6HB (01636 704943). Riverside pub with mooring for patrons, fronted by a garden. Real ales together with inexpensive home-cooked food available *L and E*. Children and dogs welcome.

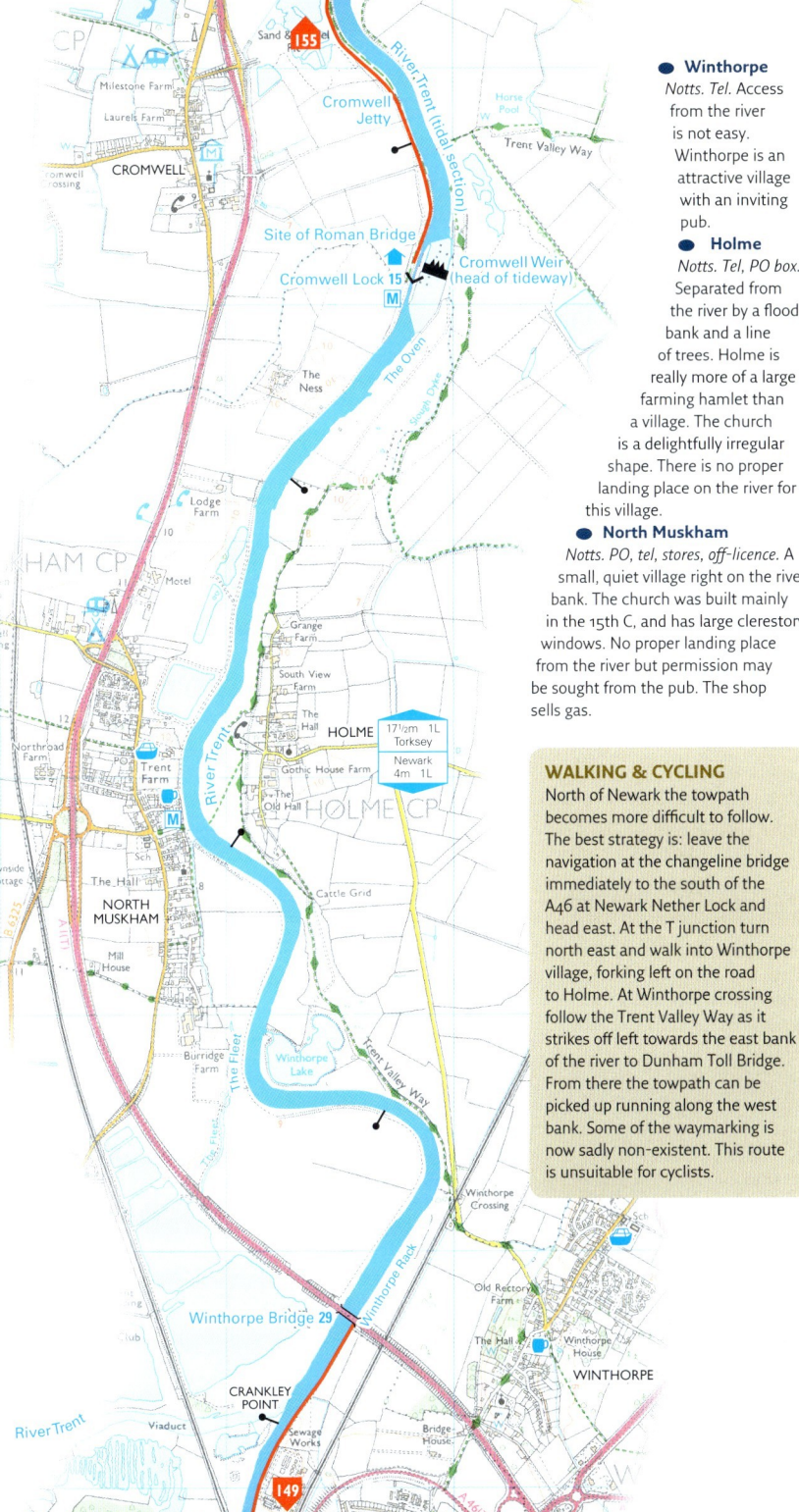

River Trent — Cromwell Lock

- **Winthorpe**
  Notts. Tel. Access from the river is not easy. Winthorpe is an attractive village with an inviting pub.

- **Holme**
  Notts. Tel, PO box. Separated from the river by a flood bank and a line of trees. Holme is really more of a large farming hamlet than a village. The church is a delightfully irregular shape. There is no proper landing place on the river for this village.

- **North Muskham**
  Notts. PO, tel, stores, off-licence. A small, quiet village right on the river bank. The church was built mainly in the 15th C, and has large clerestory windows. No proper landing place from the river but permission may be sought from the pub. The shop sells gas.

WALKING & CYCLING

North of Newark the towpath becomes more difficult to follow. The best strategy is: leave the navigation at the changeline bridge immediately to the south of the A46 at Newark Nether Lock and head east. At the T junction turn north east and walk into Winthorpe village, forking left on the road to Holme. At Winthorpe crossing follow the Trent Valley Way as it strikes off left towards the east bank of the river to Dunham Toll Bridge. From there the towpath can be picked up running along the west bank. Some of the waymarking is now sadly non-existent. This route is unsuitable for cyclists.

Sutton on Trent

This is a typical stretch of the upper section of the tidal Trent. The river meanders along its northward course, flanked by flood banks and with no bridges. The land is largely grazed as permanent pasture nurtured by the high summer water table maintained by the winter flood (now of course contained). Evidence of an ancient landscape is glimpsed, often on the inside of a sweeping bend, in the form of isolated stretches of hedgerow. These are rich in an abundance of species including ash, willow, wild roses and hawthorn – a picture of white blossom in springtime. Apart from these tantalising views there is little to see save for the occasional sand barge. Elsewhere the land yields a vast quantity of glacial gravel quarried for building and road construction. A relatively interesting place is Girton Wharf, where there are still working barges to be seen, but the moorings here are not for pleasure boats. The village of Sutton on Trent is near this wharf; so is a large converted windmill. On the east bank is Besthorpe Wharf, which is used for feeding gravel from the adjacent pits into the river barges. The Trent valley can rightly be called the powerhouse of England: electricity generating stations operating within sight of the river currently produce more than a quarter of all electricity consumed in England and Wales. This area makes an ideal site for power stations with its plentiful supply of water for steam production, as well as for cooling the spent steam once it has passed through the generating turbines. A large reserve of coal to fire the boilers was also available, until relatively recently, from the nearby East Midlands coalfield, although several of the power stations are now converted to gas. Most of them have been built since 1950, and their huge cooling towers stand out as prominent features on an otherwise largely agricultural landscape. Approximately half of all the electricity generated in the Trent valley is transmitted, via the Supergrid of overhead power lines, to London, which as a large consumer is nevertheless poorly situated for large-scale power production. Whilst waste cooling water is returned to the river, the vast output of fly ash has been used to fill nearby spent gravel pits. In an imaginative scheme it has also, in conjunction with soil from sugar beet washings, been used to reclaim worked-out clay pits at a Peterborough brickworks. These have then been returned to agricultural use. In most cases mooring along the tidal Trent is not recommended.

Pubs and Restaurants

Lord Nelson 35 Main Street, Sutton on Trent, Newark NG23 6PF. Formerly the Memory Lane, this is a comfortable, cosy inn and restaurant serving real ales and food *L and E*. Garden and children's play area. Family conservatory. B & B.

WALKING & CYCLING

Under the 1792 Trent River Navigation Act hauling rights were granted in return for an annual rent. Since the 1930s craft using the river have been self-propelled and these rights have not been exercised. Custom and practice has led to paths following the flood banks rather than the water margins. BW's legal rights are for maintenance access only, whilst they also have an obligation to maintain and erect the numerous clapper gates as necessary. On the tidal stretch of the Trent it is often possible to follow a marked footpath on either flood bank (and in some cases a minor road); therefore the towpath indicated on the map represents only the most straightforward, continuous route. In practice this offers excellent opportunities for walkers, and a combination of routes can be devised following a mix of river bank, the Chesterfield Canal towpath, country lanes and footpaths. The Trent Valley Way also parallels the river and meets the canal at Cooper's Bridge No 80. Unfortunately there is no guide for this long-distance walking trail currently in print but it is hoped that this situation will change. The bridleways along the Trent also offer the adventurous cyclist plenty of scope, although the numerous clapper gates can become somewhat tiresome.

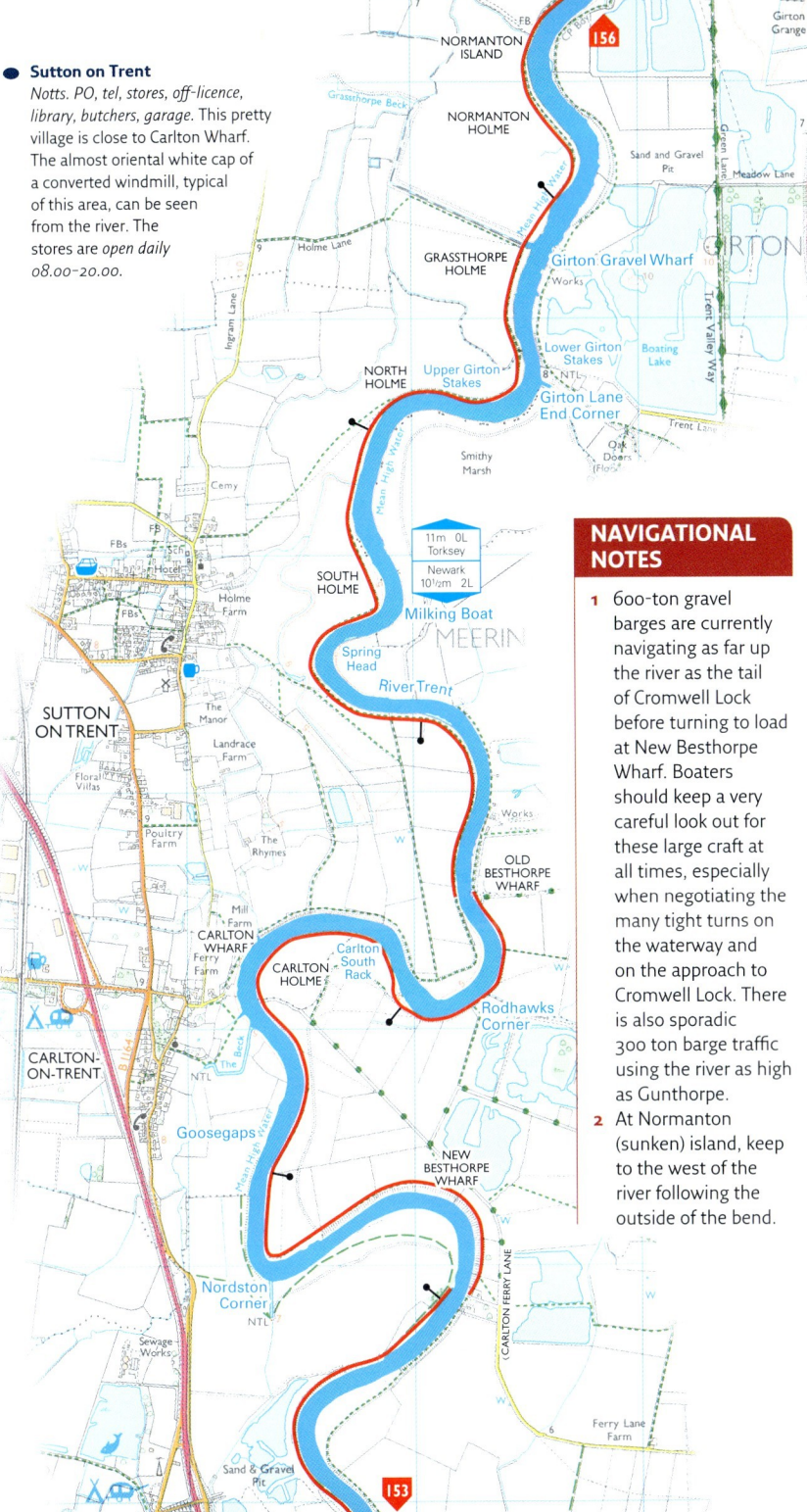

Sutton on Trent

Notts. PO, tel, stores, off-licence, library, butchers, garage. This pretty village is close to Carlton Wharf. The almost oriental white cap of a converted windmill, typical of this area, can be seen from the river. The stores are *open daily 08.00-20.00*.

NAVIGATIONAL NOTES

1. 600-ton gravel barges are currently navigating as far up the river as the tail of Cromwell Lock before turning to load at New Besthorpe Wharf. Boaters should keep a very careful look out for these large craft at all times, especially when negotiating the many tight turns on the waterway and on the approach to Cromwell Lock. There is also sporadic 300 ton barge traffic using the river as high as Gunthorpe.
2. At Normanton (sunken) island, keep to the west of the river following the outside of the bend.

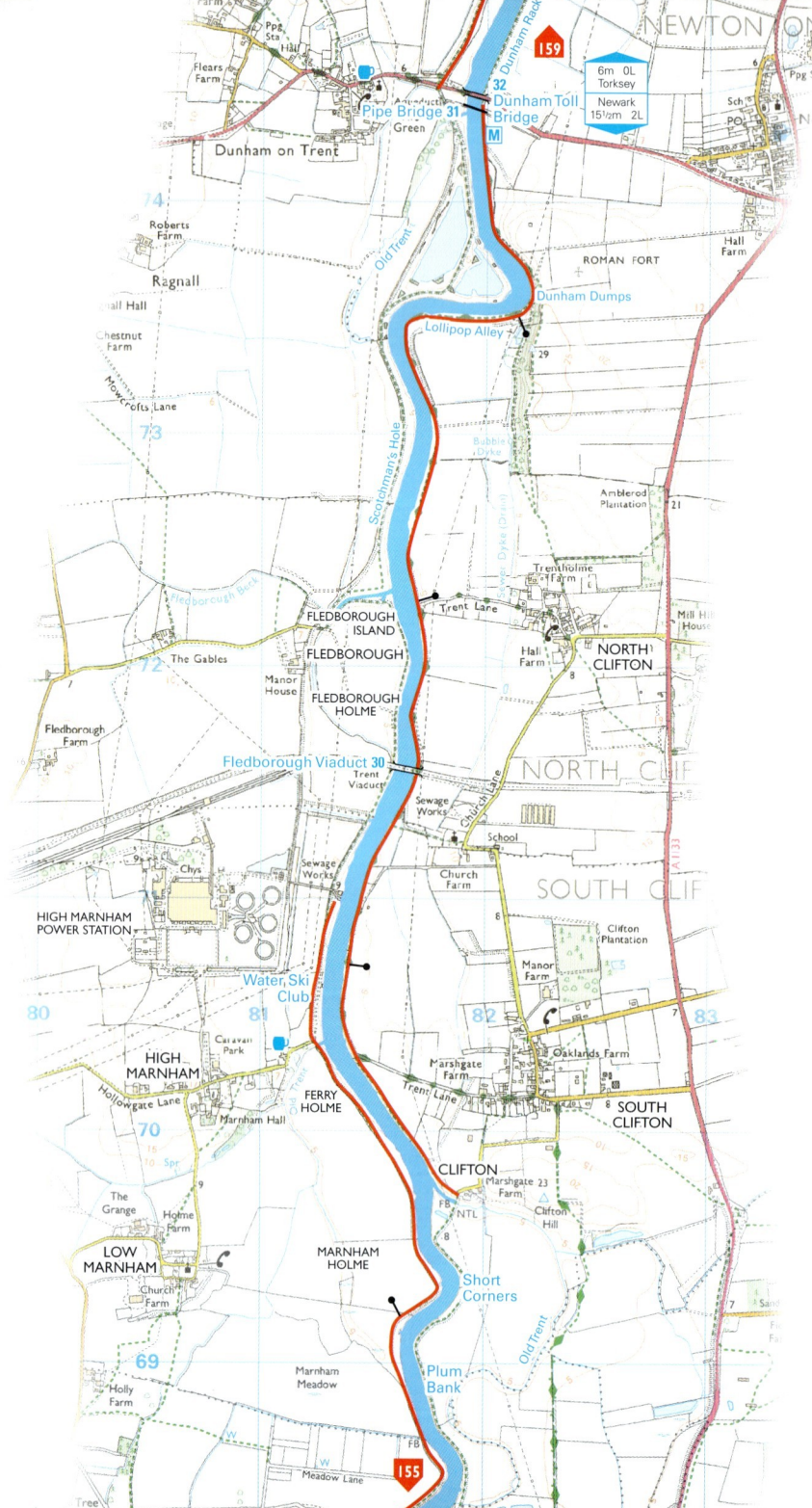

Dunham Bridge

The river wriggles around Plum Bank and Short Corners on its approach to High Marnham, passing the course of the Old Trent river. High Marnham was at one time two hamlets: Ferry Marnham and Church Marnham. The old Hall which stood between them was demolished in 1800. It was the property of the Cartwright family who held many claims to fame. Dr Edmund Cartwright invented the power loom which revolutionised the weaving industry. One of his brothers was the engineer responsible for the construction of the Ramper Road leading into Newark over raised arches. Another was an admiral in Lord Nelson's navy. Near the railway viaduct is the isolated church of St George, situated equidistant between North and South Clifton in order to serve both parishes. North Clifton once had the use of a ferry which was free to its inhabitants. 1½ miles further, the river describes a sharp S-bend as it passes a welcome little ridge of hills, pleasantly wooded. But the ridge fades away as one reaches Dunham Toll Bridge (the present structure replacing one built in 1832) and the iron aqueduct that precedes it. Once a market town, Dunham was notorious for its flooding. The Trent frequently caused buildings to be awash with up to 10ft of water. As a consequence most of the inhabitants were boat owners in order to maintain communications during the floods. Recent flood protection measures have, hopefully, made such events a thing of the past. The countryside resumes its flat and rather featureless aspect, while the river now forms the border between Nottinghamshire and Lincolnshire (as far downstream as West Stockwith). From Stapleford to Dunham the river is a birdwatcher's paradise of water meadows, pools and marshes. *Mooring* is available on a BW pontoon at Dunham, just upstream of the bridge on the east bank.

NAVIGATIONAL NOTES

At Fledborough (sunken) island, steer a line between the middle of the river and the west bank.

Pubs and Restaurants

●**The Bridge Inn** Main Street, Dunham-on-Trent, Newark NG22 0TY (01777 228765). West of the toll bridge. Real ales together with fresh, homemade meals (including breakasts) served *daily*. Children and dogs welcome. Outside seating. Occasional entertainment. *Open all day Sat and Sun*. Moorings. B & B.

●**The Brownlow Arms** High Marnham, Newark NG23 6SG (01636 822505; www.thebrownlowarms.co.uk). This family pub, with a large garden and children's play area, serves real ales and food *L and E and all day during the summer (not Mon L except B Hols)*. Boat launching facilities. Telephone for details. Also camping.

QUAY STRATEGY

Navigating the tidal Trent, the boater is constantly aware of the potential – both past and present – to move large bulk loads effortlessly. Evidence of the river's past glory as a waterways highway can be found at every tortuous twist and turn in the form of decaying wharves and abandoned jetties. The waterfront at Gainsborough, once heaving with barge traffic – often as many as three-deep – jostling for position to load or unload, is now moribund, locked in by concrete flood defences. This apparent shame at a past prosperity, one that was largely water-generated, is a telling indictment on the importance now attached to what was arguably the original form of green transport. Logic, it would appear, is completely lacking in a system that eschews the economies and scale of water transport in favour of diesel guzzling lorries. But, on reflection, is it? The more diesel consumed, the more revenue for the government. The greater the number of lorries cluttering up the roads, the greater the income from the road fund licence. Could it be that in promoting the benefits of water transport the Chancellor is shooting himself in the foot or, possibly, in economic terms somewhere far more painful?

Torksey

At Laneham the traveller will enjoy a little relief from the Trent's isolation. Here there is a church and a few houses on a slight rise near the river. A farmhouse on the river bank was built on the site of the old manor. The cellars in the building are reputed to date back even further than this to the time when the land belonged to the palace of the Archbishops of York. To the north of the village, yet another power station – Cottam – appears as the river turns back on itself to the south before swinging northwards again at the junction of the Fossdyke Navigation (marked by a pumping station). The lock up into the Fossdyke is just through the road bridge, *mooring* is below the bridge, and a *pub, petrol station* and *shop* are all near the lock. Torksey offers a haven for the boater navigating the tidal Trent with *72-hour pontoon moorings*, *water*, *toilets* and *showers*, together with *barbecue area* and *telephone*. There is also a good restaurant in the village – for further information on Torksey *see page 66*. Nearing the railway viaduct at Torksey, one sees the gaunt ruin of Torksey Castle standing beside the river. As at Newark, the façade that faces the Trent is the most complete part of the building, for the rest has vanished. (The castle has been abandoned since the 16th C.) For the first 15ft or so from the ground, the castle is built of stone – above this it is dark-red brick. In most cases mooring on the tidal Trent is not recommended.

NAVIGATIONAL NOTES

Boaters intending to break their passage to Cromwell Lock, by staying on the pontoon mooring at Dunham, are requested to inform the lock keeper at Torksey to avoid alarm at their non-arrival at Cromwell. Similarly should you change your plans and subsequently stop at Dunham, please contact a lock keeper to avoid unnecessary concern for your safety. The relevant telephone numbers are:
Cromwell Lock: 01636 821213/07887 754485
Torksey Lock: 01427 890204/07884 238781

● Laneham

Notts. Tel. Originally Lanum, the parish is divided into two areas, Church Laneham, also known as Laneham Ferry, and Laneham itself, the two being little more than half a mile apart. The church of St Peter is well worth a visit. Its wonderful Norman doorway, heavily decorated with chevron, herringbone and sunflower patterns, still contains the original Norman door, hanging on the very hinges on which it was mounted in the 11th C. The tower was once used as a watch tower over the Trent ferry. The ringing chamber of the tower contains 25 wedding rings or cheeses. These date back to the period between 1813 and 1840 when it became the custom for couples married at the church to pay the ringers a sage cheese or five shillings each for the privilege of having their initials placed in a ring.

Pubs and Restaurants

●The White Swan Newark Road, Torksey Lock, Torksey LN1 2EJ (01427 718653). Near the lock. A local village pub, popular with boaters and fishermen. Real ale is served, along with fresh, homemade food *L and E*. Children welcome, and there is a play area and garden, with moorings. Also caravan and camping site. Quiz *Sun*. Basic groceries for sale.

✕♇ The Wheelhouse Restaurant By Torksey Lock, Torksey LN1 2EH (01427 718301). A riverside restaurant, right by the moorings, serving English food *L and E (closed Mon)*. Families are welcome.

●The Ferry Boat Inn Church Laneham, Retford DN22 0NQ (01777 228350). Temporary moorings below the caravan park give access to this friendly pub which is just a short walk up from the river. Real ale is served as well as home-made food *L and E (not Tue)*. Outside seating and children welcome.

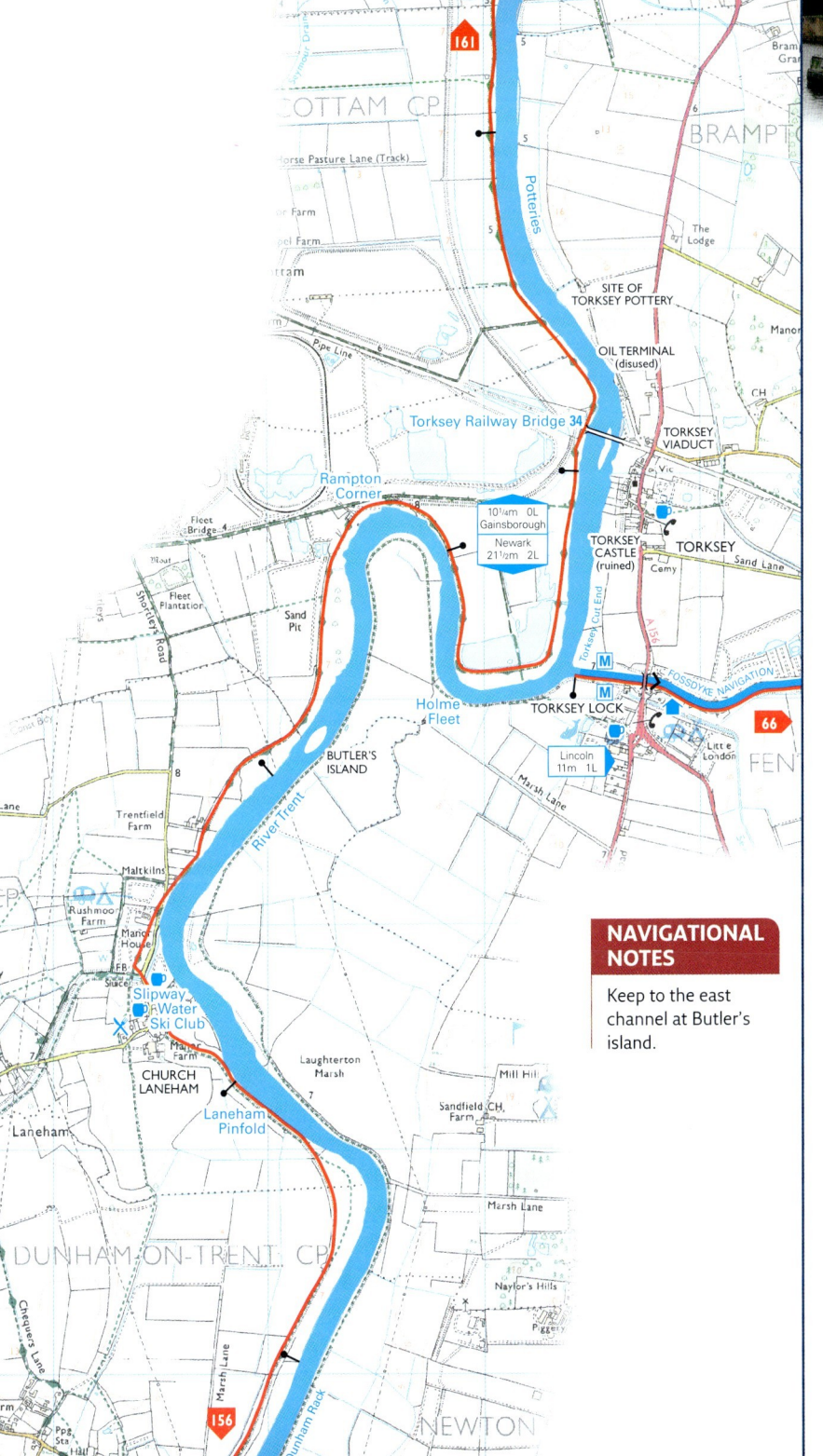

Littleborough

From Cottam, the river continues to wind northwards towards Gainsborough. This is not as dull a stretch as those further south. A windmill marks the exaggeratedly named Trent Port, which is in fact the wharf for the small village of Marton. Speedboats operate from here, but owners of any larger boats will once again find it difficult to land. Marton was important in Saxon times because of its position near the ford where a Roman road (now the A1500) crossed the Trent. This ford marked the western boundary of the ancient kingdom of Lindsay. Many historians believe that Saint Paulinus baptised some of the first Saxon Christians here in AD627. The church of St Margaret has evolved around an early Saxon church, side aisles being added to the original structure. The tapering Anglo-Saxon tower still reveals some fine herringbone masonry. In 1904 it was discovered that the entire structure was unsafe as it had been built on foundations only two feet deep made of sand and pebbles. The next place of interest is Littleborough, a tiny riverside settlement. Fortunately boats may moor temporarily at the floating jetty. Below Littleborough is a beautiful reach with steep wooded hills rising from the water's edge on the Lincolnshire side. The attractive brick and stone building set in the parkland is called Burton Château. A little further downstream, another clump of trees on the east bank at Knaith conceals a former nunnery and chapel, but mooring is only just possible here. On towards Gainsborough, the cooling towers of West Burton Power Station stand out prominently in the flat landscape on the west side of the river.

NAVIGATIONAL NOTES

Approaching Marton Mill corner from the south, the channel is on the inside (to the west) of the corner and moves across to the outside (to the north) as the river swings west.

- **Knaith**
Lincs. Temporary mooring just possible. Among the trees is the Hall and an interesting old church with a Jacobean pulpit. Both were part of a nunnery dissolved in 1539. The Hall was the birthplace of Thomas Sutton, who founded Charterhouse School and Hospital.
- **Littleborough**
Notts. An attractive hamlet with reasonably good access from the river. The little church stands on a slight rise; it is a delightfully simple Norman structure and incorporates much herringbone masonry. It is assumed from various finds, including the perfectly preserved body of a woman dug up in the graveyard, that this was the site of the Roman camp Segelocum. The paved ford dating from the time of Emperor Hadrian became visible during a drought in 1933. King Harold's army crossed this ford on its way to Hastings in 1066.

BREAKFAST AT POTTERIES

Viewed from the wheelbox of a sand-carrying barge, the Romans and their ilk were untidy fellows. Clearly they thought nothing of tossing their rubbish into the river – to make a ford or empty a failed kiln – and might be considered the forerunners of the contemporary litter lout. A heavily-laden barge lumbers down this river with difficulty, banging the bottom on even the most generous ebb, unsure where she'll finally come to rest to await the next flood tide. History's cast-offs do nothing to help the situation and invariably result in an unscheduled halt, mid-river. Piling stones on the river bed, to form a ford, might have seemed a good idea to the Romans at the time. It is not, however, an opinion widely shared amongst barge skippers of today. Littleborough doubtless offers plenty to excite the archaeologist with its wealth of antiquity, whilst a short distance upstream, connoisseurs of porcelain can wax lyrical about the decorative output from the 19th-C Torksey Pottery. The common thread lies in the debris ejected into the tideway (commemorated in the name of this reach), making it a sure-fire resting place for loaded barges and a regular bed and breakfast stop for their crew.

Gainsborough

The river moves away from the wooded slopes, passes the power station (the northernmost on the river) and heads for Gainsborough, which is clearly indicated by a group of tall flour mills. Below the railway bridge, the river bends sharply before reaching these mills, the bridge at Gainsborough and the desolate wharfs. With the completion of the new flood defences, much of this area has been changed into an attractive riverside walk with an imaginatively landscaped area just below Gainsborough Arches. Further north, handy for the town, there is a secure *pontoon mooring* accessed with a BW Watermate key. The town is set entirely on one side of the river, and is worth visiting. It was once a centre for heavy engineering and home to Marshall Tractors, manufacturers of the famous traction engines and the firm where L.T.C. Rolt (author and inland waterway campaigner) carried out his apprenticeship.

NAVIGATIONAL NOTES

1. Below Gainsborough Arches the River Trent ceases to be under the jurisdiction of BW and is controlled by the Humber Navigation by-laws. These are administered by Associated British Ports from whom a copy may be obtained by telephoning 01482 212191 (www.humber.com).
2. VHF marine band radio has become an important aid when navigating tidal commercial waterways. It allows the boater to know the whereabouts of other traffic and to maintain contact with lock keepers who listen out on channels 16 and 74, and work on channel 74. See note on page 152 for telephone contact.
3. BW request that boaters give lock keepers along the tidal river 24 hours' notice of passage. Always seek advice from lock keepers and respect their skill and experience.
4. The Trent Series Charts, published by The Boating Association (www.theboatingassociation. co.uk), are detailed charts of the tidal Trent (and the tidal Ouse and non-tidal Trent) and are available from their website (info@theboatingassociation.co.uk). Also from BW lock keepers. Charge.
5. The Aegir, or tidal bore, a tidal wave of between 1ft and 5ft in height, and breaking at the sides, may be encountered between Keadby and Torksey. It is normally only seen on spring tides of over 25ft (Hull), and arrives at the same time as the flood, although there can be a variation of half an hour each way. If you are on the river, keep a watch for it, and meet it head on, facing straight downstream and in the middle of the river. If you are anchored, use twice the normal length of warp. If you are moored, try to tie up to a pontoon mooring or large craft, which will itself rise and fall with the wave.

● **Gainsborough**
Lincs. All services, two stations. Gainsborough is best seen from the river, where the old wharves and warehouses serve as a reminder of the town's significance as a port in the 18th and 19th C. Once qualifying as Britain's furthest inland port, there is now no evidence of the boats (of up to 850 tonnes deadweight) that used to carry animal feedstuffs, grain, fertilisers and scrap metals. Elsewhere industrial sprawl and Victorian red-brick housing tend to obscure the qualities of this old market town. There are several Victorian churches, but All Saints retains its Perpendicular tower. Gainsborough was a frequent battleground during the Civil War and George Eliot described it as St Ogg's in *The Mill on the Floss*.
All Saints Parish Church Church Street, Gainsborough DN21 2JR (01427 611036). *Open during daylight hours.*
Gainsborough Old Hall Parnell Street, Gainsborough DN21 2NB (01427 612669; www.lincolnshire.gov.uk).
An attractive manor house in the centre of town, now a folk museum: it contains a medieval kitchen and Great Hall. Here Henry VIII met Catherine Parr, later his sixth wife, who was the daughter-in-law of the house. The Pilgrim Fathers also met here. *Open Mar-Oct, Mon-Fri 10.00-17.00, Sat-Sun 11.00-17.00.* Charge.
Model Railway Museum Florence Terrace, Gainsborough DN21 1BE (01427 61587). *Telephone for opening times.*
Old Nick Theatre Spring Gardens, Gainsborough DN21 2AY (01427 810616; www.gainsboroughtheatrecompany.com). *Telephone for performance details and bookings.*
Trinity Arts Centre Trinity Street, Gainsborough DN21 2AL (01427 676655). Box office *open Wed-Fri 10.00-15.30, Sat 09.30-14.00.*

River Trent
Gainsborough

West Lindsey Leisure Centre The Avenue, Gainsborough DN21 1EP (01427 615169; www.everyoneactive.com). *Open Mon-Fri 07.00-22.00, Sat-Sun 08.00-20.00.*
Gainsborough Tourist Information Centre Guildhall, Marshall's Yard, Gainsborough DN21 2NA (01427 676666; www.visitlincolnshire.com).

Pubs and Restaurants

The Trent Port Ramper Road, Gainsborough DN21 1NE (01427 612026). Just west of Gainsborough Arches. Very much a family oriented pub with indoor Fun Factory and outdoor adventure playground. Largely traditional pub food from an extensive menu available from *11.30-22.00 daily (12.00 Sun)*. Dogs welcome only in the large garden. Quiz *every Thu*.

WALKING & CYCLING

It is possible to follow the greater part of the Trent north - close to its junction with the River Ouse - along minor roads and footpaths, many of which cling to its flood banks on either side.

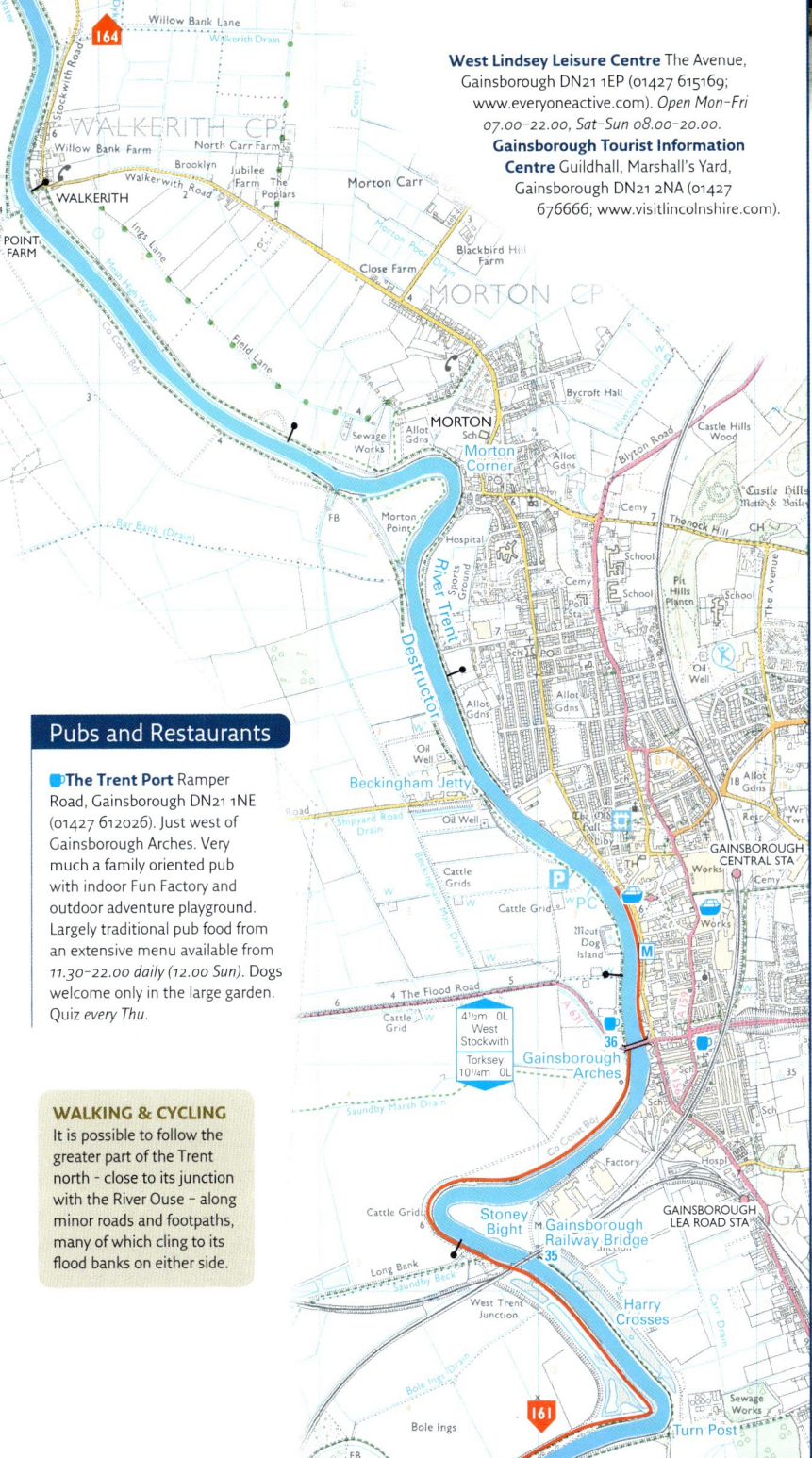

West Stockwith

On leaving Gainsborough the river passes the jetty of the Trent Wharfage and Storage Group on the left. This was the destination of the large coasters which occasionally plied the Trent above Gunness, where they discharged cargoes of ferro-metals, timber, fertilisers, bulk chemicals and animal feeds. They were able to carry loads of up to 1250 tonnes at a time, shipped from as far away as Sweden. Then the navigation bends sharply to the left, passing Morton Wharf with its Flemish gables, and winds its way past the hamlet of Walkerith towards West Stockwith. Immediately after the sharp right-hand bend in the river (below Farmers Jetty) the entrance lock into the Chesterfield Canal is visible on the left, giving access into the basin with its boatyard, moorings and friendly Yacht Club. Just downstream from the basin the River Idle, barricaded in by steel flood doors, joins the Trent beside West Stockwith's unusual 18th-C Georgian

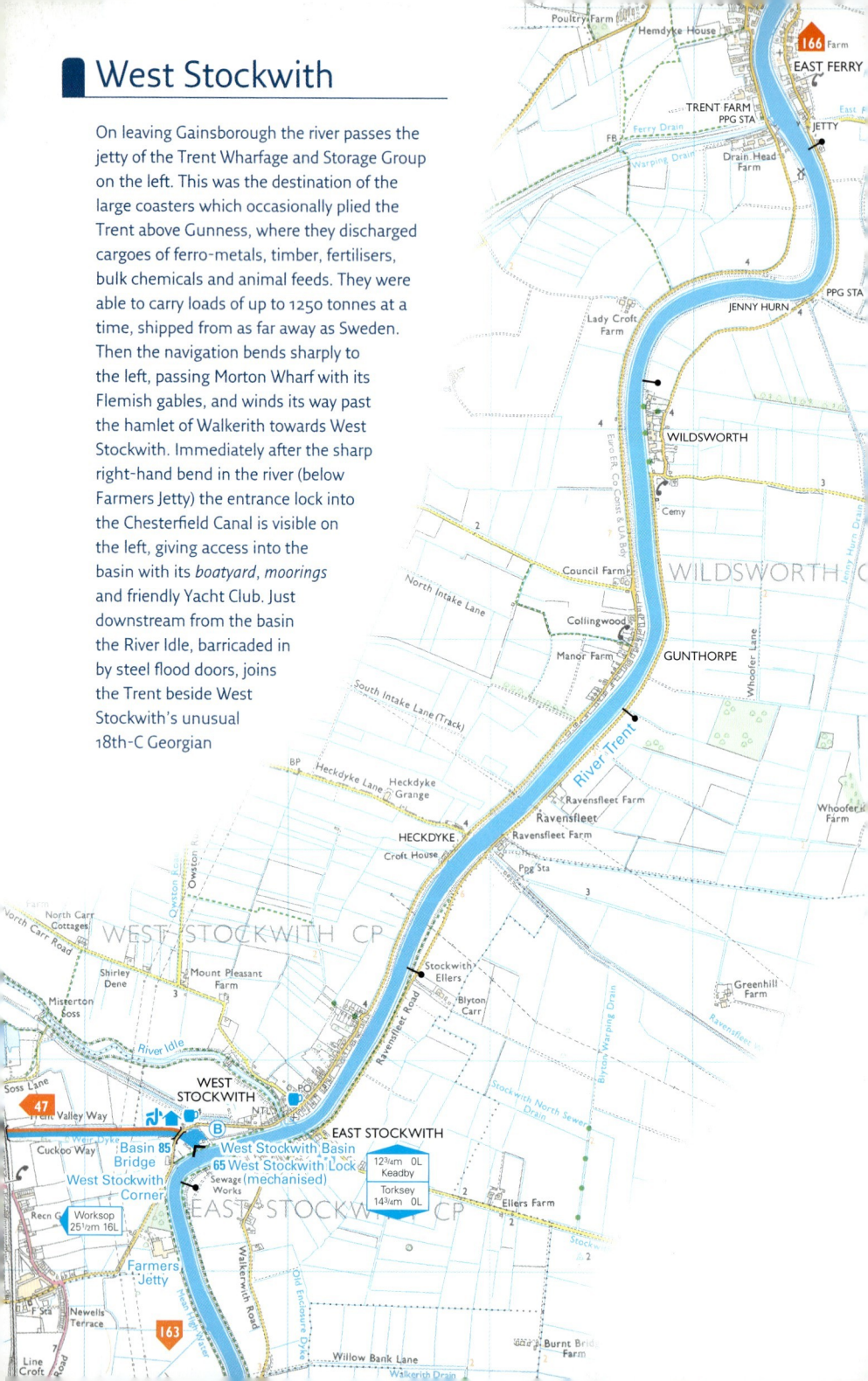

church. This was once the main highway from the industrial areas of South Yorkshire, terminating at a large wharf in Bawtry. Goods travelled to and from the town by horse and cart and, before the development of the River Don as a reliable navigation, were dependent upon the River Idle for onward transport. In draining the Isle of Axholme in the 17th C, Cornelius Vermuyden modified the course of the Idle and drastically reduced its effectiveness as a navigable waterway. From the river, West Stockwith, now a conservation area, presents a closed-in, almost intimate, aspect with its many tall three-storey buildings. It is possible to catch the occasional tantalising glimpse into the village up tiny passages, or ginnels, running between the houses. Once a thriving boat building community – there were five boatyards only 100 years ago – West Stockwith had a population of 5,000 in the 1880s; it is now reduced to 240. The brick-built church, looking more like a chapel capped with a squat bell tower, is one of only three of its kind and was completed in 1722. Inside the plasterwork is classic Adam. *See* page 47 for further details on the village. Leaving West Stockwith the Trent follows a comparatively straight course passing the isolated hamlets of Gunthorpe and Wildsworth, barely visible to the boater hidden as they are below the river's flood banks. All this area bordering the river was, in AD886, part of the Danelaw, and place names with *by* and *thorpe* endings are of Viking derivation. A sense of isolation and independence persists into the 21st C from a time when the Wash, the Trent and the Humber effectively cut this area off from the remainder of the country. In those times the inhabitants identified more with Denmark, Holland and the sea than with the rest of England.

NAVIGATIONAL NOTES

1 Entering the Chesterfield Canal from the Trent can be tricky due to the tidal flow across the entrance to the lock. A leaflet is available from BW 01636 704481 (and from most Trent locks) with instructions on how to access the lock safely – or contact the lock keeper. The lock accepts craft up a maximum size of 72' x 17' 6". The lock is keeper-operated (give as much prior notice as possible by telephoning 01427 890204/07884 238780) and passage can usually be made
2½ hours before to 4½ hours after high water. By coincidence, flood (when the tide ceases ebbing and turns to come back in) at Stockwith is the same time as high water at Hull. The flood runs for approximately 2½ hours and the direction of flow changes very rapidly.
2 Keepers at all the Trent locks can be contacted on marine band VHF radio, calling channel 16, working channel 74 – the radio is not constantly manned – or by telephone using the numbers listed below:
Cromwell Lock 01636 821213/07887 754485;
West Stockwith Lock 01427 890204/07884 238780;
Torksey Lock 01427 890204/07884 238781;
Keadby Lock 01724 782205/07733 124611.
Commercial river traffic operates on channel 6 upstream of Keadby Bridge and it is useful for VHF users to monitor this channel to establish the whereabouts of large craft.
3 Deep-draughted commercial traffic, especially coasters, require the deepest channel on the navigation at all times. Be prepared to give way to allow for this and do not necessarily expect to pass port to port when meeting craft head on.
4 Boaters intending to break their passage to Cromwell Lock, by staying on the pontoon mooring at Dunham, are requested to inform the lock keeper at West Stockwith to avoid alarm at their non-arrival at Cromwell. Similarly, should you change your plans and subsequently stop at Dunham, please contact a lock keeper to avoid unnecessary concern for your safety.

Owston Ferry

The conical tower of an old windmill on the left bank has been restored as part of a spacious new dwelling on a fairly grand scale – even to the point of having a helipad sited on an adjacent field. This feature, very much of the 21st C, contrasts strongly with the mellow buildings of Owston Ferry directly ahead. As the channel swings to the right, the pleasing scale of the riverside houses becomes apparent. Skilfully constructed using local brick and tile, they are both solid and graceful in appearance. There is something reminiscent of a Dutch painting in the views over the river seen from the lower part of the village. The church, standing a little way from the waterway, is largely medieval, but with early 19th-C Gothic additions, and inside there is an attractive rood screen dating from 1897. Although modern executive dwellings have crept into the village, generally by way of infill, it is the largely three-storey, Dutch-influenced buildings that still predominate. At Robin Hood's Well to the north west, Roman coins have been found, indicating that this is a settlement of some antiquity. Flowing northwards the river regains its isolation amidst the flat, fertile countryside behind the flood banks. Throughout history this area has been known as the Isle of Axholme – once a wetland prone to seasonal flooding and in ancient times a forest, heath and then marsh. It is a tract of low, flat land less than 100ft above sea level, some 5 miles wide and running for approximately 18 miles along the Trent's western bank. In 1625 a Dutchman, Cornelius Vermuyden, was brought over to oversee the draining of the area at a cost of £56,000. The land's natural fertility was soon realised under the Dutch and French Protestant settlers that followed him, much to the disgust of the ousted native inhabitants. After lengthy litigation the land was finally divided in 1691, the locals receiving 10,532 acres and the settlers 2,868 acres. The chief town in the area is Epworth, some 4 miles west of Kelfield and famous as the birthplace, in 1703, of John Wesley, founder of Methodism. His father was rector of the parish for 59 years. Over the years the pattern of agriculture in the area has varied, reflecting a changing society. At the time when the Wesley family lived at Epworth, flax and hemp, used in the manufacture of sacking and canvas, were amongst the principal crops. Walnut trees were plentiful along the east bank of the river, the nuts gathered as a further source of income. Today intensive vegetable growing, cereals and root crops predominate.

NAVIGATIONAL NOTES

The substantial mooring dolphins located on various reaches of the navigation – e.g. north and south of the M180 bridge – are for the safety of commercial craft and not to be used by pleasure vessels. They do not provide a way ashore.

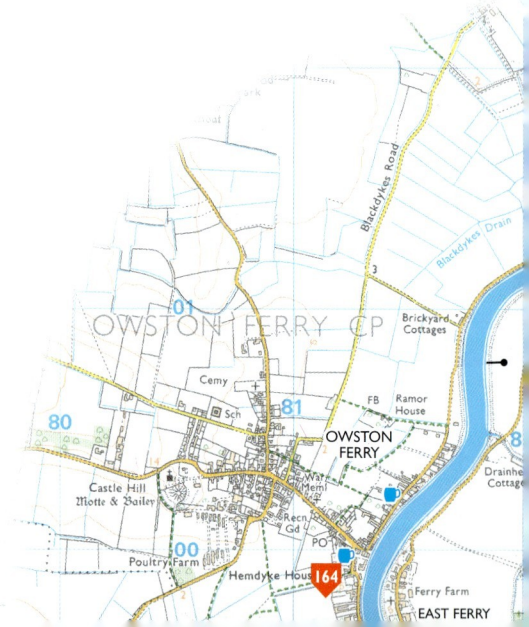

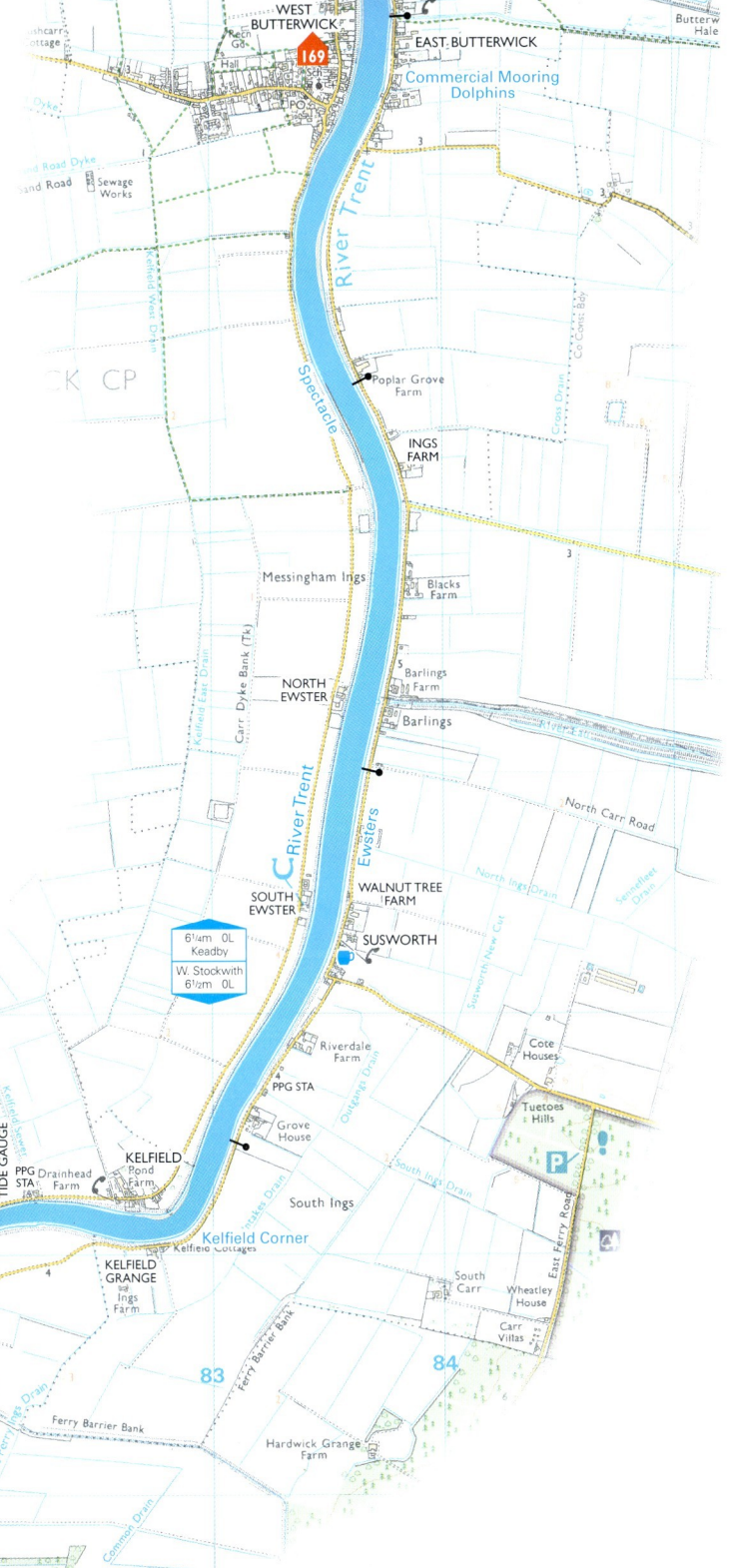

River Trent

Owston Ferry

167

Keadby

The twin villages of East and West Butterwick now come into view, facing each other across the river. As seems so often to be the case on the lower part of the Trent, the village to the west is larger than its eastern counterpart. West Butterwick is another village with a strong Dutch influence evident in the local buildings. It has an attractive church built in 1841 from creamy white brick, deceptively stone-like from a distance. It follows the Gothic style, and has a small octagonal spire together with period interior fittings. In contrast, East Butterwick is a plain place with a small church built in 1884 at a cost of £500. It was once described as being 'surrounded by root crops and often by fog'. Now the river begins to broaden out, passing under the M180 viaduct, built in 1978, and rising out of the flat countryside to clear the navigation. The scale of the river is such that the boater can now begin to appreciate just how major a watercourse the Trent really is – 150 miles long, with a catchment area of over 4,000 square miles. The river once flowed due east from Nottingham, discharging into the Wash. At some point in prehistory this channel became blocked and the river turned north, picking a course through the soft keuper marls, still evident in the many shoals along the navigation, to its present junction with the Ouse. Three thousand cubic feet of water a second discharge into the Humber, a volume greater than that from the Thames into the estuary. Throughout history the Trent has been exploited both as a trunk navigation and for its inherent fertility. For centuries farmers working the land beside the river have encouraged it to flood the fields during winter months, by directing its water along warping drains cut at right angles to the waterway. As the river water spread across the land the fertile sediment settled out, enriching the soil and raising the water-table to sustain rich summer grazing. North of the M180 two further villages sit opposite one another – behind flood embankments – before Keadby is reached. These are Burringham to the east, with its early Victorian brick and slate church squatting beside the river, and Althorpe to the west, where the church, with its late Perpendicular tower, nestles in with the houses. Dedicated to St Oswald, it owes its origins

NAVIGATIONAL NOTES

1. Three red lights are normally displayed at all times when Keadby Lock is not available. A green light will be shown when there is sufficient depth of water over the cill to work the lock. This is theoretically up to 7 hours after high water, but despite constant dredging a sand bar builds up in front of the lock and 5 hours is often the maximum realistic time after high water that passage can be effected.
2. Shelter passes are available from the lock keeper for non-registered craft using BW navigations and/or moorings for a limited period.
3. All locks and bridges on BW waterways west of Keadby Swing Bridge are now boater-operated using the BW Watermate key. This key is also required for access to the lock area itself. Keadby Swing Bridge *only opens 07.00-10.00 & 15.00-17.00.*
4. Due to the number of craft requiring the lock and the varying tide envelope, please give the lock keeper 48 hours' notice of your intention to use the lock.
5. Boaters intending to break their passage to Cromwell Lock, by staying on the pontoon mooring at Dunham, are requested to inform the lock keeper at Keadby to avoid alarm at their non-arrival at Cromwell. Similarly, should you change your plans and subsequently stop at Dunham, please contact a lock keeper to avoid unnecessary concern for your safety. VHF radio frequencies: calling channel 16, working channel 74; or telephone as below:
   Cromwell Lock 01636 821213/07887 754485;
   West Stockwith Lock 01427 890204/07884 238780;
   Torksey Lock 01427 890204/07884 238781;
   Keadby Lock 01724 782205/07733 124611.
6. Boaters navigating downstream of Keadby should check that their insurance policy covers them for this passage.
7. In order to secure your boat safely whilst using Keadby Lock, bow and stern ropes should be at least 25' in length.

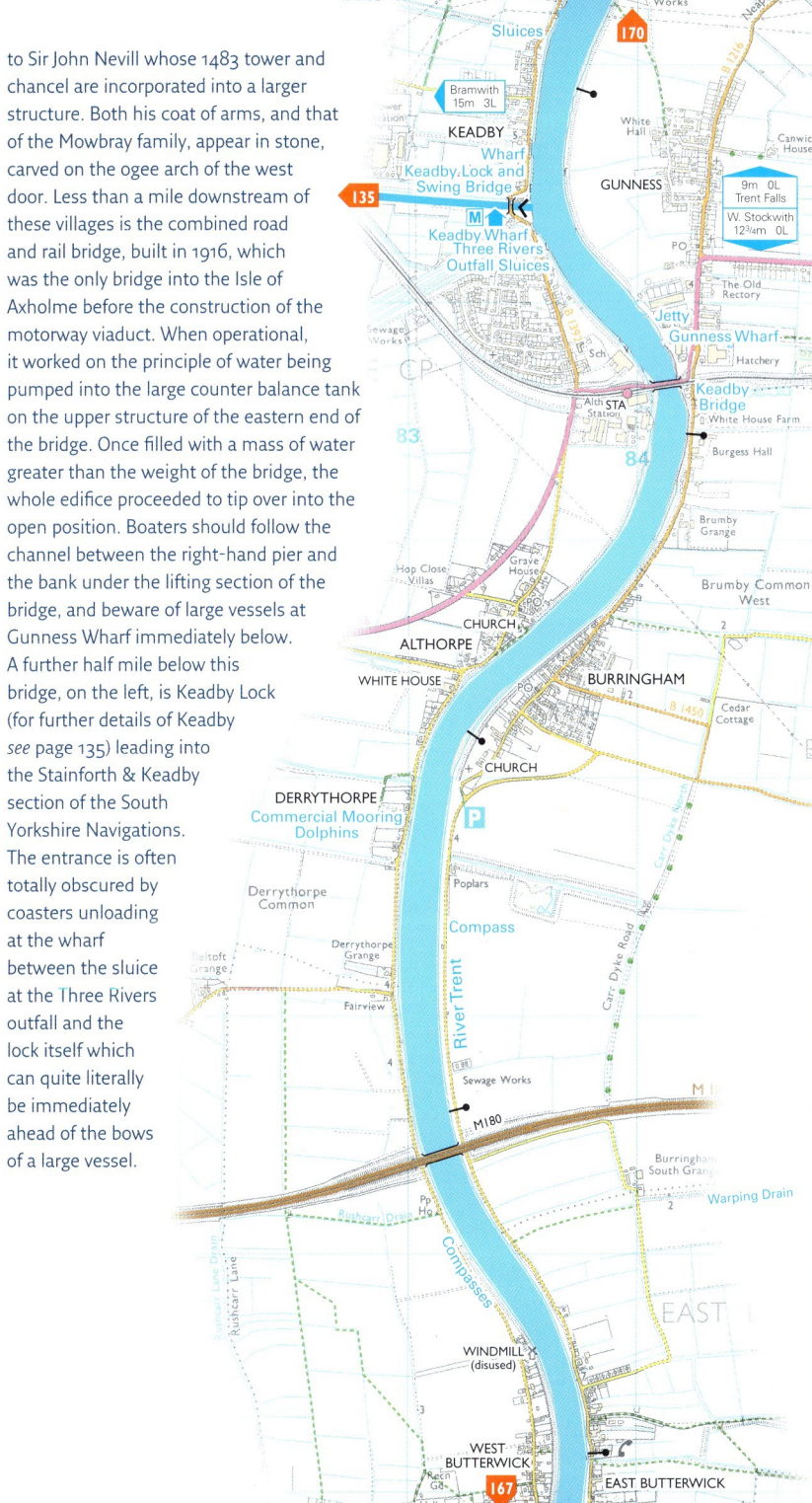

to Sir John Nevill whose 1483 tower and chancel are incorporated into a larger structure. Both his coat of arms, and that of the Mowbray family, appear in stone, carved on the ogee arch of the west door. Less than a mile downstream of these villages is the combined road and rail bridge, built in 1916, which was the only bridge into the Isle of Axholme before the construction of the motorway viaduct. When operational, it worked on the principle of water being pumped into the large counter balance tank on the upper structure of the eastern end of the bridge. Once filled with a mass of water greater than the weight of the bridge, the whole edifice proceeded to tip over into the open position. Boaters should follow the channel between the right-hand pier and the bank under the lifting section of the bridge, and beware of large vessels at Gunness Wharf immediately below. A further half mile below this bridge, on the left, is Keadby Lock (for further details of Keadby see page 135) leading into the Stainforth & Keadby section of the South Yorkshire Navigations. The entrance is often totally obscured by coasters unloading at the wharf between the sluice at the Three Rivers outfall and the lock itself which can quite literally be immediately ahead of the bows of a large vessel.

River Trent — Keadby

169

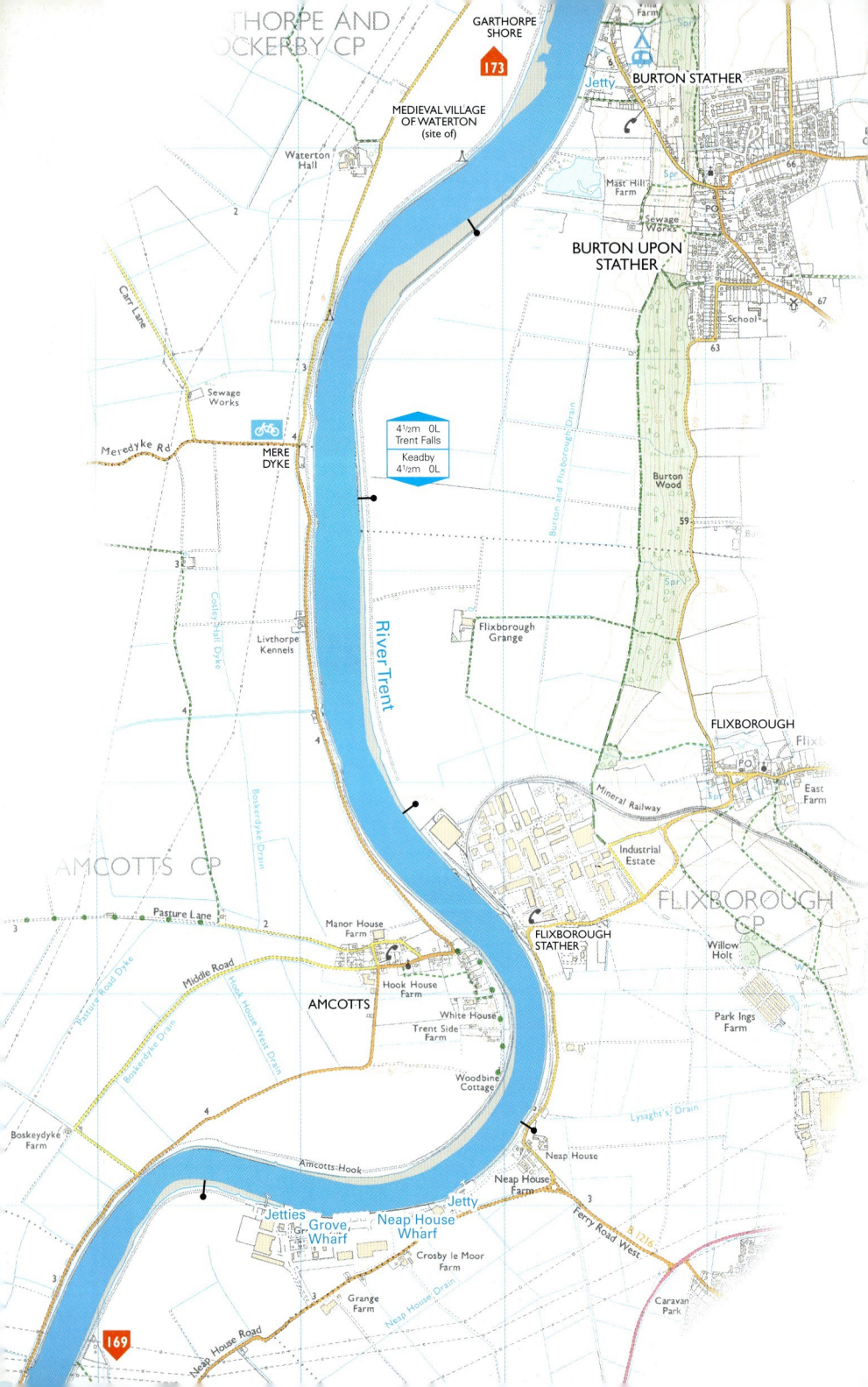

Burton Stather

This final section of the river is host to serious continental shipping and is punctuated by a series of bustling wharves. Coasters come and go with the tides carrying steel, coal and fertilisers and the constant activity of cranes, on the busy jetties, warms the heart of the true waterways enthusiast. It is perhaps not insignificant that the wharves are all in private ownership and, although relatively modest, they are nonetheless efficient for this and are clearly most cost-effective enterprises. It is probably unique for the boater, used to the prosaic names of inland pleasure craft, to be passing hulls bearing the cyrillic inscriptions of vessels registered in Eastern European ports – and beyond. Water depth for these craft is critical, even so close to the mouth of the river (it's not unusual for them to have no more than one foot of water under their keel) and all movements require very close correlation with the tide in conjunction with expert pilotage. Always bear this in mind and pay close attention to the requirements of any large vessel on the move. It is in these situations that VHF radio is an invaluable aid; or at least a comprehensive knowledge of the international sound signals. The wharves do not permit casual mooring (except in an emergency) so once past Keadby on a falling tide the boater, intending to head up the Ouse back into the inland waterways system, is, on reaching Trent Falls, committed to one of four courses of action:

1. Anchor under the lee of the training wall in the west channel, to the south of Trent Falls light.
2. Beach on Tackhammer flats.
3. Moor on Blacktoft Lay-by Jetty. *Charge*.
4. Punch the ebbing tide in the Ouse up to Goole (or beyond).

These options are examined in greater detail on the next page. Boaters passing Flixborough Stather, now predominantly engaged in steel traffic, may recall the disastrous explosion that occurred here when it was the site of a vast chemical works which was virtually flattened by the blast. To the north, beside the outfall from Meredyke, is a silt bank which, unusually, has built up on a straight section of the river, at the approach to the bite of a bend – BEWARE. Burton Stather was built and operated by the late Victor Waddington whose barges, moored on the Aire & Calder Navigation, cluster the outskirts of Goole docks awaiting incoming shipments of steel. Similarly his boats are to be found tied up several deep at Waddington Lock, on the South Yorkshire Navigations and are a testimony to his great commitment to waterways transport. His enthusiasm, often in the face of a less than co-operative bureaucracy, was only matched by the immense carrying capacity of his total barge fleet. He is alleged to have observed, about the perilous state of his home navigation, that 'The top's too near the bottom, the bottom's too near the top and there's nowt in between'. The unwary boater, failing to use the marked channel at Trent Falls, may well have occasion to reflect at some length on this observation.

Trent Falls

Now the steep wooded hills that have followed close to the east bank of the river start to peel away as the mouth of the Trent and its junction with the Ouse (to form the Humber) is approached. Large areas of low-lying ground – part mud flat, part rough grazing – accompany the waterway to its conclusion, only to be dwarfed by the vast acreage of water that is the confluence of these two great rivers. There is a lonely eeriness about so much water with only the village of Alkborough in the distance to suggest human habitation. Strangely enough the River Don, now confined to its sterile, straight, tidal channel at Goole, used to have one of its two mouths here, just to the south of Anchor Drain. When Vermuyden set out to drain the Isle of Axholme he unsuccessfully attempted to divert the river's entire output along its second branch, into the River Aire near Snaith. Nowhere else in Britain will the inland navigator be exposed to so much water and so little bank. Many boaters, regaled with tales of the fearsome nature of these waters, will do anything to avoid passage, but in reality, in a properly equipped boat, in the right weather conditions and with informed planning, Trent Falls can be navigated with comparative ease. Before passing Keadby, with its safe haven in the Stainforth and Keadby Canal, you should be clear about the channel (*see reference to Trent Series Charts, below*), the tide and weather conditions and your strategy once the Humber is reached (technically the point where Trent and Ouse meet and all points east). You should also be clear that Trent Falls is also called Trent Mouth and Apex (Apex being the name given to the lighthouse at the end of the western training wall). All three names can be heard in regular use on local shipping radio traffic. Most boaters will choose to approach Trent Falls on an ebbing tide; low-powered craft will have no option. Deep-draughted vessels will obviously plan to arrive well before low water. Only powerful boats will consider turning into the Ouse to push against the ebb to Goole. For the remainder the choices are set out below.

NAVIGATIONAL NOTES

1. Anchor in the western channel between South Trent Beacon and Anchor Drain, about 20ft out from the training wall. There is a firm bottom here and you are clear of empty sand barges risking a short cut.
2. Flat-bottomed boats can beach on Tackhammer Flats and await the flood. To perform this manoeuvre, follow the eastern channel to a point roughly mid-way between South Trent Beacon and Apex Light, turn south east at right angles to your track and head square onto the flats. The ebb will draw your stern northwards, helping to lodge the vessel securely, whilst the flood will push it southwards and help to pull you off. **Note** (a) This is not a good strategy in rough weather. The western channel anchorage provides a modicum of shelter from westerly winds. (b) If attempted at night, remember that other vessels, especially large sand barges, may also have beached, so look out for riding lights.
3. On the Ouse, west of Trent Falls (almost opposite West Ouse Beacon – the second flashing red light west of Apex Light) is Associated British Ports' (ABP) Blacktoft Lay-by Jetty which, for a fee, can be used between tides. Be prepared to share it with large commercial vessels and be sure that your vessel is powerful enough to reach it.
4. At all times read the above narrative and navigational notes in conjunction with a reputable chart such as The Trent Series Charts, published by The Boating Association (www.theboatingassociation.co.uk). Be willing to take advice from BW lock keepers and ABP staff in Goole Docks (01482 327171). **ABOVE ALL ELSE INLAND BOATERS SHOULD NOT PASS KEADBY UNLESS THEY FULLY UNDERSTAND WHAT THEY ARE DOING.**
5. Boats using Ocean Lock (into Goole Docks) and the River Ouse **MUST CARRY VHF RADIO AND HAVE AT LEAST TWO PEOPLE ON BOARD.**

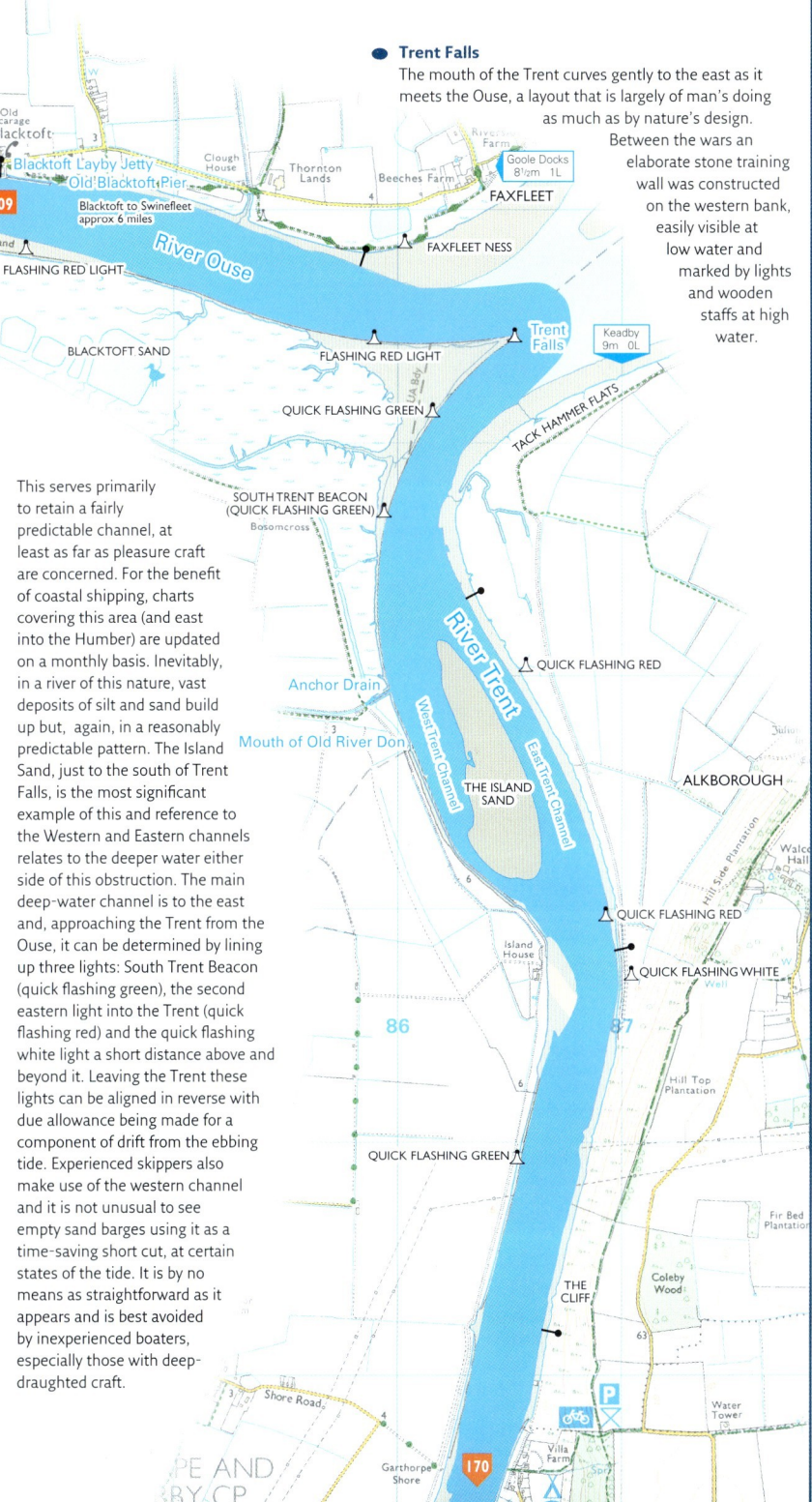

River Trent

Trent Falls

The mouth of the Trent curves gently to the east as it meets the Ouse, a layout that is largely of man's doing as much as by nature's design. Between the wars an elaborate stone training wall was constructed on the western bank, easily visible at low water and marked by lights and wooden staffs at high water.

This serves primarily to retain a fairly predictable channel, at least as far as pleasure craft are concerned. For the benefit of coastal shipping, charts covering this area (and east into the Humber) are updated on a monthly basis. Inevitably, in a river of this nature, vast deposits of silt and sand build up but, again, in a reasonably predictable pattern. The Island Sand, just to the south of Trent Falls, is the most significant example of this and reference to the Western and Eastern channels relates to the deeper water either side of this obstruction. The main deep-water channel is to the east and, approaching the Trent from the Ouse, it can be determined by lining up three lights: South Trent Beacon (quick flashing green), the second eastern light into the Trent (quick flashing red) and the quick flashing white light a short distance above and beyond it. Leaving the Trent these lights can be aligned in reverse with due allowance being made for a component of drift from the ebbing tide. Experienced skippers also make use of the western channel and it is not unusual to see empty sand barges using it as a time-saving short cut, at certain states of the tide. It is by no means as straightforward as it appears and is best avoided by inexperienced boaters, especially those with deep-draughted craft.

173

INDEX

Abbeydale Industrial Hamlet 122
Acaster Malbis 103
Acaster Selby 103
Aire & Calder Navigation 15–29, 106, 108, 109, 119, 130, 171
Aire, River 15, 18, 20, 108, 112, 114, 116, 119, 172
Airmyn 109
Aldborough 93
Aldwark 95
Aldwark Bridge 94
Aldwark Lock 124
Alkborough 172
All Saints Church, Aughton 59
All Saints Church, Cawood 104
All Saints Church, Greetwell 72
All Saints Church, Pocklington 63
All Saints Parsh Church, Gainsborough 162
Allerton Bywater 17
Althorpe 168
Anchor Drain 172
Angle Row Gallery 142
Anston Stone Quarries 36
Anton's Gowt 65, 82, 84
Apex 172
Arrows Bridge 92
Arundel Gate 122
Attenborough Nature Reserve 140, 142
Attercliffe Road 120
Aughton 59
Averham Weir 148
Axholme 24
Axholme Joint Railway Bridge 134

Bacon Lane 120
Balborough Road Bridge 35
Bank Dole Junction 112
Bank Dole Lock 15, 20, 112
Bar Convent Museum 100
Bardney 65, 73–75
Bardney Lock 74
Barlby 99
Barlby Pinfold 99
Barmby 106
Barmby Barrage Lock 51
Barmby on the Marsh 54, 60, 61, 107
Barmby Tidal Barrage 60, 61
Barnby Dun 16, 130, 131
Barnby Wharf Bridge 42
Barnsley 125
Barnsley Canal 125
Barrow Hill Roundhouse 33
Bartholomew, William 26
Barton in Fabis 137, 138
Barton Island 140
Bassetlaw Museum 42
Bawtry 30, 119, 165
Beal 114, 115
Beeston Canal 140, 142
Beeston Cut 140
Beeston Lock 136, 138, 142
Beever Bridge 24
Beighton 61
Bell Furrows Locks 89
Bell Hall 103
Belvoir Castle 143

Beningborough 96
Beningborough Hall 94, 95
Beningborough Park 94
Berwick-upon-Tweed 93
Besthorpe Wharf 136, 154
Bielby 63
Bielby Arm 62
Bishop's House 122
Bishopthorpe Palace 98
Bleasby 147
Blue Bridge 98
Bluebank Wood 32
Boatman Inn 34
Boots Estate 140
Boroughbridge 14, 88, 92, 93
Boston 58, 65, 66, 74, 82–86
Boston Grand Sluice 65, 82
Boston Guildhall Museum 84
Boston Preservation Trust 84
Boston Stump 78, 82, 84
Boundary Lock 36
Bramwith Junction 119
Branford, John 26
Branston Island 74, 75
Brayford Pool 65, 69, 70
Brayton 116, 117
Brayton Barff 116
Brayton Railway Bridge 116
Brewhouse Ward Museum 142
Brieghton Ferry 60
Brighton 73
Brindley, James 30
British Horological Institute 150
Brodsworth Hall 129
Bubwith 51, 59
Bulholme Lock 15, 16
Burningham 168
Burny Hall Gardens and Museum Trust 63
Burton Bridge 116
Burton Chateau 160
Burton Hall 116
Burton Joyce 144, 145
Burton Stather 171

Canada goose 48
Canal Corridor Study 113
Canal Head 51, 57, 62, 63
Carlton Wharf 155
Castle Donington 137
Castle Dyke Drain 84
Castle Lock 141
Castle Mills Lock 98
Castleford 17, 25, 26, 112
Castleford Junction 16
Castleford Lock 15
Caves of Nottingham 142
Cawood 104, 99
Cawood Hargreaves 16
Cemetery Lane 57
Channel Tunnel 100
Chapel Hill 78, 86
Chequer Chamber 87
Chequer Lane 28
Cherry Island Wood 89
Cherry Willingham 72
Chesterfield 30, 32, 33
Chesterfield Canal 30–50, 136, 164
Chesterfield Canal Trust 33
Church Laneham 159
Church Marnham 157
City Museum 122

Clarborough 42, 45
Clay Cross 33
Clayworth 44, 45, 50
Clayworth Bridge 30, 44
Cliffords Tower 100
Clifton Hall 140
Clifton Park Museum 123
Clumber House 41
Coates Lock 51, 57, 62
Cobb Hall 70
Cobblers Lock 78, 86
Colwick Racecourse 144
Coningsby Airfield 78
Conisbrough 126, 127
Cornelius Vermuyden 24, 165, 166, 172
Cottage Museum, The 77
Cottam 158
Cottingwith Lock 57
Cowbridge 84
Cowbridge Lock 84
Cranfleet 136, 137
Cromwell 152
Cromwell Lock 136, 152, 153
Cromwell Weir 152
Crook o'Moor Swing Bridge 133
Crow Croft Bridge 23
Crowle 134, 135
Crowle Bridge 134
Crowle Station 134
Crowle Wharf 119
Crown Hotel, The 93
Crucible Theatre, The 122
Cuddy Shaw Reach 94
Cusworth Hall Museum 129
Cutlers' Hall 122

Damselyfly, banded demoiselle 85
Danum 129
Darley's Brewery 132
Darnall Road Aqueduct 120
Darwin Iron Works 123
Dearne & Dove Canal 125
Denton Reservoir 143
Derbyshire 38
Derwent Ings 51
Derwent Mouth 136, 137
Derwent, River 51, 52, 54, 59–61, 106, 107
Devon, River 148
Dickens, Charles 128
Dixon's Lock 32
Dogdyke 65, 78, 79
Dogdyke Pumping Statin 78
Don Aqueduct 28, 130
Don, River 24, 119, 120, 124, 126, 165, 172
Don Valley Stadium 120
Don Viaduct 128
Doncaster 119, 128, 129, 131
Doncaster Town Lock 119, 128
Drakeholes 45
Drakeholes Tunnel 30, 45
Drax Power Station 107, 114
Dukeries, The 41
Dunham 157
Dunham Bridge 136, 157
Dunham Toll Bridge 157
Dutch River 24, 25, 119, 172

Ealand 135
Earth Centre, The 126
East Bridgford 146, 147

East Butterwick 168
East Cottingwith 52, 57
East Fen Catchwater Drain 84
East Midlands Coalfield 154
East Riding 63
East Stockwith 46
East Stoke 148
Eastern Channel 173
Eastwood 125
Eboracum 98
Eckington Road Bridge 32
Edinburgh 22, 129
Edlington Moor 78
Eggborough Power Station 20, 114
Ellerton 59
Elsecar Heritage Centre 123
Elsecar Power House 123
Elsecar Steam Railway 123
Elvington 54, 55
Epworth 166
Erewash Canal 136–138, 141

Fairburn 16, 17, 19
Fairfax House 100
Farmers Jetty 164
Farndon 148, 150
Fens, The 73
Ferry Bridge 86
Ferry Marnham 157
Ferrybridge 16–19
Ferrybridge Flood Lock 18
Ferrybridge Lock 15
Ferrybridge Power Stations 15, 17–19
Finkle Street 132
Fiskerton 72, 73, 136, 148, 150
Five Mile House 74
Flixborough Stather 171
Forest Locks 40, 42
Forest Recreation Ground 142
Forge Bridge 34
Fossdyke & Witham Navigations 65–87
Fossdyke Navigation 65, 66, 67, 69, 70, 72, 136, 158
Fosse Way 148, 150
Fountains Abbey & Studley Royal Water Garden 89
Frenchgate Shopping Centre 128
Frith Bank Drain 84
Fryston Colliery 16
Fydell House 84
Fydell, William 84

Gaggs Bridge 18
Gainsborough 30, 68, 160–164
Gainsborough and District Heritage Centre 162
Gainsborough Arches 162
Gainsborough Bridge 162
Gainsborough Old Hall 162
Galleries of Justice, The 142
Gautby 90
Girton Wharf 136, 154
Glory Hole 69
Godnow Bridge 133
Godnow Swing Bridge 134
Goole 15, 18, 22, 23, 25–27, 88, 108, 109, 113, 119, 136, 158, 171, 172
Goole Docks 24, 26, 108

Goole Museum and Art Gallery 27, 109
Goole Railway Bridge 108
Grantham 86
Grantham Canal 136, 141, 143
Graves Art Gallery 122
Gray's Bridge 44
Great North Road 18, 42, 93, 129, 150
Great tit 49
Green woodpecker 48
Greenland Road Bridge 120
Greetwell 72
Greetwell Hall 72
Greetwell Hall Farm 72
Grey heron 49
Greyfriars Exhibition Centre 70
Gringley 31, 45
Gringley on the Hill 47
Gunness Wharf 164, 169
Gunthorpe 146, 147, 165
Gunthorpe Bridge 136, 146, 147

Haddlesey 112, 114
Haddlesey Flood Lock 112
Haddlesey Lock 112, 114
Halfpenny Bridge 120
Halifax 54
Hambleton Causeway 112
Hardwick 66
Hargreaves 18
Harthill 37
Harthill Reservoir 30
Hatfield Chase 119
Hayton 42, 45
Hayton Low Bridge 44
Hazelford Lock 136, 148–151
Heck Bridge 20–22
Hemingbrough 107
Henshall, Hugh 30
Hewitt Hall 37
High Catton Road 52
High Marnham 157
High Marnham Power Station 157
Hollingwood 32, 35
Holme 152, 153
Holme Lock 144, 145
Holme Pierrepont 144, 145
Holme Pierrepont Hall 145
Holy Trinity Church, Acaster Malbis 103
Holy Trinity Church, Elvington 54
Holy Trinity Church, Skyehouse 28
Hooton Common 125
Hooton Road Bridge 125
Horncastle 78
Horncastle Canal 78
Houghbridge Drain 84
Hoveringham 146, 147
Howden 51
Howdendyke Island 108
Hull 112, 136, 158
Humber, River 26, 65, 88, 106, 119, 152, 165, 172, 173
Humber Ports 136

Idle, River 30, 31, 119, 165
Ings, The 54
Island Sand, The 173
Isle of Axholme 119, 165, 166, 169, 172

Jacksons Bridge 18, 20
Jessop, William 86, 112

Jorvik Centre 98

Keadby 24, 119, 130, 133–135, 168, 169, 171, 172
Keadby Canal 172
Keadby Junction 136
Keadby Lock 134, 169
Keadby Power Station 134
Keadby Swing Bridge 134
Kelfield 104, 166
Kelham 148
Kelham Island Museum 122
Kesteven 78
Kexby 54
Killamarsh 30, 34, 35
Killamarsh Reservoir 30
Kilnhurst 125
Kilnhurst Cut 125
Kilnhurst Flood Lock 125
Kingfisher 49
King's Flour Mills 18
Kings Park 42
Kirkgate 101
Kirkhouse Green Bridge 28
Kirkstead 65, 76
Kirkstead Abbey 77
Kirkstead Bridge 76, 77
Kiveton Park 37
Knaith 160
Knaresborough 88, 93
Knipton Reservoir 143
Knottingley 18, 20, 27, 109, 112, 114
Knottingley Old Hall 20
Kyme Eau 78, 86, 87
Kyme Tower 86

Lakeside Arts Centre 142
Lancaster 93
Laneham 158, 159
Laneham Ferry 159
Langley Mill 141
Langrick Bridge 80–82
Lapwing 48
Leeds 15, 112, 158
Lendall Bridge 98
Lenton 141
Lenton Chain 140
Lincoln 65, 68–72, 74, 84
Lincoln Castle 70
Lincoln Cathedral 47, 65, 69–72
Lincoln Medieval Bishops Palace 70
Lincolnshire Wolds 84
Lindsey 160
Lindum Colonia 70, 136
Linton Lock 94, 95
Linton-on-Ouse 94, 95
Littleborough 136, 160, 161
Littlethorpe 89
Lock Hill 27
London 22, 53, 84, 112, 129, 154
Long Sandall 128
Long Sandall Lock 128
Low Catton 52, 53
Low Eggborough 20
Low Lane Swing Bridge 28
Low Marnham 157
Lower Ouse 88
Lyceum Theatre, The 122

Magna Science Adventure Centre 123
Mallard duck 48
Malton 51
Manor Farm 22

Mansion House 129
Margidunum 147
Marshall Tractors 162
Marton 160
Marton Wharf 164
Mask, The 54
Mastin Moor 32
Maud Foster Drain 84
Maud Foster Mill 84
Maud's Bridge 133
Mayflower Trail 41
Mayor's Regatta 70
Meadow Lane Lock 136, 141
Meadowhall Shopping Centre 120, 123
Medge Hall 133
Medlam Drain 84
Melbourne 57
Melbourne Arm 51
Merchant Adventurers' Hall 100
Meredyke 171
Mexborough 119, 125, 126
Milby Cut 92
Milby Lock 88
Mile Long Tunnel 33
Millennium Bridge 98
Millennium Galleries 122
Millgate Museum 150
Misterton 46, 47
Moor's Swing Bridge 132
Moorhen 49
Moreby Park 103
Mr Straw's House 41
Multangular Tower 98
Murder Hole 69
Museum and Art Gallery, Doncaster 129
Museum of Costume and Textiles 142

Naburn 103
Naburn Bridge 98
Naburn Locks 103
National Bottle Collection, The 123
Navigation Wharf, Sleaford 86
Needle's Eye 120
Nether Poppleton 96, 97
New Bridge 24
New Junction Canal 15, 23, 24, 28, 29, 119, 130
Newark 146, 148–150, 152, 157, 158
Newark Branch 148
Newark Bypass 149
Newark Castle 136, 150
Newark Church 148
Newark Gilstrap Centre 150
Newark Museum 150
Newark Nether Lock 149
Newark Town Lock 148
Newark Town Treasures & Art Gallery 151
Newark-on-Trent 147
Newby 90
Newby Hall 89, 90
Newcastle 88
Newham Drain 84
Newton-on-Ouse 94, 95
Newtown 16
Nidd, River 94
Nocton Delph 74
North Clifton 157
North Duffield 59
North Muskham 152, 153
North Sea 60, 84, 136
Norwood 34

Norwood Tunnel 30, 31, 34, 40
Nottingham 34, 136, 137, 140–144, 146, 168
Nottingham Canal 140, 142
Nottingham Castle 141, 142
Nottingham Forest 141
Nottingham Goose Fair 142
Nottingham Playhouse 142
Nottinghamshire 38, 41, 157
Nun Monkton 94, 95
Nyton 93

Observatory Tower 70
Ocean Lock 108
Old London Bridge 136
Old Man Bridge 45
Old Nick Theatre 162
Osberton Hall 40, 41
Osberton Lock 30
Otter 143
Ouse Bridge 98
Ouse Gull Beck 94
Ouse, River 51, 59–61, 88, 94, 98, 104, 107, 109–113, 116, 119, 168, 171–173
Overton 96
Overton Manor 96
Owston Ferry 166, 167
Oxclose Lock 89

Peterborough Brickworks 154
Pilgrim Fathers' Story 41
Playhouse Theatre 142
Pocklington 51, 62, 63
Pocklington Canal 51, 57, 62, 63
Pollington 22, 23
Pollington Bridge 22
Pollington Grange 22
Pollington Hall 22
Pollington Lock 22
Pontefract 93
Poplar Arms Corner 141
Port Howden 108
Prior Well Bridge 41
Puddings, Tom 26

Radcliffe on Trent 144, 145
Ramper Road 157
Rampton 136
Rampton Gravel Pit 158
Ranby 40, 41
Ratcliffe Power Station 137
Rawcliffe 24
Rawcliffe Bridge 24, 25
Rawmarsh Road Bridge 124
Real Aeroplane Museum, The 61
Red Hill 137
Redshank 48
Renishaw 34, 35
Retford 30, 42, 43, 45
Retford Town Lock 30
Revolution House 33
Rhodesfield 89
Rhodesfield Lock 110–111
Rhodesia 38
Riccall 104
Ripon 88–91
Ripon Canal 89
Ripon Cathedral 89
Ripon Marina 89
Ripon Motor Boat Club Marina 118
River Derwent and the Pocklington Canal 51–64
River Ouse, River Ure and Ripon Canal 88–109

River Soar Navigation 136
Robin Hood's Well 166
Rockingham 123
Rockware Glass Works 20
Roecliffe 89, 90
Ross, River 98
Rother, River 32
Rother Valley Country Park 37
Rotherham 119, 120, 122, 124, 125
Rotherham Cut 124
Rotherham Lock 120
Ruskin Gallery 122
Ryton Aqueduct 30
Ryton Aqueduct 36

St Boltolph's Church, Saxilby 67
St Botolph Church, Knottingley 20
St Botolph's Church, Boston 82, 84
St Clement's Church, Fiskerton 73
St Everilda's Church, Nether Poppleton 96
St George's Parish Church, Doncaster 129
St Giles Church, Bielby 63
St Helen's Church, Barmby on the Marsh 61
St Helen's Church, Thorganby 57
St Helen's Church, Wheldrake 57
St John Evangelist Church, Washingborough 72
St John of Beverley Church, Wressle 61
St John the Baptist Church, Mexborough 126
St John the Divine Church, Southrey 75
St Lawrence's Church, Bardney 75
St Leonard's Chruch, Kirkstead 77
St Margaret's Church, Langrick 80
St Mary and All Saints Church, Chesterfield 33
St Mary Magdalene Church, Newark 150
St Mary's Church, East Cottingwith 57
St Mary's Church, Ellerton 59
St Mary's Church, Sprotbrough 126
St Matthew's Church, Naburn 103
St Michael and All Angels Church, Sutton-upon-Derwent 54
St Nicholas' Church, Thorne 132
St Oswald 168
St Oswald's Church, Crowle 135
St Paul's Church, Kexby 54
St Peter & St Paul Cathedral 122
St Peter and St Paul Church, Barnby Dun 131
St Peter's Church, Laneham 159
St Wilfrid's Church, Brayton 116
Sandall Grove 130
Sawley 138

Sawley Cut 137, 138
Sawley Lock 137
Saxilby 65-68
Scarborough Mills 51
Scofton 41
Selby 15, 88, 106, 107, 116, 117
Selby Abbey 107
Selby Basin 116
Selby Canal 20, 106, 112–117
Selby Dock 112
Selby Horse Shoe Walk 113
Selby Lock 113
Selby Market 107
Selby Park 107
Selby Swing Bridge 106, 116
Shambles, The 98, 100
Sheffield 23, 24, 31, 34, 119–124, 126
Sheffield Basin 119, 120
Sheffield Canal 119
Shelford 145
Shelford Manor 146, 147
Shepherds Bridge 20
Sherwood Forest 41
Shireoaks 36-39
Shireoaks Row 38
Short Ferry 74
Skeldergate Bridge 98
Skelton 96
Skew Bridge 20
Skyehouse Bridge 28
Skyehouse Village 28
Slab Square 142
Sleaford 78, 86
Sleaford Navigation 78
Smeaton, John 112
Snaith 172
Soar, River 137
South Anston 37
South Clifton 157
South Kyme 86, 87
South Kyme Tower 87
South Trent Beacon 173
South Yorkshire 119, 165
South Yorkshire Coalfield 129
South Yorkshire Navigations 28, 119-135, 136, 169, 171
Southfield Reservoir 23
Southrey 65, 74, 75
Southwell 150
Sprotbrough 126
Sprotbrough Flash 126
Sprotbrough Lock 126
Stainforth & Keadby Canal 28, 119, 135, 169
Stainforth 130–133, 172
Stamford Bridge 51–53
Stamp End Lock 69
Staniforth Road Bridge 120
Stanilands Marina 132
Stapleford 157
Staveley 30, 32, 34, 35
Steetley Chapel 41
Stockwith 47
Stoke Bardolph 144, 145
Stoke Bardolph Lock 136
Stoke Hall 149
Stoke Lock 144
Stonebridge Drain 84
Storage Group 164
Straddle Warehouse 119, 120
Sutton Bridge 54
Sutton Lock 51, 54
Sutton on Trent 154, 155
Sutton-upon-Derwent 54
Swan 49
Swinton 124, 125
Swinton Junction 119, 125

Tackhammer Flats 171
Tadcaster 104
Tales of the River Bank Visitor Centre 78
Tapton 33
Tapton Lock Visitor Cente 32, 35
Tapton Mill Bridge 32
Tattershall Bridge 78
Tattershall Castle 78
Templeborough 123
Terminal Warehouse 120
Terry Booth Farm 86
Thames, River 168
The Priory 41
Theatre Royal, York 101
Thicket Priory 57
Thoresby Park 41
Thorganby 57
Thorne 119, 132, 133
Thorne Bridge 132
Thorne Town 132
Thorpe Hall 37
Thorpe Salvin 37
Thorpe Tilney Fens 78
Three Rivers 169
Thrumpton 137–139
Thrumpton Hall 138
Thrumpton Park 137
Thrybergh Park 125
Timberland Dales 76
Timberland Fens 78
Timberland Pumping Station 78
Tinsley 119
Tinsley Flight 120, 123
Top Lane Lift Bridge 28
Torksey 65-67, 158, 159
Torksey Castle 158
Torksey Junction 136
Town Hall, Sheffield 122
Town Wharf 149
Trans Pennine Trail 32
Trent & Mersey Canal 136
Trent Bridge 136, 141–143
Trent Falls 136, 171–173
Trent Falls 24
Trent Ferry 159
Trent Hills 146, 148
Trent Lock 137, 138
Trent Mouth 172
Trent Port 160
Trent, River 24, 26, 30, 31, 46, 47, 65, 66, 119, 134-173
Trent Valley 136, 154
Trent Wharfage 164
Trinity Arts Centre 163
Tupholme 73
Turnerwood Basin 36
Tyne, River 88

Undercroft Museum 100
Universiade 120
University of Lincolnshire 70
University of Nottingham 84
Upton Hall 150
Ure, River 88, 93, 94

Varley, John 30
Vazon Swing Bridge 134
Vermuyden's Don 24
Victoria Lock 108

Waddington Lock 171
Waddington's Boats 26, 125
Wakefield 125
Wales 37
Walkeringham 31

Walkerith 164
Walton Delph 78
Wash, River 136, 150, 165, 168
Wash Lane Bridge 124
Washingborough 72, 73
Waterways Museum & Adventure Centre 26, 27, 109
Welbeck 41
Well Dressing 35
Went, River 23, 24, 28
Wesley, John 166
West Burton Power Station 160
West Butterwick 168
West Dock 26
West Fen Catchwater Drain 84
West Haddlesey 112, 114–116, 118
West Retford Church 42
West Retford Lock 42
West Riding 88, 112
West Stockwith 30, 31, 46-50, 136, 157, 164, 165
Western Channel 173
Westfields 28
Weston Mill 151
Westwick Cut 89
Westwick Lock 89
Wharf Lane Changeover Bridge 32
Wharfe, River 104
Wheldale Colliery 16
Wheldrake 57
Wheldrake Ings Nature Reserve 54
White Hart 150
Whitewood 26
Whitley Lock 20
Whitwood 136, 158
Wildsworth 165
Willington Power Stations 137
Winthorpe 153
Wiseton 45
Wiseton Park 45
Witham 82
Witham Lodge 80
Witham Navigable Drains 82, 84
Witham Navigation 69, 70
Witham, River 65, 69, 72, 78, 82, 84, 86, 136
Witham Valley 72
Wolds, The 62
Woodhall Reservoir 30
Woodhall Spa 76, 77
Worksop 30, 40, 41
Worksop Museum 41
Worksop Town Lock 30, 40
Wressle 51, 61
Wressle Castle 61
Wykewell Lift Bridge 132

Yedingham 51
York 88, 96, 98-101, 103, 112, 158
York Castle 100
York Castle Museum 101
York Minster 100
York Dungeon 100
Yorkshire 20, 38, 93
Yorkshire Air Museum 54
Yorkshire Coalfield 15
Yorkshire Garden World 114
Yorkshire Law and Order Museums 89
Yorkshire Ring 125
Yorkshire Wildlife Trust 51